Teaching for Impact

Teaching for Impact

Critical thinking, Creative thinking and ACT Responsibility as defining features of contemporary Bildung in Academic Law Schools

Hedwig van Rossum

eleven

Published, sold and distributed by Eleven
P.O. Box 85576
2508 CG The Hague
The Netherlands
Tel.: +31 70 33 070 33
Fax: +31 70 33 070 30
e-mail: sales@elevenpub.nl
www.elevenpub.com

Sold and distributed in USA and Canada
Independent Publishers Group
814 N. Franklin Street
Chicago, IL 60610, USA
Order Placement: +1 800 888 4741
Fax: +1 312 337 5985
orders@ipgbook.com
www.ipgbook.com

Eleven is an imprint of Boom uitgevers Den Haag.

ISBN 978-90-4730-183-7
ISBN 978-94-0011-351-0 (E-book)

Illustrations by L.M. van Rossum

Table of Contents

Abbreviations

ACT Responsibility	The three-stage rocket prospective, personal and non-personal responsibility that is proposed in this research for academic legal professionals. It includes Awareness, Choice making and Taking action
ALE	Academic Legal Education
CHR	Corporate Historical Responsibility
CRP	Creativity Relevant Processes
CSR	Corporate Social Responsibility
CTRP	Critical Thinking Relevant Processes
DRS	Domain Relevant Skills and Knowledge
ECHR	European Court of Human Rights
ECTS	European Credit Transfer and Accumulation System
EU	European Union
GDP	Gross Domestic Product
ITAC Method	Thinking method in which the student identifies the Issue, explores relevant Theory, Applies the theory and makes Conclusions
NGO	Non-Governmental Organization
SLE	Skeptical Legal Education, a type of academic legal education proposed by Van Klink and De Vries
TAPS	Thinking Aloud Pairs, a thinking routine proposed by Ogilvy and Holley
UN	United Nations
UNESCO	United Nations Educational, Scientific and Cultural Organization
UTQ	University Teaching Qualification (in Dutch: Basis-kwalificatie Onderwijs, BKO)
VaKE method	Value and Knowledge Education method
WICS system for leadership	Sternberg's system, in which effective and creative leadership results from a combination of Wisdom, Intelligence and Creativity that have to be Synthesized
ZPD	Zone of Proximal Development (Vygotsky)

Note for readers

The title of this book is 'Teaching for Impact'. It explores how educators in academic legal education could contribute to their students' academic development. Because of its ability to support the understanding of readers and listeners, so-called 'dual-coding' increases an educator's impact.[1] By communicating in two ways – in written words and in images, for example – educators are able to strengthen their message's impact. For that reason, this book includes, in addition to its written text, visuals, graphs and schemes to support its message.

1 See: Caviglioli, Odijk, Bruinen & Van Rossum 2021.

"I find the lure of the unknown irresistible."
– *Sylvia Earle*

Introduction – Into the Unknown

"And I must continue to follow the path I take now.
If I do nothing, if I study nothing, if I cease searching, then, woe is me, I am lost.
That is how I look at it – keep going,
keep going come what may."
– *Vincent van Gogh*[1]

The Quest

Stepping into the unknown can be challenging, frightening but also exciting. Since the future is unknown and, additionally, the fast pace of change and opportunities of our times demand endless choices from every individual, we – educators, students, academically educated legal professionals and global citizens – all constantly have to take that brave step forward into the unknown. Like Van Gogh, we have to keep going, keep searching – come what may.

The learning process, too, is a step into the unknown. It is fascinating and often a lifelong process in which the ultimate outcome continues to be a mystery. Questions such as what will we learn; how might what we learn change us, and what might we do with the things we have learned, remain unknown throughout the process. Contemporary life also consists of a constant interaction with the tantalizing unknown, since we almost never fully know all the possible consequences of our choices and following actions. The uncertainty that comes from having to deal with the unknown can be quite daunting and is a globally shared issue.[2] In the context of the university, educators in law schools might

1 Letter from Vincent to Theo van Gogh (written in Cuesmes, July 1880). Translated by J. van Gogh-Bonger. Available at http://www.webexhibits.org/vangogh/letter/8/133.htm, last visited November 12th 2022.

2 Uncertainty is inextricably linked to human existence. After all, not only our individual futures, but also the collective future of humankind is essentially uncertain: it is an open horizon (Nowotny 2016, pp. 1, 26). Human society in itself is inherently uncertain, since others are unknown, and therefore uncertain, entities in daily life. This is in particular the case in individualistic societies in which social bonds have been loosened (see Bauman 2005-3, pp. 76-77). Bauman speaks of strangers mismeeting while wearing masks and of people constantly moving through cloakroom communities – single purpose and short term communities – that individuals temporarily visit without truly having shown who they really are (see Bauman 2000, pp. 95, 199-200). Beck refers to the disconnectedness, loneliness and isolation of the individual (see Beck 1997, p. 94). The fact that uncertainty is part of human life is not new. However, in contemporary society the level and character of uncertainty has altered. The reason for this development is the increasing complexity of contemporary global society. This complexity is the result of technological innovations that offer a constantly increasing number of choice opportunities. Decision making – whilst knowing that those decisions are often made based on incomplete information – between countless

recognize this experience of uncertainty in student behavior. For example, we see students attempting to avoid or banish uncertainty through a constant search for practice-exams and information about their upcoming assessments, which often distracts them from their actual learning. Nevertheless, in many popular past-times such as games, theater plays and movies the aspect of an unknown future results in a very different – and much more helpful – response. There, the uncertainty makes us feel excited, stimulates us to engage and sparks our creativity. Would it not be great if law students experienced the same during their learning process?

Academic education in law has a long history. Indeed, law was one of the first domains to be studied at the mother of all universities, the university of Bologna, which was established in 1088. Until this day, the interest in and importance of the academic study of law remains: Studying law at the university is meaningful and it is something many people aspire to. The ambition to become a law student can be based on all sorts of reasons. For example, aspirant law students might long to understand the law and its relationship to society or hope to contribute to society and/or to justice in their future lives. Others aspire to studying law because of future career prospects – they want to become lawyers, notaries, judges or prosecutors. Also, a number of new students want to study law because of its broad and societally relevant object of study which will not limit their options of choice with regard to studying and working in the future. For all these reasons, studying law at a university can be an excellent idea. And, fortunately, in current society and academia, it is possible for many of those who aspire to an academic education in law to realize their dreams. Since the modern university of the 19th century aimed at emancipation of the people through transmission of knowledge, universities and academic law schools have welcomed large numbers of students with open arms every academic year. In the last decades, the number of students entering academic legal education seems only to have grown.

But is *academic* legal education still what we are all looking for? There are some concerns about this. For instance, scholars have uttered worries about the status of the academic component of legal education due to the current societal marketization that

---

possibilities has become a heavy obligation. Indeed, any choice may very well result in unimaginable dangers for an unknown number of unidentified others. The awareness of contingency – the fact that every choice *could* have been different – results in a wide-spread sense of uncertainty, because the chooser remains unsure about whether the choice is good or bad (Beck 2015, p. 8. See also: Francot 2014, p. 206). The privatization of risk, in which individuals are held personally responsible for the risks connected to all kinds of choices and decisions, further contributes to this sense of uncertainty (Bauman 2000, p. 8. See also: Geldof 2011, p. 44). Another reason for the change in uncertainty in current society, is our altered perspective on time (Nowotny 2016, p. ix.). The increasing pace of technological and social change diminishes time scales. Not in a few decades or a couple of years, but *tomorrow* everything could be different (see, on three categories of social acceleration: Francot & Mommers 2017, pp. 278-279). Not knowing our imminent future(s) makes the experience of uncertainty constantly urgent.

influences the university. These scholars argue that market values such as profit, effectiveness, efficiency and speed could have detrimental effects on academic values and aims. For instance, academics are in need of time to be able to think and reflect, whereas a marketized environment seeks to gain results as fast as possible. This is often pursued through a focus on administration, by making outcomes quantifiable and through standardization. All of these are recognizable in universities to the concern of both educators and students. Students, for example, are worried about experiencing a one-size-fits-all education and becoming 'cookie-cutter-graduates'. This is opposite to the students' ambition of developing as individual learners. Furthermore, a learning environment and learning culture focused on profit may jeopardize the university's traditional mission of supporting the development of autonomous, critical thinkers in their search for knowledge and truth.

Another worry regarding the question whether or not academic legal education is still what we are looking for relates to the observation that the many changes occurring in society demand new abilities and skills from its citizens. In other words, contemporary life as an academically educated legal professional probably requires other abilities and knowledge than that traditionally taught in law schools. The current lives of all global citizens are influenced by relatively new societal processes such as globalization, fast-paced change and digitalization. These processes manifest in our educational context, for example, in the use of social media by almost every one of our students (and many educators as well). The habit of scrolling through short videos, soundbites and stories written in shorthand affects students: It may have developed their level of visual literacy, but also seems to result in a limited attention span and diminished levels of writing skills and comprehensive reading skills. Furthermore, the societal processes have their effect on all sorts of daily choices and actions, such as what people eat; what they wear; how they travel; how they have relationships; what kind of work they do, and; where, when and how they work. It is clear that technology and globalization have brought global citizens – including academically educated legal professionals[3] – an abundance of choice opportunities in all of these cases. The current societal circumstances resonate in the daily lives of academically educated legal professionals: Their work has become more and more digitalized, has often gained a global aspect and includes the necessity of having to deal with uncertainty. For example, now that digitalized systems (including AI)[4] and

3 With the denominator 'academically educated legal professional', I refer to every individual who has graduated from an academic law school and is active as a professional in a domain that relates to law. This description includes, but is not limited to: legal scholars, educators in legal education, policy makers, politicians, lawyers, prosecutors, judges, notaries, legal counsels, tax specialists, legal advisers and legal designers.

4 At this moment (May 2023) Artificial Intelligence confronts higher education (including ALE) with some serious challenges in, for example ways of assessment. Reason for this is that everyone – including students – could use the recently developed ChatGPT to answer open-ended questions or write an essay.

professionals from other domains have started to take on some of the traditional tasks of lawyers, academically educated legal professionals search for ways to redefine their vocation and seek further specialization. Also, in contemporary complex society, the problems legal professionals face are often complex. In explanation, a judge may have to make decisions in complex cases characterized by a multitude of problems. In these moments, the consequences of the choice could be far-reaching and are often not (fully) known at the moment of choice.

The seemingly limitless choice opportunities of contemporary life result in a globally shared sense of uncertainty, since any choice made might have been different *and* since any choice may have far-reaching, unknown consequences.[5] Importantly, the sense of uncertainty is the result of all kinds of choices, including many personal choices regarding purchasing, consumption, transportation, education etcetera. Because of uncertainty's comprehensiveness, managing uncertainty has become one of the most important personal abilities in contemporary society. However, law, lawyers, law students and academic legal education are not typically known for their tolerance of uncertainty or the unknown. They much prefer to deal in certainties. And, often, legal professionals are particularly qualified for providing certainty to others. For example, legal agreements, such as prenuptial agreements or employment contracts, make it clear what parties may expect under specific conditions. This provides certainty for the future. Also, law makers (or policy makers) create clear rules on what people should and should not do in specific circumstances. Judges even more clearly end disputes with their judgments, thereby influencing future behavior and providing a sense of certainty. In the same way, notaries offer their clients certainty for the future by, for instance, finalizing a will. Through these actions, academically educated legal professionals bring a type of certainty to society. Being in a prolonged state of uncertainty may therefore seem especially counterintuitive and uncomfortable for actors in the legal domain. And indeed, uncertainty can leave a person feeling uncomfortably aware of all sorts of risks and dangers they would like to avoid. It is a feeling many seek to deny, ignore, evade or banish. Still, accepting, tolerating or even using uncertainty may be much more helpful in contemporary life. The challenge for educators in law schools is then to prepare aspiring academically educated legal professionals for their future lives as legal professionals and members of contemporary

---

Educators in higher education are searching for ways to deal with this new technology. See, for example, https://www.iesalc.unesco.org/wp-content/uploads/2023/04/ChatGPT-and-Artificial-Intelligence-in-higher-education-Quick-Start-guide_EN_FINAL.pdf, last visited May 24th 2023; https://vu.nl/nl/nieuws/2023/omgaan-met-chatgpt-in-het-hoger-onderwijs, last visited May 24th 2023, https://theconversation.com/chatgpt-is-the-push-higher-education-needs-to-rethink-assessment-200314, last visited May 24th 2023. This development is very recent, which is the reason why I will not further address this new technology in this book.

5 See footnote 2.

society. To be able to support the development of contemporary law students, academic legal education might require some alterations.

The concern about whether academic legal education still entails what we aim for and the aforementioned circumstances of contemporary life raise questions such as what an *academic* education in law actually means and what this should currently consist of. Also, one might wonder what educators in law can do to support the academic development of their students. Answering questions such as these could fill a potential void in the educational visions of law faculties. It might also help educators in legal education to identify and explicate their own educational mission and could provide them with a number of possible suggestions, formats, structures or ideas that they could use in their own educational practice to accomplish their aim. This is a meaningful mission that has real impact on our students, since an academic education in law often takes place at a fascinating and crucial moment in the life of young adults: For them, it is a step into the unknown of their futures. Their time at the university is a transition from youth to adulthood which holds the promise of growth. Educators in law schools have the opportunity to play an important role during this developmental process from teenager to novice legal professional who is ready to take on the world and make their mark.

With this book, I invite the reader, and especially educators in academic legal education, to join me in a search for the meaning of legal education's academic core in contemporary society. During this journey we seek, first, a sound theoretical foundation for legal education's academic core and, secondly, we pursue appropriate practical ideas and instructional interventions that educators could use in their everyday practice of teaching and designing courses and classes. However, as any true quest, ours is not easy. The endeavor appeals to our courage to reflect on our current practice and to possibly initiate change. Also, our quest compels us to step outside the legal domain, as it takes us through a varied and intriguing landscape of concepts concerning academic legal education, stemming from domains such as educational philosophy, theoretical sociology and social psychology.

Since an important aim of this book is to inspire and support the educational work of colleagues in academic legal education, I hope that many of them will embark on this journey to further develop legal education and strengthen its academic core.

Main Question and Methodology

The unlimited choice, uncertainty, digitalization and marketization that are features of contemporary times result in various challenges for academic legal education which could jeopardize its academic core and the academic development of its students. This neglect of the academic element of legal education is problematic, since it could hinder the growth of our students' higher order thinking abilities, such as (self-)reflection, critical thinking and creative thinking. In consequence, this may obstruct the legal professional's ability to fulfill their civic and professional roles in contemporary life. Thus, the search for strategies to safeguard legal education's academic component and to strengthen the academic development of law students is of importance. This research therefore aims to explore how educators could contribute to the academic development of their students in contemporary legal education. The main research question of this project is:

> *How can educators in contemporary academic legal education contribute to the academic development of their students?*

Demarcation of this research's scope

This question specifically focuses on academic legal education (ALE). This type of education looks at a specific object of study – the law – and is traditionally taught through practicing how to solve legal cases and by using the 'Socratic Dialogue'-method (see Chapter 1). This research has both a theoretical and practical focus. I seek to contribute to the 'theory of legal education' by defining current ALE's theoretical foundations. Building upon these foundations, this research develops practical suggestions and possible models applicable to the practice of legal education that educators in law schools might use as a source of inspiration. However, the relevance of this research is not limited to the education provided by the staff of academic law faculties. It also deals with the question of what an 'academic' education consists of and may therefore also be of interest for educators in other academic disciplines.

To answer the main question, I conduct a literature study from a multidisciplinary perspective that, overarchingly, can be depicted as belonging to the field philosophy of education, but additionally draws on insights stemming from the domains of law, theoretical sociology, history, philosophy (including legal and educational philosophy), educational studies and social psychology. Each domain adds an understanding of (part of) one or more key elements of ALE. In explanation, the domain of law provides the context in which law students and educators in ALE operate. It is also the domain in which students enrolling in ALE will become professionals. Consequently, the legal domain is my point of departure. Secondly, theoretical sociology offers the societal context in which legal education and all global citizens are situated: It depicts the current societal circumstances of unlimited choice, detrimental effects of marketization (and consumerism) on society – including education – complexity, uncertainty and the necessity of individual and collective responsibility. Thirdly, philosophy (including the philosophy of education and legal education) lays the foundation of the content of concepts such as play, critical thinking, responsibility and *Bildung*. In its turn, the historical domain provides further depth to the content of concepts such as *Bildung*, critical thinking, creative thinking and responsibility, since it allows us to consider the historical context and development of these concepts. Finally, educational studies and social psychology provide insight into the developmental stages of children and young adults, the content of critical thinking, creative thinking, play, playfulness, and the range of possible instructional interventions educators might use. Together, this multidisciplinary approach for answering the main question results in a rich body of knowledge that underpins this research. Although I regularly refer to my own experience or to examples from the Dutch context, the sub questions that are raised in this research and the literature that was studied transcend the national boundaries of the Netherlands, so that the ideas and suggestions this research provides are also applicable to ALE beyond the Dutch borders. By connecting insights from such a diverse and rich body of research stemming from various disciplines and by including my own 12 years of experience as an educator in ALE, I aim to offer a well-grounded educational vision of ALE paired with practical recommendations and suggestions that are possible to apply in the daily practice of educators.

The main question *'How can educators in contemporary academic legal education contribute to the academic development of their students?'* focuses specifically on what *educators* in legal education are able to do in order to support the academic development of law students. So, all recommendations resulting from this research will be aimed at factors educators could influence, such as the content of their own classes, the design of their own courses and the curriculum. Consequently, ideas or suggestions for strengthening the academic core of legal education on the level of, for example, national policy do not fit into the scope of this research. Also, the research question is directed at educators and at student development in *academic* legal education, in other words, in legal education as offered at academic universities. Consequently, it does not include a study in the learning of students in vocational legal education, such as a legal education at a university of applied sciences (in Dutch: *hogeschool*).

Research questions, sources and structure of the research

Together, the following six chapters aim to answer the main question '*How can educators in contemporary academic legal education contribute to the academic development of their students?*'. The object of this research question is the *academic development* of law students. The fact that the research concerns *academic* education and *academic* development gives rise to questions such as: What did the *academic core* of a university education historically entail?, what are the circumstances of contemporary universities and ALE? and what do law students need to develop to become academics capable of civic and professional life in contemporary times? These questions are answered in the first chapter that ultimately depicts the circumstances in which educators in contemporary ALE operate and the current neglect of the academic component of legal education. For this purpose, I draw on the work of academics studying the traditional values and aims (and their deterioration due to marketization) of the university such as Rolfe, Reading, Nussbaum, Collini and Bok. Insight into developmental theory on children and (young) adults is found in the work of scholars such as Piaget, Vygotsky, Kuhn and Kegan. For insight into the various instructional techniques that might be used in ALE, I draw on the work of legal scholars such as Cedrone and Stolker.

The depiction of the current circumstances of legal education – in which its academic core seems to be neglected – necessitate an exploration of what the academic component of *contemporary* legal education could consist of. Hence, the second chapter seeks an answer to the question what guidelines a contemporary interpretation of the 19th century educational ideal of *Bildung* can offer for the content of the academic core of current legal education. To find out how the academic core of legal education could be defined, I propose a renewed interpretation of the 19th century educational concept of *Bildung*, after answering the question how *Bildung* is historically depicted and used in education. In this context, I draw on the work of (educational) philosophers from 18th and 19th centuries such as Humboldt, Schiller, Nietzsche and Kant, because their interpretations give insight in *Bildung*'s interpretation during the time when the ideal laid the foundation for the modern western universities. For a further understanding of the historical meaning of *Bildung*, I draw on historical research on Romanticism and *Bildung* conducted by Horlacher, Beiser and Lechner. Importantly, by incorporating the notion of *Bildung* into ALE, this research implicitly embraces the notion that Academia holds an important position in society, namely the role of educator of young individuals in connection with society and also *for* society. In other words, student learning and development is not merely seen as important in itself, but also important *because* it allows graduates to contribute to society. Indeed, by virtue of their academic education, academically educated legal professionals are able to actively engage with a complex society and be part of discovering, understanding and solving societal problems regardless (or even because) of the accompanying sense of uncertainty.[6] In answer to the question central to the second chapter, I propose the reinterpretation of *Bildung* as the academic component of contemporary legal education. This component consists of three essential elements for academically educated legal professionals in contemporary life, namely critical thinking,

6 There are also scholars who disagree with this viewpoint. For example, Van Klink explicitly agrees with Oakeshott's interpretation that acquiring knowledge (which according to Oakeshott consists of information and judgment) should happen without instrumentality. In other words, acquiring knowledge should only be done for the sake and worth of knowledge in itself.

creative thinking and responsibility. Additionally, play and playfulness are recognized as impactful ways of teaching for academic learning.

The three elements of my reinterpretation of *Bildung* will each be explored in a separate chapter: Critical thinking in Chapter 3, creative thinking in Chapter 4 and responsibility in Chapter 5. In all three chapters, three questions are answered, namely: What does the element entail?, What depiction of the element is relevant in the context of ALE? and, finally, How may the element be practically integrated into ALE? To answer these questions, each chapter first defines the element central to it (critical thinking, creative thinking or responsibility). This is followed by an interpretation of that concept for legal education. Finally, practical recommendations and suggestions are provided to incorporate critical thinking, creative thinking and responsibility in ALE. In these chapters, I draw on research from experts that are recognized as such in their respective fields. The research of these experts supports the understanding of what critical thinking and creative thinking entails and how it can be taught. This provides the foundation for developing ideas on how to integrate critical and creative thinking into ALE. In case of critical thinking, I draw on research of Ennis, Davies & Barnett, Bailin, Facione, McPeck, Siegel and Paul & Elder. Van Klink's and De Vries's work provide insight and inspiration on critical thinking in Dutch legal education. With regard to creative thinking, I draw on the work of experts in the field of creativity research, such as Amabile, Csikszentmihalyi, Cropley, Jeffrey, Craft, Boden, Kaufman & Beghetto and Bailin. Additionally, the poet John Keats provides inspiration on 'negative capability', which is the artist's ability to manage uncertainty. For the exploration of responsibility, I draw on research from Francot & De Vries, Matravers and Davis and I touch upon the work of, in particular, Strawson, Wallace, Frankfurt, Go, Weber, Levinas, Bauman and Jonas. Inspired by these conceptions of responsibility, I propose ACT Responsibility as the responsibility for academic legal professionals. It is a prospective, personal and non-personal responsibility that includes Awareness, Choice making and Taking action. The sixth and final chapter seeks an answer to the question *how* educators in ALE can teach critical thinking, creative, thinking and ACT responsibility. In this chapter, play and playfulness are explored as essential strategies for teaching *and* for students to learn how to manage uncertainty within a safe learning environment. Research by play theorists and experts in the field of play and playfulness such as Huizinga, Caillois, Csikszentmihalyi, Sutton-Smith and Bennett provide the basis for the definition of both play and playfulness.

Finally, the Concluding Remarks provide a summarized answer to the main question of this research, which is a conclusion based on the answers to the questions in the six chapters.

An outlook on the upcoming chapters

With the aim of providing readers with a reading guide, the last section of this Introduction offers a short summary of each of the upcoming chapters. In the following, the key points of each chapter are offered.

The first chapter 'Battle of the Tower' seeks to identify the academic core of legal education and explores the challenges that this core faces in contemporary times. With that aim, my starting point is an inquiry into the history of the university. I seek to flesh out its traditional values and aims. This itinerary depicts the development from the pursuit of knowledge, free from state and social pressure to a focus on economic rationality and its central values of efficiency, effectiveness and speed. I will argue that these economic values cannot suffice for an *academic* (legal) education in contemporary times, in which globalization, interconnectedness, interdependence and uncertainty demand more than just vocational and practical skills of law graduates. Even more so, I hold that marketization has had many detrimental effects on the university and academic law schools. Directed towards efficiency and quantity, there is no room nor time left for academic curiosity and the development of an academic attitude. The central question I will address in this chapter is: *How* are educators in legal education able to contribute to their students' intellectual, personal, professional and academic development? This, as I will show, requires knowledge about developmental stages of young adults and a focus on their learning process instead of on how we teach and the broadening of our palette of pedagogical techniques/ instructional interventions. Furthermore, a renewed balance between the vocational and academic component of ALE is necessary, by giving more emphasis to the latter. In this first chapter, I argue that a 'good academic' entails an academic who is a global citizen and is capable of responsibility, critical thinking and creative thinking. These notions are based on a renewed interpretation of the 19th century education ideal of *Bildung*.

The second chapter 'Something There' explores how a renewed interpretation of *Bildung* might function as a safeguard for the academic core of legal education. The chapter seeks to answer the question how *Bildung* might be reinterpreted for contemporary ALE. It aims to identify key components of *Bildung* that are relevant and of importance for current ALE. With that aim, the chapter starts with an exploration of the history of the concept, starting with the middle ages and traveling to the Enlightenment and Romanticism. It becomes clear that *Bildung* entails the holistic development and complete self-realization through constant self-examination of the individual in the context of society. After describing leading interpretations of *Bildung*, the chapter continues with a description of some of the criticisms made against *Bildung* and parries these criticisms. Consequently, an interpretation of *Bildung* is proposed for contemporary ALE. Based on this renewed depiction of *Bildung*, the chapter concludes with the description of three key elements that are of importance in the context of contemporary ALE, namely supporting our students' development of critical thinking skills, creative thinking skills and responsibility. These abilities might be taught through another key element within the conception of *Bildung*, namely through play and playfulness.|

The third chapter 'The Bare Necessity' dives into the first of the key elements of *Bildung* identified in the second chapter, namely critical thinking. The central question this chapter aims to answer is 'How can we integrate critical thinking into ALE?'. To answer this question, the chapter first seeks to define what critical thinking entails. This exploration commences with a description of the historical development of critical thinking. These historical depictions are further explored in the consecutive part of the chapter, which looks at investigating critical thinking's aims and definition. In addition to the importance of critical thinking in the search for truth and knowledge, I argue that it is important to pursue critical thinking because of its worth as an ability that enables self-authored thinkers to define and take their responsibility. Consequently, I propose an interpretation of Robert Ennis's critical thinking definition and corresponding abilities and dispositions in the context of ALE. I find that *decision* (or: judgment) is this definition's center of gravity, which means that the decision about what a person understands to be the truth or right (in their opinion) is the primary aim of critical thinking. To come to such a decision, one goes through a mental, rational endeavor that uses reason, reasons, reasoning or arguments. Building upon this definition and the abilities and dispositions researchers have identified as crucial for critical thinking, the chapter seeks to provide educators with practical suggestions for teaching critical thinking. With this aim, it offers an initial model for incorporating critical thinking in law schools. After introducing the model, the chapter elaborates on ten practical suggestions that educators may choose from if they are interested in incorporating critical thinking in their students' legal education.

In the fourth chapter 'The Spark of Creation' creative thinking is investigated as the second key element of *Bildung*. This chapter seeks to answer the question 'how can we integrate creative thinking into ALE?' and begins with a consideration of the importance of creative thinking skills in addition to critical thinking skills for contemporary academically educated legal professionals. To understand what creative thinking consists of, the chapter starts with exploring the concept's history. Based on the insights of leading theorists in the field of creativity and creative thinking the chapter understands creativity and creative thinking as a human endeavor that encompasses a specific (creative) state of mind concerning possibility thinking and can take place in any domain. Furthermore, creativity involves the generation of something *novel* that has *value*. I argue that educators in ALE interested in supporting their students' creative thinking could aim for the development of little-C level creativity and in building the foundation for their students' pro-C level creativity. To provide insight into the workings of the creative thinking process, the chapter dives into Amabile's depiction of this process. After mapping out the elements of the creative thinking process, the chapter continues with describing a model for incorporating creative thinking into ALE. In its final section, the chapter offers a further elaboration on the eleven practical suggestions for integrating creative thinking into ALE.

Responsibility, the third element of *Bildung*, is investigated in the fifth chapter 'History Has Its Eyes On You'. The chapter seeks to outline the kind of responsibility that it is relevant to teach in contemporary ALE. In order to do so, the chapter explores the concept of responsibility by, first, diving into its development throughout history. The chapter continues its exploration of responsibility by mapping out various dominant interpretations of the concept and presenting them in a Four-Axis Graph to provide more insight. The graph categorizes four groups of responsibility: Retrospective personal responsibility; retrospective non-personal responsibility; prospective personal responsibility and prospective non-personal responsibility. The responsibility-concepts central to these groups are investigated so that it becomes possible to pinpoint the group to which the responsibility concerning academically educated legal professionals belongs. Inspired by the insights gained from the Four-Axis Graph, I propose so-called *ACT responsibility* as the relevant responsibility for academically educated legal professionals. The final section of the chapter aims at answering the question how educators might integrate ACT responsibility into ALE by offering suggestions for learning goals regarding ACT responsibility.

After exploring the three elements of the reinterpretation of *Bildung*, critical thinking, creative thinking and ACT responsibility, the sixth chapter 'Anyone Can Whistle' elaborates on *how* an educator might teach these elements in ALE and I propose play and playfulness as useful strategies for teaching in academic law schools. The sixth chapter therefore seeks to answer the question how *play* and *playfulness* can be defined within the context of legal education and how these concepts could provide educators with tools for supporting student learning in the daily practice of legal courses. To answer the first of these questions, the chapter starts with defining play and playfulness. After an elaboration on both definitions, the chapter continues with investigating how these concepts could be integrated into ALE. To offer insight into some of the categories that play consists of, the chapter outlines five categories of play, which I count as being part of the 'playful approach to ALE'. Readers who wish for more elaboration on possible instructional interventions that fit into one of these play-categories will find a detailed description of 19 examples in the appendix to Chapter 6.

This concludes the outlook on the following chapters. From here, I invite readers to travel with me through the chapters and join me on the quest in search of the meaning of legal education's academic core in contemporary society. Our departure point is the first chapter which will start with an exploration of the university's traditional values and aims.

1 Battle of the Tower. Safeguarding the Academic Core of Legal Education

"When old age shall this generation waste,
Thou shalt remain, in midst of other woe
Than ours, a friend to man, to whom thou say'st,
'Beauty is truth, truth beauty,' – that is all
Ye know on earth, and all ye need to know."
– *John Keats*[1]

Introduction

Keats's famous verse inspires a reflection on the university. It is astounding to think of how much the academic institution must have been able to withstand in its almost thousand year long history. It has remained and it has evolved, in the midst of all sorts of changes and challenges. Despite everything, it has always held onto its quest for truth and learning. The Introduction offered a first illustration that the proverbial 'Ivory Tower' of Academia is in stormy weather: Late modernity confronts the university, academic law schools and the legal profession with challenges. At the root of these challenges are at least two processes, namely globalization and the realization that science is fallible, which result in the question of allocating responsibility.[2] Our current, marketized society is subjected to constant (and increasing) change, which poses the challenge to remain upright whilst being open to change. In response to these social circumstances in which academic legal education (ALE) is situated, I suggested that aligning ALE with late modernity's demands on academically educated legal professionals is a necessity. These adjustments could be found in teaching students strategies for dealing with uncertainty through a renewed emphasis on legal education's academic core – including the development of critical thinking, creative thinking and responsibility.

At the moment, however, it seems that the (aspiring) academic legal professional must most of all be in possession of practical legal knowledge and skills.[3] To ensure that law

---

1 Keats 2001 (Ode on a Grecian Urn), pp. 221-222.

2 See for a further exploration of these circumstances of ALE, academic legal professionals and law students: Van Rossum 2018-1.

3 See, for example, the practical suggestions made by Susskind on the most relevant skills and knowledge needed by lawyers in the 21st century in 'Tomorrow's lawyers' (Susskind 2016).

graduates are able to acquire jobs and can immediately contribute as members of the working force to legal practice and to day to day life in society, vocational skills are emphasized within the curricula of law schools, at the expense of the students' academic and personal development. In the context of the marketized university, ensuring that law graduates are not only capable professionals, but also proficient academics, may seem a lost battle. In contrast to this trend, I argue that in the ever-changing, uncertain, and complex global society, ALE has an important role to play: It can offer its students an education that prepares them for professional life and for their societal roles in contemporary society and it can support their personal development. To do so, educators in legal education require an understanding of the attitudes and skills necessary for living in contemporary society. Furthermore, they require knowledge of the students' learning process and developmental stages and are in need of instructional tools to support their students' growth. The content of ALE could be characterized by its duality of teaching: On the one hand, the practical skills a legal professional needs, and, on the other hand, the academic core that provides law schools with their *academic* identity. Whereas the former is focused on training professional skills, the latter is often associated with teaching students a life attitude of critical thinking and reflection. Both are needed, but the balance between these two parts of legal education is often difficult to maintain. Especially in the last years, due to a corporatization of society and the university, the focus has turned more and more to training measurable, vocational skills.[4] In the Netherlands, law schools emphasize the training of practical legal knowledge and skills, such as procedural law, legal tech or legal writing in their Bachelor's programs. This is a result of their focus on student workability and job-readiness, which often undervalues a student's *academic* development. However, this approach to an academic legal education is insufficient for supporting students' development for life in the current global society. Consequently, the balance between the vocational and academic components is jeopardized. This calls for a battle to recapture the focus on the *academic core* of legal education.

To further understand ALE and its current challenges, this chapter aims at gaining more insight into legal education's *academic core*. Here, questions to be answered are what the academic core of higher education and legal education consists of and what challenges the academic component of legal education faces in contemporary times. To answer these questions, the chapter begins with a study of the roots of the university, searching for its origins and the ideals and aims of the first modern university. This is followed by an exploration of the way in which the phenomenon of societal marketization as it appeared since the second half of the 20th century affects these traditional values and aims of academic institutions. Next, the chapter turns explicitly towards the practice of academic

4 See, for instance, Van Klink & De Vries 2016, p. 9.

legal education: After visiting learning and developmental theories, some possible blind spots in the pedagogy of ALE are explored, its vocational and academic components are clarified, and the current problematic balance between these two components is pointed out.

In search of the University's soul

Origins

The western university's roots can be traced back to Ancient Greece. Plato's Academy and Aristotle's Lyceum were informal, open and non-hierarchical gatherings. These gatherings focused on the pursuit of truth and understanding, and free theoretical exchange through dialectical conversation in debates and discussions. This strategy of learning empowered the learner in reasoning and was aimed at the full development of learners in all their facets. In this learning process, the teacher acted as a role model who facilitated the inquiry process of his students in a Socratic debate. The teacher himself did not need to know all the answers, since the aim was rather for the student to surpass the tutor in knowledge of a particular subject.[5] Aristotle connected teaching with research in the sense that research preceded teaching: Through discussing research findings in the context of teaching, sound judgments and decisions could be made.[6]

Opposite to this type of education, was the instruction given by the Church in the Middle Ages. The education's content consisted of a *trivium* and a *quadrium*, which were both focused on preparing priests for their vocation.[7] The *trivium*'s grammar, rhetoric, and logic helped priests to preach eloquently and convincingly and the skills and knowledge acquired through the *quadrium*'s arithmetic, geometry, astronomy and music were meant to enable priests to manage the church's estates.[8] Not only the content and aim, but also the method of educating varied from those of the Ancient Greeks. Instead of individual learning through dialogue in a non-hierarchical setting, the church's training consisted of an instructor reciting important texts that were then literally copied by his students. During this monastic learning experience, a definite hierarchical relation existed between the knowledgeable teacher and his subordinate student.[9]

5 Izak, Kostera & Zawadzki 2017, p. 1-2.
6 Izak, Kostera & Zawadzki 2017, p. 2.
7 See Izak, Kostera & Zawadzki 2017, p. 3. See also Readings 1996, p. 56, Collini 2018, p. 17.
8 Izak, Kostera & Zawadzki 2017, p. 3. See also Bauman 1997, p. 17.
9 Izak, Kostera & Zawadzki 2017, p. 3.

In resistance to this unidirectional way in which the churches taught, universities were institutionalized in the late 11th and early 12th centuries.[10] The mother of all universities, the Bologna University, was founded in 1088. There, scholars were able to freely teach and pursue knowledge – independent of state and church.[11] The political times demanded debates and deliberation on the relations between state and church, which was the reason why law was central to the University Bologna's areas of study.[12] Reaching back to education's aim in Ancient Greece, the goal of studying at the university was to develop as an individual thinker, speaker and researcher. Learning was stimulated through, for example, debating and criticizing by use of the scholastic method. Freedom of inquiry and independence from particular ideologies or social pressures became defining principles of the university.[13]

The birth of the modern *university*

The university as many of us know it today is based on the ideals of the Enlightenment. Intellectual inquiry was perceived to have its own intrinsic value because it was a product of Enlightenment: Knowledge resulted from Enlightened spirits. It was also a way of maintaining the Enlightenment project of universal knowledge and progress through science and reason by producing and spreading the cultural norms and values of the nation state. In these circumstances, the university's purpose could be defined as *fostering culture*.[14] *Culture* (i.e. *Bildung*) became the immanent unifying principle of the university's disciplines in order to strengthen 'the people' of the nation state.[15] Two contrasting grand narratives of the Enlightenment legitimized the university: (1) *emancipation* of the masses by conveying knowledge and (2) *truth*, through the pursuit of knowledge for its own sake. The latter narrative became especially central to the university during the 19th century,[16] in which the search for and transmission of knowledge was emphasized.[17] The Humboldt

10 Izak, Kostera & Zawadzki 2017, p. 3.

11 https://www.unibo.it/en/university/who-we-are/our-history/university-from-12th-to-20th-century, last accessed 23 November 2018.

12 https://www.unibo.it/en/university/who-we-are/our-history/university-from-12th-to-20th-century, last accessed 23 November 2018.

13 See Izak, Kostera & Zawadzki 2017, p. 3. See also Rhodes 2017, p. 20. However, the struggle for academic freedom has been ongoing ever since, the university fighting for its independence from either the state or the church, see Rhodes 2017, pp. 20 & 22-24.

14 Rolfe 2013, pp. 4-5.

15 Readings 1996, p. 15.

16 Rolfe 2013, p. 5.This quote from T.H. Huxley in 1894 illustrates the emphasis on the grand narrative of *truth*: '*The primary business of universities has to do merely with pure knowledge and pure art – independent of all application to practice; with the advancement of culture and not with the increase of wealth or commodities.*' See Collini 2018, p. 16.

17 Collini 2018, p. 17.

University, founded in Berlin in 1809, was the first to be called *modern* and was based on German idealism and German Romanticism. It equated truth with beauty and, consequently, favored the arts over the sciences (which were included under the denominator of 'the liberal arts').[18] In contrast to the natural sciences, the arts believed in and were focused on absolute 'truth', in understanding (*verstehen*) the essence, instead of the scientific and empiric belief in 'facts' and the explaining (*erklären*) of the appearance.[19] Therefore, the modern university valued the comprehensive development of the student by offering a liberal, broad education that highlighted aesthetics. Here, the aim was to educate students into citizens that could contribute to democratic society.[20] Humboldt's university also distinguished itself from its contemporaries through its focus on a community of learners that required close relations between educators and students and in its emphasis on the combination of education and research.[21] Whereas previously, teaching and research were two separate activities that existed within separate organizations and had separate staff members – a *University* for education and an *Academy* for research – Humboldt suggested combining the two into one University.[22] All throughout Europe and the Americas, the example of this *modern* university was followed.[23]

Post-war reforms and Marketization

During the 20th century the shine of this ideal of a modern university – and the belief in pursuing knowledge and truth for their own sake – faded. The practical usefulness of scientific research became apparent during the Second World War. It was discovered that knowledge and technology could be used for freedom, justice, and the end of suffering (i.e. war) by, for example, deciphering encrypted texts, developing medicines, or engineering nuclear bombs. In the United States, this realization resulted in great government investments in the natural sciences.[24] The emphasis on the emancipatory (utilitarian) narrative of the Enlightenment – using knowledge for practical results – led to a focus within the university on the natural sciences, medicine, biology, and political studies. These were the research areas in which 'scientists' could find explanations and practical solutions for society's problems. At the same time, the Second World War resulted

18 Rolfe 2013, p. 5.
19 Rolfe 2013, p. 6.
20 Collini 2018, p. 18.
21 Collini 2018, p. 18.
22 Humboldt 1970, pp. 247-248, see also Rolfe 2013, p. 73.
23 Readings 1996, p. 7. See also: Horlacher 2016, pp. 72-73. Currently, however, many universities in European countries offer specialized education, in which students focus on one specific area of study, instead of the liberal education that is customary in American universities, see Nussbaum 2016, *preface*, p. *xix*.
24 Bok 2003, p. 11.

– according to Rolfe – in a complete distrust of *all* grand narratives, since the emancipation project had also led to technological innovations that caused horrifying atrocities, such as the deaths of millions and dehumanizing scientific experiments on humans beings in concentration camps.[25] As a result of this distrust, the two grand narratives of the Enlightenment, *truth* and *emancipation*, were abandoned in favor of the sole – and 'thankfully' amoral – narrative of *the market*.[26]

In contemporary society the distrust of the grand narratives of the Enlightenment still lingers, as technology is demystified as the creator of risks such as pollution of ocean and air, the greenhouse effect, and wildlife extinction.[27] Further characterized by interconnectedness and interdependence,[28] the global society is focused on reducing the fear brought on by constantly present uncertainty. According to Francot, this uncertainty is rooted in an abundance of choice opportunities that demand selection.[29] However, the choice that has to be made between options might have far-reaching, uncontrollable consequences, which induces a sense of uncertainty and fear in every individual's everyday life.[30] Bauman describes that the desire to manage uncertainty has made information on risks and protection against the manifestation of risks highly sought after and valuable.[31] However, even though risks affect *all* world citizens, access to relevant information on risks or resources for protection against risk manifestation is not equally distributed. The rich have more access to information and more resources to protect themselves than the poor. This introduces a new type of social inequality.[32] In these circumstances, the democratic nation-state seems increasingly powerless, and neo-liberal values and capitalism have become leading factors.

Liberal capitalism and its preference for valuing anything that produces profit has resulted in a comprehensive marketization of society: market values have gained center stage in contemporary life. In industries originally inclined to value very different things – like health care, law, and education – marketization becomes a challenge. According to Rhodes, the marketization process flattens out society's theoretical and normative foundations as it only focuses on economic rationalization.[33] Business interests seem to have become immune to all values other than the maximization of profit.[34] However, recently, a slight change can be observed in this trend. Corporate Social Responsibility

25 Rolfe 2013, pp. 7-8.
26 Rolfe 2013, p. 8.
27 Beck 1992, p. 156.
28 Bauman 2008, p. 26.
29 Francot 2014, pp. 204-205.
30 Beck 1992, p. 46.
31 Bauman 2011, p. 21.
32 Bauman 2011, p. 5.
33 Rhodes 2017, p. 25.
34 Bauman 2011, p. 22.

(CSR) becomes a new part of entrepreneurship. Businesses are developed with strategies on social and environmental responsibility[35] and now and again businesses are even created solely aiming at, for example, sustainability or social integration.[36] Be that as it may, market values are still a central factor of life in contemporary society and the market has gained power that was previously reserved for the nation state.[37] The drive to privatize has resulted in weakened social bonds and, in its wake, social control and solidarity have decreased. The individual is the central 'hero' of this society's narrative and finds itself under pressure from the global market and individually held accountable for all-encompassing, socially produced risks such as air pollution or global health hazards. However, since single individuals are not nearly resourceful enough to deal with these problems, they might feel inadequate and overwhelmed by the accompanying uncertainty. The widespread mental health problems resulting from the 2020 and 2021 covid-crisis illustrate the pressure that individuals are under in times of uncertainty.[38] Feelings of loneliness, inadequacy and helplessness in the face of global, socially produced risks may result in a decreasing sense of responsibility for these risks as citizens become dulled, jaded, and numb.[39]

Academic Education's peril

After the Second World War and the Cold War, scientific research lost its usefulness for warfare and gained a new goal: Furthering the economy and public welfare through technological innovations, such as electronics and computers. Especially in the United States, this change in the function of scientific research was furthered by the economic slowdown of the late 1970's that demanded strong economic and technological competition with Europe and Japan. The marketization of the university, an institution embedded in

35 See, for example: https://mvonederland.nl/, last accessed March 5th, 2023. This shift from a sole focus on economic growth towards a focus on human well-being and sustainability is also noticeable in Ecological Economics, a subfield of Economics that has been developing since the early 1990's, but currently seems to be gaining momentum. See: Victor 2010, p. 244 and Constanza et al. 2015, pp. 87-89.

36 See for example, the Ocean Cleanup, https://www.theoceancleanup.com/, last accessed March 5th, 2023, or restaurants and lunchrooms run by employees with Down's Syndrome, for example http://www.downeys.nl/downeys/index.html, last accessed March 5th, 2023.

37 Bauman 2011, pp. 22-23.

38 See for example: www.bbc.com/news/explainers-55957105, last visited June 23rd 2021, https://nos.nl/artikel/2352807-ggz-mentale-gezondheid-in-gevaar-door-corona-jongeren-kunnen-door-ijs-zakken, last visited June 23rd 2021.

39 Blocking out in the sheer effort to avoid the constant appeal to their empathy and responsibility while not being able to control the situation or able to offer a valuable contribution is, for example, the case for individuals who were constantly confronted with news on the covid-19 crisis: www.ctvnews.ca/health/coronavirus/compassion-fatigue-making-people-numb-to-daily-covid-19-case-counts-experts-1.5400438, last visited December 8th 2021.

the changing political and societal structures, began.[40] According to Bok, one of the reasons for the corporatization of the university was the close connection with the businesses that inevitably arose due to the university research's stimulating role in the economy.[41] The corporative culture within these companies left its mark on the university. Other causes that Bok pinpoints for the marketization of the university are the cutbacks in government funding,[42] the prominence of entrepreneurship in general society from the 1980's onward, the lack of clarity of the university's intrinsic values – which left the door wide open for capitalistic values, i.e. profit – and the increased competition between academic institutions. Above all, the corporatization of the university is due to increasing technological developments in the past decades that created profitable opportunities for universities, such as possibilities for patenting, developing education for professionals in need of new skills and knowledge, and offering Massive Open Online Courses (MOOCs).[43] However, business opportunities and opportune secondary jobs that are sought after and accepted by academic researchers or professors bear the risk of being Trojan horses. Notorious cases that have recently been highlighted in the Dutch media show that the danger linked to funds promised by foundations or commercial corporations could lead to a breach of the University's 1000 year old defining principle of independence from ideologies and social pressure. In other words, external funding carries the risk of drifting away from the university's quest for *truth*, since a business proposal may come with constraints or expectations for the research and the researchers, such as the expectation for a Dutch research group in Human Rights receiving funding from a Chinese foundation to publicly support the human rights policy of the Chinese government,[44] the risk of an implicit appeal to a professor in geopolitics and energy with close connections to stakeholders in the fossil industry to lobby for that industry,[45] or a tax law professor whose

---

40 Rolfe 2013, p. 3. Teixeira & Dill 2011, p. VII. See also Zeleza 2016, pp. 111, 139.

41 Bok 2003, p. 11.

42 For example, in the Netherlands a new financing model for higher education was introduced in 2008 (Uitvoeringsbesluit Wet op het Hoger Onderwijs en wetenschappelijk onderzoek, https://wetten.overheid.nl/BWBR0006152/2018-09-01, & Regeling financiën hoger onderwijs, https://wetten.overheid.nl/BWBR0024005/2018-11-09). In this model, all universities receive a basic amount of money (all though this amount is less than it was previously). Additionally, universities receive a sum of money related to their output, i.e. measured by the number of students graduating within a certain amount of time. The financing of higher education has been met with criticism and a cutback of 25 percent per student can be noticed since 2000, while student numbers have grown by 68 percent (See: https://vsnu.nl/dalende-rijksbijdrage.html). So, universities struggle to educate an increasing number of students towards their timely graduation while receiving less money to do so sufficiently and qualitatively. In 2018, concerned staff and students at Dutch universities organized themselves in the collective *WOinActie* (Higher Education in Action, https://woinactie.blogspot.com/), to protest against these developments.

43 Bok 2003, pp. 12-13, 15.

44 https://nos.nl/artikel/2413702-china-financiert-onderzoek-naar-mensenrechten-aan-vu, last visited May 16th 2022.

45 https://nos.nl/nieuwsuur/collectie/13896/artikel/2424146-de-hoogleraar-en-de-connectie-met-de-fossiele-industrie, last visited May 16th 2022.

research in tax reduction possibilities for real estate investors was sponsored by a lobby, which jeopardized the independence of his research.[46] Especially in law, an academic domain with close connections to its professional practice, relevant secondary jobs of the academic staff are appreciated for their value for education.[47] Nevertheless, since connections outside Academia may lead to issues of integrity, educators and researchers in legal education need to remain watchful to maintain their academic independence.

In the 21st century, there are more universities worldwide than ever and their role has become central in society's economy. Furthermore, the number of students enrolled in universities has grown exponentially.[48] Universities are organized and run as major businesses and are commercially active in, for example, selling executive programs or refresher courses for professionals (e.g. for lawyers or doctors), trading research results, and patenting scientific discoveries.[49] Within its walls, the increasing corporatization of the university is noticeable in the frequently heard 'values' of effectiveness and efficiency.[50] Academia's 'profit' seems achievable by educating at low cost a constantly increasing number of students in as few years as possible with the aim of delivering employable professionals. The university's profit can be increased by decreasing the input, for example by spending less money on the education of each student.[51] The university's corporatization also comes to the fore in its need for 'impact' and the emphasis on measurable (research and educational) output.[52] Apart from the fruits of research, the university's output is its students that graduate and start contributing to society as members of the work force. To maximize this output, the marketized university needs to make sure that it prepares as many students for a vocation as possible. Altbach argues that this mass education, focused on the quantity of diplomas in the shortest amount of time, inevitably leads to a decrease in the quality of the education offered by universities.[53] Although mass education makes access to higher education widely possible, which might at first glance be in accordance with the Enlightenment's grand narrative of emancipation, it also comes with pitfalls. According to Altbach, for example, mass education together with an economic rationality that revolves around customers and service workers, brings along the idea that higher

46 https://nos.nl/nieuwsuur/collectie/13896/artikel/2426919-hoogleraar-uva-neemt-ontslag-na-heimelijke-constructie-met-vastgoedlobby; last visited May 17th 2022. See also: https://www.folia.nl/actueel/151620/vertrokken-hoogleraar-belastingrecht-niet-vijf-maar-acht-jaar-betaald-door-lobbyclub, last visited May 17th 2022. See also: https://www.folia.nl/actueel/150313/zuidaskantoren-oefenden-invloed-uit-op-publicaties-medewerkers-belastingrecht, May 17th 2022.

47 https://www.folia.nl/actueel/150313/zuidaskantoren-oefenden-invloed-uit-op-publicaties-medewerkers-belastingrecht, May 17th 2022.

48 Collini 2012, pp. 3-4. See also Berg & Seeber 2016, p. 3.

49 Rolfe 2013, p. 3. Bok 2003, pp. 83-84.

50 Rolfe 2013, p. 11.

51 Altbach 2013, p. X. See also: Zeleza 2016, p. 93.

52 Szadkowski 2017, p. 40. See also Zeleza 2016, p. 58.

53 Altbach 2013, pp. X, 9.

education is a private good – an individual privilege – instead of a public good that benefits the whole of society. Therefore, the state's financial support of the university could be in jeopardy, since financing their higher education is then believed to be the responsibility of privileged individuals and not the responsibility of society at large.[54] Another pitfall might be that the possibility for every person to have access to an education that befits them gets confused with the idea that *everyone* should be able to successfully complete an *academic* education. The latter is not case, since certain standards and characteristics are central to Academia. Therefore, it should be noted that, although everyone has a right to education, there is not a subjective, demandable 'right' to a *university* education.

Although few scholars will immediately applaud the marketization of institutions of higher education, the development might have some positive effects. For instance, competition, a prerequisite for a healthy market economy and more and more a part of academic life,[55] might lead to better research and innovations in education.[56] On the other hand, many voices can be heard criticizing the marketization of the university. Students complain that universities have become 'cookie cutter'- factories that 'produce' graduates as fast as possible and educators and researchers struggle to educate and research effectively and efficiently while still maintaining or even improving quality.[57] So, although marketization might have some positive results, it is problematic in the context of the university. It results in a one dimensional interpretation of life and of the university: Solely focused on measurable income and output; on gain and efficiency. Not only does this lead to complaints of burn-out and personal discontentedness by overburdened students and staff,[58] but – more fundamentally – it renders higher education one-dimensional. Because of the rationality of economic calculation, values that do not immediately result in useful – measurable – output are slowly fading into oblivion. As a result, the corporatized university neglects the values and aims that many deem essential for a university education, for example the academic value of the advancement of knowledge and science.[59] Other

---

54 Altbach 2013, p. 8.

55 Szadkowski 2017, p. 40. Researchers, educators and students see themselves competing for grants, trainee positions, and future jobs.

56 Bok 2003, pp. 27-28, 62-63.

57 Educators, too, are concerned with the university's turning into the so-called 'knowledge factory'. See Bok 2003, p. 16.

58 To illustrate, studies show that a large number of students in the Netherlands experience stress-related problems, like burn-out, anxiety or depression. In the last few years, many news articles can be found on this topic in the Dutch media. For example: https://www.trouw.nl/samenleving/angst-depressie-en-zelfmoordgedachten-studenten-gaan-er-aan-prestatiedruk-onderdoor~a8336942/ (April 2018), last accessed 13 December 2018, https://www.rtlnieuws.nl/editienl/artikel/3703816/driekwart-van-studenten-uitgeput-aan-alle-kanten-werd-aan-me-getrokken (2017), last accessed 13 December 2018, https://lsvb.nl/wp-content/uploads/2016/10/Onderzoeksrapport_Psychische_klachten.pdf.

59 Rolfe 2013, p. 3.

goals and aims, such as academic freedom,[60] and the university's project to promote culture and educate students to become responsible and critical citizens in a democratic society[61] are under pressure as well. Even though many students start a university education, their sheer numbers prevent their educators from being able to support their full development as critical, creative and responsible academics. There is simply not enough time, nor is every one of the aspiring students able or prepared to start an *academic* education. The damage to the university's values and aims is sustained by the loss of foothold suffered by the humanities e.g. philosophy, art, history, and cultural studies. With that, Nussbaum argues, crucial aspects of an academic education, such as fostering imagination, creativity, and critical thought, disappear.[62] In economic terms, the disciplines that help support the development of these competences are deemed unprofitable. In their stead, disciplines that are thought to be useful for the economy and that have a clear (immediate and practical) sense of purpose, for example business schools, the natural sciences, and empirical studies flourish.[63] Antagonistically, at the same time that budget cuts are being made that result in a decimation of the humanities, the value attributed to the competences supported by these disciplines increases. This is the case because citizens are in dire need of, for example, critical reflection skills, the capability to take on various viewpoints, and a notion of responsibility in order to be able to face the challenges of the 21st century.

Marketization wounds the soul of the university, since it dismisses the original values that form the university's beating heart. Profit takes the place of the *modern* values of the university and, as a consequence, higher education is turned into a consumer good. Rolfe states that, due to this rationale, educators become salesmen and students consumers and customers paying to receive a degree. Similar to a factory, the university (and its students) focus on education's output instead of on the process of learning.[64] This 'factory of higher education' values *fast* results in research as well as in education. In sharp contrast to this economic rationality, the ideal of the *modern* university relied on the belief that its value lies in the non-instrumental cultivation of scholarship and science, and on the acceptance that the influence of the university's scholarship on everyday life could be indirect and

60 Where the university has long since fought for its freedom from church and state, it now has another battle to wage: Freedom from the economic market. With corporations financing research, the job market demanding a certain set of skills to be trained during the university education, and an institution run by managers highly skilled in the use of corporate language and acquiescing in capitalistic values, the question arises if freedom of the economic market is possible at all.

61 See, for example, Nussbaum 2016, pp. 6, 9.

62 Nussbaum 2016, p. 3.

63 Bok 2003, pp. 5-6

64 Rolfe 2013, p. 11. See for a study of the impact of marketization on the experience of the (consumer-) student in the UK: Nixon, Scullion and Hearn 2018.

long-term.[65] Liberal capitalism, on the other hand, demands speed and *immediate* engagement with and usefulness in the 'real world'. This undermines the foundations of the modern university, as it denies the necessity of making time for seemingly 'unproductive' work. In stark contrast to the seemingly constant scarcity of time within the contemporary university's walls, Berg and Seeber argue in *The Slow Professor* that time is an essential resource for thought, reflection, and creativity.[66] Furthermore, they state that the lack of time resulting from the corporatization of the university has led to standardized learning and a damaging sense of urgency.[67] Learning, deliberation, reflection, dialogue and creation require deceleration instead of the pressing acceleration and demand for quick results.[68] These processes are rooted in introspection and consideration, and aim at long-term results. Those results, reflections and ideas are very necessary as there is a need for critical citizens able to take responsibility, rethink society and create new solutions for the challenges that all world citizens face. Without those citizens, the danger arises that only law abiding, uncritical professionals remain: Quick to follow the issues of the day, but unable to question and reflect on current practices, and without the capacity to (re) discover creative new ways of solving contemporary difficulties.

In addition to the focus on fast and increasing profit, the concept of 'excellence' has gained in popularity and importance within the university. According to Readings, 'excellence' has turned into the legitimizing idea of the contemporary university, whereas the university envisioned by Kant was guided by the concept of *reason*[69] and the modern university founded by Humboldt was legitimized by the idea of *culture* (i.e. *Bildung*).[70] Thus, the contemporary university can be denominated as a 'University of Excellence'. Even though this might sound nice – 'excellence' seems to suggest that it is a 'good' university – Rolfe argues with Readings that 'excellence' is actually a hollow notion. It does not express a value but is merely a unit of measurement. What is measured as 'excellent' can vary, and therefore excellence has no content in itself. For instance, a Bachelor's program can be deemed 'excellent' because of the many students graduating every year, or because of the strict selection of only high scoring freshman students, because of the large number of contact hours offered, or rather because of the number of MOOCs and knowledge videos available for home studying. So, the designation 'excellence' depends on one's own perspective on the content of that concept. Therefore, the concept in itself remains meaningless. Furthermore, Collini explains that the concept of 'excellence' in contemporary society and university is reduced by its current 'no standing still'

65 Collini 2018, p. 18.
66 Berg & Seeber 2016, pp. 27, 89-90.
67 Berg and Seeber 2016, pp. 6-8.
68 See Berg and Seeber 2016, p. 11.
69 Readings 1996, p. 54.
70 See: Readings 1996, pp. 63, 65. See also: Rolfe 2013, p. 4.

interpretation. This means that every activity must improve at a certain rate,[71] which entails that quantitative standards – or benchmarks – must always be surpassed.[72] Within a university aimed at individual learning processes and in-depth research this demand cannot be fulfilled. Moreover, instead of the professor, the central figure in a 'University of Excellence' is the administrator,[73] since excellence is ensured by standards checked upon by administration.[74] However, academic staff can ensure the quality of their research and lectures, but an administrator cannot. Quantity is therefore often chosen over quality, since the administrator is only able to examine compliance with standards in terms of quantity.[75] For example, the 'quality' of academic education seems to be measurable by the quantity of graduating students, the number of academic staff, student attendance numbers, or the number of positive student evaluations. Adding to the difficulties the new role for the administrator brings to the actual quality of teaching is the low tolerance the administrative culture of control has for uncertainty. In contrast, scientists and academics work in a culture of trust that is very much at ease with uncertainty. Even more so, according to Nowotny, scientists work together on the 'cusp' of uncertainty to seek new knowledge.[76] In addition, the learning process is in itself uncertain and a step into the unknown, since it is never clear from the start – notwithstanding their level of effort – if the individual will truly be able to learn, deeply understand and appreciate the nuances of the material. The uncertainty of the process offers excitement, endless opportunities for the learner and makes learning worthwhile. Success, in the sense of high grades or passing exams – is therefore never a given, nor should it be.[77] This shows that the marketized university's turn towards a central role for administrators is at odds with and may be even harmful to the fundamental activities of the academic community.

It seems clear that the marketization of society is changing the university. For instance, the corporatization of the university – in which the university turns more and more into a profitable business – causes its roots in academic freedom, objectivity, and the unconstrained quest for truth to deteriorate, since Academia becomes subject to market forces. It can be said that academic culture requires 'rising above what's ailing society',[78] which in current circumstances would mean not going with the accelerating flow of marketization and the search for profit. Instead, it calls for making time for collaboration, learning, thinking, reflection, in-depth research, and thoughtful teaching.[79] Yet, the

71 Collini 2012, p. 109.
72 Berg & Seeber 2016, p. 9.
73 Berg & Seeber 2016, pp. 4-5.
74 Rolfe 2013, pp. 8-9.
75 See also Collini 2012, p. 108.
76 Nowotny 2016, p. xii.
77 See, for example, Biesta 2013, pp. 1-4.
78 Berg & Seeber 2016, p. 71.
79 Berg & Seeber 2016, pp. 72, 89.

opposite often seems to be happening within the university. Moreover, the corporate focus on output – i.e. delivering as many students to the workforce in as little time as possible – prevents an individualized education, only permitting a pre-fabricated education that essentially forces all students to develop in a uniform manner. That results in a 'dime a dozen' graduate: Ready to be put to work in the knowledge economy, but certainly not a human being who is in the process of developing all of their capacities during a university education. However, the latter will be able to thrive in late modernity, while the former cannot. Furthermore, the scholar in search of knowledge and insight is replaced by administrators and the ideal of a scientist able to deliver useful results that lead to profit and quick societal impact. Consequently, Rolfe argues, the intellectual craftmanship – the art – of the scholar disappears: Their desire for knowledge and their intrinsic motivation are challenged by the pressure of grant competition and the market.[80]

The university finds itself in the middle of societal change and is adjusting accordingly. However, the question remains whether the adaptions made to the institution are undesirable since they are uprooting the traditional values and aims (and with that, the *academic* core) of the university. This necessitates a reconsideration of these starting points and a search for the future-proof and fitting values and aims of the contemporary university. In the following, the focus of this chapter shifts to *legal* education as it explores the specific challenges ALE faces in the context of contemporary society.

Meeting Academia's challenges in legal education

The study of law has belonged within Academia from the time it became one of the first disciplines of study in the University of Bologna in 1088. Academic legal education therefore has a long history in which it was aimed at developing individual thinkers, speakers and researchers. In this context, ALE is rooted in the original academic values of the search for truth and independence from state and societal pressure. Since the 19th century, emancipation of the masses and fostering culture were added as important goals for any academic education. Nevertheless, due to the 20th and 21st century marketization of society and the ever expanding university, ALE seems now primarily focused on producing output, revenue, quantification, 'customer'-satisfaction and quick results. Subsequently, the university has been criticized for not being able to support the (time-consuming) full development of individual human beings, and that, instead, academic institutions are rapidly producing cookie cutter graduates. This has wounded the *academic* character of the university and of legal education.

80 Rolfe 2013, p. 11.

Societal changes have, undeniably, their effect on ALE. Legal educators recognize in their law school's organization, for instance, the use of marketized concepts such as output or profit when referring to the 'success' of their students, individual courses or Bachelor's programs. Furthermore, a shift of focus is noticeable towards training vocational skills at the expense of the development of academic qualities such as critical thinking or reflection. In spite (or may be: because) of this situation, many legal academics hold that an academic ability such as critical thinking is crucially important for (future) academic legal professionals.[81]

In an effort to rethink the necessary knowledge and abilities needed by lawyers in contemporary times, legal professionals and legal educators have recently conceptualized various types of lawyers such as the 'T-shaped lawyer', 'Delta-shaped lawyer' and the 'O-shaped lawyer'. Most of these descriptions of the professional abilities of lawyers focus on the necessity of in-depth and broad knowledge (which are part of so-called Domain Relevant Skills, see chapters 3 and 4). According to Amani Smathers, who originally introduced the idea of the T-shaped lawyer in 2014, T-shaped lawyers are able to think analytically and have the ability to connect ideas across disciplines. For this ability, she argues that lawyers need broad (not in-depth) knowledge of various areas, such as data analytics, business, project management, design thinking and technology (the horizontal line of the T) in addition to in-depth legal knowledge and skills (the vertical line of the T).[82] However, Amani Smathers seems mainly to see merit in these abilities of the T-shaped lawyer because they enable *professionals* (it seems as if this denominator is mostly applicable to lawyers – i.e. members of the Bar – employed by large legal firms) to better meet their clients' demands and to better tap into untried possibilities for financial gain and profit.[83] This focus on the corporate merits and economic gain also seems the aim of the UK-based initiative of the 'O-shaped lawyer'[84] and the US-based model of the 'Delta-shaped lawyer'.[85] To illustrate, the O-shaped lawyer framework describes the ideal lawyer as original, open-minded, having ownership, an being opportunistic and optimistic. It attributes this lawyer with, for instance, courage, empathy, resilience, and skills in collaboration, synthesizing, problem solving and simplifying complexities.[86] Generally,

81 See on the importance of critical thinking (and the faculty of critical judgment) for legal academic education: Van Klink & De Vries 2016, p. 6; Van Klink & Francot 2019, p. 54; Witteveen 2005, pp. 191-192; Bosch-Boesjes 2005, p. 26; Knigge 2005, p. 73; Mak 2017, p. 30; Schwartz, Hess & Sparrow 2013, pp. 24-27; Mudd 1983, pp. 705-706; Cownie 2004, pp. 76, 78, 83; Ahsmann 2016, p. 9; Brouwer 2005, p. 5.

82 Amani Smathers 2014, pp. 35-36.

83 Amani Smathers 2014, pp. 35-36.

84 See: www.oshapedlawyer.com, last visited May 18th 2021.

85 See: www.legalexecutiveinstitute.com/delta-model-personal-effectiveness-skills, last visited May 18th 2021.

86 See: *The O-shaped lawyer. Core competencies.* Available at: http://static1.squarespace.com/static/5e73266f0be3ab3148757f25/t/5f9aa7f8ea9b437e19774bf3/1603971065143/The+O+Shaped+Competency+Framework.pdf, last visited May 19th 2021.

this seems to correspond with some of the attributes that are explored later in this research as part of *Bildung*, ACT responsibility, critical thinking and creative thinking. Nonetheless, the overarching aim of the framework of the 'O-shaped Lawyer' is to 'make the legal profession better', which basically means making legal services more customer centric.[87] All three models of the ideal lawyer (be it T-, Delta- or O-shaped) seem to focus on, in Mak's vocabulary, the image of the 'rational legal professional'. This was a dominant image in the second half of the 20th century that had replaced the traditional image of the lawyer-statesman.[88] Mak argues that this image of the rational legal professional is connected to economic values such as efficiency and effectiveness,[89] but has shifted in the 21st century into the idea that the law, and thus legal professionals, may play a role in creating societal change.[90] This idea is connected to contemporary values such as social justice and sustainability.[91] In the sixth chapter, I argue that it is part of the role responsibility of *all* academics, including academically educated legal professionals, to actively develop their awareness of their responsibility regarding the great challenges of our time such as sustainability and social justice and formulate their own position towards it (see Chapter 6). However, while I affirm the *great lawyer*'s social responsibility and therefore wholeheartedly agree with Mak on the overall aim (realizing societal change) and the values of social justice and sustainability for academically educated legal professionals of the 21st century, I do not concur that these can be labeled part of the notion 'T-shaped lawyer'. The reason for this is that, originally, the T-shaped lawyer's abilities and goals are economic[92] and not social or related to the holistic educational ideal of *Bildung* and the T-shaped lawyer's abilities are, at heart, focused on improving legal services for customers and not on improving (or: contributing to) society, humanity or the natural environment that sustains mankind. By merely ascribing attributes to legal professionals to better their performance in their professional capacity to, ultimately, generate more profit, the images of the T-shaped lawyer, Delta- and O-shaped lawyer focus on the *persona* – in other words, only one of the roles (or: masks) played by the lawyer instead of on their whole *person*. In contrast to only developing their professional *persona*, academics are required (and able) to develop their whole *person* and lead an examined life in which their ideals, beliefs, and convictions are congruent with their actions in any capacity. This renders depictions of the lawyer that focus on developing profitable professional skills unsuitable for answering the

87 Research report O-shaped lawyer, *Transforming the training & Development of Lawyers*, February 2020, p. 5. Available at: http://static1.squarespace.com/static/5e73266f0be3ab3148757f25/t/5e736114824c026bd67da1e1/1584619820423/O+Shaped+Lawyer+-+In-House+Report+%28February+2020%29.pdf, last visited May 19th 2021.

88 Mak 2017, pp. 13-15.

89 Mak 2017, p. 15.

90 Mak 2017, p. 17.

91 Mak 2017, pp. 17-18.

92 Amani Smathers 2014, pp. 35-36.

call for an *academic* model for educating academically educated legal academics that focuses on *Bildung*, entailing the inner development of all a *person*'s abilities and talents.

Nevertheless, many educators in legal education may recognize the difficulty of teaching students academic attitudes. The very context in which we are tasked to teach this to our students seems unhelpful. That is, unfortunately it does not pay for students in ALE to develop their character or academic abilities such as critical thinking. Instead, it makes much more sense for them to resort to rote and surface learning. Mathiasen and Andersen express this concern and argue that this problem is caused by the marketization of the university (the university of the administrator) and its administrative focus on performance indicators. Those indicators are merely able to measure goals attained in the short term, but are unable to provide room for long term goals such as personal development and critical thinking ability.[93] Those goals require time and an individual approach to student development and student learning which are not (yet) always made a central focus in higher education. With regard to legal education, Thornton observes that marketized law faculties focus on doctrinairism, known knowledge and 'right answers', which outshouts the academic focus on developing a questioning voice.[94] This learning culture influences our students' learning strategies. Stolker illustrates this point by saying that one of legal education's biggest problems in these times of mass education is formed by its students who are focused on getting the right answers and passing the exam, are ill prepared and uninterested in discussions with their educators or peers.[95] In truth, we cannot blame our students for adapting to a context that we have created and help to sustain. The current teaching environment often causes students to feel that surface learning (through rote learning) is much more effective than deep learning to live up to what is expected of them, namely to give the right answers, pass the exam and gather EC-points as quickly as possible. Perversely, this is currently regarded as a success and the Faculty is funded accordingly. Since these consequences are unhelpful for teaching students an academic attitude, it is time to turn the tide.

As the title of this chapter already suggests, we are called to battle to regain the academic character of the university and legal education. Although a crucial step towards a higher education that prioritizes quality over quantity and long term over short term goals has to be made at the level of national policy makers: Educators can support this development by repeating the message that the current system results in undesirable consequences. Educators do have influence within their institution, Faculty, curricula, courses and classrooms, and thus may be able to shift the focus more and more to long term learning and development goals, such as critical thinking, creative thinking,

93 Mathiasen & Andersen 2020, p. 41.

94 See Appleby, Burdon & Reilly 2013, p. 345.

95 Stolker 2014, pp. 168-169.

responsibility and character formation. Of course, the question is *how* are educators in legal education able to contribute to this kind of academic development? To answer these questions, we first need to understand how learning works and with that in mind, revisit the traditional pedagogy of legal education.

Understanding how learning works

Our first step entails a shift of focus. According to Rochette's research, educators in ALE are mainly focused on how teaching works instead of on how student learning works.[96] However, teaching may be viewed as a social, communicative event with the ultimate goal of nourishing our students' learning process.[97] Changing our focus towards the *learning process* of our students may therefore be very helpful for our pedagogy and didactics.

If we want to gain insight into how students learn and develop, it is useful to explore the ideas of psychologists of development and learning. Ambrose et al. describe learning as a *process* that leads to *change*, which occurs through *experience*.[98] This means that learning is not a product or outcome, but a process[99] and that the result of the learning process is a change in, for example, the way the learner views the world. Furthermore, this definition reveals a preference for the so-called experiential learning theory. Kolb defines this theory as a holistic perspective on learning that combines elements of two central theories of learning: The behavioral theory and the cognitive theory.[100] Although in-depth study of the literature, concepts and ideas of established legal scholars, philosophers and scientists is important for learning in higher education, supporters of the experiential learning theory hold that students learn though experience. This means that students construct knowledge by having direct encounters with the issue or problem they study and are not merely thinking about the issue.[101] The experiential learning theory is widely supported and its influence can currently be recognized in, for example, competence

96 Rochette 2010, p. 296.
97 Mathiasen & Andersen 2020, p. 41.
98 Ambrose et al. 2010, p. 3.
99 See also Kolb 2015, p. 37.
100 Kolb 2015, p. 31. The *behavioral theory of learning* is based on the culture in psychology called 'behaviorism' with leading theorists such as Thorndike and Skinner. The theory relies on objective observation of human behavior and empirical data to gather knowledge of human psychology (and learning). According to behaviorists, learning means acquisition of new behavior and the method of learning is through conditioning. The behavioral theory rejects the notion that unconscious and subjective experience are important for the learning process. In education, behaviorism leads to educator-centric teaching methods: 'the traditional teaching style'. See Kolb 2015, p. 31, Tomic 1993, pp. 38-40 and Pritchard 2009, pp. 3, 5-6. The cognitive theory is based on rationalist, idealist epistemology and finds that learning involves acquisition, manipulation and recall of abstract symbols. See Kolb 2015, p. 31.
101 Kolb 2015, p. 5.

based education and the life-long learning movement.[102] Many see John Dewey (1859-1952) as the founding father of the principles of experiential learning and the father of the *progressive Education Movement*.[103] This movement in the late 19th and early 20th century was inspired by, for example, Rousseau's Emile and its followers believed in the worth of experience as a way of gaining knowledge. However, to avoid some progressives' dismissal of literature, many contemporary experiential educationalists in higher education combine experiential instructional techniques with traditional teaching methods, such as literature study and discussing literature.[104] Another renowned proponent of the experiential learning theory was Jean Piaget (1896-1980). Piaget was a developmental psychologist known for laying the foundations of cognitive constructivism which includes his analysis of the stages of the cognitive development of children.[105] Cognitive constructivists hold that individual learning results from mental construction. In other words, learning is an active mental endeavor in which a person learns[106] by having experiences in their environment that result in new information that has to be added to (or built into) their existing structure of knowledge, understanding and skills.[107] Therefore, any experience with the world supports a student's learning and (cognitive) development. In harmony with this assertion, Cedrone argues that every form of experience (be it role-play experience, a field trip or group work) supports the development of habits of mind and supports the course of a student's development. *Reflection* on the experience especially has transformative power and functions as a means of learning.[108] That is, students may experience a specific problem or issue, for example, they recognize several problems surrounding legal guardianship in cases of dementia. Through reflecting on such issues and on the ethics that accompany the complex legal content, the student's development may be furthered. In some cases, this results in a transformation in the way the student perceives the world and/or their position in the word. This transformation leads to a new step in the student's development.

Piaget found that every child goes through the stages of development at an age-related pace. This meant, according to Piaget, that progression through the stages has a natural flow that could not be accelerated.[109] This is different from the theory of the social

102 Kolb 2015, pp. 5, 18.

103 Dewey was also one of the few educational philosophers who paid attention to the developmental dimension of learning. Overall, the developmental dimension is underexposed in educational philosophy. See Kuhn 1999, p. 18.

104 Kolb 2015, p. 5.

105 Kolb 2015, p. 12, see also Pritchard 2009, p. 20.

106 For constructivists, there are four areas of learning namely knowledge, concepts, skills and attitudes. See: Pritchard 2009, p. 18.

107 Pritchard 2009, pp. 17, 20. See also: Kolb 2015, p. 12, Kuhn 1999, p. 18 and Ambrose et al., p. 44.

108 Cedrone 2013, pp. 833-834.

109 Pritchard 2009, p. 115.

constructivist Lev Vygotsky (1896-1934), who is most known for his description of the 'zone of proximal development' (the 'ZPD').[110] The ZPD is a space just above the level of understanding of a person: It is the level of understanding to which the learner will progress next. Vygotsky advocated that development may occur through collaboration between a student and a more knowledgeable other in this ZPD.[111] In other words, in educational settings, the educator (or a more experienced peer) may nurture and support the development of children by offering support and appropriate challenges in the pupil's ZPD.[112] For instance, educators may nudge students towards a subsequent stage in their development by scaffolding specific assignments that let students practice on the edge of their understanding to expand their horizons.

For constructivists, learning is a personal journey: Although educators may act as facilitators, learners have to come to their own ideas and knowledge.[113] Biesta offers some criticism on this notion of constructivism, which he views as the foundational theory of the so-called 'learnification' of education. According to Biesta, 'learnification' places learners and their learning at the center of education instead of, for example, educators or the curriculum. In short, Biesta's criticism comes down to his concern that constructivism's belief that learning is a strictly *personal* process makes learning within an educational context empty. Biesta finds that this is the case, because without a context – often offered by the institution, curriculum or educator – that consists of a purpose (*why* is the student learning), content (*what* is the student learning) and relationship (*for whom* is the student learning), 'learning' in an educational setting is void of substance.[114] The *purpose* of education has especially been extensively (and famously) described by Biesta, who sees the purpose as threefold, namely 1) qualification, (2) socialization and (3) subjectification.[115] With Biesta's warning in mind, it may be wise for educators in ALE to adopt a balanced position that considers learning an individual process that may be stimulated and nurtured by educators who provide the educational context.

Piaget's and Vygotsky's research focuses on the development of children. To gain understanding in the development of *adults* (including young adults, as most of our students are), we may find inspiration and insight in developmental theories such as those

110 See Smagorinsky 2018, p. 71.
111 Pritchard 2009, p. 115.
112 Pritchard 2009, p. 25.
113 See Pritchard 2009, pp. 32-33. See also Biesta 2020, p. 91.
114 Biesta 2020, p. 91.
115 Biesta 2020, p. 91. According to Biesta, education has three purposes. The first is *qualification*, which consists of transmission of knowledge and skills. The second purpose is *socialization*, which looks at the implicit or explicit (re-) presentation of cultures, traditions and practices. Finally, the third purpose is *subjectification*. This concerns the development of the self as a human being with 'qualified' freedom (freedom that is connected to their existence in and with the world, other human beings, living creatures and the physical environment). The individual is then capable of self-action and becomes a subject of his or her own life, not just an object steered by others or external factors. See Biesta 2020, pp. 92-94.

described by Kuhn and Kegan. These theories build upon the ideas of Piaget and describe how adults develop their thinking and how their way of making sense of the world transforms.[116] Even though Kuhn and Kegan describe the development in different terms and Kuhn describes four levels of epistemological understanding whereas Kegan describes five orders of consciousness, both descriptions have a similar build-up. The basic idea of both theories also resonates with other descriptions of the intellectual development of adults, such as those of Perry; Belenky, and; Baxter-Magolda.[117] The main ideas shared by these theories may be helpful to educators in legal education. For this reason, both theories will be discussed in the following.

Kuhn describes four levels of epistemological understanding. In other words, she defines four levels on which individuals can view, experience and gain knowledge of the world around them. The level of understanding on which a person stands determines how they perceive reality, how they view knowledge and to what extent they are able to think critically.[118] The first level is the level of the *realist*. Someone on this level (often a young child between the age of 3 to 5 years) starts with the understanding that things that people say or write express that person's beliefs, which are direct reflections of reality. In other words, what people say about reality is seen as true.[119] The realist believes that reality can be directly known and that knowledge is absolute and given by an external authority. Since any assertion made is undoubtedly true, critical thinking is not necessary on this level.[120] In contrast, on the second level of epistemological understanding, the *absolutist* regards an assertion as a mere, though factual representation of a person's belief about reality. The main difference with the realist's awareness is that for an absolutist, this belief may be different from physical reality and can therefore be either true (in accordance with reality) or false (different from reality). Knowledge claims can be tested against reality as being true or false with the help of evidence.[121] On this absolutist level, reality is knowable, knowledge absolute and given by an external authority. Furthermore, critical thinking has a limited use as merely a process that tests if an assertion is true or false.[122] A small number of people do not progress beyond this absolutist state during their lifetimes. For these people, conflicts between assertions presented to them may occur but are solved by appealing to an authority.[123] However, by being confronted with experts who disagree on

116 See Kegan 1994, p. 9.

117 These theories share, for example, the idea that the higher levels of development are characterized by an increased tolerance for uncertainty, personal authorship of knowledge and the development of judgment based on evidence. See Ambrose et al. 2010, p. 163. See also Cedrone 2013, p. 816 (footnote 181).

118 Kuhn 1999, p. 23.

119 Kuhn 1999, p. 19.

120 See Kuhn 1999, p. 23.

121 Kuhn 1999, pp. 19, 22.

122 Kuhn 1999, p. 23.

123 Kuhn 1999, p. 22.

important topics, most people progress – often in their adolescence – towards the *multiplist* stance. On this level, people lose their absolutist belief in certain truth. This results in the conviction that every opinion is the result of the subjective preferences of the person expressing them and all opinions have their own worth and the same status: No one opinion is better than any of the others. On this level of epistemological understanding, a person does not have a yardstick to critically compare the various opinions on their strengths: This means that critical reflection on opinions and assertions is not possible. This level of understanding might be recognized in those lively discussions between active participants on social media where some people find that 'everyone has their own truth', 'science is just one other opinion' and speak of 'fake news' in the context of mainstream news media. According to Kuhn, many people remain on this third level of epistemological understanding for the rest of their lives. Nevertheless, a number of people do progress towards the fourth, *evaluative*, level. On this level, people have the understanding that opinions are unequal and standards can be used to evaluate the worth of expressed opinions. Gaining knowledge is seen as a process that involves argumentation, evaluation and judgment, resulting in an informed opinion. In other words, on the evaluative level, truth remains uncertain, but evaluation of opinions is possible through reasonable argumentation. On this level, critical thinking is the path towards an informed opinion.[124]

Comparable to this outline of the developmental path, Kegan introduces five ways of constructing reality, which he calls orders of consciousness or the five developmental stages of learning.[125] Just as is the case for Kuhn's four levels of epistemological understanding, people progress through these orders during their lifetimes, but not all people reach the highest levels. Young children function within the *impulsive* order, until they go through a transformation of the mind between the ages of 5 and 10 and progress into the second, *instrumental* order, which enables them to control their impulses and view reality beyond simply their own perception.[126] This level seems to largely correspond to Kuhn's absolutist level. Signs that students are functioning in this instrumental order will probably be recognizable for educators in secondary and higher education. For educators in ALE, this might especially be familiar in the behavior and communication of first-year students. A student in the instrumental order of consciousness looks for an external authority to provide knowledge, they want to do things right, but crave to hear from the authority – the educator – in more detail exactly what is expected of them and what the 'right answer' is. Other people are seen as either instrumental for the achievement of personal goals or as obstacles to the fulfilment of their own individual needs.[127]

124 Kuhn 1999, pp. 22-23.
125 See Kegan p. 313 and Scott Fruehwald 2020, p. 3.
126 Scott Fruehwald 2020, pp. 3-4.
127 Cedrone 2013, p. 812.

For example, a third-year student in my Moot Court course complained that she should have been given not only instructions and assessment criteria, but also an exact and detailed example of the brief I asked her to write. In addition, she protested that she had to explain some legal concepts to a team member and found that this student was a liability to her success. This behavior signals that the student (for the time being) resides in the second order – the instrumental order – of consciousness. Although they cannot see a number of things and cannot abstract a main theme from a body of information, people functioning in this second, instrumental order are able to control their impulses, deduce cause and effect, create narratives of events and can construct fixed mental categories in which concepts and people are placed.[128] In this second order, knowledge is pursued instrumentally: It is a way to achieve a concrete result,[129] such as a career or pass an exam. Most people progress into the third order by the age of twenty. However, according to Kegan, approximately 10 percent of people do not develop further than this second order of consciousness.[130] The ones that do, progress toward the *socializing* order where they become more capable of abstraction and 'theory'.[131] Cedrone claims that this level is especially important for law students, since it enables them to consider assumptions for the sake of the argument, make hypotheses that can be tested, and reflect on their own thinking.[132] Furthermore, in this third order, people can view themselves in relation to others, identify the Self in relation to their social context and are able to put the needs of others before their own. Still, knowledge is viewed as coming from an authority. Because knowledge is pursued to meet the expectations of others from whom they need acceptance – such as peers, educators or parents – students in the third order of consciousness may perceive feedback as an attack on their self-worth.[133] According to Cedrone, law students functioning in this order cannot see that the law is just one system or method of viewing the world (which is a limited view) and, for example, try to apply legal reasoning and concepts to all areas of life.[134] Kegan raises a fundamental concern with regard to the third order: It makes socialization possible but also makes people vulnerable to the negative effects of socialization, namely a lack of criticality. In explanation, because the community becomes of great importance for the development of the individual's Self, they are unable to criticize the community's system. In our context, this means that merely focusing on the development of the socializing order of development in law schools might undermine students' ability to think critically about the law, society and themselves. To counter this

128 Cedrone 2013, p. 811.
129 Cedrone 2013, p. 812.
130 Cedrone, p. 811, See also: Scott Fruehwald 2020, p. 4.
131 Cedrone 2013, p. 814, Scott Fruehwald 2020, p. 4.
132 Cedrone 2013, p. 814.
133 Cedrone 2013, pp. 814-816, Scott Fruehwald 2020, p. 4.
134 Cedrone 2013, p. 816.

risk, Kegan suggests aiming at the development of the fourth order of consciousness in higher education.[135] This is the *self-authoring* stage, which Kegan relates to life in modern times. In this stage – which may only be reached by one half or one third of all individuals[136] – knowledge is seen as constructed by the individual Self through experience, reflection and analysis, based on the careful consultation of multiple sources, such as literature and educators.[137] In this order of consciousness, individuals are able to reflect upon their social context and their role in that context. Also, the individual's identity remains stable and is not subjugated to social circumstances. Students who function in this order of consciousness are self-directed learners and have a level of autonomy and self-determination. They can critically reflect on the law, the legal system and their role within that system. Furthermore, these students view feedback as an opportunity to grow and do not feel threatened by it.[138] Finally, the fifth level of consciousness as formulated by Kegan is the *self-transforming* order. According to Kegan, this level can only be reached later in life and only by a select few, since it requires vast life-experience and insight. It is a level on which individuals see themselves as a complex system subjected to constant change. They are able to reflect on and doubt their own identity and fundamental beliefs and consider themselves a perpetual work-in-progress that is never finished or whole.[139]

Every step on the 'ladder' of development stages is related to the specific way individuals at that stage make sense, understand and construct knowledge of the world. When there is a change in their functioning and in the way they see the world and themselves in the world, individuals are able to progress to the next step of development. This is a *qualitative* change – a change in how people view the world.[140] Nevertheless, not all individuals will be able to reach the highest levels of epistemological understanding or orders of consciousness. Parallel with Vygotsky's assessment, Ambrose et al. argue that while the intellectual development of young adults cannot be forced, it *can* be nurtured and encouraged in higher education by providing support and appropriate challenges (in the zone of proximal development). Kegan, too, maintains that an individual can be supported in developing toward a subsequent order of consciousness and argues that higher education's aim is to support students' development towards the fourth level of consciousness.[141] Based on Kegan's research, Cedrone proposes a developmental approach to legal education in which students are taught more than just 'thinking like a lawyer'. According to Cedrone, the aim of this approach is for legal education to trigger a change

135 Kegan 1994, p. 287.
136 Scott Fruehwald 2020, p. 4.
137 Cedrone 2012, p. 819.
138 Cedrone 2013, pp. 819-820.
139 Kegan 1994, pp. 311-313.
140 Cedrone 2013, pp. 805-806.
141 Kegan 1994, pp. 44, 287.

in the students' worldview and for the student to develop the ability to have creative legal ideas in complex, human situations.[142]

To be able to support student cognitive development – and, according to Kuhn, in order to teach critical thinking[143] – educators require an understanding of the developmental stages.[144] This understanding helps recognize what a student's responses reveal about the developmental stage they may likely be in. This provides educators with the opportunity to develop appropriate challenges or instructional interventions that support the student's further development. As such, the levels of development may function as guide posts in legal education: Insight into a student's development level steers the educator in the direction of effective strategies to support the student's further growth.[145] This means that educators could scaffold legal education to support our students' development towards the self-authoring and evaluating stages in which students are capable of academic abilities such as critical thinking, reflection and responsibility. In this situation, the educator's role is to facilitate student learning by creating meaningful experiences. The student's learning is then constructed by individual study – for example, by reading and processing literature, or by listening to an educator's explanation – and experiences.

Still, there will be graduates leaving university at earlier stages of development. Many of these students will travel through the following stages at their own pace, for example through experiences in the work place.[146] Importantly, the fact that not all students will be able reach the final stage(s) of cognitive development before they leave their law school calls for educators to have realistic expectations of what a student can achieve in their few years of study. That way, educators will be able to set appropriate goals and will hopefully not be discouraged when a number of students are (yet) unable to show mastery of the highest level(s) of development.

Revisiting the signature pedagogy of legal education

In addition to understanding the students' learning process, it is important for educators in legal education to have insight into the pedagogy that could be used in legal education. This helps educators in the preparation of their courses or individual classes, when they choose which instructional interventions they want to employ. Abrami et al. describe four categories of these interventions, namely: individual study; dialogue; authentic/anchored

142 Cedrone 2013, pp. 788, 823.
143 Kuhn 1999, p. 24.
144 See also Kuhn 1999, p. 24.
145 Kuhn 1999, p. 24. See also: Cedrone 2015, p. 821.
146 Ambrose et al. 2010, p. 166.

instruction; mentoring. Individual study concerns students who – while being alone – are reading, watching, listening to an educator explaining knowledge, reflect on new information and individually solve complex problems. Students engage in individual study during, for instance, lectures in large groups, which aim at knowledge transmission.[147] In these situations, for example during a lecture for 400+ students, there is often no space for real interaction between the educator and the students (or between the students). Instead, the students mostly listen to the educator's explanation and take individual notes.[148] The second category of instructional interventions, dialogue, starts with the belief that students learn through discussion. The discussion may be held in an adversarial or cooperative setting and can either be written or oral. Abrami and his colleagues describe the many subcategories of dialogue, such as: The educator asking the student questions; students asking their educator questions; students discussing the content in pairs with or without an educator; whole class discussions with or without an educator; group discussions with or without the educator; formal debates; student presentations with complementary discussion; the Socratic dialogue.[149] Stolker finds that forms of dialogue are possible during seminars given to smaller groups of a maximum of 30 students that have prepared the material in advance.[150] The third category, authentic/anchored instruction, seems related to experiential learning theories which takes us back to Rousseau, Dewey and the *Progressive Education Movement*. The idea is that students are confronted with authentic problems and their exploration and analysis of these problems results in engagement and inquiry. Authentic/anchored instruction may be employed in various ways, namely through applied problem solving (for example, by giving students real life dilemmas), case studies, simulations, playing games and roleplay.[151] Stolker finds that project work, blended learning and practical skills training provide opportunities for authentic/anchored instruction and experiential learning in ALE.[152] In law schools in the Netherlands, notable examples of anchored instruction are the curricula (and courses) that are structured around problem-based learning at Maastricht University and Erasmus University. In an ideal situation, in which the educator scaffolds the students' learning, educators provide increasingly complex problems and challenges during the course and the curriculum.[153] Finally, the fourth category of instructional techniques is mentoring. This is an intensive intervention that requires one-on-one interaction between a student and an expert, during which the expert models the desired behavior and provides the

147 Abrami et al. 2015, p. 289.
148 Stolker 2014, pp. 162-163.
149 Abrami et al. 2015, pp. 289-290.
150 Stolker 2014, pp. 162-163.
151 Abrami et al. 2015, pp. 290-291.
152 Stolker 2014, pp. 162-163.
153 Cedrone 2013, p. 831.

student with detailed feedback. Forms of mentoring are one-on-one educator-student interaction, internships and pairing with a more experienced peer.[154] In legal education, mentoring may take place during tutorials in which an educator supervises one or two students.[155]

Dialogue is currently the dominant category of instructional techniques used in legal education. Since Christopher Langdell introduced the Socratic dialogue as an instructional intervention in legal education at Harvard University in the 1880's,[156] this has become known as the 'signature pedagogy' for law schools. In the United States, the Socratic dialogue is often used within the Case Dialogue method. Here, the focus is on court cases that are studied and discussed during class in order to analyze the case law and find underlying legal principles.[157] This is a method that befits the US legal and legal educational system, since it is based on a common law system and American legal education is a *professional* education. However, the pedagogy of dialogue, including the Socratic dialogue, is also commonly used in Dutch legal education, which is based on the Dutch civil law system and is primarily an *academic* education. In the Netherlands, many educators use dialogue techniques in their lectures or seminars: Students study literature, the legal code and case law at home and during class individual students are asked to answer (often prepared) questions posed by the educator. In response to the student's reaction, the educator will either ask a follow-up question (to the same or another student), approve of the answer, or point out fallacies in the answer. This is a commonly used instructional method in Dutch ALE, which shows that dialogue (and often Socratic dialogue) is also the 'signature pedagogy' in the Dutch practice of legal education.

A signature pedagogy is a characteristic form of teaching and learning through which newcomers are introduced and trained in the discipline or domain.[158] The signature pedagogy defines what the field sees as 'knowledge' (and what not) and also prescribes how domain relevant knowledge (see also chapters 3 and 4) is analyzed and criticized.[159] The signature pedagogy functions as an introduction to the so-called conversation of the domain and is based on an archetype of the ideal professional.[160] Signature pedagogies are most strongly represented in professional education and focus on (the development of) three dimensions: The cognitive dimension (thinking), technical/practical skills dimension (performing) and the moral dimension (acting with integrity/ethical professional role).[161]

154 Abrami et al. 2015, p. 291.
155 Stolker 2014, pp. 162-163.
156 Stolker 2014, p. 164. Cedrone 2013, p. 796. See also: Trousdale 2010, pp. 31-33.
157 Trousdale 2010, p. 32.
158 Shulman 2005, p. 52. Cedrone 2013, p. 790.
159 Shulman 2005, p. 54.
160 Cedrone 2013, p. 793.
161 Shulman 2005, pp. 52, 58. Cedrone 2013, p. 792.

The Socratic Dialogue is a form of dialogue that takes place between the educator and a student: The educator asks a question that the student answers. After the student answers, the educator may ask follow-up questions. There are at least two essential elements in this instructional intervention: First, the unexpectedness of the question(s) a student is asked, which they have to answer immediately. Secondly, the necessary student preparation (reading literature, reading case law) in order to join and follow the dialogue during the seminar.[162] The underlying archetype is that of an ideal lawyer who is well-prepared, able to think on their feet and has quick insight into the legal issues of a case.[163] Importantly, the Socratic Dialogue nurtures the idea that the educator is the authority who has the knowledge that the students are required to learn, which results in the educator's voice being dominant in the classroom. In addition, there is very little room for student-student interaction in class, since most communication takes place between the educator and the student who is singled out to answer questions. Even though they may not be called upon, the idea behind this pedagogy is still that *all* students are actively involved in learning: The students that are not asked question(s) need to be well prepared to be able to mentally answer the question(s) asked. However, this will only be possible if all students are sufficiently prepared and the questions are indeed asked unexpectedly of random students in the room. If this is not the case, active students will quickly become passive.[164] A strong point of the legal signature pedagogy is that it enables newcomers to quickly adapt and learn to analyze reality through the legal filter consisting of legal constructs. This is because signature pedagogies focus on teaching students certain routines: 'Thinking like a lawyer' becomes a habit of mind that makes dealing with new problems or challenges easier.[165] Also, the Socratic Dialogue is an instructional technique that can be used with groups that are quite large, which is most definitely practical when regarding the great number of students studying law.

However, the Socratic Dialogue also comes with some pitfalls. First, the pedagogy gives center stage to the *cognitive* development of students because (especially in the Case Dialogue Method) it places the procedural and formal qualities of legal thinking at the forefront.[166] Indeed, in 2007, the Carnegie Foundation for the Advancement of Teaching published a study on law schools in which they concluded that most American law schools mainly focus on intellectual development (knowledge and thinking). However, the Carnegie Foundation strongly recommends legal education to emphasize not one, but *all three* dimensions of development. The attention to intellectual development in legal education underexposes the other two dimensions (technical/practical skills and ethical

162 Cedrone 2013, p. 793, footnote 62.
163 Cedrone 2013, p. 793.
164 Cedrone 2013, p. 793, footnote 62.
165 Shulman 2005, p. 56.
166 Cedrone 2013, p. 790.

reflection on the professional role).[167] In Dutch legal education, too, it seems that the cognitive development of students has been taking center stage for a long time, due to a focus on the transmission of knowledge. In the past years, technical skills (especially writing skills) training has gained attention, although the attention for professional skills development may be less substantial than in the US. The reason for this is that the legal educational system in the Netherlands offers a separate, additional professional training *after* a student's completion of the university's Bachelor and Master programs. However, it seems that attention to ethical development is still in its infancy. In short, the American and Dutch law schools share a tendency to favor the development of cognitive skills. The second pitfall of the Socratic Dialogue method is that one of its goals is socialization: Through this pedagogy, students learn from more experienced members of the community how to participate in the conversation of the domain. Just as is the case with Kegan's socialization order of consciousness, this *socialization* aspect can be met with some skepticism, since some say that it results in a lack of criticism. This critique is illustrated by Trousdale who describes how he adapted to the system but utterly lost his own voice during his legal education in which the case dialogue method was utilized.[168] When socializing – in other words, when becoming part of the domain – is the most important aspect of a pedagogy, it will be next to impossible for new members to become able to contribute, criticize or change the domain. A third pitfall of the Socratic dialogue is that it is prone to creating a competitive atmosphere in class, because students are motivated to give their educator the 'right' answer and might try to compete with one another. Unfortunately, this atmosphere can threaten the safe learning environment. An unsafe learning environment could have serious negative consequences for students, for example, Rhode describes increased stress levels, lowered self-esteem and the silencing of students belonging to minorities.[169] Fourth, a pitfall that may accompany the Socratic Dialogue is related to the setting in which it is often employed. Lectures – in very large groups, but also in smaller groups of approximately 30 students – are often the chosen instructional form. To a certain extent, this is fine: As said before, lectures for large groups may be quite effective for transmitting information. However, research shows, too, that lectures are not an effective means of teaching students values, behavioral skills, or how to think. Also, lectures often fail to inspire students.[170] Consequently, the way the Socratic Dialogue is taught is not helpful for teaching students critical thinking, engaging students or teaching them to find their way in ethical dilemmas. Finally, it seems that the way in which the Socratic dialogue is often used is not fully able to support our students' progress towards

167 See also: Cedrone 2013, pp. 795-796.
168 Trousdale 2010, p. 30.
169 Stolker 2014, p. 166.
170 Stolker 2014, p. 163.

the highest developmental stages: The self-authoring order of consciousness and the evaluative level of epistemological understanding. This could specific situation be the case, when the educator is the central persona in the classroom, students are trained to understand that the educator has the answers and has full insight into the knowledge they have yet to learn, and the students' focus lies on giving the educator the correct answers. These attitudes correspond with the position taken by people functioning on the realist, absolutist, instrumental, and socializing levels of development. In contrast, in order for students to function on the higher levels of development – the evaluative or self-authoring stage of development – they will have to understand that knowledge is not absolute and are required to construct their own knowledge. However, this seems not to be an attainable goal considering how the Socratic Dialogue is currently practiced in legal education lectures. This observation gives reason to call for adding other pedagogical strategies to the use of the Socratic dialogue in legal education.

With Stolker, Cedrone and the Carnegie Foundation,[171] I call for a change in legal education: ALE may gain much from using more variation in the teaching methods (instructional interventions) that are used.[172] Educators in ALE could find inspiration in theories of experiential learning and create a broad variety of experiences to support their students' learning. Possible teaching methods for legal education that are rooted in experiential learning, may relate to play, such as role-play, simulations, quizzes, and story-telling. Others may entail instructional interventions using dialogue, such as the Socratic method, small group discussion, oral presentations or written papers; techniques using technology, such as including videoclips, *virtual reality* or online cooperation; interventions that bring professional practice closer to the students, for example field trips, internships or guest speakers; techniques that focus on thinking strategies, such as one minute papers, think-pair-share, mind-maps or other thinking habits.[173] These experiences we create for our students can be based on any of the categories of interventions: From dialogue, to individual study, anchored instruction to mentoring. Combining two or more categories in one experience is also possible. Indeed, research has shown that combining dialogue, authentic/anchored instruction and mentoring has the most influence on student learning.[174]

To summarize, we could engage our students and support their learning and development by providing more variety in teaching methods. While wandering off the

171 Cedrone 2013, p. 796. Stolker 2014, pp. 159-160.

172 Stolker 2014, pp. 159-160.

173 Stolker gives many of these suggestions in his plea for more variation in the teaching method(s) of legal education. See: Stolker 2014, p. 161. Interestingly, educators in higher education responded with virtually the same sort of techniques to the question which types of activities were used to teach critical thinking, see Bellaera et al. 2021, p. 9.

174 Abrami et al. 2015, p. 302.

well-worn path of the traditional Socratic Dialogue, educators in legal education might discover that other techniques, such as the many possibilities of authentic/anchored instruction effectively support our students' academic abilities, including their abilities of critical thinking, creative thinking and responsibility.

Restoring the balance between the vocational and academic components of legal education

The previous sections show the current state of ALE, which is characterized by its emphasis on cognitive development and gaining knowledge of black letter law. Also, due to the marketization of academic education and by means of the Socratic Dialogue, legal education predominantly focuses on training students' vocational abilities and skills, so that they may quickly and successfully join the workforce. Consequently, the development of a student's character and academic abilities moves to the background. In other words, the balance of legal education has shifted towards vocational abilities and skills. In order to support the *full* development of our students, a shift in legal education's predominant focus on the development of vocational skills is necessary. In the following, the distinction between legal education's two components (the vocational and academic component) and the current problematic balance between the two will be further explicated.

In general, a distinction can be made between vocational education and academic education.[175] Students in the U.S. who want to obtain a law degree at a university, start with four years of study in an academic, broad (liberal) undergraduate degree course (without specific content on law), followed by a vocational, graduate education in law. This graduate law degree – the JD – is focused on training students for the Bar and the practical legal profession. In contrast, in the Netherlands (and in many other countries), Bachelor students enroll from the very start in a specific area of study, be it Economics, Medicine, or Law. The fact that the Dutch educational system does not typically know the American broad undergraduate degree means that Dutch law students start off with an immediate in-depth study of law. This law degree is not only considered vocational, but also *academic*: It prepares them not only for professional life as an attorney or prosecutor, but also for life as an academic.[176] In all cases, legal academic education consists of a vocational and an academic component. Law – the legal academic's object of study and the focus of legal education – is a societal phenomenon that has its own specific role and practice. After graduating law school, students will often find themselves working within a practice as legal professionals. Hence, it is not surprising that ALE has a vocational component that

175 Horlacher 2017, pp. 60-61. See also Ahsmann 2016, p. 16.
176 Stolker 2014, pp. 17-18.

teaches students practical legal knowledge and skills, in order for them to be prepared for professional life. In this sense, Dutch legal education can be viewed as professional training. This vocational component is recognizable in black letter law courses such as Criminal Law, Contract Law, Migration Law, Administrative Law, and courses on Procedural Law. These courses teach practical relevant information about current law, that the students will be able to apply in their future occupation as legal professionals. In many of these courses – and in some cases in specialized courses (for example, moot court courses) – legal skills are trained. The skills that are being trained and tested during the Bachelor and/or Master program are specifically relevant to the (traditional) legal profession, for instance argumentation, language and analytical skills, reading and analyzing case law, legal writing, oral pleading, and legal reasoning.

In these times of globalization, increasingly fast technological innovations and corporatization of legal practice,[177] it might be argued that other – less traditionally legal – skills and knowledge become relevant for professional life as well,[178] now that some of the academic lawyer's traditional tasks can be executed through faster or less expensive options, for instance through digitalized information and automated processes (e.g. online legal information or e-courts),[179] or be performed more cost effectively by transferring originally legal tasks to non-lawyers who work at lower cost.[180] I concur with Susskind that these changes will bring new challenges to the lawyer's doorstep, because they will have to be able to deal with legal issues but also with *non*-legal issues such as (global) economics, business management, and project management.[181] Furthermore, Susskind argues that contemporary and future society will require legal professionals to reinvent their occupation, since their traditional role is subject to change. As new legal roles Susskind suggests consultant, business adviser, legal systems engineer, legal data systems organizer, legal data analyzer, or legal risk manager.[182] Moreover, legal design and legal tech are becoming more known as new areas that legal professionals need to be competent in. It is clear that these possibly future roles and areas of vocation of the legal professional also require different knowledge and skills, for example in programming, data analysis, design thinking, visualization, risk management, organizational psychology, and business management.[183] In the (near) future, these could therefore be part of the *vocational*

177 See Susskind 2017, p. 126.

178 See Mak 2017, p. 7.

179 See for example, Hildebrandt, M. (June 24th 2011). Although not undisputed (see www.mr-online.nl/juristen-laten-weinig-heel-van-werkwijze-e-court/, last visited May 24th 2023), experiments with digitalized judgments are on their way, for instance in the Netherlands where a privately established 'E-court' (www.e-court.nl) gave judgment in cases of unpaid insurance premiums.

180 Susskind 2017, pp. 34-35, 37.

181 Susskind 2017, pp. 126-127.

182 Susskind 2017, pp. 135-137, 140.

183 See, for instance, Mak 2017, pp. 25-26.

component of legal education and would call for a broader, multidisciplinary legal education.

Vocational – in other words *professional* – training is part of a legal education. This holds true for legal professionals trained at an academic university level, as well as for the professionals who received their legal education at a non-academic institution. In the Netherlands, for example, a Bachelor's degree in law can be achieved at an Academic University as well as at a University for Applied Science. Universities for Applied Science offer their students a non-academic legal education that focuses on a practical, vocational training for their future legal profession.[184] The career options for legal professionals trained at a University for Applied Science are different from those for academically educated lawyers, since without additional *academic* education, the former cannot pass the Bar and are excluded from some occupations, such as those of judge, prosecutor, or attorney. Other differences between the academic law school and the non-academic vocational training at a University of Applied Science are, for instance, the level of prior education required of freshman students, and the content and focus of the curriculum. In short, vocational education offers professional training, teaches *practical, factual* legal knowledge and legal skills, and provides a more specialized education so that the graduate is ready for professional life. In this sense, *education is useful*.[185] From a vocational point of view, the purpose of the law school is to produce good (relevantly skilled) lawyers.[186]

However relevant for the legal practice and legal profession, an *academic* legal education requires more than vocational training.[187] It necessitates a component that makes that education specifically academic. The academic component complements and transcends vocational legal education, as it adds its own purpose to legal education. Namely, that ALE is not just about producing good lawyers, but also about educating good citizens capable of responsibility, critical reflection and creative problem solving.[188] This aim requires specific skills, knowledge, and the life attitude that characterize academics. I argue that the core characteristics and dispositions of academics in the 21st century come down to the academic's comprehensive *attitude of responsibility*, which includes that critical thinking ability necessary to a perpetual search for truth and the academic ability to create novelty.

---

184 See, for example, https://studiegids.hva.nl/studiegids?edu=hborechten-vt, https://www.hu.nl/voltijd-opleidingen/hbo-rechten/tijdens-de-opleiding, https://www.hanze.nl/nld/onderwijs/economie/instituut-voor-rechtenstudies/opleidingen/bachelor/hbo-rechten, last accessed 10 January 2019.

185 Horlacher 2017, p. 60. Horlacher argues that *usefulness* and, thus, vocational training was seen as the primary goal of education by 18th century philanthropists in Germany and educators from the era of Enlightenment. She contrasts this view with the German Romantic's aim of *self-realization*.

186 Cownie 2004, p. 31.

187 See, for example, Collini 2012, p. 7.

188 Cownie 2004, p. 31. See also Nussbaum 2016, pp. 6, 9.

Becoming a 'good citizen' of 21st century global society demands that academic lawyers obtain additional skills and knowledge relevant to the practice of their profession. This quest to educate students for global citizenship[189] calls for nurturing a notion of responsibility for that society and the critical, autonomous – or rather – self-authored,[190] and reflective thinking[191] that is often brought forward as a defining *academic* characteristic.[192] The idea that this type of thinking is specifically *academic* becomes clear in the light of Academia's historical (and systematic approach to the) search for truth. According to Martin, the capacity for critical questioning makes the pursuit of truth possible, and he finds that it is therefore the core of academic capability.[193] And surely, one of the concepts closely related to critical thinking is *truth*, since knowledge claims are judged on – amongst others – logic, which detects whether a statement or an argument (and its premises) is in accordance with truth. Simply stated, when judging (legal) arguments, it is of importance to decipher the truth-value of the claim, which in its most minimalist interpretation means that it is in correspondence with 'the way things are'.[194]

For a legal academic to be able to be a self-authored thinker with reflective and critical skills, it can be argued that knowledge of and familiarity with various disciplines is needed.[195] Indeed, being reflective, skeptical, or doubtful[196] of someone else's, your own, and your professional field's ideas, practices, or traditions requires constructing an examined, self-authored and somewhat detached point of view. This can only come into existence if an individual reaches towards higher levels of development and acquires further knowledge to extend his or her own horizon. In particular, interesingly, being

189 Nussbaum 2016, p. 7. See also Smits 2005, p. 8 and Witteveen 2005, pp. 192-193.

190 Van Klink argues that instead of talking about autonomous thinking, we should phrase this as 'intellectual and moral integrity'. No one is able to separate their thought process completely from their own background, which colors a person's convictions and ideas, hence making them not completely separate, or autonomous. What any academic should rather aim for instead of autonomous thinking, is 'using one's own faculty of judgment' in reflection and discussion to understand and question that background so that old assumptions might be replaced by new insights. Van Klink 2016, p. 21. Since I agree with Van Klink's analysis, I also suggest using a different denominator than 'autonomous thinking'. Therefore, in the context of developmental theory, I suggest using 'self-authored thinking'.

191 Critical thinking can be described as a process with the goal of making reasonable decisions about what to believe or what to do. See: Ennis 1996, p. XVII. The concept of critical thinking is further explored in Chapter 3.

192 See on the importance of a critical attitude and critical thinking for academics and, more specifically, for lawyers: Cownie 2004, pp. 76, 78, 83, Mak 2017, p. 30, Ahsmann 2016, p. 9, Van Klink & De Vries 2016, p. 6, Brouwer 2005, p. 5, Witteveen 2005, p. 191, Bosch-Boesjes 2005, p. 26, Knigge 2005, p. 73.

193 Martin 1999, p. 97. See also: Cownie 2004, p. 78.

194 Bowell and Kemp 2010, pp. 60-61.

195 See Ahmann, p. 9.

196 Ulrich Beck describes 'the art of reflexive doubt' as a liberating endeavor and as a starting point for relativism, tolerance and flexibility. It requires (re-)examination of one's own ideas and convictions and is often accompanied by some discomfort and self-disillusion. See Beck 1997, p. 162. See also: Van Rossum 2018-1, p. 249.

skeptical towards your own field of expertise's traditions and practices can be a challenge for lawyers, since it is ingrained in the legal domain, the lawyer's occupation and legal education's signature pedagogy that a higher authority exists with a claim to objective (legal) truth: Namely the law, the judge's decision or the law professor's opinion.[197]

Critical thinking is the process necessary for making decisions in matters of consequence.[198] This faculty of judgment is often regarded as a necessary academic skill for law students to develop.[199] In the marketized, contemporary risk society interlaced with a permanent sense of uncertainty, this faculty is all the more important for our students to develop, since decision-making has become increasingly difficult. Indeed, an unambiguously *right* choice seems hard to make, because any selection out of the many options of choice may have unforeseen and far-reaching consequences for an unknown number of people.[200] For example, relatively small life choices such as using plastic bags for groceries, driving a non-electric car, eating meat regularly, or ordering products on AliExpress already negatively influence environmental conditions on earth, which may have all sorts of consequences for millions – if not billions – of people now *and* in the future. In professional life, too, difficult choices await. In the process of making these personal and professional choices, the individual is increasingly in need of a highly developed faculty of judgment and decision-making skills. Therefore, they need to be able to judge knowledge (information) on its truth-value, sufficiency, and relevancy, which – as said – presupposes skills in reflective and critical thinking. These skills are of importance for *all* global citizens, but can specifically be required of *academically* educated individuals, who can be expected to be skilled in dissecting truth from falsehoods, critical thinking and making sound judgment calls.

In this context, creative thinking ability, too, is of importance, since creativity necessarily succeeds the practice of the capability of judgment and decision-making. For example, after critical reflection on a current practice and deciding that it is not desirable, a *new* idea of how it *should* be must be created. In other words, *new* alternatives must be contemplated. This requires creative ability.[201] Also, defining the problem and judging the

197 See Kant 1996, p. 251.

198 See Ennis 1996, p. XVII.

199 See on the importance of the faculty of judgment for legal academic education: Van Klink & De Vries 2016, p. 6. Here, Van Klink and De Vries connect the faculty of judgment with critical thinking skills. See also on the importance of critical judgment: Witteveen 2005, p. 192, Bosch-Boesjes 2005, p. 26 and Knigge 2005, p. 73. For academic legal professionals, for instance judges, attorneys, prosecutors, and civil servants, decision making skills are off course also highly relevant for their vocation, which points out that decision-making is not only an *academic* skill necessary for citizenship of the global society, but is also a *vocational* skill, useful for (and necessary in) the legal profession.

200 Francot 2014, pp. 204-205, Beck 1992, p. 46.

201 Ennis 1996, p. XVII. Interestingly, most of the legal academics (here meaning academic staff in universities) that were part of Cownie's research defined critical thinking as the principle aim for legal education, but almost none mentioned creativity as an important ability in their *own* occupation. This might be

worth of the created possibilities for a solution require critical thinking. In this way, both capabilities are closely connected. In short, critical and creative thinking are therefore important for the legal academic who wishes to propose change or alternatives and as such takes their responsibility in contemporary society. Furthermore, for legal *academics* to be able to take professional and civic responsibility in the face of the complexity, increasingly fast change and uncertainty of contemporary society, they need to be able to understand and adjust to changing circumstances.

Various scholars, including Nussbaum, argue that a liberal – or broad – education, which entails the humanities and the arts, is able to provide the academic component of education, enabling students to think critically, reflect, judge, and create.[202] However, the balance between vocational training and academic schooling in academic law schools is a matter of ongoing debate and at the moment the emphasis seems to lie on the vocational component.[203] This debate on the balance between vocational and academic schooling in the university is not new. It was already ongoing at the dawn of the modern university. German Romantics of the 18th and 19th centuries identified self-realization as an important aspect of education, which contrasted with vocational training's aim of *usefulness*. These thinkers thought that the academic component of education could be found in this ideal of human completeness.[204] During the 19th century, this ideal of a liberal education – or *Bildung* – prevailed over vocational training. As a consequence, 'useful' training was seen as teaching irrelevant and practical skills and 'useful' branches of study, such as technology and economics, were perceived as less valuable and had to make way for the humanities and their promise of moral development.[205] Recently, the balance between vocational and academic learning in ALE (and – as has been argued – also in the university in general[206]) has shifted the other way: Towards the vocational component of higher education. Center stage is given to practical legal knowledge and skills training.[207] This shift is unsurprising in a globalized society revolving around business values, such as profit, effectiveness,

---

problematic, since educators in higher education model behavior for their students, for whom creativity, following critical thinking and decision-making, is an important civic and professional skill. See Cownie 2004, p. 82.

202 Nussbaum 2016, p. 7.

203 Ahsmann 2016, p. 16.

204 Horlacher 2017, p. 60.

205 Horlacher 2017, p. 63.

206 This can be noted in publications by concerned academics. See for example: Nussbaum 2016, Collini 2012, Readings 1996, and Donoghue 2018.

207 See, for example, Van Klink & De Vries 2016, p. 3. Although Cownie's research, in which she questioned legal academics (i.e. academic staff in universities), points out that her respondents all claimed that they found critical thinking in their students (part of the academic component) of the utmost importance (Cownie 2004, pp. 76-78), marketized society pushes law faculties to invest in the training of practical legal skills at the cost of the academic component.

efficiency, and transparency,[208] since these 'useful' skills and knowledge are more easily measured and can immediately be put into action in any corporate legal business (i.e. lead to *profit*). These skills and knowledge help graduates to secure a job and earn money (i.e. lead to *profit*).[209] Another reason that law schools to focus on professional skills training is the criticism frequently made by legal practitioners (the future employers of law students) of ALE for not sufficiently preparing students for the legal profession.[210]

The shift towards the vocational component is noticeable in the curricula of law schools, where black letter law courses and legal skills training are favored at the cost of a more reflective approach to law. In Dutch academic law schools, a reason for this shift can be found in the requirements of the so-called 'civiel effect', which is a specific certificate required for students to be able to practice law as attorneys, judges, or prosecutors in their future careers. The stipulations of the '*convenant civiel effect*' are focused on training in practical legal knowledge and skills.[211] Under the influence of the Netherlands Bar – the Counsel of the Judiciary and the Netherlands Public Prosecution Service – the conditions of the 'civiel effect' are considerable and Dutch law schools are obligated to include more practically useful knowledge and skills into their curricula.

The profit-based vocational focus of higher education, and specifically in law schools, entails training students in the skills necessary for their future vocation in as short a time as possible. The result of fulfilling these demands in the three short years of a Bachelor's degree in law, means that a selection has to be made in the content of the curriculum. At the moment, that choice seems to jeopardize the academic core of legal education. Problematically, a possible oversight of this component in ALE might give reason to law students, the legal practice, and other academic disciplines to raise doubts regarding the *academic value* of legal education and legal scholarship. More fundamentally, neglecting the academic component in favor of market-based values that may be met through a vocational education disregards the time needed for thinking and the process of

208 Mak 2017, pp. 14-16.

209 Job security and employability have become major goals of higher education, and are highly sought after by students. This is noticeable in, for instance, the results of the Dutch Student Inquiry 2018 (Nederlandse Studenten Enquete, NSE), which shows that students are (still) quite unsatisfied regarding preparation for their future professional careers.
See: http://www.studiekeuzeinformatie.nl/wp-content/uploads/2018/06/factsheet2018_WO_EN.pdf In 2022, this had not changed significantly as Dutch law students once again pointed out that they do not feel that their education prepares them sufficiently for their professional careers. See: https://www.studiekeuze123.nl/nse/dashboard, last visited March 7th 2023. Interestingly, this student experience seems to contradict the university's efforts to support the development of useful, professional skills and the noticeable vocational turn of ALE.

210 Susskind 2017, p. 161. See also: Smits 2014, p. 5.

211 Mak 2017, p. 28. See the convenant 'Civiel Effect', 22 March 2016. Accessible at: https://www.advocatenorde.nl/afgestudeerd-oude-stijl-rechtsgeleerdheid. See for criticism of the effect of the covenant: https://www.mr-online.nl/civiel-effect-mag-verdwijnen/, last accessed 8 November 2018.

understanding, is unable to support students in fundamental and full personal development, and renders ALE one-dimensional. The current disbalance between legal education's two components is therefore of concern. In contrast to these developments, many legal academics argue that the vocational and academic components should *both* be important factors, which means that sufficient time and focus must also be given to the *academic* component of legal education.[212]

To teach students professional skills that are relevant to the legal practice *and* to support them in their development towards becoming critical, reflective, decisive, creative and responsible citizens of contemporary global society, both the vocational and academic component are of importance. Therefore, I argue that a balance between the two components is needed. Since the balance is now off-kilter, the balance between the currently highlighted vocational component and the understated academic component must be restored. For this, we are required to emphasize and give further substance to legal education's academic component.

In the next chapter, *Bildung* is introduced as a theoretical concept that may help educators to emphasize and develop the academic component of academic legal education. *Bildung* may provide educators insight into what they could aim for when trying to find the balance between the vocational and academic components. Furthermore, *Bildung* offers the theoretical groundwork for placing the development of critical thinking, creative thinking and responsibility at the heart of an *academic* legal education. In addition, *Bildung* provides a conceptual context that integrates the importance of student development and experiential learning, which leads to a greater variety of pedagogical interventions that might be employed by educators to support law student's development and academic learning.

212 See for example Cownie's study in which responding academic staff members of law schools state that critical thinking for them is the main aim of legal education (Cownie 2004, p. 76-78), but also Brouwer's observation that practical, legal skills such as analyzing, reasoning, and communicating are also of importance for law students (see Brouwer 2005, p. 2). See also Susskind 2017, p. 160.

2 Something There. Exploring *Bildung* to Re-build Balance in Academic Legal Education

"Who is the happy Warrior? Who is he
That every man in arms should wish to be?
– It is the generous Spirit, who, when brought
Among the tasks of real life, hath wrought
Upon the plan that pleased his boyish thought:
Whose high endeavours are an inward light
That makes the path before him always bright;
Who, with a natural instinct to discern
What knowledge can perform, is diligent to learn;
Abides by this resolve, and stops not there,
But makes his moral being his prime care."
– *William Wordsworth (1770-1850)*[1]

Introduction

Taking a cue from this poem by William Wordsworth, who would the 'happy Academic' be? What determines this person's inward light that brightens the path before them and provides them with guidelines for action? This chapter examines how *Bildung* could offer an answer to these questions. The previous chapter explored the predicament of academic legal education (ALE), and specifically problematized the marketized university as an environment in which it becomes difficult to develop and offer students an *academic* legal education. The reason for this is the contradiction between what is needed for the academic study of a domain – for example, reflection and time – and what is important in a marketized environment – such as fast results, measurability and standardization. To illustrate the struggle of offering students an academic education in law schools, the first chapter mapped out the disrupted balance between the vocational and academic components of legal education. To restore this balance, legal education's academic core requires strengthening. This chapter aims to answer the question of how to do this in

1 Fragment of 'Character of the Happy Warrior', written by William Wordsworth, an English romantic poet, who wrote this poem in 1806. See Wordsworth 1994, p. 588.

contemporary times, by drawing on the concept *Bildung*. The reason for this choice is that *Bildung* is the fundamental idea on which the first *modern* university in the early 19th century is based. This university, the University of Berlin (now: the Humboldt University[2]) was established by Wilhelm Von Humboldt and was – in its time – seen as the pinnacle of the modern university: It focused on the integration of research and education and integrated the natural sciences with the humanities. Since the modern university held the academic schooling of its students in high esteem and its educational example was praised and copied throughout the world,[3] this example may give us guidance in how to revalue academic learning in contemporary law schools. Humboldt's conceptualization of *Bildung*, formulated in an attempt to (re-)discover and reconnect with academic values in times of disenchantment, have shaped the university for the past 200 years and may help define and practically construct the academic core of contemporary legal education in a time in which marketization has caused another kind of disenchantment within academic education. At the moment, *Bildung* is still a central part of education in Germany[4] and can also be recurrently heard as a notion in Dutch (tertiary) education.

Bildung could safeguard *academic* education against the strong force of marketization that pulls it away from its original academic values towards the capitalistic and neo-liberal value of profit, which contributed to the emphasis on vocational training. In legal education, this pull is very much felt, because of the discipline's strong connection to society and the legal practice, including the legal profession. This could potentially disrupt the balance between the vocational and academic components of legal education and, hence, safeguards are necessary. As such a safeguard, *Bildung* enables the reinforcement of the academic component of legal education and could contribute to a harmonization of these two components. To be able to understand to what extent and how *Bildung* could contribute to a restored balance between the vocational and the academic components, a further exploration of this rich but rather ambiguous concept is required.

Therefore, the concept's historical roots and various meanings will be scrutinized in the following. The focus in that scrutiny will mainly be on the meaning given to the concept by Wilhelm von Humboldt, in which center stage is given to the development of the unique human being. In contrast to focusing mainly on training vocational skills and knowledge, *Bildung* aims at the complete self-realization of the human being through self-examination. In answer to the challenge of finding a renewed balance between the vocational and academic component of ALE as described in the previous chapter, this chapter reconsiders the concept of *Bildung*. It concentrates on several of *Bildung*'s essential aspects in order to build them into a concept that can be applied to contemporary ALE to

2 See: https://www.hu-berlin.de/en/about/history, last visited 2 October 2018.
3 Von Humboldt 1970, p. 242 (introduction).
4 See Masschelein & Ricken 2003, pp. 140-141. See also Zuurmond 2020, p. 19.

strengthen its academic core and find a renewed balance between its vocational and academic components.

THE IDEAL OF *BILDUNG*

Making sense of Bildung

Developed by various German thinkers in the 18th and 19th centuries, *Bildung* is a broad and ambiguous concept whose interpretations are manifold.[5] In general, *Bildung* is associated with ideas of grandeur and splendor[6] and is related to concepts such as human dignity, liberty and salvation.[7] Also, *Bildung* is known as being focused on more than utility[8] and knowledge: It aims at establishing a better society.[9] As a concept, *Bildung* is untranslatable. The literal meaning of the German word is 'formation', but in various contexts it might also be understood as 'development', 'education' or 'culture'.[10] In short, *Bildung* is an ideal that fits perfectly into the tradition of liberal education,[11] which highly values the holistic, personal development of individuals within the context of society.[12] This should be understood as a holistic development since individuals need to develop all their natural capabilities and should develop those into a harmonious, balanced whole.[13] *Bildung* aims to achieve this development in students by offering a broad education, which means an education that is not just focused on developing professional knowledge and skills (such as legal knowledge and skills) but also on a broader, more individual development of knowledge (and skills) from other disciplines, such as philosophy, psychology or medicine. In the context of the current vocational turn of legal education, concerned scholars and students have renewed their interest in *Bildung*.[14]

The educational meaning was given to the concept by Wilhelm von Humboldt,[15] who integrated the ideas of many of his contemporaries in his description of *Bildung* in the late 18th and early 19th centuries. Ever since, *Bildung* has been an established ideal at all levels

5 See: Horlacher 2004, pp. 409-410, Horlacher 2017, p. 1, Francot & Corrias 2016, p. 36.
6 Horlacher 2004, p. 409.
7 Prange, 2004, p. 501 and Horlacher 2004, p. 410. See also: Horlacher 2017, pp. 1 & 3.
8 Horlacher 2017, p. 1.
9 Horlacher 2004, p. 410.
10 Prange 2004, pp. 501-502. See also: Beiser 2003, p. 26.
11 Giesinger 2012, p. 3.
12 Lechner 2003, p. 104.
13 Beiser 2003, pp. 26-27. See also: Horlacher 2004, p. 410.
14 An example of the interest in *Bildung* is the foundation of the Dutch *Bildung* academy in 2015, which offers many additional courses for students and educators alike. See: http://debildungacademie.nl/open-bildung-academie/, last visited on September 26th 2018.
15 Giesinger 2012, p. 3.

of education – primary, secondary or higher – in German-speaking countries. Universities in other countries have followed Germany's example.[16] In the following, the historical development of the concept of *Bildung* will be explored.

Bildung*'s early formation*

The concept of *Bildung* originates in the Middle Ages. German theologian Meister Eckhart (1260-1328) created new words while translating Latin Biblical scriptures, since occasionally there were no corresponding words in German for the Latin originals. To describe the experience of 'sinking into Christ' while contemplating oneself as an image of God in order to reach true humanity, Eckhart chose the term *Bildung*.[17] According to Eckhart, the spiritual and religious ideal was for every human being to try to develop themselves in the image of God ('*Gottes Ebenbild*').[18] With the dawn of early modern times, *Bildung* grew further apart from its religious starting point and could also be interpreted as '*Bildung* through science'. In this interpretation, *Bildung* was able to achieve a central position in the culture of science.[19]

In the late 17th century, the development of the concept of *Bildung* continued. Anthony Ashley Cooper, third earl of Shaftesbury (1671-1713), travelled through Europe during a Grand Tour, which inspired him to initiate a theory of the 'virtuoso'. According to Shaftesbury, a virtuous man is an erudite, self-educated ('polite') gentleman whose actions are *rational*, but based on *affection* for the common good.[20] Here, reason and sensibility were combined in the description of a virtuous human being. The self-knowledge and self-examination as practiced by these gentlemen were an inner 'forming' or 'formation' in the light of the promise of every human being's perfectibility. This inner formation was later translated in German as *Bildung*.[21] To Shaftesbury, *Bildung* meant the development of individual powers (in other words, capabilities) into a harmonious whole. If a human being achieved that balanced unity of natural powers, their character was perceived as beautiful.[22] As such, *Bildung* had a close connection to the ideal of a beautiful soul. This was especially the case in the context of 'the fine arts', where *Bildung* was initially embraced, and later also in pedagogy.[23] The inner self-formation gives literature and art an important

16 Humboldt 1970 (introduction), p. 242. See also: Horlacher 2017, pp. 1-2.
17 Horlacher 2017, p. 8.
18 Giesinger, p. 2. See also: Horlacher 2017, p. 8, Karlsohn 2018, p. 109, Oelker 2013, p. 1, and Francot & Corrias c, p. 37.
19 Oelker 2013, p. 1. See also: Francot & Corrias 2016, p. 37.
20 Horlacher 2017, pp. 39-40.
21 Horlacher 2017, p. 41. See also: Francot & Corrias 2016, p. 38.
22 Lechner 2003, p. 62.
23 Horlacher 2004, p. 411.

social role, since these disciplines are helpful for the inner development of aesthetic self-understanding, which is the basis for moral goodness.[24]

Shaftesbury's ideas on inner formation were influential in the 18th century, since German philosophers, thinkers and artists saw (some of) their own ideas reflected in Shaftesbury's viewpoints. The thoughts of these 18th century writers and practitioners of the fine arts would later be recognizable as ideas belonging to *Bildung*.[25] The concept of *Bildung* was not unique to any specific German group of thought in the 18th century, but rather was part of the general German tradition. The concept was repeatedly discussed in movements such as the *Aufklärung* (e.g. Wolff, Mendelssohn, Kant and Fichte), *Sturm und Drang* (e.g. Herder) and *Weimarer Klassik* (e.g. Winckelmann, Schiller, Goethe and Humboldt).[26] It was in these times and under the influence of the German idealists that *Bildung* received its humanistic connotation and the individual was given center stage.[27] In the time of the French Revolution (1789-1799) and its consequent political mayhem in France, German thinkers such as Humboldt, Herder, and Schiller criticized totalitarian regimes, but did not see revolution as the solution to these kind of governments. Rather, they believed *Bildung* – individual development, emancipation of the individual – was the answer because they thought that political reform could only be achieved if the people's beliefs, attitudes and customs matched the reforms. In their opinion, the chaos of the French Revolution and atrocities committed during it would not have come to pass if the people would have been educated. These German thinkers believed that the ideals of *liberté, egalité* and *fraternité* could be accomplished through individual *Bildung*.[28]

The first contours of Bildung *in the 18th century – Herder*

German writer and pastor Johann Gottfried von Herder (1744-1803) was one of those inspired by Shaftesbury.[29] Herder could be called the founder of the German theory of *Bildung*,[30] since his interpretation of the concept increasingly dominated other interpretations during the 18th century.[31] Shaftesbury's concepts of 'inwardness', 'inner form' and 'beautiful soul' found resonance in Herder's ideology of Lutheran Pietism, which was a prominent religious movement in Germany from the late 17th until the middle of the 18th century. Pietism had followers in influential societal positions and organizations,

24 Horlacher 2017, p. 43.
25 Horlacher 2017, pp. 30-31. See also: Lechner 2003, p. 100.
26 Beiser 2003, p. 28.
27 Oelker 2013, p. 1.
28 Beiser 2003, p. 89. See also: Lechner 2003, p. 115.
29 Horlacher 2017, p. 11.
30 Horlacher 2004, p. 420.
31 Horlacher 2014, p. 421.

such as the universities. This explains *Bildung*'s success in these times: It was an ideal that many could closely relate to. Herder saw *Bildung* as non-political. For him, it was focused on the inner process of self-realization and self-cultivation by the individual. Herder's *Bildung* is therefore based on introspection and self-examination.[32]

As a logical consequence of his earlier years when he was a member of the *Sturm und Drang*-movement,[33] Herder critiqued the omnipotence of rationality as well as the Enlightenment's rejection of intuition, sensibility and experience. During the 18th century, the intellectual legacy of Enlightenment was noticeable in the German schooling system. The aim of this Enlightened education was to convey knowledge, which included clear and distinct concepts.[34] In short, the *Geist* of Enlightenment focused on cultivating the intellect.[35] Herder objected that Enlightenment's rational abstraction and generalizations hindered an individual and subjective view of the human being.[36] Furthermore, he thought that education's focus on rationality broke off any possibility for spontaneity of thought and prevented students from thinking for themselves. Instead, it treated students as passive consumers of the thoughts of others. Therefore, Herder positioned *Bildung* as a counterweight to this part of the Enlightenment and highlighted the significance of individuality, sensibility, experience, art, and culture.[37] Herder saw virtue not just as being rational, but also as having sensibility.[38] Additionally, Herder thought that man was also a being that experienced through the senses.[39] Since Herder's idea of an educated man is that he is a preacher of the virtue of his own age[40] that person embraced not only his rationality, but more importantly, his sensibility. This person was an 'enlightened, educated, sensitive, reasonable, virtuous, and enjoying man'[41] who strived for humanity. Achieving that humanity was possible, but the *striving* – in itself – for humanity was the core of being human.[42] Humans had, according to Herder, a limitless ability to develop. They should be given freedom so that they could develop themselves toward their perfection: Humanity.[43] Herder connects the fine arts ('Schöne Wissenschaften') to *Bildung*, by which he meant that the arts and sciences 'make us *human*'.[44] In other words, they give us the opportunity

32 Horlacher 2004, p. 421.
33 Lechner 2003, p. 56.
34 This contrasted with the vagueness of the *Bildung* ideal. See: Horlacher 2017, p. 19.
35 Beiser 2003, p. 94.
36 Lechner 2003, p. 57.
37 Horlacher 2017, p. 11. See also: Lechner 2003, pp. 57, 61.
38 Horlacher 2017, p. 12.
39 Lechner 2003, p. 57.
40 Horlacher 2017, p. 11.
41 Horlacher 2017, p. 11. See also: Horlacher 2014, p. 420.
42 Lechner 2003, p. 60.
43 Lechner 2003, p. 60.
44 Horlacher 2014, p. 423.

to develop ourselves towards our humanity. Herder thought that the beauty of the fine arts cultivated and educated human beings, and so, through art, people become *gebildet.*

Uniting views on Bildung *in the 18th century – Humboldt*

Where Herder was the first to give the concept of *Bildung* a general content with religious roots in the 18th century, Wilhelm von Humboldt (1767-1835) became the father of the *Bildung* ideal and its specific meaning for education.[45] Humboldt established the first modern university that promoted freedom of education and research.[46] According to Humboldt, scholars and students needed to be able to pursue knowledge without constraints. The university was required to offer the possibility of self-formation, free from state intervention,[47] since intellectual freedom was vital for the individual development of students.[48] Humboldt integrated ideas from the Enlightenment (*Aufklärung*), *Sturm und Drang* and *Weimarer Klassik* into his secular, pedagogic description of *Bildung.*[49] Like Herder, Humboldt emphasized the individuality of every person and, through the concept of *Bildung*, promoted the inner development of every unique, reasonable and sensible individual. This humanist focus on individual human beings, their authenticity, creativity, and beauty stood in stark contrast to the Enlightenment's emphasis on reason and its focus on a more abstract definition of 'man'.[50] Since the start of the industrialization, the individual subject had become degraded to an object and the Enlightenment's focus lay on the human race as an abstract whole instead of on the individual.[51] In contrast, Humboldt advocated a broad education that focused on the *individual* development of the human being through an education with a tendency towards depth and breadth.[52] Furthermore, the connection between the individual and the world was of significance in Humboldt's interpretation of *Bildung*: In order to develop their individual selves, human beings needed to connect with the world by discovering and shaping it.[53]

In the following, three themes central to Humboldt's theory of *Bildung* will be further examined: 1) its penchant for the classic, Greek culture, 2) its belief in human perfectibility, and 3) the connection between reason and sensibility.

45 Francot & Corrias 2016, p. 37. See also: Horlacher 2017, p. 15.
46 Lechner 2003, p. 103.
47 Humboldt 1970, p. 245.
48 Nietzsche 2016, (notes to lecture V, note 6), p. 120. See also: Francot and Corrias 2016, p. 39 and Giesinger p. 7.
49 Lechner 2003, p. 99-100. See also: Horlacher 2017, p. 15.
50 Lechner 2003, p. 49, 113.
51 Lechner 2003, p. 112-113.
52 Humboldt 1970, p. 245.
53 Lechner, 2003, p. 104.

Influence of the classics

Humboldt thought that ancient Greek culture and the Latin and Greek languages should be at the center of the curriculum in gymnasia, which were thought to be the exclusive entrance level for an university education.[54] In the late 17th and early 18th century, including classical culture in education was not an uncommon idea, since it was a social tradition for gentlemen to partake in the Grand Tour. During that journey through Europe, these 'virtuoso'[55] encountered ancient Italian and Greek works of art, which was the reason that ancient art became an authority and role model for the visual arts. At the same time, studying the ancient world gained in importance and had prestige.[56]

Humboldt's inspiration to include the worth of ancient art and culture into the concept of *Bildung* was the work of Johann Joachim Winckelmann (1717-1768) who also inspired Herder, Goethe and the movement of *Weimarer Klassik* with love of the classics.[57] From Shaftesbury, Winckelmann borrowed the concept of 'beautiful soul' and saw the manifestation of that soul in Greek art.[58] Winckelmann thought that the ultimate ideal of beauty – which is traditionally equated with moral goodness – could be discovered by studying ancient art[59] because Greek society was not yet advanced, and therefore close to nature, unspoiled and uncorrupted. Greek artworks were therefore also ideal for educational purposes. According to Winckelmann, this was also the task of contemporary artists: Their works of art should instruct spectators, offer inspiration and help them find the ideal of beauty – i.e. moral goodness.[60] In other words, art supported the development of a person's morality. As a result, artists gained an important position since they were mediators between the ideal (art) and the audience, whom they taught in matters of beauty. As such, the artist was responsible for the *Bildung* of their audience.[61] The curricula of the early 19th century gymnasium and university – with in their cores Latin, Greek, Literature, Mathematics and History – combined this ideal of art's role in developing moral goodness with Humboldt's concept of *Bildung*.[62]

---

54 Lechner 2003, p. 103.

55 'Virtuoso' was the word that indicated German gentlemen with a love of classical knowledge and science. See: Horlacher 2017, p. 26.

56 Horlacher 2017, p. 26.

57 Lechner 2003, p. 86. See also: Horlacher 2004, pp. 418-419 and Giesinger, p. 4.

58 Lechner 2003, p. 88. See also: Horlacher 2004, p. 418.

59 Which he himself did profusely: Winckelmann can be named the 'father of art history'. See: Prettejohn 2005: pp. 15-16.

60 Horlacher 2017, pp. 27-28.

61 Horlacher 2017, p. 28.

62 Horlacher 2017, p. 59.

Perfectibility

The second theme recognizable in Humboldt's *Bildung* ideal can be traced back to John Locke's (1632-1704) and Jean-Jacques Rousseau's (1712-1778) faith in the perfectibility of humankind. These ideas are the basis of both Herder's and Humboldt's conceptualizations of *Bildung*.[63] Central to Herder's and Humboldt's ideal is the belief that every individual has the capability for improvement – and the ability to achieve perfection by honing their natural abilities. This inner self-realization of the individual human being into a balanced whole is the highest good of humanity.[64] Here, the ideas of Shaftesbury and Herder are recognizable in how the inner, beautiful soul is developed.[65] The individual's task is to become an original person.[66] This viewpoint of inner development results in endless possibilities for the progress of human beings: It is a perpetually ongoing process. Through education (*Bildung*) this process can be supported. According to Humboldt, every human being has an inner desire to develop, since that development is a defining characteristic of humanity. Without a possibility of self-formation, individuals are alienated from themselves.[67]

Humboldt's interpretation of perfectibility as an *individual* ethical development of character and strengths differs from philosophers belonging to the Enlightenment, such as Immanuel Kant (1724-1804). For Kant (1724-1804), the 'perfect' human being is capable of determining his purpose in accordance with his *duty*.[68] That emphasis on duty and reason reflects Kant's wish for uniformity: All human beings will understand their duty equally as a result of their rationality. This illustrates the romantic complaint that the Enlightenment generalizes and disregards the individuality of every human being. Similarly to Humboldt, Kant states that education's goal is for mankind to achieve perfection, as "man can only become man by education".[69] However, their interpretations of 'perfection' differ. Kant proposes disciplined instruction for students, so that they are polished through opposition.[70] In other words, disciplined instruction helps students to develop themselves. Human nature improves through education and it is the duty of human beings to improve themselves.[71] Interestingly, just as Humboldt argues that – through knowledge and culture – education 'builds' human beings over generations,[72] Kant equates education to an *art* that develops over generations as every generation

63 See: Horlacher 2017, pp. 19-23.
64 Beiser 2003, p. 26.
65 Lechner 2003, pp. 104-105.
66 Humboldt's ideal of *Bildung* valued individuality and originality. See: Giesinger, p. 7.
67 Humboldt 1964, p. 7.
68 Kant 1900 (introduction), p. XVII.
69 Kant 1900, pp. 6-7.
70 Kant 1900, p. 5.
71 Kant 1900, p. 11.
72 Humboldt 1964, p. 7.

transmits another layer of knowledge to the following. Therefore, from Kant's position, education improves and stimulates the human race's progress over time towards its destiny, which is doing *good*.[73] Humboldt's *Bildung* ideal calls on the human race and on the individual to develop and become human. This is achievable through self-realization, namely the development of all one's characteristic powers.[74] Because *Bildung* – education and culture – enables this development, it is viewed as the highest good.[75]

In addition to the inward dimension of *Bildung*, which is focused on the inner self-formation of the individual, the ideal also has an outward dimension.[76] That is, without social interaction, individual development is not possible. So, the human being needs to connect to the outside world, for example to a community or nation. Through the interplay between the individual and the outside world understanding arises and individual development continues.[77] In the context of the university, this entails that free collaboration between scholars and students is a requirement. The reason for this is that, during collaboration, the intellectual successes of one person may awaken intellectual progress and enthusiasm in another.[78]

Reason and Sensibility

The third theme that can be recognized in Humboldt's ideal of *Bildung* is its emphasis on both reason *and* sensibility. The Enlightenment regarded reason as the most important human capacity. This is prominent in Kant's envisioned University, which consisted of three higher faculties, namely Theology, Law and Medicine, and the lower faculty: Philosophy (which included the humanities). For their content, the higher faculties depended and focused on the practice of religion, law, and medicine. Therefore, Kant deemed these higher faculties not *autonomous* (i.e. free from state intervention) since they relied not directly on reason, natural law, or the physiology of the human body for their teaching, but rather on the authority of something else: The Bible, legal provisions, or medical regulations.[79] In contrast, the so-called 'lower' faculty of Philosophy had no direct link to societal practices or regulations. Thus, Kant thought philosophers capable of reason, of *free rational inquiry*. Although called the 'lower' faculty, it is clear that Kant thought the faculty of Philosophy was very valuable for the university, since the faculty of philosophy was autonomous and educated its students in *reason*.[80] However, the

73 Kant 1900, p. 11-12.
74 Beiser 2003, p. 91.
75 For instance, see Schlegel (1799): 'the highest good is culture (*Bildung)*', in: Beiser 2003, p. 88. See also: Beiser 3003, p. 91 and Francot and Corrias p. 42.
76 Francot and Corrias 2016, p. 40.
77 Humboldt 1964, pp. 6 & 8.
78 Humboldt 1970, p. 243.
79 Kant 1996, p. 4
80 Readings 1996, pp. 56-57.

preeminence of reason in Kant and the Enlightenment was critiqued and contradicted in the 18th century by an emphasis on sensibility.[81] In this context, the *Sturm und Drang*-movement functioned as a very helpful environment for the further development of the ideal of *Bildung*. It focused on emotions and sensibility as important human attributes in addition to reason.[82] *Bildung*, too, equally values both human capacities of reason and sensibility.[83] Since *Bildung* requires individuals to develop *all* their natural capacities into a harmonious whole, reason and sensibility needed to be developed in equal measure. This human development towards excellence is seen as beauty.[84] Here, beauty is equated with goodness and virtue, corresponding to Plato's theory of forms, in which beauty is the highest idea and, therefore, morally good.[85] Consequently, within the ideal of *Bildung*, beauty is a virtue and human development towards the aesthetical can be regarded as ethically right. Although, traditionally, a strong connection existed between virtue and beauty and many scholars in the 18th century embraced that idea, Kant's enlightened theory rejected the connection between morality and aesthetics or pleasure. According to Kant, moral action was the result of reason without any involvement of sensibility. Observing art and beauty only led to a subjective contemplation of the observer,[86] but beauty could not be an objective feature of the object itself. Johann Christoph Friedrich von Schiller (1759-1805), a friend of Humboldt's[87] and part of *Sturm and Drang* early in his life,[88] responded to this criticism with a reinterpretation of the concept of beauty, in the hope of objectifying the concept. In this new interpretation, something is deemed beautiful if it is self-determined and independent from constraints. Here, beauty and perfection are understood as *freedom*.[89]

The artist and their art are given an important task in human development – in human emancipation[90] – since art, flowing from the artist's creative imagination, is the *creator* of the human being.[91] This is the starting point for German Romanticism: The artist is a

81 Beiser 2003, p. 94. Importantly, although *reason* takes central stage, Kant *does* leave room for *feeling*. In his depiction of human nature, Kant finds that all humans are capable of genuine fellow feeling in the sense of sympathetic joy or sorrow. For Kant, morality requires conscience, love for others, self-respect and moral feelings. According to Kant, these feelings appear naturally when human beings live near one another. Kant calls these feelings sensible feelings of pleasure and displeasure, in other words, they are *aesthetic*. See Wilson 2014, pp. 445-446.

82 Karlsohn 2018, p. 104.

83 Beiser 2003, p. 92.

84 Beiser 2003, p. 96-97.

85 Horlacher 2017, p. 24. See also: Beiser 2003, p. 27.

86 Beiser 2003, p. 98.

87 Lechner 2003, p. 102.

88 Schiller's later works are characterized as belonging to *Frühromantik* and Romanticism, see: Beiser 2003, p. 28.

89 Beiser 2003, p. 29.

90 Horlacher 2017, p. 24.

91 Lechner 2003, p. 96.

'genius' or, more in tune with the definition of Shaftesbury, a 'virtuoso'.[92] In the view of *Sturm und Drang*, art becomes an aesthetic role model. For example, reading literature was seen as advantageous for the development of the soul, since it motivates the reader to good behavior.[93] Schiller, too, promoted art as inspiring the beholder to act according to reason and thus morality: When one regards art, the artwork can act as a stimulator of morality,[94] but this will mostly only have its effect on already virtuous individuals.[95] Therefore, Schiller argues that *Bildung* does not arise through by works of art, but by humans developing their characters into works of art.[96] Here, creating human perfection (*Bildung*) is equal to creating a work of art. As a reward for this virtuosity, the individual will experience aesthetic pleasure.[97]

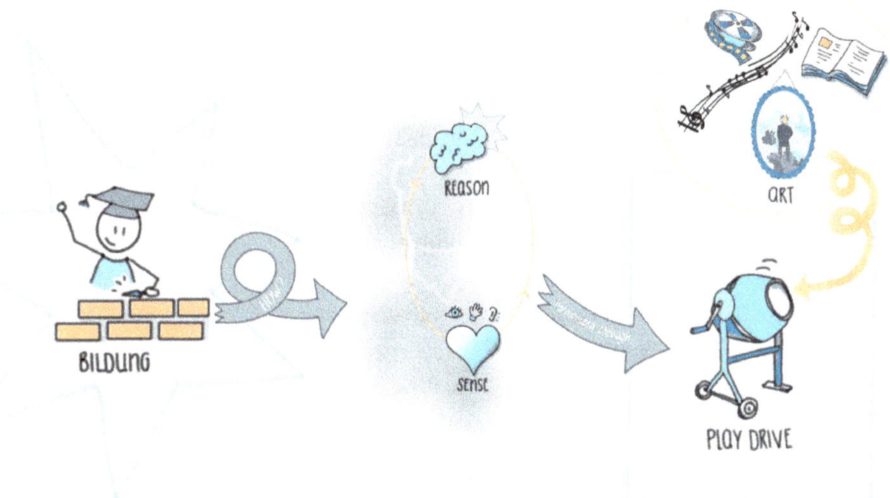

As shown in the visual above, Schiller introduced three human drives in order to be able to develop not only the senses or reason, but the whole human soul.[98] This idea was a reaction to Kant's dichotomy of nature and morality. According to Schiller, every human being has three drives: A *sensuous drive*, corresponding to the determining sphere of

92 Horlacher 2017, p. 24.
93 Horlacher 2017, p. 24.
94 Beiser 2003, p. 95.
95 Schiller, Letter 10. See also Beiser 2003, p. 96.
96 Beiser 2003, p. 96.
97 Beiser 2003, p. 97.
98 Horlacher 2017, p. 17.

nature and a *formal drive*, corresponding to the sphere of morality, where categorical imperatives could be discovered through the formal process of reason. In between, the *play drive* operates as a unifying force for reason and sensibility.[99] Especially through 'playing with art' it is possible to connect the two seemingly contrasting drives of sensibility and reason and thus for human beings to develop their whole selves. In explanation, people perceive art and aesthetic beauty through their senses: They feel it, see it or hear it and the work of art appeals to their emotions and/or desires. When someone then *contemplates* the art's beauty, for example, when that person asks themselves which feelings a painting elicits in them and what those feelings say about their values or position in the world, the senses that perceived the beautiful artwork connect with the thoughts and reason involved in contemplation. In that moment, sensibility and reason are in harmony and the form of the individual's reason is unified with the content of the individual's sensibility.[100] This means that the process of contemplating art enables morally or reasonably inclined individuals to *feel* and it allows individuals that are inclined to sense, to think and reason. Therefore, both types of people develop an aesthetical sensibility which completes their human selves and, through that, they *liberate* (i.e. beautify) themselves.[101]

Developers of theories of *Bildung* were in agreement with the legacy of the Enlightenment and thought that morality is only possible by suppressing the sensuous nature and impulses of the human being through reason. This requires an education of the emotions. When their emotions are brought into harmony with reason people reach excellence and become 'beautiful souls'.[102] Excellence, i.e. human perfection or self-realization, could be achieved through an aesthetic education.[103] Schiller was aghast at the violence of the French revolution and – like other German thinkers – saw a solution in *Bildung*.[104] Through beauty and an *aesthetical* education society could be improved, since it could inspire people, touch their hearts and arouse their imagination as nothing else could since the decline of religion's primacy.[105] Equal minded contemporaries of Schiller's thought that the goal of an aesthetic education is to develop every individual's nature as a spontaneous and free subject.[106] As such, *Bildung* (the aesthetical education) leads to

99 Horlacher 2017, p. 17. See also: Lechner 2003, p. 95,
100 Beiser 2003, p. 96.
101 Beiser 2003, p. 29.
102 Wertz 2005, p. 81. See also: Beiser 2003, p. 96.
103 Beiser 2003, p. 93.
104 Horlacher, 2017, p. 17. See also: Beiser 2003, p. 94.
105 See Beiser, p. 94. See also: Horlacher 2017, p. 17.
106 Beiser 2003, p. 29.

autonomy, individuality and originality.[107] In other words, *Bildung* is the development of independence,[108] which corresponds to the interpretation of beauty as freedom.

In contrast to Enlightenment's aim to solely develop the individual's capacity for reason, aesthetic education is focused on the cultivation of reason *and* sensibility, by 'romanticizing the senses'.[109] In the late 18th century, a sense of alienation from natural feeling and sensibility arose as a result of industrialization (division of labor) and the one-sided focus on reason. With the denial of sensibility's importance, a part of the human being was disregarded. Therefore, individuals were alienated from their whole self.[110] Since *Bildung* is essentially a holistic ideal, it contains the value of unity with oneself, others and nature. Consequently, individuals should feel comfortable with themselves, in harmony with society and with nature.[111] If there is no unity – as was the case because of the denial of sensibility – individuals feel separated and are alienated from themselves, society and the world.[112] The *Romantics* believed that art could regenerate this unity. It could also reunite society because of its ability to awaken love[113] and could enable individuals to see the ordinary as extraordinary. This would allow them to perceive the wonder and mystery of the world.[114] In the words of Schiller: "*It is the mystery that enchants*".[115] This re-mystification through restoring nature's mystery, magic and beauty reunites and reconnects human beings with themselves and the world.[116]

Aesthetical education is not easily obtained: It takes discipline and the training of virtue.[117] Through an aesthetical education – through *Bildung* – a taste for and perception of beauty (which is linked to morality) is developed. By experiencing art and beauty a person learns to recognize the idea of beauty.[118] Here, art becomes the main instrument of the education – and thus liberation – of human beings.[119] Art was seen as a positive and productive power that stimulated morality and inspired people to act according to reason because it appealed to imagination and emotions.[120] Just as art is a unity of form and content, human perfection is, too, since it requires individuals to develop the multiplicity

107 Beiser 2003, p. 29.
108 Beiser 2003, p. 100.
109 Beiser 2003, p. 100.
110 Schiller, Letter I, p. 10. See also: Lechner 2003, pp. 96-97.
111 Beiser 2003, pp. 31 & 102.
112 Beiser 2003, pp. 31 & 102.
113 Beiser 2003, p. 54.
114 Beiser 2003, pp. 100 & 101.
115 Schiller, Letter I, p. 11.
116 Beiser 2003, p. 102.
117 Beiser 2003, p. 97.
118 Horlacher 2017, pp. 24-25.
119 *"For art has to leave reality; it has to raise itself boldly above necessity and neediness; for art is the daughter of freedom"* in: Schiller, Letter II, p. 13. See also: Beiser 2003, pp. 93 & 97.
120 Beiser 2003, pp. 53 & 95.

of their natural powers – reason and sensibility – into a harmonious whole.[121] This results in the formation of a beautiful soul.

CRITICISM ON THE PRACTICE OF *BILDUNG*

The concept of *Bildung* is not undisputed and has met with criticism since it became the foundational ideal of Humboldt's University of Berlin in 1809 and turned into a dominant interpretation in education during the 19th century. For example, Marx found that *Bildung* – which is heavily rooted in ideals of the Enlightenment such as autonomy of the individual – was just another ideology invented by the dominant, wealthy class to disguise the actual, unfair situation of the proletariat. Not the education of the masses, but only a political revolution would be able to end the inequality between classes.[122] Other criticism of *Bildung* mostly focuses on what it attempted to achieve in education, such as Nietzsche's opinion that mass education would degrade *Bildung*; the idea that *Bildung*'s focus on life-long learning reduces people to eternal children, and criticism of the tension between the inward and outward dimensions of *Bildung*. Since these comments on the practice of *Bildung* may provide insight into how we could strengthen the concept in its contemporary use, the following section will further explore and review those criticisms in the current context of *Bildung* in higher education.

Within the university as envisioned by Humboldt, students and educators enhanced one another's growth by challenging each other in their research efforts.[123] Although students learned how to conduct research, Humboldt thought that studying at the university had a societal significance since it furthered a student's professional development. But, in the end, an academic education was *more* than professional training: Its ultimate goal was to develop humanity.[124] *Bildung* promised to be achievable for everyone.[125] And that claim seemed true. After the German empire was proclaimed at Versailles and the *Gründerzeit* (1871-1873) began, rapid industrial growth and the expansion of the educational system followed.[126] More students – also from less distinguished backgrounds – were welcomed in Academia and student numbers in German universities climbed rapidly. However, these developments were not uncontested. For example, *Bildung* was seen as a state affair: The German state was responsible for the education of its people. This led to an increasing amount of criticism by supporters of anti-establishment groups, who

121 Beiser 2003, p. 96.
122 Horlacher 2017, p. 68.
123 Reitter & Wellmon 2016, p. XIII.
124 Reitter & Wellmon 2016, p. XIV.
125 Horlacher 2017, p. 61.
126 Horlacher 2017, p. 70.

criticized the dominant role of the state in the development of so many citizens and the concern that education was being degraded to mediocrity.[127] Also, the practice of the ideal of *Bildung* was increasingly subject to criticism, amongst others from Friedrich Nietzsche (1844-1900),[128] whose criticism seems to be reflected in current complaints about academic education. Because of their relevance for contemporary higher education, the following will briefly describe some of Nietzsche's criticisms on *Bildung*'s practice in the 19th century.

Instead of *Bildung*'s romantic and idealistic promise of a broad education meant for personal development of the individual, utility had returned as the center of attention.[129] The task of education in the 19th century had become, according to Nietzsche, to form people as fast as possible into as much valid currency as possible in order for them to be able to earn money in professional life.[130] As such, the real meaning of *Bildung* was betrayed and only used as an instrument for economic and political purposes.[131] This led to a narrowing of education: The only skills and knowledge necessary were the ones that rapidly let people make money.[132] Nietzsche disapproved of the decline of the educational practice: He found that it had sunk beneath the educational heights the German system had once reached by virtue of Winckelmann, Goethe, Schiller, and Lessing.[133] According to Nietzsche, the inclusion of the middle class in educational institutions was to blame for this deterioration: The educated middle class was insensitive to real culture and only valued virtues such as loyalty, obedience, reliability, orderliness and sense of duty. In consequence, these people were not able to improve the world by developing a genuine and productive culture.[134]

Nietzsche also criticized the university's dependency on the state and critically reflected that the growth of universities and the development and the broadening of university education would lead to the weakening and deterioration of the *Bildung* ideal.[135] For instance, Nietzsche expressed his displeasure with the university's loss of connection with art and qualities related to art (originally part of the *Bildung* ideal), such as artistic

127 Horlacher 2017, p. 68.
128 Horlacher 2017, p. 68.
129 Horlacher 2017, p. 69.
130 Nietzsche 2016, (Lecture I), p. 16.
131 Horlacher 2017, p. 69. The main problem in this corrupted interpretation of *Bildung* appears to be the phrasing of its aim. No longer was education a place for individual development striving to further humanity, to establish a better society or to contribute to the common good. If the common good was at all aimed at, then it was only defined in utilitarian and monetary terms and therefore degraded. In contemporary times, this teaches us the importance of keeping the true aims of *Bildung* in sight, so that we will not make the same mistake. However, we need to remain vigilant, since the mistake is easily made especially in our times where the ideal of *Bildung* can be (and is) used in a context where education is permeated with economic values such as competition and 'excellence'. See Zuurmond 2020, p. 19.
132 Nietzsche 2016 (lecture I), p. 17.
133 Nietzsche 2016 (lecture II), p. 30.
134 Horlacher 2017, p. 70.
135 See: Nietzsche 2016, pp. 78 & 92 and Oelker 2013, p. 3.

thinking, learning, striving for humanity and comparative analysis, which Nietzsche found lacking in university schooling in 1872.[136] True education, according to Nietzsche, offers its students "goals, masters, methods, models, companions and the invigorating, uplifting breath of the true German spirit".[137] Furthermore, Nietzsche found that it needed Greek antiquity, language, art, and philosophy.[138]

Moreover, Nietzsche advocated a separation between education (*Bildung)* and training, with the former having an exclusive and elitist status. Education aimed at the creation of enduring cultural products and advocated critical thinking and aesthetic achievement.[139] Nietzsche thought that true education (*Bildung*) should be exclusively for the elite and should be elitist.[140] In spite of the 19th century acceptance of 'academic freedom' and its disapproval of hierarchy, Nietzsche states that all education starts with obedience to a leader and with discipline. Without leadership, he argues, nothing extra-ordinary can come from a group of people. Under the leadership of a genius, however, humans are immediately transformed and can accomplish beauty and improve the world.[141] In his fifth lecture at Basel, given on March 23rd 1872, Nietzsche explains this with a musical metaphor. He sees the ideal educational institution as an orchestra. Without a conductor or with a mediocre conductor, an orchestra cannot perform exceptional music. It will be flawed: For example, the timing will be inaccurate and the intonation incorrect. If, however, the inept conductor is replaced with a genius, the whole orchestra and its music will be lifted to a higher level and the possibility of incredible music is created. For educational institutions this meant that students could only achieve new heights when led by genius.[142] Unfortunately, Nietzsche deemed most of his contemporaries hopelessly incompetent as academic educators: He accused them of only wanting to avoid the true work and demands of education and – in a time where the rights of genius were democratized – evading the hard work required for genius. Therefore, Nietzsche thought those academic lecturers unable to lead their students to excellence.[143] To remedy this problem, Nietzsche proposed that academic educators should be better selected.[144] Then, scholars can become true guardians of *Bildung*, and defend the ideal against utility.[145]

Although Nietzsche's criticism of educators in higher education may come across as quite harsh, the situation of the 19th century university he describes and his criticism of

136 Nietzsche 2016, p. 78.
137 Nietzsche 2016, p. 82.
138 Nietzsche, 2016 (lecture II), p. 23. See also: Nietzsche 2016, p. 79.
139 Horlacher 2017, p. 69.
140 Nietzsche 2016, p. 79.
141 Horlacher 2017, p. 70.
142 Nietzsche 2016, pp. 26, 85-86.
143 Nietzsche 2016, pp. 14-15.
144 Nietzsche 2016, pp. 30, 44.
145 Horlacher 2017, p. 70.

mass education and of the discourse of utility are not unfamiliar and find a resonance in the previous chapter. Does this show a repetition of history, or perhaps a constantly present pressure on the foundations of Academia? Whichever it is, it gives us warning to remain vigilant to breaches of the academic core of legal education and urges us to continue to be on the alert for possible corrosion of the *Bildung* ideal.

In our times, interpretations and criticisms of the *Bildung* ideal are also noticeable. For instance, even though she agrees that the university should abandon the focus on utility and profit, Huijer's article in the Dutch newspaper *Trouw* seems to provide ideas that give a nuance to Nietzsche's (and Humboldt's) insistence on including Greek art and literature in the education of young adults. Huijer's – as well as Taylor's – point is that *Bildung* is a mobile concept that should not be politicized but rather be *contextualized*. This means that the foundations of *Bildung* should be interpreted in the context of the time and place, in other words, to fit the educational setting.[146] For example, although the 19th century ideal was for students to contemplate Greek literature and art, in the contemporary globalized world in which diversity has become an important aspect and asset of life in and outside the classroom, students might 'build' themselves through reading literature and studying art from all corners of the world. After all, the reason for studying Greek texts and art was to find beauty – to seek morality. The idea was for the student to become an autonomous moral thinker within the context of society and, at the time, the Greek tradition was seen as the exceptional example of that which was unspoiled and good. In our current society, globalization and technology have led to a social space where people from diverse backgrounds and ideologies assemble and where knowledge is widely available. All this input of information may lead to a renewed understanding of modern-day morality. To uncover and contemplate a morality befitting contemporary life, a melting pot of literature and art from across the globe can be studied.

Another contemporary criticism with regard to implementing *Bildung* in educational institutions concerns the tension that might be perceived between its inward and outward dimensions. This results in the concern that *Bildung*'s outward dimension might lead to the development of only uncritical citizens. *Bildung* traditionally highlights its inward dimension, namely the importance of inner self-formation of the individual.[147] Gur-Ze'ev illustrates this in his description that the core of *Bildung*'s aim is "the elevation of the independent, creative, autonomous individual".[148] On the other hand, *Bildung*'s outward dimension looks at the development of the human being in the context of society. Bauer describes this as a creative, critical and transformative process that changes the relationship

146 Huijer 2015 and Taylor 2017, p. 423.
147 Gur-Ze'ev 2002, p. 391. See also Biesta 2017, p. 2. See also: Bauer 2003, p. 211.
148 Gur-Ze'ev 2002, p. 392.

of the Self and the world in combination with a changing social and material environment.[149] To summarize, *Bildung* entails becoming a person – in other words, subjectification – and becoming a person *within* society – socialization, but the balance between these components is sometimes perceived as problematic. Criticism of the balance between these elements of *Bildung* could also be heard in the context of American primary education during the progressive period in the 1910's and 1920's. In this era, the *Progressive Education Movement* gained a footing with leading educationalists such as John Dewey, Theresa Montessori and Friedrich Fröbel. According to Raber, in progressive primary education, *Bildung* was interpreted in the context of Goethe's and Schiller's work: As an individual, spiritual development that was utterly intertwined with the development of society. Raber observes that critics argue that the *Progressive Education Movement* in the 1910's and 1920's resulted in young children developing into conformists under the flag of *Bildung* through their primary and secondary education. The reason for this was what Raber calls 'classical *Bildung*', which was dominant in progressive education and equated individual development and social development.[150] Therefore, young students were not taught to be able to distinguish between their own morality and society's norms. In that sense, critical reflection upon social norms was not possible and these young children – who would grow up to become members of society – were silenced into conformity from the start. Some critics find that this also holds true for the use of *Bildung* in contemporary education, be it primary education, secondary education or higher education.[151] However, certainly not all theorists agree with the notion that *Bildung* leads to law abiding and uncritical citizens. For example, some – such as Thomas Mann in the 1930's – argued that since *Bildung*'s core centers on the inward dimension, *gebildete* individuals could actually be a danger to the establishment: They would be able to resist the normalized norms and codes of the current social order.[152] Others too, like Van Klink, find that criticality does not necessarily exclude being part of society. On the contrary, Van Klink describes that criticality starts from an uncritical background of shared opinions and beliefs: By joining the ongoing conversation of the domain, law students gradually discover their own voices which could be different from those of their educators.[153] Furthermore, Raber argues that in the beginning of the 20th century this 'classical' or 'Goethe/Schiller' type of *Bildung* (Raber's terminology) was dominant in progressive *primary* education, but not in higher education. There, he finds that another interpretation, namely the 'Von Humboldt'-interpretation stood at the center, which was more focused on *Bildung*'s inner formation

149 Bauer 2003, p. 212.
150 Raber 2018, p. 6.
151 See Zuurmond 2020, Huijer 2015.
152 Gur-Ze'ev 2002, p. 391.
153 Van Klink 2016, p. 21.

instead of on socialization. According to Raber, this led to an emphasis on, for example, academic freedom in higher education.[154]

In addition to the criticism of creating a generation of uncritical citizens, Raber also states that the aforementioned 'classical *Bildung*' interpretation presupposes that the individual 'never grows up', since *Bildung* remains a life-long ideal to strive towards but will probably not be achieved. In that sense, individuals always continue to be children in need of instruction and examples and are not 'fully human'.[155] Biesta argues a similar point with regard to (mostly) primary education. Biesta finds that when educators aim for *Bildung*, they almost always have a notion of what the child is being *gebilded*, for example, being aware of social problems. In this sense, children are not free to develop themselves and to find a motivation to become their own person, but are being 'built' by their educators – according to Biesta – as *objects* rather than subjects of *Bildung*. Here, Biesta finds that *Bildung* becomes more socialization than subjectification.[156] To counter the misinterpretation of *Bildung* as mere socialization, Biesta suggests wielding the concept of *Erziehung*, which he finds includes more freedom for the child – or individual – to choose their own developmental goals, which would lead to *subjectification*. In the light of the description of *Bildung* in this chapter (which obviously differs from what Raber calls 'classical *Bildung*'), the observation that *Bildung* cannot be attained and that life-long learning presupposes that all humans remain eternal children does not hold. The fact that life-long learning is inherent in *Bildung* and, in life, individuals are in a process of continuous learning does not mean that *Bildung* is never achieved, nor does it mean that people do not become adults. Continuous learning, reviewing and self-revision are part of an examined adulthood and the achievement of *Bildung* lies in the ongoing process of development and not in the end result. The beauty lies not in the destination of an '*ausgebildete*', but in in their continuing journey since *Bildung* is not a goal but an ongoing process.

Furthermore, in contrast to Biesta's interpretation of *Erziehung*, other theorists, such as Masschelein and Ricken, hold that *Erziehung* has become a 'dirty term' that specifically centers on the socialization of citizens and has an affirmative character which makes individuals incapable of criticism, whereas *Bildung* looks at self-realization within society which enables the individual to disagree with applicable norms.[157] It is clear that Masschelein and Ricken take note of *Bildung*'s original center of gravity: The inward development of the human being. In the context of vocational education, Van der Ploeg defines *Bildung* as self-responsibility, which means that *gebildelte* persons are able to live

154 See Raber 2018, p. 6.
155 Raber 2018, p. 14.
156 See Biesta 2017, pp. 2-3. See also Zuurmond 2020, pp. 23-24.
157 Masschelein & Ricken 2003, pp. 140-141.

life in a manner they judge to be right and develop their own personality and become autonomous with an authentic morality.[158] In addition to this interpretation of *Bildung*, Van der Ploeg sees educational importance in the formation of citizenship (in Dutch: *burgerschapsvorming*), which – in contrast to self-responsibility – he calls shared-responsibility. This shared-responsibility seems similar to the outward dimension of *Bildung* and also to what is aimed for through *Erziehung* in the interpretation of Masschelein and Ricken, namely the socialization of the person to become a person – a citizen – within the community. If this interpretation of *Erziehung* is adopted, a tension between *Bildung* and *Erziehung* becomes noticeable. To resolve this tension, Van der Ploeg proposes 'self-responsible shared-responsibility'. In other words, he finds that authentic autonomous citizenship can be achieved when individuals make their own choices (subjectification) as to how they realize their shared-responsibility in society (socialization). Van der Ploeg finds that critical thinking is the act that results in this 'self-responsible shared-responsibility.[159]

It might be true that, because of *Bildung*'s current wide popularity in education, the interpretation of the concept is sometimes far removed from its original meaning,[160] which results in an uncharacteristic focus on socialization. However, this cannot be a reason to abandon the concept altogether, but rather calls for the introduction of a more nuanced interpretation that is true to the original focus on both inner development and development within society in equal measure. The outward dimension of *Bildung* means interacting with the culture of a society. Nevertheless, this need not be assimilated with 'socialization'. The individual has to study and/or experience a social context before being able to either agree with the social norms of the context or swim against the tide of that culture.

In short, the criticisms uttered against the educational practice of *Bildung* looks at the problematic consequences of mass education for actual individual *Bildung*; the idea that the ongoing learning process that *Bildung* entails reduces individuals to eternal children, and; the concern that socialization – as part of the outward dimension of *Bildung* – takes precedence over inner development, which would turn *gebildete* individuals incapable of critical thinking. These concerns indicate possible weak spots in various interpretations and practical utilizations of *Bildung*, which can now be kept in mind when developing an interpretation of *Bildung* to battle the challenges of contemporary ALE. To provide students with strategies to manage contemporary life's uncertainty and to counter the consequences of marketization in legal education, including the disbalance between its vocational and academic components, a nuanced interpretation of *Bildung* can be helpful. In the following section, such an interpretation of *Bildung* will be explored.

158 Van der Ploeg 2019, p. 3.
159 Van der Ploeg 2019, pp. 4-6.
160 Zuurmond 2020, p. 19. Masschelein & Ricken 2003, p. 141.

At the tipping point of *academic* legal education: *Bildung*

In this chapter, I explored and reinterpreted *Bildung* to offer an answer to ALE's current predicament. First, it may be so that the omnipresent societal sense of uncertainty – which turns managing uncertainty into one of the most important skills of contemporary life – requires educators in ALE to adjust their way of teaching to better prepare students for their future lives. Secondly, the unbalanced emphasis lying on ALE's vocational component – due to, among other influences, the marketization of higher education – calls for a strengthening of legal education's academic core. A focus on *Bildung* offers a foundation for embracing uncertainty and supporting our students' ability for managing uncertainty, because it includes a constant confrontation with the uncertainty of the learning process. Moreover, *Bildung* can function as a counterweight to the vocational turn and safeguard the academic component of legal education, since at its core *Bildung* is focused on the inner development of all the individual's capabilities, and not solely on teaching useful knowledge and skills.[161] Based on the previous sections, several aspects of *Bildung* can be put forward as guidelines for contemporary ALE to emphasize its *academic* core in order to restore and maintain the balance between its vocational and academic components. This sought-after balance between the components of legal education seems to resound in the 'harmonious unity' that *Bildung* aims for in the individual. In short, the academic core can be emphasized by approaching academic education as only *a part* of the student's life-long individual development, aimed at developing an attitude of responsibility (ACT responsibility, see Chapter 5) which entails critical and creative thinking ability and is made possible by a connection with others and the world, and playful interaction with, for example, others, art and culture.

Bildung: *self-realization in the context of society*

Central to *Bildung* is self-realization: The personal, holistic development of the virtuous human being in the context of society. As human being and citizen, the individual needs to develop their capabilities into a harmonious, balanced whole. This inner development is a striving for perfection, namely the development of *all* of an individual's capabilities and talents. A one-sided development in a person's character is undesirable.[162] By developing *all* of their capabilities, the individual works on self-realization, which is the result of ongoing self-examination. This self-examination process requires in-depth and broad knowledge; critical thinking (including doubt and questioning), and sensibility, emotions and intuition. The self-examination results in a person's own constantly

161 Horlacher 2017, p. 43.
162 Lechner 2003, p. 109.

re-examined view of – and position towards – themselves and the world. Based on this, the individual is able to make thought-through judgment calls and take congruent action. Because every person has their own capabilities and process of self-examination, this development is deeply personal. Therefore, the individual in the process of constant self-realization is unique and original. He or she is a self-authored and independent thinker, since individuals constantly liberate themselves from presuppositions and unexamined knowledge and thoughts. *Bildung* celebrates the uniqueness of every human being and the diversity of individuals in society, since this diversity in talents between people is the first precondition of mankind to evolve. According to Humboldt, mankind will be more perfect if there is more diversity between individuals.[163]

This striving for originality and uniqueness stands in stark contrast to the current accusation directed at universities that they offer fixed curricula in which they educate their students into undistinguishable 'dime a dozen' graduates. In an attempt to counter this criticism and to embrace the originality required for true *Bildung*, educators in ALE could strive to approach every student as an individual, teach small groups, and make an effort to develop differentiated teaching. The individual development of *all* the student's capabilities (more than developing vocational skills and the understanding of legal concepts) also entails offering a broad education, because the student's self-realization and self-examination requires more than just legal knowledge and skills to develop as a human being, academically educated legal professional, and citizen.

Bildung requires a virtuous human being to *strive* for humanity. Within the ideal of *Bildung*, individual development is seen as a process, not focused on a specific outcome but on the journey of development.[164] Therefore, that endeavor has no finish line: It is a life-long process.[165] So, for academic law students, graduating law school is not the end of a development, but rather one milestone in a whole life full of learning and development. The student's personal and professional insights and competences will perpetually change and expand. The academically educated legal professional's life-long learning might take place naturally, at home or at the work place, and also more formally in post-academic or post-graduate education courses.[166] The education provided by law schools is an important step in the process of life-long learning and one of its challenges is to prepare students for this ongoing journey of self(re-)discovery.

The continuous process of self-realization and re-examination inherently means that individuals find themselves in a situation of constant change. Furthermore, the uniqueness of every person's development entails that there is not one fixed point of success. For

163 Lechner 2003, p. 108.
164 Lechner 2003, pp. 107-108.
165 Lechner 2003, p. 108.
166 See also Susskind 2017, p. 164.

everyone, the development is uncertain.[167] This might call for other forms of assessment in ALE. Instead of focusing on summative assessment – which is a focus on end results – it might be helpful to incorporate formative evaluation into our courses and curricula. Formative evaluation appreciates the learning process and better enables educators to scaffold the learning of individual students. Contrary to the current societal and educational focus on predictable, measurable, and quantifiable results, *Bildung* entails creativity, unquantifiability, and a degree of randomness,[168] and, therefore, comes with uncertainty and risk. To manage this uncertainty, individuals have to possess a considerable degree of flexibility in order to be able to adjust to change. The same quality is of importance to cope with the uncertainty of societal life. For academically educated legal professionals, too, flexibility is valuable: New insights, scientific or otherwise, may give reason to search for corresponding adjustments in legal practice.

As I argued in the first chapter, academic law schools seem to try to banish as much uncertainty as they can from their students' lives. We are therefore at risk of banning all mystery, uncertainty and magic that learning and studying at a centuries old institution might entail from the lives of our students – and our own. It seems that standardization has resulted in a straight path from the start of the Bachelor's program to the end – the receiving of a degree and starting to work in legal practice. For instance, students are taken by the hand as (overly) clear learning goals are formulated, fool-proof instructions are written for writing papers or answering exam questions, and additional training in taking exams is offered. Furthermore, transparency and measurability is demanded from educators who are grading papers or exams. However, all this 'certainty' only seems to make students all the more insecure. They apprehensively search for 'right' answers, examples of previous exams, or lecture recordings that they can memorize and then copy during exams or in papers to prove their 'mastery' of the subject.[169] In this mechanized and unbearably shallow interpretation of studying at an academic institution that rules out uncertainties and failures, no side routes, surprises, (self-)discoveries and true self-realization are possible. Distracted by others and external yard sticks, students are approached solely on the level of lower developmental stages, and are alienated from their own learning process and maybe even from themselves. A renewed place for *Bildung* in ALE, however, may be able to bring the educator's and student's focus back towards their own development that inevitably sometimes comes with uncertainty and the necessity of

167 Lechner 2003, p. 106.
168 Horlacher 2017, p. 43.
169 In some cases, unaware students even capitalize on these word-by-word transcriptions (and thus copyrighted material) of their professor's work by selling and sharing them to other students on websites such as www.studeersnel.nl or www.stuvia.com. In addition to breaching their educator's copyright to their fruits of thought and time-consuming labor, this practice does not stimulate in-depth contemplation of the chosen field of study.

being flexible. These are part of human – and thus of a student's – self-realization. Through a re-mystification of legal education – which entails the cultivation of forms of uncertainty – the law student's self-realization will be supported, and the skill of managing uncertainty will also be helpful to them later in life.

Responsibility

According to Humboldt, every individual has the duty to develop their own natural talents and every unique person contributes to the whole of humanity. This duty is a responsibility for self-realization that lies with the individual. By developing themselves, individuals own up to their responsibility, and at the same time become able to contribute to the whole of society, to humanity. Autonomous learning and character formation[170] are responsibilities belonging to every individual. For legal education, this entails that students are responsible and accountable for their own self-realization during their time at the university. Academic institutions and educators are responsible for *supporting* students in their individual processes and to scaffold their learning, but they are *not* the responsible agents for this learning process. So, students have to own responsibility for their individual learning processes, and for their life-long learning, even though this process is often uneasy, complicated, and without guaranteed results. It is a challenging – but in the end, rewarding – endeavor.

Responsibility has become even more challenging, since defining your own responsibility and taking responsibility as an academically educated global citizen and as an academically educated legal professional who has to understand and appoint legal responsibility has become complex, but very significant, in contemporary society. Also, the possibility of manifestation of risks leads to uncertainty and a call for security that can be (temporarily) alleviated by allocating responsibility. Legal professionals, par excellence, are able to offer this kind of security. Furthermore, citizens of contemporary global society have great power in the sense that the smallest life choices may have far-reaching consequences and, thanks to technological innovations, they are able to reach out to millions of others through (social) media. This grants citizens of the global network society great power, individually and collectively, and with that power comes responsibility. As a citizen, the individual is responsible for gaining knowledge, critically reflect on that knowledge, and making (life) decisions and acting congruently on those decisions.

The significance of responsibility in contemporary society gives rise to consider responsibility the defining virtue of the 21st century. In the words of Herder, who argued that a virtuous human being was the preacher of the virtue of his age, this would mean that

170 Prange 2004, p. 509.

a virtuous human being of the 21st century has a sense of responsibility. This requires rationality, sensibility, and the ability to make decisions and act accordingly. Building on the observation that responsibility becomes a crucial ability for contemporary society, I propose it as the unifying principle for the university. The University of Responsibility could be the 21st century successor of Kant's University of Reason, Humboldt's University of Culture, and the market's University of Excellence.[171] Responsibility will then act as a guiding concept and as a unifying principle for the university's various disciplines.

In the responsibility for the furthering of society a prerequisite for *Bildung* can be noticed: The necessity of a connection with others and the world (the outward dimension of *Bildung*). Through self-examination, which is the basis of self-realization (the inward dimension of *Bildung*), the human being discovers and shapes the world. This is visualized in the image below.

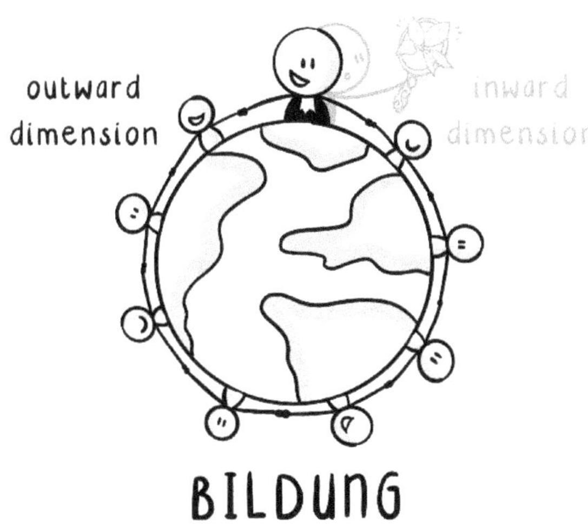

According to Humboldt, *Bildung* – in other words, self-examination and independent thinking – is only possible through social interaction. For students in legal education this means that their *Bildung* is supported by collaboration and group work, and by an academic community in which ideas are shared and discussions are welcomed. Also, *Bildung* requires the individual to *connect* with the world, which for academic law students might entail connecting and discovering global society *during* academic legal education. This could take shape in considering and experiencing societal challenges during courses and in the classroom, (legal) volunteer work, studying abroad and/or internships.

171 Readings 1996, pp. 14, 21, 54, 65.

Not only the connection with others and the world is of significance for *Bildung*. *All* the individual's talents can only be developed equally if both capacities of reason and sensibility (or feeling) are appealed to and further developed in equal measure. This would lead to a beautiful, in other words, good or virtuous, human being. Furthermore, this individual is independent, self-determined and self-authored, that is *free*. According to Schiller, through playful interaction with art (or: culture), the individual's reason and sensibility connect, resulting in the development of the whole human being. In the context of ALE this requires cultivating the student's reason, but also their sensibility.[172] In contrast with Plato's theory of forms and the romanticist belief, currently, beauty is not (always) equated with goodness. However, a beautiful appearance might still have the deceiving effect of suggesting goodness or quality – which is, for example, used for profit in advertising and movies. The university, in contrast, should be beyond these shallow appearances. In ALE the focus needs to be on true beauty: The development of unique and self-authored individuals capable of independent thinking and responsibility. To achieve this, we might have to take a risk and leave our *rational* comfort zone and include sensibility, feeling, emotion, and intuition in academic education. In our lectures and classrooms, playful interaction with not only art and culture, but also with the study subject(s) and peers is a means to enable the student's simultaneous development of both reason *and* sensibility.

If the academic law student takes on the challenge of constant self-realization, they are creating a unique work of art. In this sense, life in itself is a work of art. True artists challenge themselves again and again to attempt the impossible and set high standards for themselves. The artist can only hope (and trust) that they are to match those individual standards of 'excellence'.[173] Taking on this challenge, this responsibility, requires discipline, but will also bring the life-long learner a sense of pleasure, because their character develops towards an aesthetic, harmonious whole and they are capable of congruent action.

As has been argued above, it is clear that *responsibility* for yourself, for others and for the world resides at the heart of a notion of *Bildung* designed for contemporary ALE. This responsibility requires critical thinking and creative thinking, which are both abilities of importance for *Bildung* as well. In education, play and playfulness can be used as teaching strategies to support the student's development of critical thinking, creative thinking and responsibility. Having discovered this, we are able to continue our journey in search of the foundations of the academic core of legal education. In the following chapters, the three key elements of *Bildung* – critical thinking, creative thinking and responsibility – will each be further considered in the context of ALE. The third chapter explores critical thinking, the fourth chapter focuses on creative thinking and the fifth chapter examines responsibility.

172 This sensibility refers to emotion, feeling and sense. Beiser 2003, p. 100.

173 See also Bauman 2008, p. 17.

In the sixth chapter, play and playfulness are investigated as strategies for educators in ALE to teach critical thinking, creative thinking and responsibility.

3 The Bare Necessity. Infusing Critical Thinking into Academic Legal Education

"The fool doth think he is wise,
but the wise man knows himself to be a fool."
– *William Shakespeare*[1]

Introduction

This line from Shakespeare's 'As you like it' is reminiscent of critical thinking, which entails for an individual to be capable of continuous critical reflection upon their opinions and to change those if warranted. Critical thinkers therefore always remain vigilant of what they consider truth and are aware that they do not know everything. In the previous chapter, critical thinking was introduced as one of the key elements of contemporary *Bildung* and as a crucial part of every academic's abilities. All academics, including academically educated legal professionals, need the ability to manage our time's complexity and the accompanying sense of uncertainty. However, this is not an easy feat. The Introduction and the first chapter described the challenges contemporary lawyers face and the peril of (legal) academic education. I have argued that the *academic* core of legal education is currently in jeopardy due to the marketization of academic education and the tendency to avoid uncertainty at all costs, which results in the existing focus on measurable outcomes and the development of useable vocational skills. To rediscover a balance between the vocational and academic components of legal education the second chapter proposed a renewed interpretation and practice of various aspects central to *Bildung*, namely critical thinking, creative thinking and responsibility. This chapter explores the first of these aspects, namely critical thinking.

When discussing what characterizes an *academic* education, many (legal) academics propose *critical thinking* as a key concept.[2] Critical thinking is considered by most to be the bare necessity of an *academic* education in law. For example, Mathiasen and Andersen regard the development of critical thinking as the central mission of all educational institutions, since it ensures that students become responsible citizens who think ethically

---

1 William Shakespeare in 'As You Like It', Act 5, Scene 1.

2 Davies & Barnett 2015, p. 2, Arum & Roksa 2011, p. 35, Barnett 1997, p. 2. Van Klink 2016, p. 15, Van Klink & Francot 2019, p. 54. Adriansen 2010, p. 82, Cownie 2004, pp. 81-83, Scott Fruehwald 2020, p. 1.

and take the public good into account when they act.[3] However, according to Davies and Barnett, when 'employability' became increasingly important as a goal of academic education, 'critical thinking' disappeared into the background, or was understood solely as an *economic* value instead of a social and civic value.[4] Furthermore, even though critical thinking is – in the words of Mulnix – *'all the rage'* in academic institutions,[5] the content of the concept and what is involved in critical thinking often remains unclear or unexplained in the practice of higher education.[6] It seems that many consider the notion of critical thinking and all it entails self-explanatory. However, this is not the case. In my experience as an educator and as a tutor of novice educators, the concept is scarcely made explicit to students and often remains underexposed in the professional training of educators in legal education, such as during the University Teaching Qualification (UTQ) in the Netherlands (Dutch: *Basiskwalificatie Onderwijs*, BKO), although there is attention for the concept of deep learning and for Bloom's six levels of thinking. Even for those who do not immediately consider this lack of a shared and discussed understanding of critical thinking problematic, the situation will become daunting in the light of recent research. For example, Arum and Roksa show in their *Academically Adrift* that the quality of higher order cognitive thinking skills – which include critical thinking – of university students has diminished since the 1970's and 1980's. Furthermore, a vast number of students do not improve their critical thinking skills during their years of study.[7] Of the more than 2300 students in Arum and Roksa's sample, a staggering 45 percent did not significantly improve their skills in critical thinking, complex reasoning and writing in their first two years of college. Graduating students did not fare much better.[8] In other words, many students that graduate are not (yet) sufficiently capable of higher order cognitive processes, including critical thinking. To refer back to Kuhn's description of the developmental stages of young adults (Chapter 1): These graduates seem to not have risen beyond the absolutist or multiplist stages. Consequently, an ability that many academics regard as key to an academic education fails to become part of our graduates' abilities. Based on these insights and bringing our focus back to legal education, we might ask if our graduating law students are currently sufficiently capable of becoming responsible citizens and lawyers in

---

3 Mathiasen & Andersen 2020, p. 39.

4 See Davies & Barnett 2015, pp. 1-2.

5 See Mulnix 2012, p. 464.

6 Scott Fruehwald states that college staff lack a substantive concept of critical thinking, see: Scott Fruehwald 2020, p. 1. Mathiasen and Andersen, too, notice the lack of consensus between educators, students and tutors on what critical thinking entails. See Mathiasen & Andersen 2020, p. 40.

7 Scott Fruehwald, p. 2. See also: Arum & Roksa 2011, p. 36.

8 Arum & Roksa 2011, pp. 35-36. The authors add that this percentage is probably even larger: When using the standard error of the CLA (College Learning Assessment) 2005 score, the percentage of students that did not show significant growth of their critical thinking, reasoning and writing skills within their first two years of college might be 53% (Arum & Roksa 2011, p. 219, note 15). See also Davies and Barnett 2015, p. 4.

contemporary society. One reason for our students' insufficient capability to think critically might be found in the lack of a shared understanding of what critical thinking entails and how this can be taught.

In this chapter, I therefore seek to answer questions such as if and why critical thinking is important for contemporary academically educated legal professionals; how critical thinking can be defined for legal professionals; what is required of law students to be able to think critically and, finally, how critical thinking could be further incorporated into the teaching in academic law schools. To answer these questions, I draw on the ideas of well-known theorists in the domain of philosophy of education and critical thinking, such as Ennis, Bailin, Davies and Barnett, and Paul and Elder, since these theorists have studied the content of critical thinking and how to teach critical thinking in (higher) education. To bring the concept of critical thinking closer to home, namely to our law schools, I find inspiration in the ideas of academics researching critical thinking in the context of legal education, such as Cedrone, Van Klink, De Vries, Corrias and Francot. This chapter first investigates why critical thinking is of importance for *academically* educated legal professionals in the 21st century. Then, a definition of critical thinking for lawyers is sought, followed by a description of which knowledge, skills, and dispositions law students who aim to be critical thinkers require. Finally, the chapter offers a first draft of how to explicitly create space for critical thinking in academic legal education (ALE) on the organizational levels of 1) learning culture and environment; 2) curriculum design; 3) course design and; 4) teaching method and teaching style. This final part of the chapter also includes an overview of and practical suggestions for educators in legal education.

On the critical importance of critical thinking for lawyers

As said earlier, many academics, including legal academics, state that the ability for critical thinking is a key ability to be learned in any academic education. There are good reasons to perceive critical thinking as a crucial ability for academically educated lawyers of the 21st century. In the following, four of these reasons are further explicated.

First, lawyers require critical thinking skills, because they regularly decipher and compose arguments. Also, they defend their point of view and are able to understand argumentations made by others. To do so, lawyers need the skills to distinguish between assumptions and conclusions, and discover fallacies in another's and their own argumentation. These skills are all part of critical thinking. Furthermore, based on information that they judge as true, valuable, convincing, or trustworthy, legal professionals have to be able to make inferences and construct hypotheses. For example, based on pieces of evidence, a prosecutor constructs a convincing story of what exactly has happened, who is accountable and what legal consequences should follow. Moreover, academically educated legal professionals need to be open-minded to alternatives, and have to be able to adjust their opinion when evidence calls for it in order to critically reflect on *inter alia* laws, judgments and the legal system as a whole. After all, they need to be able to question and look beyond the *status quo* and – if the situation calls for it – search for alternatives. During this chapter it becomes clear that all the aforementioned abilities and dispositions are elements of critical thinking, which is therefore important for legal professionals to develop.

Secondly, lawyers engaging in the process of critical thinking constantly practice with being in a state of uncertainty, since critical thinking involves constant doubt and questioning. The critical attitude that lawyers ingrain through continual practice makes them better equipped to manage uncertainty in other aspects of life as well. This is because critical thinking requires open-mindedness and the inherent willingness of critical thinkers to change their viewpoints if evidence warrants it. Critical thinking basically consists of questioning your own ideas and prejudices, the convictions of others, and also the ideas and opinions that form the conversation of the domain (such as Law). Therefore, law students have to learn to wonder about the information they come across and ask questions. When they develop the ability to question the information they are confronted with, students see that information is often colored and perspectives on reality are manifold. A critical attitude changes how students perceive, judge and apply information. Furthermore, the ability to question – which entails allowing the sense of uncertainty into their minds – explicitly shows law students that, although there are starting points and there is knowledge fundamental to the domain, knowledge is still only a construction resulting from a perpetual critical thinking process between the participants in the domain. Consequently, there will be times in which ideas that are now undisputed could be – and, possibly, should be – questioned and the possible answers to those questions might lead to a change in the domain. The experience of constant possibility of change in the domain may support a student's ability to deal with a sense of uncertainty.

Third, critical thinking is an important ability for all citizens in these times of information overflow, disinformation, 'personal truths', and 'fake news'. It is important that individuals are able to judge the value, quality and truthfulness of information and that they use doubt and think for themselves and make self-authored decisions. Good citizens of contemporary times are not 'obedient' citizens that believe quickly without checking the relevant sources and the quality of information but, instead, are critical thinkers able to come to an informed opinion. Since legal professionals live and work in contemporary society, they too, have to be able to think critically and make self-authored judgments rooted in reasoning and argumentation about what they regard as truth. Moreover, from academically educated legal professionals one may expect that they are especially capable of self-authored thinking and critical thinking in the domain of law, since they have in-depth knowledge about the law and are trained in argumentation skills.

They are, for example, able to use relevant legal and academic sources and check the credibility of sources used by others and are able to detect fallacies in the arguments of others. For legal professionals, self-authored thinking consists of other abilities as well. In explanation, the complex contemporary society requires academically educated legal professionals who do not meekly abide by rules and do not just 'go with the flow', but people who question the status quo: To critically reflect on the law, its theoretical foundations and practice and on the legal profession. In other words, they require the courage and ability to swim against the tide and stand for what they believe even if at times it seems they stand alone. This, for example, necessitates the ability to observe and judge the legal system from some distance, which is part of critical thinking ability.

Finally, critical thinking is an important ability for being able to define and take responsibility, which is – as argued in the second chapter – part of *Bildung* and part of the *academic* component of legal education. This involves managing uncertainty, making deliberate choices and acting on those choices. Responsible citizens – which ideally includes academically educated legal professionals – are expected to make impactful choices based on their informed opinion stemming from available information. This requires skills in judging the worth and truthfulness of information unfazed by – but aware of – its incompleteness and/or complexity. It also requires decision making skills: Since upon judging information, legal professionals are obliged to make choices and *act* based on those decisions. For them to be able to do so, lawyers require critical thinking.

These reasons underpinning the conviction that critical thinking is a crucial ability for academically educated legal professionals in the 21st century also relate to *Bildung*, which I argue is key to managing uncertainty and being responsible in contemporary times. Indeed, self-authored thinking, (self-) reflection and the art of doubt are all elements of *Bildung* as well as critical thinking. Nevertheless, the concepts are not the same: Critical thinking is only one aspect of *Bildung*. Hence, in order to better understand what contemporary *Bildung* consists of, we require a better grasp of critical thinking. To that aim, the next part of this chapter explores the content of critical thinking.

What is critical thinking?

A short history of critical thinking in education

In short, critical thinking may be sketched as 'a skilled activity of thought that includes commitment to reason'.[9] This shows that critical thinking is at its core rooted in reason and

9 Mulnix 2012, p. 471.

reasoning.[10] Reason has long been a philosophical theme, central to and also preceding the thinking of Socrates,[11] Plato[12] and Aristotle.[13] After the Middle Ages, it was revalued in Early Modernity.[14] During the Enlightenment, Immanuel Kant asserted the importance of reason and stated that free thinking – resulting in critique – was only possible through education. Which meant that an individual could only become a free human – in other words, an individual independent of another's ideas – through education. Education was therefore seen as a liberating force required for fulfilling the human destiny of '*Sapere Aude*'.[15]

Throughout history, philosophers, scientists and lawyers have been using sound reasoning for developing and communicating their ideas.[16] Consequently, using reason and trust in the human capacity for reasoning is most certainly not new. However, critical thinking only became a popular theme for *educationalists* in the early 20th century, when well-known educationalist John Dewey (1859-1952) brought the theme into the open by describing it as 'reflective thinking'.[17] This was later renamed by progressive educationalists as 'critical thinking'.[18] Dewey is therefore regarded as the founder of the contemporary movement of critical thinking in education.[19] In addition, Dewey advocated experiential learning and was also a leading figure in the American *Progressive Education Movement*.[20] This movement, which promoted critical thinking,[21] developed in the late 19th century. It has its roots in Romanticism, Rousseau's *Emile*[22] and also found inspiration in the *Bildung*

---

10 Adriansen 2010, p. 68.

11 The 'Socratic method' (still) consists of finding knowledge through dialogue: By responding to questions that shed doubt on their first assumptions and beliefs, individuals slowly but steadily advance their knowledge through logic reasoning.

12 Socrates and Plato both used logic, in the sense of *dialogical thinking*, to judge if an argument was sound. According to Plato, only *philosophers* were able to achieve absolute, true *knowledge* of reality through the hard process of thinking, whereas all others were only able to achieve relative *beliefs*. The *Ideas* (objective realities) provide philosophers with criteria that make them able to judge, for example, the beauty or truth of a statement. See: Thayer-Bacon 1998, p. 124 and Biesta and Stams 2001, p. 57. See also Mulnix 2012, p. 472.

13 See Biesta and Stams 2001, p. 58. See also Mulnix 2012, p. 472.

14 See Biesta and Stams 2001, pp. 57-58. See also: Thayer-Bacon 1998, p. 124.

15 Biesta and Stams 2001, pp. 58-59. See also: Van Klink 2016, p. 15. Kant refers to 'Sapere Aude' (dare to think) as the call of the Enlightenment in his famous essay *Was ist Erklärung?*.

16 Thayer-Bacon 1998, p. 124.

17 Reflective thinking was defined by Dewey as 'the kind of thinking that consists in turning a subject over in the mind and giving it serious and consecutive consideration.' See Dewey 1933, p. 3.

18 See Ennis 2015, p. 31. See also: Ennis 2011a, p. 4. Philosopher Max Black was most likely the first author to use the words 'critical thinking' as the book title of his 'Critical Thinking: An Introduction to Logic and Scientific Method' in 1945. See Ennis 2011a, p. 6, Ennis 2016, p. 10. See also: Ennis 2015, p. 30.

19 Ennis 2016, p. 10. See also Dumitru 2019, p. 872.

20 See Kolb 2015, p. 22.

21 Ennis 2011a, p. 5.

22 See Reese 2001, pp. 2-3, 6.

ideal.[23] Other driving forces for the movement were European educationalists Johann Heinrich Pestalozzi (1742-1827, known for the *head, heart, hand* approach in – preferably – vocational education),[24] Friedrich Fröbel (1782-1852, best known as the creator of the *Kindergarten*)[25] and Maria Montessori (1870-1952, known for her *Montessori* primary school system).[26] Following in the footsteps of these thinkers, the *Progressive Education Movement* rejected traditional education – which was seen as passive,[27] uniform and unnatural – and emphasized the importance of experience, nature and diversity for the development of individuals and especially children. In the view of the movement, education was meant for human development and important for creating a democracy in which all citizens participate. For this endeavor, critical thinking was paramount.[28] This resulted, for example, in the inclusion of play – including games – stories, and informal learning in the education of children.[29] However, some followers of the *Progressive Education Movement* can be criticized as being anti-intellectual.[30] These progressives rejected, for example, the teaching of literature. Since he did not agree with all its viewpoints, Dewey protested against being called the father of the *Progressive Education Movement*.[31] Nevertheless, he *was* responsible for a well-known progressive experiment in primary schools in the U.S. called the Eight Year Study. Developing critical thinking was part of this experiment, but the publication of the results of the Study did not gather much attention due to the focus on the Second World War at the time. After the War, the results of the experiment were shared at the pinnacle of America's defeat in the war on space when the Russians were first in launching their satellite 'Sputnik'. This caused the results to go by unnoticed. More importantly, progressive schools were held accountable for the failure of winning the war on space since they were blamed for not educating students appropriately on subject matter. As a result, the *Progressive Education Movement*, including its focus on the development of critical thinking skills, fizzled out during the 1950's.[32]

23 Horlacher 2017, pp. 73-74.

24 Reese 2001, pp. 11-13.

25 Reese 2001, p. 15.

26 Reese 2001, p. 8.

27 See Reese 2001, p. 2. In contrast to what the progressives envisioned, in many universities in the late 19th century, passive memorization and traditional recitation were important skills for successful graduation. See: Reese 2001, p. 10.

28 Ennis 2011a, p. 5.

29 Reese 2001, p. 16.

30 Reese 2001, p. 17-19.

31 See Reese 2001, pp. 1-2, 23. Dewey did not agree with a the romantic, rose-colored glasses through which young children were typically viewed by the progressives and he did not share the opinion that children should just do as they please in educational settings.

32 Ennis 2011a, p. 6. In our times, there seems to be a renewed interest in the viewpoints of the Progressive Education Movement, which seem to be currently linked to intrinsic motivation, experience, participation in society and 21st century skills. In Dutch academic legal education this renewed interest can be seen in the University of Amsterdam's project in experiential learning (started in 2018) which looks at the inclusion of

Still, interest in teaching critical thinking in schools remained a topic for educationalists and philosophers, many of whom have contributed to the discourse on critical thinking in educational settings.[33] In 1956, Bloom introduced his taxonomy of educational objectives, which included 6 categories of the cognitive domain, namely (1) knowledge, (2) comprehension, (3) application, (4) analysis, (5) synthesis and (6) evaluation.[34] In 2001, Bloom's taxonomy was reconsidered by a group of experts. In this revised form, called the *Taxonomy for Learning, Teaching and Assessing*, the six categories have received an update. Now, they are more actively defined and 'creating' has become part of the taxonomy. So, the contemporary taxonomy's categories of educational objectives are: (1) remember; (2) understand; (3) apply; (4) analyze; (5) evaluate, and (6) create.[35] In the 1956 version as well as in the revision of 2001, critical thinking is thought to be an element of categories two to six, since these are part of what is often called higher order thinking. Critical thinking is therefore *part* of what is typically called higher order thinking,[36] but the two concepts are not interchangeable. As the taxonomy shows as well, higher order thinking includes more types of thinking in addition to critical thinking, such as creative thinking and problem-solving.[37] Currently, the revised taxonomy is applied extensively in higher education. For example, the Bloom taxonomy is studied during the University Teaching Qualification program for junior educators at the Vrije Universiteit Amsterdam and most courses in the law faculty use the taxonomy for their assessment matrixes. However, Bloom's 1956 taxonomy did not specify what critical thinking was and it also received criticism of the six categories which some believe to be non-transferrable between disciplines.[38]

The field of critical thinking in education was advanced in 1962, when Robert Ennis published an article that is seen by many as a reference work on critical thinking and what

---

experiential learning in their legal Master programs. See: Amsterdam Law School, *Amsterdam Law Practice. Experiential Legal Education Programme Handbook*, January 2023. See also: https://www.uva.nl/en/about-the-uva/organisation/faculties/amsterdam-law-school/education/masters-programmes/amsterdam-law-practice/amsterdam-law-practice.html.

33 Well-known contributors to the field of critical thinking in the second half of the 20th century were, for example, Ennis, Siegel, McPeck, Paul, Bailin and Thayer-Bacon.

34 Bloom 1956, p. 18. See also: Lucassen, 2018: https://www.vernieuwenderwijs.nl/de-taxonomie-van-bloom-vaak-verkeerd-gebruikt-maar-zo-werkt-het-wel/, last visited March 28th 2023 and Draaijer 2023: https://vu.nl/nl/nieuws/2023/goed-nieuws-hogere-orde-kennis-en-vaardigheden-bestaan-niet, last visited March 28th 2023.

35 Anderson & Krathwohl 2001, p. 28.

36 Importantly, discussions of the topic of the denominators 'higher' and 'lower' order thinking have recently become noticeable. Some educationalists argue that these words mistakenly frame remembering and understanding as unimportant, whereas these categories of educational objectives are in themselves valuable. See: Draaijer 2023: https://vu.nl/nl/nieuws/2023/goed-nieuws-hogere-orde-kennis-en-vaardigheden-bestaan-niet, last visited March 28th 2023.

37 See also: Facione 1990, p. 5.

38 Ennis 2011a, pp. 12-13.

it entails.[39] In his article, Ennis defined critical thinking as '*the correct assessment of statements*'[40] and continued to describe twelve aspects of critical thinking and three dimensions.[41] The article mainly focused its description of critical thinking on the skills required, which Ennis called 'the characteristics' of critical thinking. Other thinkers in the domain were inspired and from this publication onward, Ennis became recognized as one of the leading experts on critical thinking and the pedagogy and assessment of critical thinking.[42] In education, the influence of Ennis's description, which was at the time mainly focused on necessary skills for critical thinking, seems apparent in the so-called 'first wave' of critical thinking in education. In explanation, critical thinking pedagogy during the '70s mainly focused on teaching reasoning, logic and argumentation skills, on the premise that arguments are logical structures that can be identified and evaluated. If one was able to use the logical structure of argumentation(s), one was perceived as a critical thinker.[43]

In the years of the Cold War, critical thinking was regarded in the United States as politically important for withstanding communist indoctrination and finding truth, which – in the eyes of Western states – would lead to a just society.[44] In the 1980's – at the end of and after the Cold War – attention to critical thinking within philosophy and educational studies, especially in the U.S., soared.[45] Illustrative of this scientific interest is the conduct of the *Delphi Project* in 1988 and 1989.[46] Under the direction of Peter Facione, a group of 46 experts in the field of critical thinking, mainly including philosophers and educationalists (including Ennis), formulated a definition of critical thinking.[47] At this time, the main focus on critical thinking shifted from considering it a necessary tool in the tension

39 See Ennis 2011a, p. 6. Biesta and Stams 2001, p. 59; Thayer-Bacon 1998, p. 123; Thayer-Bacon 2000, p. 56; Davies & Barnett 2015, p. 27. McPeck 1981, p. 2.

40 Ennis 1962, p. 83.

41 These twelve characteristics of critical thinking were: (1) grasping the meaning of a statement; (2) judging whether there is ambiguity in the line of reasoning; (3) judging whether certain statements contradict one another; (4) judging whether a conclusion follows necessarily; (5) judging whether a statement is specific enough; (6) judging whether a principle establishes a statement that is alleged to be an application of it; (7) judging whether an observation statement is reliable; 8) judging whether an inductive conclusion – for example, a generalization – is warranted; (9) judging whether a problem has been identified; (10) judging whether something is an assumption; (11) judging whether a definition is adequate; (12) judging whether a statement made by an (alleged) authority is acceptable. The three dimensions of critical thinking Ennis describes here are the logical, criterial, and pragmatic dimensions. Each of the twelve characteristics falls into one, two or three of these dimensions. See Ennis 1962.

42 In addition to his many publications on critical thinking and critical thinking pedagogy, Ennis was also involved in creating and further developing the very influential *Cornell Critical Thinking Tests.*

43 Davies & Barnett 2015, p. 7.

44 Thayer-Bacon 1998, p. 123.

45 Ennis 2011a, p. 8.

46 Ennis 2011a, p. 8.

47 In consensus, the experts of *the Delphi Project* defined critical thinking as '*purposeful, self-regulatory judgment which results in interpretation, analysis, evaluation, and inference, as well as explanation of the evidential, conceptual, methodological, criteriological, or contextual consideration upon which that judgment is based*'. See: Facione 1990, p. 2.

between East and West, to approaching it as a valuable ability for economic growth and the production of wealth.[48] In these years, Ennis adapted his definition of critical thinking into the practical definition '*reasonable reflective thinking that is focused on deciding what to do or believe*'.[49] According to Thayer-Bacon, this also changed the definition's center of gravity from focusing only on the skills relevant for critical thinking to a broader interpretation of the concept, including dispositions relevant for critical thinking and a differentiation between the process (assessing) and product (*correct* assessment) of critical thinking.[50] This broader interpretation of critical thinking is also recognizable in the 'second wave' of critical thinking education which regarded critical thinking as an ideological issue and focused on the development of the student as a *complete* human being instead of only focusing on enabling students to mechanically decipher and construct argumentations.[51] A subgroup within this second wave called 'critical pedagogy' found inspiration in the critics of the Frankfurt School, and interpreted 'criticism' as 'critique'. For education, this meant that the ideal was for students to learn to question the hidden meanings behind all sorts of social structures and to be the active sources of radical social change.[52]

In the 90's of the previous century and first decades of this century, critical thinking became increasingly important on the agenda of institutions of higher education.[53] A third wave of the critical movement in education became visible in the first decade of the 21st century. This wave united the ideas of the previous two waves and focused on connecting the importance of developing critical thinking skills, such as argumentation skills, with the development of other aspects of the human being such as emotions, imagination and creativity.[54] Especially in the U.S., courses on critical thinking became mandatory in the curricula of universities.[55] I do not recognize this practice in universities in the Netherlands, even though there are teaching method initiatives that implicitly and explicitly focus on the development of autonomy and autonomous thinking and learning, such as *problem-based learning* which has long been a practice at Maastricht University and is also used at the Erasmus University in Rotterdam. However, a comprehensive and – above all – practical definition and explication of critical thinking, that functions as a spot on the horizon and road map for the learning and assessment of our students and our educators'

48 Thayer-Bacon 1998, pp. 124. See also Barnett 1997, p. 3.
49 Ennis 1987, p. 10.
50 Thayer-Bacon 2000, p. 57.
51 Davies & Barnett 2015, p. 7.
52 Davies & Barnett 2015, pp. 7, 9.
53 The reason for this interest in critical thinking in higher education is the conviction that learning subject matter is not enough for becoming an academic who is able to critically reflect on their professional, civic and personal life. See Ennis 2011a, p. 8.
54 Davies & Barnett 2015, p. 8.
55 Ennis 2015, p. 31.

teaching, eludes us still. This absence seems to be reflected in the rather disheartening results of Arum and Roksa's study on the lack of development of students' critical thinking skills.[56]

These disappointing reports notwithstanding, our complex, global society and legal practice are in dire need of critical thinkers, since critical thinking enables people to search for the truth value of knowledge claims and opinions, while remaining open minded to alternatives. Yet, it seems that, at the moment, higher education is more focused on the employability of students than on the development of crucial academic abilities, such as critical thinking, even though the latter was one of the fundamental aims of the 19th century blueprint of the university.[57] Although it might be worthwhile to support a student's development as a future employee in the legal field, this is not and should not be the main focus of an *academic* legal education. In the Netherlands, vocational education is already being provided by the Netherlands Bar's vocational training and in legal oriented curricula provided by colleges or Universities of Applied Sciences (*hogescholen*). After all, what distinguishes ALE from these other types of legal education if not its academic orientation? Therefore, I argue that it is necessary for ALE to explicitly create time and space for the development of law students' critical thinking. Helpful to that goal is, in the first place, a clear (and shared) understanding of the aim of critical thinking, a useful definition of critical thinking and insight into the necessary skills and dispositions that law students require to be capable of critical thinking. Thus, I will describe the aim, definition, and scope of critical thinking. Based on these findings, suggestions will be explored for the further incorporation of critical thinking in legal education.

The aim of critical thinking

So what is the aim of critical thinking? In contrast to the economic aims ascribed to critical thinking in the last two decades of the 20th century, in the complex and uncertain contemporary society of our time, critical thinking should not be valued because of its effect on economic growth.[58] Rather, it should be pursued for its worth as an ability that is

56 Arum & Roksa 2011, pp. 35-36, 219.

57 Davies & Barnett 2015, pp. 2, 6.

58 Some may probably still hold that critical thinking is mainly of importance as an economic commodity. See Davies & Barnett 2015, p. 2. From the end of the Second World War onward, the growth of the economy became the main goal of many governments and international organizations. However, this one-sided focus on economic growth (especially in the domain of Economics) has been met with criticism since the early 1990's (see Victor 2010, p. 244). For example, in academic literature, attention is drawn towards uneconomic growth and the problems related to focusing solely on growth in economics (see Daly 2013). Alternatives are offered by the field of ecological economy and, for instance, in Raworth's visualization of the 'donut economy' (Raworth 2017). These alternatives attempt to refocus Economy's aim from economic growth to human well-being and sustainability, since these are seen as the most urgent problems to be

an essential part of the overarching ACT responsibility (chapter 5) and enables self-authored thinkers to define and take their responsibility for themselves, others, society and the natural environment. I therefore argue that critical thinking for the academically educated legal professional enables defining and taking responsibility in the world and is aimed at becoming a self-authored thinker capable of making decisive judgments.

Critical thinking is aimed at becoming an independent, self-authored thinker. This is especially relevant for academics, who are regarded as especially capable of thinking for themselves because of their educational background and because of the possible roles they might take on in society. This includes being capable of making deliberate and independent personal and professional choices and being open to doubting and revising one's own and others' beliefs and opinions when warranted. As said before, making choices is part of every individual's daily life in contemporary global society. These choices often have to be made based on incomplete or even incorrect information and one has to decide what to consider accurate and what to do based on these decisions. Critical thinking is crucial for decision-making in matters of consequence, since it is based on careful consideration.[59] Furthermore, to prevent building upon false ideas and unquestioningly following suggestions, opinions and convictions, academics require the ability to judge the truthfulness of knowledge claims and this is possible through critical questioning. Therefore, Martin finds that critical thinking is the core of the academic capability.[60] According to Siegel, the aim of critical thinking is not so much to achieve truth, but to give a rational justification, in hopes of approaching truth.[61] So critical thinking enables individuals to give rational justifications for their beliefs (or: opinions/ideas/convictions) and prevents them from deciding and/or acting on false or incorrect assumptions. In this sense, the experts of *The Delphi Project* called critical thinking a liberating force and a "powerful resource in one's personal and civic life".[62] Critical thinking frees us from being constrained by others and by our own shortsightedness, prejudices, and lethargy: it enables, but also *necessitates* deliberate, contemplated, personal choice. Importantly, this means that when critical thinking is taught in education, what should be taught is *how* to think critically, and not *what* to think. The content of what is thought, and the resulting

solved by humanity in these times. According to Constanza et al., the field of ecological economics intends to tackle these problems and achieve the three goals of sustainable scale, fair distribution and efficient allocation through transdisciplinary dialogue and cooperative problem solving (Constanza et al. 2015, pp. 87-89). It seems that in the current context of an increased urgency of the call for sustainability, criticism of the economic and political focus on economic growth is also noticeable in the mainstream (not solely academic) media. See, for example, Stegehuis and Rammelt 2022.

59 See Ennis 1996, p. XVII.

60 Martin 1999, p. 97. See also: Cownie 2004, p. 78.

61 Siegel 1991, pp. 24-25.

62 Facione 1990, p. 2.

beliefs and actions are independently constructed.[63] This results in academics who seek to lead their own *examined life*: a life in which they make their own contemplated choices and in which critical thinking abilities and dispositions have become part of their character. Paul has called this ability to critically reflect on not just another's, but also your own position, arguments and worldview 'critical thinking in the *strong sense*'.[64]

Critical thinking – definition and scope

Knowing the aim of critical thinking is not the same as having a clear definition of the concept. Hence, the following section seeks to offer such a definition. However, one only has to meander through the vast jungle of the literature on critical thinking to come across an abundance of definitions of the concept(ion). Although the many variations might at first deter newcomers to the field, on closer inspection many interpretations overlap. Many theorists working on finding a definition of critical thinking seem to agree that, at its core, critical thinking is about reasoning and rationality. Many of these definitions also postulate that it is a mental process of reasoning that will result in judgment.[65] When 'critical thinking theorists' describe what someone needs in order to be able to think critically, again, the language used may be different, but the content of what is meant appears similar.

According to Barnett, there are currently three movements noticeable regarding critical thinking in higher education, namely the *critical thinking movement*, the *criticality movement*, and the *critical pedagogy movement*. The first, the *critical thinking movement*, can be related to the earlier described 'first wave'. It regards critical thinking mainly as a cognitive process that involves skills and dispositions. In education, this *critical thinking movement* focuses on developing the inward dimension – the individual dimension – namely the individual's personal development of the cognitive and affective elements involved in critical thinking.[66] In other words, it looks at the skills and dispositions central to critical thinking. Barnett places educational philosophers such as Ennis, Siegel and McPeck within this movement.[67] The *criticality movement*, of which Barnett himself is a passionate spokesperson, aims to show the extent to which education can truly support the development of students. In contrast to the *critical thinking movement*, the idea is that student develop their characters and not only their rationality during their education by

63 Mulnix 2012, p. 466.

64 Davies & Barnett 2015, p. 13 and Mason 2007, p. 341.

65 For the separate definitions, see Ennis 2016, pp. 8-9. Here, Ennis has clustered 14 definitions of critical thinking.

66 This dimension seems quite similar to the inward dimension of *Bildung*, since both focus on the individual's inner development.

67 Davies & Barnett 2015, p. 14.

not just developing one – specifically *thinking* – but multiple aspects, namely thinking (critical thinking), being (critical self-reflection) and acting (critical action).[68] These are all part of 'criticality'. Barnett thinks that higher education should aim at developing this criticality in its students, since it is the capacity of the 'critical being'. *Criticality* has emancipatory power since a critical being is not just subjected to the world, but able to think and act autonomously and with purpose in the world.[69] Therefore, in addition to the development of students' skills and dispositions – which is the inward, individual dimension – the *criticality movement* regards critical doing and participation in the form of *action* a part of 'criticality'. This action takes place in the context of society – in other words, the outward, socio-cultural dimension.[70] Consequently, the *criticality movement* argues that criticality has an inward and outward dimension, which are both of importance. So, the *criticality movement* interprets critical thinking more broadly than the *critical thinking movement*, so that it involves a cognitive, ethical and active dimension.[71] Finally, the third movement of critical thinking takes things several steps further: This *critical pedagogy movement* sees education as a way to critically and actively engage with ideology. It also views higher education as a device for radical social change, assuming that people who are educated in 'critique' become activists able to withstand ideologies, and especially the ideology of capitalism. Similar to the *criticality movement*, the *critical pedagogy movement* views 'critical thinking' broadly as skills, dispositions, ethics and action. However, in this movement, 'action' justifies radical, all-encompassing societal change, whereas the *criticality movement* sees 'action' as a student's personal ability to react to events.[72]

I consider Barnett's assessment of these three movements to be insightful, because it provides an opportunity for this chapter to clarify its position in the light of these three movements. I disagree with the critical pedagogues' extreme and instrumental position of using higher education solely as an instrument for social change and propagandizing the danger of ideology and the necessity of radical social change to every student. Firstly, this is an ethical opinion, which should be the result of a student's own, self-authored critical thinking process and not the standard and thus indoctrinated result of a university

68 This brings back memories of Pestalozzi's (one of the progressive education's inspirations) head, heart, hand approach in primary education and the three dimensions that are the focus of signature pedagogies: The cognitive dimension (thinking), technical/practical skills dimension (performing) and the moral dimension (act with integrity/ethical professional role).

69 Barnett 1997, p. 4.

70 This outward dimension of critical thinking seems similar, or perhaps complementary, to *Bildung*'s outward dimension. The outward dimension of *Bildung* is aimed at self-development and becoming a part of society through connection with the outside world and others. The outward dimension of critical thinking (in the words of Barnett) might add to this description that the self-development and becoming a citizen involves taking action and active participation.

71 Davies & Barnett 2015, pp.15-18. See also: Barnett 1997, p. 4.

72 Davies & Barnett 2015, pp. 19-20.

education. This would mean that higher education would miss its purpose of teaching critical thinking. Secondly, all academically educated legal professionals are participants in the legal domain and are participants in its ongoing conversation. Although encouraging change in a conversation is interesting and inspiring, it is not beneficial to any conversation to ruthlessly insist on radical change. The same holds true for many legal professionals who work in relatively conservative environments. Here, managing change has a greater chance of success through approaching topics with critical sensitivity than by taking the radical offensive. Considering these arguments, the *critical pedagogy movement's* point of view does not seem an appropriate route to follow for ALE.

In many aspects, however, ideas central to Barnett's *criticality movement* resonate with the arguments brought forward in the earlier chapters of this research, such as its insistence on the importance of the full development of the individual and the positive role higher education could have in this process. I also concur with Barnett's view that taking action is based on decisions and judgments which are the result of critical thinking skills and dispositions. However, I argue that Barnett's character formation, consisting of a student's thinking, being and acting, are all elements of what I have identified as 'ACT responsibility' (see chapter 5), instead of 'critical thinking'. I think that what Barnett calls 'criticality', which he describes as a broader interpretation of critical thinking, is not part of the concept(ion) of 'critical thinking' but is, in fact, *Bildung*.[73] Stretching the concept of 'critical thinking' in order to encompass action and an outward dimension that looks at participation in society therefore seems unnecessary and might result in needless confusion between concepts.

So, even though I agree with Barnett on the importance of character formation in the context of society and recognize that critical thinking is of importance in this process, I do not include this as part of the concept of critical thinking. Rather, character formation in the context of society is part of the overarching concepts *Bildung* and ACT responsibility for which critical thinking is a precondition. In addition to the reason and rationality connected to critical thinking, *Bildung* and ACT responsibility also include awareness, action taking and creativity (sensibility). To distinguish critical thinking clearly from both *Bildung* and ACT responsibility, I understand critical thinking as a concept based in reasoning and rationality in the 'traditional sense', in accordance with the *critical thinking movement* and referring to the development of reason, rationality, judgment, skills and dispositions. As said earlier, there are many similarities between the various definitions of critical thinking in this sense. However, for ALE, the definition that seems to be the most helpful as a starting point is Ennis's compact and clear description of critical thinking: '*reasonable reflective thinking that is focused on deciding what to do or believe*'. For educators

73 Barnett's *criticality* dimensions, too, show remarkable similarities to the inward and outward dimensions of *Bildung*.

in legal education, who already have to distribute their limited time and attention over many responsibilities, such as their research, the Faculty's organization and politics, the content of their courses, and their students' development and well-being, this clear and memorable description will be helpful. Nevertheless, Ennis's short definition is more encompassing and more complex than one might suspect at first glance. In explanation, the definition is broad in the sense that it includes thinking and deciding on topics within *and* beyond the legal domain, which is a necessary ability in our times of complex, multifaceted problems that transcend the legal domain. Also, the definition '*reasonable reflective thinking that is focused on deciding what to do or believe*' can only be understood in full by being aware that the mentioned reasonable and reflective thinking necessitates specific abilities and dispositions (in other words, critical thinking relevant processes).

In our context of ALE, I understand the label '*reasonable*' as used in Ennis's definition not as 'what is commonly understood as practical, fair or sensible'[74], but in a meaning closer to the philosophical idea of 'ratio', namely as 'using reason, reasons, reasoning or arguments'. This means that critical thinking is a process in which reflection, or contemplation, is grounded in sound reasoning with a judgment or decision at the end of the thinking process. This interpretation reinforces that critical thinking is a process of rationality and reason. As mentioned earlier, reasoning consists of the process of searching for reasons and the process of giving reasons. The latter requires the ability to recognize inferential connections holding between statements.[75] However, critics concerned about a possible bias – such as a gender or cultural bias – in the current description, have questioned whether critical thinking should be defined in broader terms, transcending its core of reason and rationality. Thayer-Bacon is one of these critics.[76] To counter a bias, Thayer-Bacon argues that critical thinking should not only involve reason – which she believes is biased towards men[77] – but also contain emotion, intuition and imagination.[78] Purists of the concept 'critical thinking' reject this proposition and may already find Ennis's renewed definition '*reasonable reflective thinking that is focused on deciding what to do or believe*' a bit too broad, since it encompasses creative thinking as well.[79] Nevertheless, even though Ennis explicitly allows room for creativity in his conception, he also makes it clear that its emphasis lies on reasonableness, rationality, reflection and decision making.[80]

When defining critical thinking and seeking the boundaries of its scope, it is important to notice the differences and similarities between critical thinking and creative thinking.

74 See Van Klink 2023, p. 8.
75 Mulnix 2012, p. 472.
76 See also: Biesta and Stams 2001, p. 59.
77 Thayer-Bacon 1998, p. 125.
78 Thayer-Bacon 1998, p. 144.
79 Thayer-Bacon 2000, p. 57.
80 Ennis 1991, p. 6.

In this research I differentiate between critical thinking (the topic of this chapter) and creative thinking (the next chapter). At first glance, critical thinking seems to be completely different from creative thinking.[81] Critical thinking is then viewed as an analytic process that produces judgments within a specific framework, whereas creative thinking is seen as an imaginative mental process that transcends or breaks out of a framework.[82] Paul and Elder argue that cultural stereotypes of critical thinkers and creative thinkers are the reason for the fact that critical thinking and creative thinking are commonly – but mistakenly – seen as complete opposites.[83] Illustrative of this argument are the stereotypes of critical thinkers as serious and hard workers and creative people as emotional scatterbrains. In line with these ideas, the abilities required for critical and creative thinking would be very different. In practice, however, the opposite is the case and various abilities are relevant for both critical and creative thinking. To bring this discussion closer to our context of legal education, most legal academics questioned by Cownie on the qualities of the good academic lawyer did not mention creativity or imagination as valuable analytical skills. However, they *did* mention the importance of having an inquisitive mind; being reluctant to take things at face-value; being skeptical, open-minded and curious; and the desire to hear competing arguments and not accepting answers and explanations without questioning them first.[84] These abilities and characteristics seem similar to those belonging to critical thinking and (as the following chapter will show) are also a necessary part of the creative thinking process. Consequently, it seems that there might be a fluid boundary between critical thinking and creative thinking since, although the two concepts are separate, at some points they have similarities. For instance, critical thinking and creative thinking are both products of thought and are processes of higher order thinking.[85] Additionally, critical and creative thinking share characteristics and prerequisites such as an attitude of curiosity and open mindedness,[86] the ability to question and the importance of delaying judgment.[87] Also, critical thinking and creative thinking both require asking questions.[88] Moreover, both are often focused on solving problems.[89] In agreement with Paul, Elder, Mulnix and Bailin, I hold that critical thinking and creative thinking are processes of thought that are neither

81 Bailin 1987, p. 24.

82 Bailin 1987, pp. 23-24. Importantly, Bailin puts this notion of 'rule-breaking creativity' into perspective, as she notices that most creative work is done *within* the boundaries of the domain or only *tweaks* the existing boundaries without breaking them. See Bailin 1987, p. 25.

83 Paul & Elder 2012, p. 4.

84 Cownie 2004, pp. 81-82.

85 Paul & Elder 2012, pp. 5. In this context, Paul and Elder speak of 'high quality thinking'.

86 Cownie 2004, pp. 81-82.

87 See Dewey 1910, p. 74.

88 Adriansen 2010, p. 78, Van Klink 2016, p. 21. Dewey 1933, p. 16. See on suspension of judgment for creative thinking: Bailin 1987, p. 24.

89 See Adriansen 2010, p. 68.

the same nor oppose each other, but should complement one another.[90] For instance, creating something new *requires* critical thinking not only for finding a problem that is in need of a novel solution, but also for reflecting on the value of the innovation. Thus, creativity entails critical thinking.[91] Therefore, Paul and Elder state that the generative power of creativity and the sense of critical thinking are both required for purposeful thinking.[92] They seem to agree with Bailin on this matter, who argued in 1987 that teaching students critical and creative thinking would help them become effective and better thinkers able to solve problems.[93] According to Bailin, disciplines such as law are not static bodies of knowledge but have to be understood as conversations that constantly develop. Criticism is of the utmost importance in this context, because it makes it possible to join in the domain's conversation.[94] Therefore, it enables the further evolvement of that discipline, since the critic's remarks call for answers to questions and could also offer hypotheses if used in combination with creative abilities for further investigation. As such, current knowledge can be recognized as the result of a domain-conversation, indeed, as the result of critical thinking. In this view, it is important for students to understand that any domain consists of knowledge that is a man-made creation and can be developed further through the questioning voice and sound reasoning of criticality in combination with creative thinking.[95] I concur with Mulnix that broad(er) descriptions of critical thinking encompass all kinds of thinking/mental processes, such as creative thinking, imaginative thinking, emotion-based thinking, or problem solving and are therefore not critical thinking, but 'thinking' in the broad sense.[96] However, I advocate that there is nothing wrong with including many types of thinking in education. In fact, I suggest doing exactly that in ALE. Bailin, too, embraced the combination of teaching students critical and creative thinking, which she both included under the denominator of '(effective) thinking skills', even though she differentiated between critical thinking and creative thinking.[97] Still, when focusing on one particular type of thinking – as this chapter does with regard to *critical* thinking – it is clearer to regard critical thinking in its traditional

90 Mulnix 2012, p. 478. Bailin 1987, p. 27. Paul and Elder argue that critical thinking and creativity are both needed for good thinking. In their words: '(...) creativity without criticality is mere novelty. Criticality without creativity is bare negativity.' Paul & Elder 2012, p. 20.

91 See also: Bailin 1987, p. 25. Bailin also states that critical thinking requires creativity to a certain extent, for example, for deciding what to do or believe (see Ennis's definition of critical thinking) one is in need of some imagination (and thus creative capacity) in order to imagine the possible consequences of any decision. Bailin 1987, pp. 25-26.

92 Paul & Elder 2012, pp. 5-7. According to the authors, high quality thinking means purposeful thinking that 'requires posing problems and reasoning through intricacies'.

93 Bailin 1987, pp. 23, 27.

94 Bailin 1987, p. 28.

95 Bailin 1987, p. 28.

96 Mulnix 2012, p. 471.

97 Bailin 1987, p. 23.

sense, with its focus on rationality and reason. Other forms of thinking – that are considered to be more feminine, traditionally speaking – such as creative thinking, emotion, intuition, are not necessarily less important when speaking of *Bildung*'s focus on 'the *full* development of the complete human being', but they *are* different from critical thinking. They involve more than just critical thinking and should therefore not be included in a straight description of *critical* thinking. This is why I propose to use Ennis's description of critical thinking in legal education: '*Critical thinking is reasonable reflective thinking that is focused on deciding what to do or believe*'.

Now that a definition of critical thinking has been chosen and its scope has been explored, this chapter dives deeper into the content of critical thinking by looking at the critical thinking process and the abilities and dispositions that critical thinking necessitates.

Critical thinking – process, skills and dispositions

To be able to incorporate critical thinking (as defined above) into academic education, we require a further exploration of this fairly broad definition. A more detailed interpretation of the concept will provide educators in legal education with practical and useable tools. The first elaboration Ennis offers is a description of the critical thinking process, which consists of the stages and prerequisites of the decision-making process.[98] This could be of use for practical instruction in higher education. Ennis's depiction of the process is as follows:

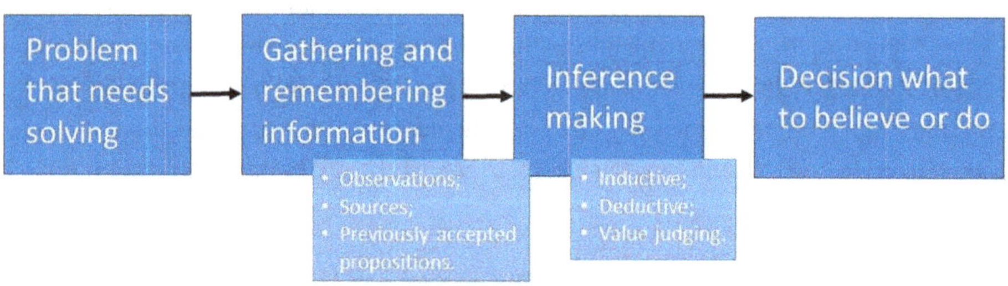

The image shows on the far right that the critical thinking process aims at deciding (or: judging) what to do or believe.[99] On the left, the image illustrates how the critical thinking process often starts with the identification of a problem that is in need of a solution. At least there has to be an issue that will be considered in order to make a decision. In this

98 Ennis 1991, p. 7.

99 In other words, the aim is to be able to *judge* what to do or believe. Bailin and Battersby, too, affirm that critical thinking is focused on making reasoned judgments. See Bailin & Battersby 2009, p. 1.

'problem-solving context' the critical thinker sets off with (1) gathering information through observations or by consulting sources, for example, literature, the opinion of an expert, web pages, or social media. It is also possible to start off with previously accepted propositions that are already acceptable conclusions and do not require additional information: They are part of widely accepted and uncontested knowledge and are therefore seen as valid or factual. For instance, most people do not need to conduct an experiment or check the literature to know that water boils at 100 degrees Celsius in case they wish to boil an egg.[100] Based on the information or the previously accepted proposition(s), the critical thinker is able to (2) identify inferences holding between statements. This means that the person goes beyond the information that they have gathered to come to a conclusion. These inferences can be inductive such as generalizations or hypotheses that are supposed to explain the facts,[101] or deductive, like a prediction. Another form that the inference might take is what Ennis calls a value judgment. Finally, the inference leads the person to (3) a self-authored decision about what to believe or do in the context of the problem that needed solving. *Taking action* based on what the critical thinker now judges to be true or necessary to do is *not* part of the critical thinking process, but rather part of *Bildung*, which also involves creative thinking and ACT responsibility (see chapters 4 and 5).

One might wonder what a person who commences a critical thinking process needs in order to go through its stages and, ultimately, come to a decision. The visual below shows two important prerequisites. According to Ennis, during the three steps of the critical thinking process it first remains essential to communicate with clarity, so the critical thinker has to use *clear language* when explaining what they mean.[102] Additionally, Ennis advocates that the critical thinker must constantly *remain open to considering alternatives*.[103]

100 However, this uncontested knowledge differs from shared opinions in the sense of accepted cultural or social norms within a specific community. In explanation, shared ideas within a community on for instance religious matters or individual virtue cannot be seen as uncontested *outside* the community nor are the ideas factual. Therefore, it seems quite possible to form alternative ideas on these matters though a critical thinking process.

101 Ennis 1991, p. 17.

102 Paul and Elder, too, assert the importance of clarity for critical thinking. For them clarity is part of the Intellectual Standards (in addition to accuracy, precision, relevance, depth, breadth, logic, and fairness). See Paul & Elder 2020, p. 12. In addition, the *Delphi Project* endorses the importance of clarity as well, see: Facione 1990, p. 2.

103 Ennis 1991, p. 7.

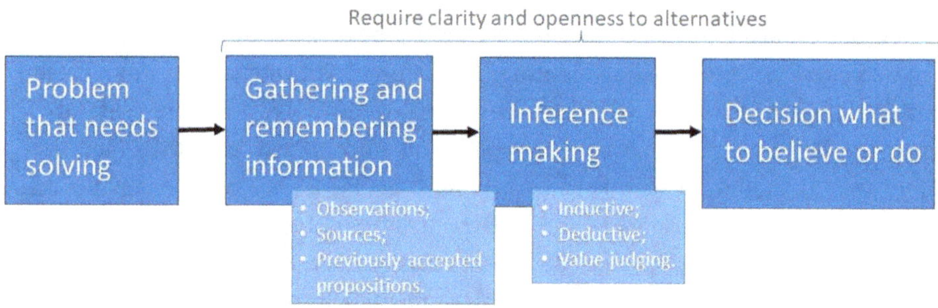

However, this is not all. The image below provides additional prerequisites for various stages of the process. The graphic is based on Theresa Amabile's visualization of the componential model of creative thinking, which shows the creative thinking process and its prerequisites (chapter 4).[104]

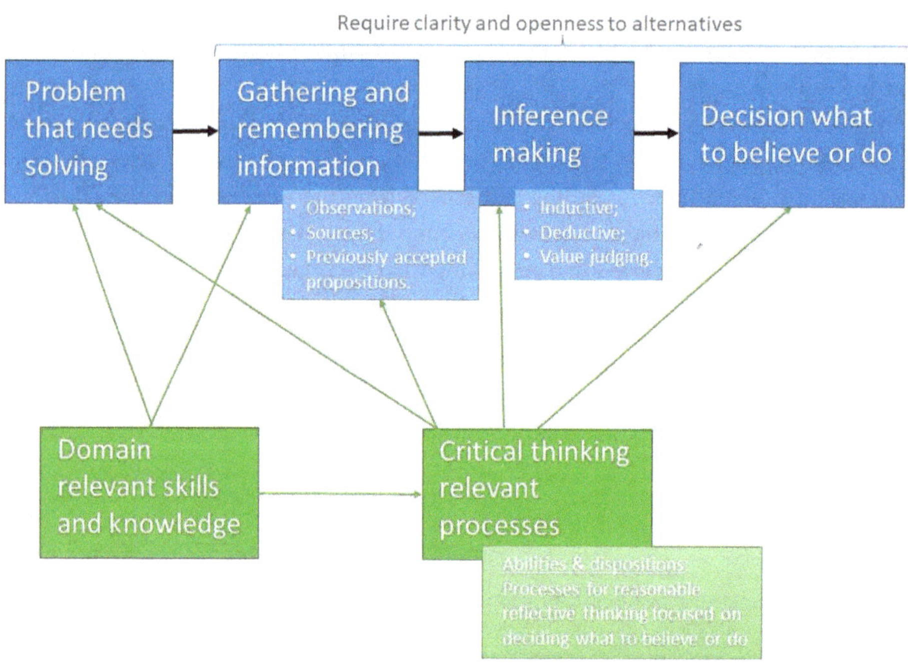

104 Amabile 1996.

Inspired by Amabile's terminology, I refer to the two additional prerequisites, marked in green above, as Domain Relevant Skills and Knowledge (DRS)[105] and Critical Thinking Relevant Processes (CTRP). The green arrows show for which stages of the process each of the two prerequisites is important. In the following, the DRS and CTRP will be further clarified.

Domain relevant skills and knowledge

First, Domain Relevant Processes (DRS) form the basis of all a person performs in a domain[106] and include an in-depth (factual) knowledge of the domain, which means that a person needs to be aware of conventions, opinions, and paradigms; the symbolic system and procedures; and the important ideas and concepts of a domain. For example, academically educated legal professionals require knowledge of key concepts such as the rule of law, *trias politica* and fundamental rights and need to be aware of important institutions with essential functions for the domain. For lawyers (in the European Union) that includes an understanding of the EU, ECHR, national Supreme Court and their national system of law making. DRS also involves knowing the problem solving strategies that are commonly used within a domain (so-called 'performance-scripts'), for example, understanding how to solve a legal case. In addition, the technical skills required in the domain are also part of DRS, for instance, the ability to search for legal documents, read case law, or argumentation techniques. Along with knowledge of a domain and an appropriate skillset, DRS contains a person's special domain-relevant natural ability, for example, a law student's natural predisposition for presenting their point convincingly or a lawyer's natural ability to structure information.

Although a student's level of DRS partly relies on their natural talents relevant to the domain,[107] formal and informal education are important factors in acquiring DRS.[108] Providing a formal education in the domain of law is at the heart of ALE. To become good lawyers, our students require knowledge of the legal domain and have to acquire the skills necessary for legal professions. This provides students with a reservoir of knowledge that enables them to identify problems in the legal domain and enables them to employ specific legal performance scripts (for example, the steps every lawyer takes when solving a case). Of course, the fact that law students are in need of legal knowledge and skills seems only logical and it is hard to imagine an academic law curriculum that does not include these.

---

105 Ennis emphasizes that background knowledge is essential for critical thinking, see: Ennis 1991, p. 18. Bailin, too, insists on emphasizing the mastery of disciplinary knowledge and skills, see: Bailin 1987, pp. 28-29.

106 Amabile 1996, p. 83. A domain consists of a set of symbolic rules and procedures, see Csikszenthihalyi 1997, p. 27.

107 These include innate abilities and skills, natural perceptual and motor skills, see Amabile 1996, p. 84.

108 Amabile 1996, p. 84.

However, relatively new skills that have become necessary in the fast-changing legal domain, such as legal design skills or even programming skills, could also be included in contemporary legal education. Furthermore, it seems insufficient to only acquire knowledge and skills that belong to one domain if a person is to find solutions to complex, multifaceted problems and tasks.[109] Therefore, in addition to expertise in one domain – in our case, law – *broad* knowledge spanning multiple domains is required for critical thinking.

As illustrated in the graphic, Domain Relevant Skills and Knowledge are of importance in the critical thinking process for identifying a problem. For example, one's in-depth knowledge of the law allows recognizing legal problems and questions. Furthermore, DRS support the development of Critical Thinking Relevant Processes. For instance, asking questions is part of CTRP and background knowledge of a domain is paramount in formulating fundamental questions, which is an ability of critical thinkers.

Critical thinking relevant processes

In the graphic above, the green arrows between 'Critical thinking relevant processes' and all stages of the critical thinking (indicated in blue) show that CTRP are required for all elements of the critical thinking process. In other words, they are essential for understanding the problem; understanding and judging information and previously accepted propositions; making inferences, and; decision making. Insight into these CTRP is of importance for ALE. But what is meant by Critical Thinking Relevant Processes? If these are identified, we gain knowledge about what to teach and how to teach if we wish our law students to become critical thinkers.[110] First of all, there seems to be consensus between a number of experts in the field of critical thinking, including Ennis, the experts in the *Delphi Project* and Paul, that critical thinking – which can be interpreted in this context as Critical Thinking Relevant Processes – consists of two components. Other authors might not explicitly speak of two components, but their suggestions are almost always allocated to one or both of these two. Paul and Scriver describe one component as (1) 'a set of information and belief generating and processing skills' and the other as (2) 'the habit based on intellectual commitment, of using those skills to guide behavior'.[111] This relates directly to Siegel's (1) *reason assessment*, which consists of abilities and skills relevant to the proper understanding and assessment of reasons, claims and arguments and (2) *critical spirit*, described by Siegel as a complex of dispositions, attitudes, habits of mind and character traits. At first glance, Ennis – similar to the *Delphi Project*[112] – seems

109 Nygaard, Courtney & Holtham 2010, p. 2.
110 See also: Mathiasen & Andersen 2020, p. 39.
111 See Mulnix 2012, p. 465.
112 The *Delphi Project* calls the components cognitive skills and dispositions. See: Facione 1990, p. 2.

to keep the definition of the two components short and depicts them as (1) *abilities*, in other words, skills and (2) *dispositions*, also known as affective dispositions, by which he means frame of mind or habits of mind necessary for using skills.[113] Nevertheless, Ennis continues by describing no less than 18 abilities and 12 dispositions.

What are these abilities and dispositions that are part of critical thinking? 'Abilities' refers to *skills*. Each of these skills may be executed with the help of a disposition,[114] which can be defined as frame of mind, habit of mind,[115] or virtue.[116] In other words, a disposition is the aptitude to use a skill. For example, a person has to be open minded in order to ask good questions or to be able to evaluate arguments. According to the experts of the *Delphi Project*, once someone has developed affective dispositions connected to critical thinking, they are more inclined to use their critical thinking skills/abilities than someone who has not developed these dispositions.[117] Therefore, teaching the affective dispositions in addition to cognitive skills enables our students to become practicing critical thinkers. Harvard's Project Zero apparently employs a broader interpretation of the concept of 'disposition'. According to the researchers of the project Making Thinking Visible, a disposition is a habit of mind that consists of skills (ability), inclination (motivation), and sensitivity (recognizing moments when it is appropriate to employ the skill).[118] Others argue that a disposition is constructed by a critical attitude and the desire to express the attitude or by a moral orientation that motivates critical thinking.[119]

Many authors have written about the specific skills and dispositions that are part of critical thinking, which we could call 'critical thinking relevant processes'. For the sake of clarity, these abilities and dispositions as described by Ennis are listed below.[120] In the following, Ennis's lists will be considered against descriptions given by other experts in the field of critical thinking.

---

113 Davies & Barnett 2015, p. 13.

114 Facione 1990, p. 11. In this research, the dispositions are also referred to as 'affective dispositions'.

115 Davies & Barnett 2015, p. 13.

116 See Bailin & Battersby 2015, pp. 367-368.

117 Facione 1990, p. 13.

118 Ritchhart & Church 2020, p. 18. See also, more general information on Project Zero and Making Thinking Visible: https://pz.harvard.edu/projects/visible-thinking, last visited January 20th, 2022.

119 Mason 2007, p. 343.

120 Ennis 2015, pp. 32-33.

Abilities (skills of critical thinkers)

An ideal critical thinker is able to:

1. Have a focus and pursue it.
2. Analyze arguments.
3. Ask and answer clarification questions.
4. Understand and use graphs and math.
5. Judge the credibility of a source.
6. Observe, and judge observation reports.
7. Use their background knowledge, knowledge of the situation, and previously established conclusions.
8. Deduce, and judge deductions.
9. Make, and judge, inductive inferences and arguments.
10. Make, and judge, value judgments.
11. Define terms, and judge definitions.
12. Handle equivocation appropriately.[121]
13. Attribute and judge unstated assumptions.
14. Think suppositionally.
15. Deal with fallacy labels.[122]
16. Be aware of, and check the quality of, their own thinking.[123]
17. Deal with things in an orderly manner.
18. Deal with rhetorical strategies.[124]

---

121 According to Ennis, this looks at a particular type of ambiguity, namely at shifting between an interpretation of a concept/definition in the midst of an argument. See Ennis 2011a, p. 12.

122 For example: circularity, bandwagon, post hoc, non sequitur, hearsay, appeal to authority. See: Ennis 2015, p. 43.

123 In addition to the already extensive list of 15 essential abilities, Ennis defines three abilities that he finds helpful (but not essential). In this overview the helpful abilities are grey-colored and the essential are visualized in black.

124 In order to avoid being deceived by rhetorical experts.

Dispositions (the critical spirit)

An ideal critical thinker is disposed to:

1. Seek and offer clear statements of the thesis or question.
2. Seek and offer clear reasons.
3. Try to be well informed.
4. Use credible sources and observations, and usually mention them.
5. Take into account the total situation.
6. Keep in mind the basic concern in the context.
7. Be alert for alternatives.
8. Be open minded: a. seriously consider other points of view, and b. withhold judgment when evidence and reasons are insufficient.
9. Take a position and change a position when evidence and reasons are sufficient.
10. Seek as much precision as the situation requires.
11. Try to "get it right" to the extent possible or feasible.
12. Employ critical thinking skills.

Many of the abilities and dispositions documented by Ennis are also listed by other theorists as belonging to critical thinking. For example, skills such as having focus and pursuing it (1);[125] analyzing arguments (2);[126] asking questions (3);[127] the ability of judgment (5, 6, 8, 9, 10, 11, 13);[128] inference making (9);[129] managing fallacies (15), and metacognitive skills (18)[130] are mentioned regularly by other experts. The dispositions as

125 *The Delphi project* refers to being focused in inquiry and persistent in seeking results. Facione 1990, p. 2.

126 The experts of *the Delphi Project* divide analysis in three sub-skills, namely examining ideas, identifying arguments and analyzing arguments. See Facione 1990, p. 6. Davies and Barnett find that critical thinking includes reasoning skills, such as recognizing and constructing arguments (this combines Ennis's analyzing arguments and making arguments). See Davies & Barnett 2015, p. 5.

127 Davies and Barnett refer to 'asking questions for clarification', see Davies & Barnett 2015, p. 12.

128 See, for instance, Davies and Barnett, who state that academics are required to be able to form their own authentic judgment and to evaluate arguments. Davies & Barnett 2015, pp. 2, 12. Instead of judgment, the *Delphi Project* uses the term 'evaluation'. This includes sub-skills such as assessing claims and assessing arguments. See Facione 1990, p. 8.

129 For example, Mulnix' *recognizing (and making) inferential connections that hold between statements*. See Mulnix 2012, p. 467. See also Davies & Barnett 2015, p. 12. Paul and Elder, too, find that 'inference' is part of an element of critical thinking, namely of 'Elements of thought'. The other two elements associated with critical thinking are, according to Paul and Elder, Intellectual standards and Intellectual traits. See Paul & Elder 2020, p. 12. The experts of *the Delphi Project*, too, include inference in critical thinking. In short, they describe the ability for inference as the ability to identify and secure elements in order to draw reasonable conclusions. In their view, inference also involves forming hypotheses and distilling possible consequences of, for example, statements, beliefs or data. Identified subskills of inference in *the Delphi Project* are: querying evidence; conjecturing alternatives, and drawing conclusions. See: Facione 1990, p. 9.

130 Kuhn refers to meta knowing skills, which involve metastrategic knowing, metacognitive knowing and epistemological knowing. See Kuhn 1999, p. 18. *The Delphi Project* speaks in this context of self-regulation,

thought out by Ennis, too, receive endorsement by others, for instance, try to be well-informed (3);[131] take into account the total situation (5);[132] alertness to alternatives (7);[133] open mindedness (8);[134] flexibility in a position that is taken or considered when warranted (9).[135] Some experts have added dispositions to this list. For instance, Paul and Elder include what they call 'intellectual traits'. These traits consist of, for example, intellectual courage, intellectual empathy and intellectual perseverance.[136] In addition, tolerance of ambiguity[137] and willingness to suspend judgment when the circumstances require this are important dispositions for critical thinkers.[138]

Any of the skills or abilities as listed by Ennis can be assimilated on different accomplishment levels. An academically educated legal professional's level of ability to *'make, and judge, inductive inferences and arguments'* could – and probably should – therefore be more accomplished than their level of *'understanding and using graphs and math'*. Importantly, teaching critical thinking is part of (academic) skills training and – as with any skill – it cannot be solely learned from books, but has to be practiced, and practiced often.[139]

How will these lists of skills and dispositions help educators in legal education in their quest to teach academic law students critical thinking? According to Ennis, the list of abilities/skills and dispositions could be used as a checklist for developing curricula for critical thinking.[140] I suggest expanding the list with the additions of other experts and use it in law faculties as a source of inspiration when revising the final attainment targets of curricula. It would be advisable to develop a learning trajectory for critical thinking for

---

which is directed at the cognitive process of critical thinking and concerns the analysis and evaluation of one's own cognitive processes. Self-regulation is divided into two sub-skills, namely self-examination and self-correction. Facione 1990, pp. 10-11. Davies and Barnett, too, refer to metacognition and self-regulation as important skills for critical thinkers. See: Davies & Barnett 2015, p. 12. Some connect metacognitive skills to 'reflective thinking', as it reflects on one's own thinking process. See Robinson 2011, p. 276.

131 *The Delphi Project* mentions inquisitiveness, eagerness for reliable information, being well-informed and diligence in seeking relevant information. Facione 1990, pp. 2, 11, 13. Davies and Barnett speak of the disposition of inquisitiveness. Davies & Barnett 2015, p. 13.

132 Davies and Barnett refer to 'seeing both sides of an issue', see: Davies & Barnett 2015, p. 13.

133 Davies & Barnett 2015, p. 13.

134 Facione 1990, p. 2, Davies & Barnett 2015, p. 13.

135 Facione 1990, p. 2. See also: Robinson 2011, p. 275.

136 In total, Paul and Elder describe eight such traits: Intellectual humility; intellectual courage; intellectual empathy; intellectual autonomy; intellectual integrity; intellectual perseverance; confidence in reason; and fair mindedness. See Paul & Elder 2020, p. 12. See also: Mulnix 2012, p. 466. Davies and Barnett also view intellectual humility, intellectual courage, intellectual integrity, intellectual empathy, and perseverance as important dispositions for critical thinking. See Davies & Barnett 2015, p. 13. The experts of *the Delphi Project* endorse confidence in reason (which includes trust in the process of reasoning and confidence in one's own ability to use reason) and fair mindedness. See: Facione 1990, p. 2.

137 Davies & Barnett 2015, p. 13.

138 Robsinson 2011, p. 275.

139 Mulnix 2012, p. 467.

140 Ennis 1991, p. 8.

Bachelor's and Master's programs in law in which the complexity of critical thinking increases (related to the developmental stages of students and the attainment goals of the curriculum) and is taught, practiced and assessed per phase of study. However, the list is possibly somewhat too extensive for everyday use by educators and students, for example in class or in the study materials. My experience with using very detailed assessment criteria is that many students and educators do not read, use and internalize these, since they find them *too* time consuming to study. As an alternative to demanding educators study extensive lists, it would be advisable to regularly discuss critical thinking and all it entails in the context of the curriculum as a whole and in specific courses among teams of educators. Also, in individual courses and syllabi, the so-called 'super-streamlined conception', which is shorter than Ennis's 1991 streamlined conception,[141] could be utilized. This compact version mixes dispositions and abilities, and is more manageable for individual students and educators.[142] However, the super streamlined conception lacks some detail, which the original definition *does* provide, so if it is used by educators and students, it is important that they understand this lack and are aware of this simplification. The use of the compact, less detailed version of the conception hopefully encourages more students and educators to actively seek (student)development in critical thinking. Another route to help educators to become more aware of what critical thinking entails of and how to teach it in the various phases of the students' legal education is to include the list and the model for integrating critical thinking in legal education (see below) in the curricula of the University Teaching Qualification (in Dutch *Basis Kwalificatie Onderwijs*, BKO).

Critical Thinking in Academic Legal Education

The previous section proposed some preliminary suggestions for the incorporation of critical thinking into ALE. These suggestions stem from the guiding principle that it is essential to teach critical thinking, since critical thinking is a crucial academic characteristic, in the sense that one can only be a 'good' academic if one is capable of critical thinking.[143] In addition, critical thinking can be viewed as vital for society, for it is

141 In the super streamlined conception of critical thinking, Ennis describes that the critical thinker: 1. Is open minded and mindful of alternatives; 2. Desires to be, and is, well-informed; 3. Judges well the credibility of sources; 4. Identifies conclusions, reasons, and assumptions; 5. Asks appropriate clarifying questions; 6. Judges well the quality of an argument, including its reasons, assumptions, evidence, and their degree of support for the conclusion; 7. Can well develop and defend a reasonable position, doing justice to challenges; 8. Formulates plausible hypotheses; 9. Plans and conducts experiments well; 10. Defines terms in a way appropriate to the context; 11. Draws conclusions when warranted – but with caution; 12. Integrates all items of the above eleven points. Ennis 1991.

142 Ennis 2011a, p. 12, Ennis 2011b, p. 6.

143 See, for instance, Davies & Barnett 2015, p. 2, Arum & Roksa 2011, p. 35, Barnett 1997, p. 2. Adriansen 2010, p. 82.

beneficial for a democratic society if its public servants and citizens participate, which they can do through critical thinking. Critical thinking enables meaningful discussion between opposing beliefs, opinions or ideas, because of the open mindedness and perpetual openness for alternatives that are central to critical thinking.[144] It is therefore not surprising that many legal academics underline the importance of incorporating critical thinking in law schools. To illustrate, in 1996, the British Lord Chancellor's Advisory Committee on Legal Education and Conduct stated that intellectual integrity and independence of mind was the main aim of legal education. In order to be capable of these things, students needed to become self-motivated; autonomous (or: self-authored), critical thinkers; self-directed learners; self-aware and self-critical; committed to truthfulness; open to other viewpoints and able to think of alternative possibilities, and able to give reasonable arguments for their viewpoints.[145] These are ambitious objectives and as ambitious is the objective to teach law students how to go through the critical thinking process and to support their development of necessary skills and dispositions as described earlier in this chapter. The importance of critical thinking makes the effort worth our while. However, the question is: how to teach our students critical thinking? Next, Van Klink's and De Vries's *skeptical legal education* will be considered as a possibility for incorporating critical thinking in legal education by highlighting its aim and preconditions.

Van Klink and De Vries argue that the need for critical thinking development – or, in the words of these authors, the development of the faculty of judgment and reflection – calls for *skeptical legal education* (SLE).[146] This approach to legal education aims for students to develop a critical attitude towards the material they read and the things they are told.[147] Furthermore, it requires students to reflect upon their own learning process and on the social context.[148] Through a skeptical legal education, students learn to think for themselves, unencumbered by the pressure of others and develop their faculty of judgment. This faculty of judgment involves at least two things. In the first place, students learn to make their own assessment of information by building their own standards of evaluation. They require this ability for assessing if an assertion is convincing – through reflection on the evaluating standards (in other words, the beliefs and opinions) that are customary to the conversation of the legal domain. In the second place, students learn the moral and intellectual integrity to use their own faculty of judgment.[149]

144 Mulnix 2012, p. 472.

145 Appleby, Burdon & Reilly 2013, p. 360. De Vries also emphasizes the importance of independence of mind, see De Vries 2021.

146 See Van Klink & De Vries 2013, p. 42; Van Klink 2016, p. 20, and; Van Klink, De Vries and Bleeker 2017.

147 Van Klink 2016, p. 15.

148 Van Klink and De Vries 2013, p. 37.

149 Van Klink 2016, p. 20.

If law educators want to incorporate *skeptical legal education* into their curriculum, they have to be aware of three prerequisites. These preconditions of skeptical legal education will be further explored and considered in the following. Firstly, SLE requires active student engagement during classes. Van Klink refers to Oakeshott, who holds that the faculty of judgment can only be taught implicitly through modeling by the educator: During class, students observe and listen and are therefore submerged in the Conversation of the domain.[150] Here, Van Klink adds that students learn about the legal Conversation not only through individual study by listening to their educator and reading the material, but also by *actively* discussing the material. In class, the students actively practice joining the Conversation of law and practice how to make their own judgments and assessments. In other words, they actively practice – and therefore develop – their faculty of judgment. Van Klink and De Vries suggest the use of small classes and instructional interventions in the categories dialogue and anchored/authentic instruction, such as group discussions, moot courts and presentations or extracurricular reading groups.[151] In addition to these helpful suggestions for legal education, I propose to actively develop and integrate teaching strategies that let students *practice* their critical thinking and supports their development.

The second prerequisite of skeptical legal education requires educators to remain objective towards or detached from the content they discuss with their students.[152] They are also expected to primarily focus on questioning and unmasking ideologies and not support any of their own.[153] The reason for this is that, when the educator objectively presents viewpoints and argumentations, the students become able to make their own conclusions and opinions unrestricted through intended or unintended pressure by the educator. If educators express their own subjective opinion, Van Klink and De Vries believe it imperative that educators give their students notice that what they are sharing is their own opinion based on specific arguments.[154] With Van Klink and De Vries, I agree that it would be desirable for educators to be aware of their possible influence on the students belief systems and that educators should be careful to offer students the necessary space to come to their own conclusions and examined opinions. Nevertheless, it is not always desirable to expect educators to approach their teaching disconnected from the content and without sharing their commitment to beliefs that are an essential part of their examined, self-authored identities. The reason for this is that – if the goal of ALE is to support the development of young adults towards becoming academically educated legal professionals and citizens that are able to manage uncertainty and define and take their responsibility in the complexity of contemporary society – *this* behavior has to be modeled

150 Van Klink 2016, p. 20.
151 Van Klink and De Vries 2013, p. 42 and Van Klink 2016, p. 22.
152 Van Klink 2016, p. 23. See also Van Klink & De Vries 2013, p. 43.
153 Van Klink 2016, p. 21.
154 Van Klink & De Vries 2013, p. 43.

by their educators. A part of being a responsible individual (and a part of ACT responsibility, see chapter 5) is to develop an examined life – in which a person's skills and dispositions have become deeply rooted in their personality and are part of their character –[155] through critical thinking. In order for the educator to model this desired behavior of examined living through critical thinking and decision making, it is important for them to share their own journeys and conclusions with their students. This requires space for educators in legal education to show their true colors and to discuss with their students why they are committed to their beliefs – as long as the educators remain open minded to alternatives and are critical towards their own position(s). Of course, this is not the same as brainwashing students to committing to the same beliefs as the educator's: The goal of sharing and explaining one's opinion is for the students to understand that an educator takes a position and why, so that the students are able to embark on their own personal journeys to build their beliefs through critical thinking and reflection.[156] This could, for example, be supported by experimenting with the so called VaKE method in teaching which is thought to support the development of critical thinking skills and dispositions. *Va*KE stands for Value and Knowledge education and is aimed at preparing students to become responsible citizens in society, able to think critically and evaluate the implications of their choices. It is a route towards providing students the tools to develop their (legal) knowledge as well as their moral compass. Nevertheless, the latter is formed by the students themselves, without forcing the opinion of the individual educator or the institution on the student.[157] Another reason for allowing educators to express their opinions and beliefs is that detached and forced objective teaching may not be fruitful for engaging and inspiring students in class. Engagement and a shared learning experience require all parties involved in the learning process to share to a certain extent who they are so that the members of the learning community are able to relate to one another. Also, employing self-depreciating humor regarding the personal opinions or world view of the educator can be an effective strategy in creating a playful and safe learning environment that stimulates students' critical thinking ability and creativity (see chapter 6). Finally, passionate and therefore inspiring educators are often exactly that because specific beliefs

155 Davies & Barnett 2015, p. 13.

156 It is important to note that, hopefully, an educator's knowledge claims and value judgments are rooted in well thought through reasoning resulting from critical thinking. In contrast to Van Klink and De Vries's argument that these knowledge claims and value judgments as solely fallible opinions (see Van Klink and De Vries 2013, p. 45), it seems that these examined claims therefore deserve a different status and treatment than a random opinion of, for example, a student who has read an article on social media. The worth of various opinions, knowledge claims and value judgments can be measured by the standards of the critical thinking process.

157 Pnevmatikos, Christodoulou and Georgiadou have experimented with this method in the domain of Psychology. Their preliminary results are promising: Student understanding of the content expanded as well as their critical thinking skills and dispositions. See Pnevmatikos, Christodoulou & Georgiadou 2019, pp. 899-900.

and convictions motivate them to share their observations, ideas, arguments and points of view with their students. Asking these educators to leave part of themselves and one of their main reasons for teaching out of the classroom might have a negative effect on their enjoyment and the beauty of their teaching.

In the previous sections, two prerequisites of *skeptical legal education* were considered. This leads us to the third and final prerequisite of SLE that Van Klink and De Vries have described. This involves the necessity for a diverse educational context in which a plurality of voices exists. In a mixed community consisting of students and educators from a wide variety of backgrounds and in a curriculum that highlights, for instance, legal theory, legal history, legal philosophy and legal sociology, students are confronted with all kinds of ideas, arguments, opinions. There, they discover that in Academia, many ideas are not set in stone, but are up for doubt and reasonable discussion.[158] This relates to the call for a broad curriculum in legal education. Through the introduction of the skeptical legal education approach for law schools, Van Klink and De Vries have developed and brought together various possibilities that support the further development of critical thinking.

Critical thinking as part of Bildung *in Academic Legal Education*

Although I recognize that Van Klink and De Vries's skeptical legal education may support the development of law students' critical thinking, I think that – if ALE is to succeed in teaching its students to become critical thinkers – we are first in need of a shared conception of critical thinking. Then, we require further practical guidelines for teaching and learning

158 Van Klink 2016, pp. 24-25. Van Klink & De Vries 2013, p. 44.

critical thinking in legal education. The previous sections of this chapter have outlined what critical thinking *is* and which skills and dispositions it entails. Also, some preliminary choices for further incorporating critical thinking in legal education were made, such as the definition '*critical thinking is reasonable reflective thinking that is focused on deciding what to do or believe*'. The following builds upon these insights and further explores the incorporation of critical thinking in ALE. With this aim, a model for incorporating critical thinking in legal education will be introduced. Before introducing this model for ALE, it is important to address some ideas and concepts, introduced earlier, in the context of critical thinking. This especially concerns the (im)possibility of critical thinking in the light of student developmental stages (chapter 1) and the apparent tension between critical thinking and *Bildung*'s outward dimension (chapter 2).

First, it is of importance to note that the perceived necessity and the ability for critical thinking is closely connected to the developmental stage of the individual and their level of metacognition. Kuhn holds that meta knowing – in the words of Paul 'the Art of thinking about your thinking'[159] – is the cognitive skill most closely connected to critical thinking and is therefore important for our students to develop. Meta knowing can be divided into: 1) *meta strategic knowing*, which entails a form of knowing that selects and monitors strategies that can be employed to achieve goals; 2) *meta cognitive knowing* that concerns an individual being aware of what they know and how they know it, and; 3) *epistemological knowing* which is more philosophical and has to do with a person's broader awareness and understanding of knowing and knowledge.[160] To support their students' development of critical thinking, educators could offer information and create relevant assignments that implicitly or explicitly help students practice their meta knowing skills. Research has shown that law students, too, wish for an education that focuses on transformative personal development and not solely on knowledge transmission.[161]

To be capable of the type of critical thinking as described in this chapter, students have to travel towards Kegan's self-authorizing stage or Kuhn's evaluative level. Ideally, students become self-directed learners capable of reasoning, communicating, researching and intellectual discipline.[162] However, students start their legal education at their own developmental stage, and most will not yet have progressed towards the highest stages. Consequently, not every student will be capable of critical thinking and a large number of students will struggle with being a critical thinker. In accordance with Stolker's description of problematic law students, many educators in legal education will probably recognize that not all students seem 'ready' to be critical, self-authored thinkers. I recognize this

159 Kuhn 1999, p. 17.
160 Kuhn 1999, p. 18.
161 See Appleby, Burdon & Reilly 2013, p. 361.
162 Appleby, Burdon & Reilly 2013, p. 363.

primarily in some freshman students, but sometimes also in the behavior of more senior students, even up to the level of masters students. For example, in my mandatory course in legal philosophy, I see first year students who are extremely focused on getting the correct answers by repeatedly asking me to recapitulate topics that already are collectively discussed by their peers. They seem to view the educator as an oracle tasked with providing answers that can then be copied and stored for future recounting during the exam. This shows that these students expect to be assessed on Bloom taxonomy's level of knowledge or remembering (and may be understanding), but not on the categories of applying, analyzing, evaluating or creating. However, through this behavior students deprive themselves of the opportunity to practice how to think for themselves. Furthermore, they seem to be struggling with thinking critically about the course content while being unaware of it. Analyzing this behavior in the context of developmental theories, these students seem to reside in the instrumental stage. They are looking for precise instruction, right or wrong answers and view others as helpful instruments or annoying obstacles on their way to success: The concrete result of passing the exam. Furthermore, these students' epistemological understanding is either on the level of the absolutist or multiplist (see chapter 1), which means that they have limited critical thinking ability. In other words, students on these levels of development are either only able to use critical thinking to judge if a statement is true or false according to a standard that they view as absolute, or they cannot reflect critically on various assertions because of a lack of evaluative ability that provides a standard by which to judge. Instead of being irritated by these students' behavior, developmental theory helps educators to understand where the student's reaction stems from: It is not unwillingness to study or deliberate inappropriate behavior within the university's walls, but the developmental stage that at a given time limits a student's ability to think critically or reflect on their own actions. Additionally, the behavior students show is the result of the existing learning culture of earlier experiences educational contexts where risks have been avoided, sometimes due to national educational policies that do not truly support development and learning. To further their students' development, educators could include teaching methods and a teaching style that scaffolds the learning, engages students and challenges them in their zone of proximal development (ZPD). For example, educators in ALE might offer students struggling with critical thinking some assignments that help them communicate in a shared language about their critical thinking and practice relevant thinking strategies. Kuhn proposes that educators approach the development of their students in two ways: By providing students with many opportunities to practice with critical thinking skills and by teaching them what critical thinking entails and which intellectual values are connected to critical thinking. Because this enables students to develop meta cognitive and meta strategic control, they will further their knowledge of their own minds. This will help them to, in time, assimilate critical thinking dispositions.[163]

The second idea in the context of critical thinking which it is important to address, is the apparent tension between critical thinking and *Bildung*'s outward dimension (chapter 2). The next two paragraphs delve deeper into this discussion and its consequences for teaching critical thinking in ALE. In this research, *Bildung* is the overarching educational ideal that provides us with the theoretical foundation for including responsibility, creative thinking, critical thinking and play and playfulness in the academic education of law students. In other words, critical thinking is part of the umbrella concept of *Bildung*. By contrast, Barnett uses the term 'criticality' to include skills, dispositions *and* taking action. According to him, responsibility – which within this research includes being able to *act* – is part of critical thinking. However, I advocate that critical thinking is a cognitive and affective (dispositional) element of *Bildung*, that consists of reasonable and reflective thinking focused on deciding what to do or believe. Developing critical thinking abilities and dispositions is a part of the *Bildung* of the individual. This is in accordance with Mathiasen's and Andersen's view that academic *Bildung* is the formation of a person as a responsible citizen and as an independent thinker in education and in life in general.[164] What is required for this interpretation of *Bildung* and for becoming an academic is high quality thinking, which means purposeful, effective and serious thinking. Paul and Elder argue that this requires critical thinking and creative thinking.[165] In this context, Van der Ploeg understands critical thinking as *responsible thinking*, since by examining their standpoints and doubting and revisiting their viewpoints, people take responsibility for their own thinking.[166] In combination with the other elements of *Bildung* – responsibility and creative thinking – critical thinking will be key for our law students to be able to define and take responsibility in contemporary society and thrive in the current and future legal profession that are both characterized by a sense of uncertainty.

Nevertheless, as has already been discussed in the second chapter, the notion of *Bildung* has countered criticism. The criticism of the supposed tension between the inward dimension and the outward dimension of *Bildung* is of particular interest for critical thinking, since some claim that *Bildung*'s aspect of socialization makes it impossible for *gebildete* students to be true critical thinkers. According to these scholars, the inner development – in other words 'subjectification' – of the person, implied by *Bildung*'s inner dimension, is at odds with the outward dimension that focuses on being part of society, which some equate with 'socialization'.[167] Biesta, for example, holds that since the mission

163 Kuhn 1999, p. 24.
164 Mathiasen & Andersen 2020, p. 39.
165 Paul & Elder 2012, p. 6.
166 Van der Ploeg 2019, pp. 5-6.
167 See Zuurmond 2020, pp. 22-24.

of *Bildung* in educational settings often has an aim, such as achieving independence or a specific moral sense, it lacks true freedom to become a person as the student themselves wishes to be. Because it aims for development in a specific direction, Biesta believes that in these situations *Bildung* becomes only socialization.[168] Zuurmond points out that Dutch policy on Education seems to be primarily focused on the 'socialization' dimension of *Bildung*.[169] The main concern here is that this focus on 'socialization' does not just mean 'becoming a person within society', but rather implies that students are solely trained to think and act in accordance with the rules of the dominant culture or tradition within their society. This concern is also recognizable in the criticism made by Rideout and Ramsfield of social constructivism in education. According to them, the social view in an education should not be used for indoctrination or acculturation only, and that professors should not choose community over critical thinking.[170] However, the risk of doing exactly that, is present. Consequently, the concern brought to light by Zuurmond, Rideout and Ramsfield implies that *gebildete* individuals won't be able to be truly critical, are not able to achieve that self-authoring stage of development, and are unable to take on contemporary problems that require fundamental change. Yet, I argue that the importance of critical thinking and autonomous – in other words, self-authored – thinking for the *Bildung* concept diminishes the source of this concern.[171] As explained in the second chapter, the development of the human being – the inward dimension – is crucial for *Bildung*. This analysis aligns with Mann, Zuurmond and Bauer's observations that *Bildung*'s rich history results in a concept with depth, in which critical thinking is of great importance and the connection with society does not mean that members of society always have to agree with the traditions and rules of that society. It merely means understanding the rules and traditions in their context. On this basis, a *gebildete* individual is able to critically question and reflect and by doing so, they (re-)shape their society.[172] By giving attention to the development of our students' ability for critical thinking, we support them in becoming critical individuals able to be self-authoring and to act with purpose, instead of them being subject to the world and unable to go against the tide of dominant cultures.[173]

Having addressed these two preliminary issues concerning critical thinking in ALE, the next section will offer a model for integrating critical thinking into that education.

---

168 Biesta 2017, p. 5.

169 Zuurmond 2020, pp. 26-27.

170 See Cedrone 2013, p. 802.

171 See, for example, Gur-Ze'ev who emphasizes that the core of *Bildung* is its inward dimension. See: Gur-Ze'ev 2002, p. 391.

172 Gur-Ze'ev 2002, p. 391. Zuurmond 2020, p. 31.

173 See: Barnett 1997, p. 4.

A Model for Integrating Critical Thinking into Academic Legal Education

How can educators in ALE further support their students' development of critical thinking? My goal is to aid educators in their effort to further incorporate critical thinking in ALE. With this aim, I will provide an initial outline of a model for incorporating critical thinking on various levels of ALE's educational structure. In explanation, educators are able to influence very directly how they teach, how they organize their lectures/working groups and how they construct their courses. In addition, educators are able to influence (sometimes more indirectly, or more within the playfield of the university's politics and policies) the construction of the curriculum. Furthermore, they have the ability to contribute to the overarching learning culture and environment within the university, the law faculty, Bachelor/Master programs and their lectures or working groups. Thus, if categorized from the most broad to the most concrete levels of 'educator influence', these levels are 1) the learning culture and – environment; 2) curriculum design; 3) the course design, and; 4) the teaching method and teaching style of educators. With regard to the latter, this research calls for a legal education in which a wide variety of teaching methods is used, offering students experiences on which they reflect. By doing so, the student's way of viewing the world may be transformed, resulting in the student progressing to their next developmental step. This idea of transforming through experience recalls the ideas of Dewey and the *Progressive Education Movement* (see chapter 1) as well as of Schiller's description of *Bildung* through 'playing with art' (see chapter 2).[174] Because of their continuation to a subsequent level of development, the student will be better equipped to think critically.

In the following, the initial model for integrating critical thinking into ALE is outlined. The idea is that it is a perpetually evolving model that can be adjusted and added to by educators. At the moment, the model provides ten practical suggestions for the integration of critical thinking into ALE that are structured on the previously mentioned four levels that educators may influence. The dots in the chart show the level(s) on which each given suggestion supports the development of the students' critical thinking. Some of the suggestions can be used on multiple levels, for example on the level of curriculum design as well as on the level of the course design. In further explanation of the model and its content, each of the ten practical suggestions is elaborated on later in this section. Before diving into a further explanation of the suggestions and their contribution to the critical thinking process, the model is presented below:

174 After all, according to Schiller, the rational reflection on the sensory impulses human beings experience while studying an art work resulted in a further development of individuals.

Initial Model for Integrating Critical Thinking into Academic Legal Education

	I want to improve on the level of → You can↓	Learning Culture & Environment	Curriculum Design	Course Design	Teaching Method & Teaching Style
1	Aim to develop deep and broad knowledge		•	•	•
2	Be open minded	•			•
3	Delay Judgment	•			•
4	Reward courage			•	•
5	Model desired behavior and attitudes				•
6	Make time	•	•	•	•
7	Create opportunities for practice and feedback, through appropriate instructional interventions, assignments and assessment.			•	•
8	Use play and playfulness	•	•	•	•
9	Emphasize the focus on the development of critical thinking and critical thinking relevant processes	•	•	•	•
10	Aim to develop the faculty of judgment		•	•	•

The visual provided earlier on the critical thinking process showed that there are two components that support the critical thinking process, namely domain relevant skills and knowledge (DRS) and critical thinking relevant processes (CTRP). DRS enable a person to define a problem that needs solving and helps with gathering and remembering information. CTRP are essential for all four stages to the process: identifying a problem, gathering information and remembering information; inference making and decision making. To illustrate, the visual can be seen once more below:

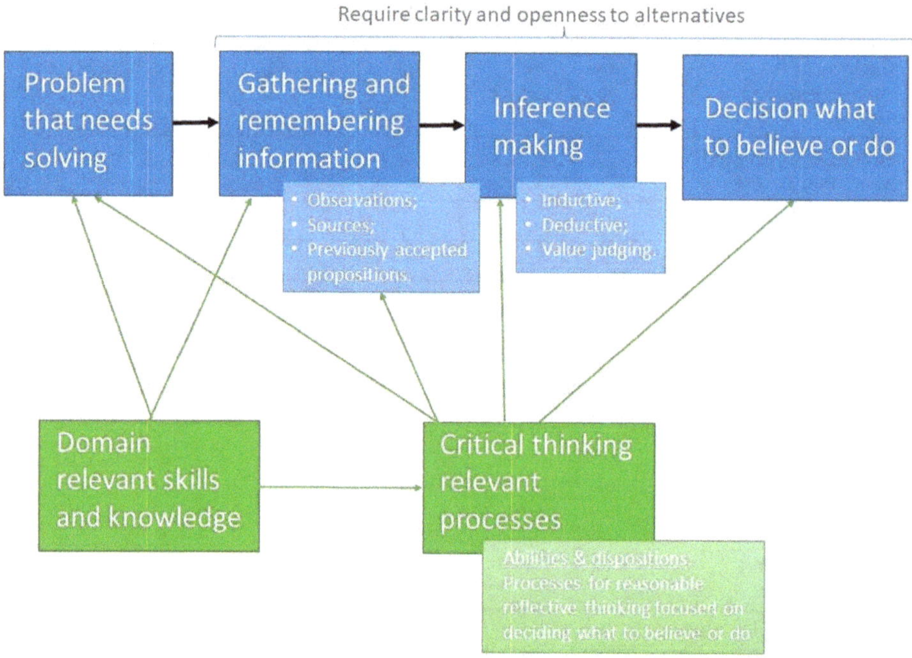

In the following final part of this chapter, each of the ten suggestions as presented in the model for integrating critical thinking into ALE is further explored. The ten suggestions are all related to the components of the critical thinking process (visualized in green above). Some suggestions support the development of domain relevant skills and knowledge, while others are beneficial for the development of critical thinking relevant processes. Moreover, some of the suggestions support the development of both components. At the start of the explanation of each of the ten suggestion below, the component that is supported by a suggestion is indicated by a yellow check mark.

No. 1 – Aim to develop deep and broad knowledge

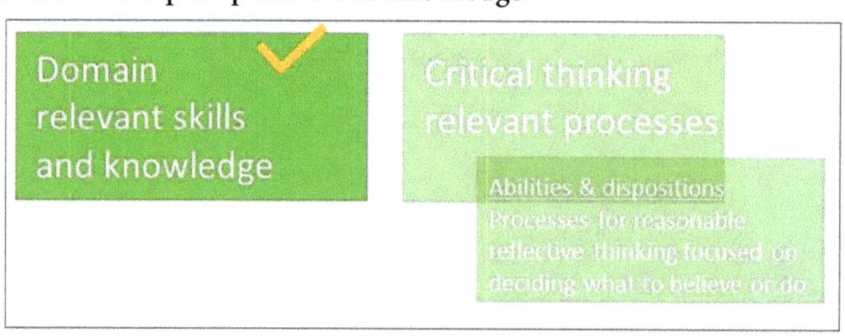

After exploring the critical thinking process and its prerequisites earlier in this chapter, some things have become clear. For example, in order for our law students to be able to go through the critical thinking process, they require knowledge of what critical thinking is. Also, they are in need of developing critical thinking skills and dispositions. Additionally, as was shown in the visual on the critical thinking process, domain relevant knowledge is necessary for critical thinking. Bailin, too, argues that academic education should emphasize the mastery of disciplinary knowledge and skills in order for students to think critically and creatively. According to Bailin, this means that students in a specific domain – in our case law – require knowledge of their domain's current body of information; principles and procedures; methods of inquiry; standards for assessing opinions and argumentations, and the overarching aims and deep questions of the domain.[175]

This calls for developing in-depth knowledge of the law. Since the legal profession has become more complex, in the sense that the topics and problems legal professionals have to deal with vary widely and often transcend the legal domain, academically educated legal professionals require deep, specialist legal knowledge as well as broad knowledge of the legal domain and other domains. For that aim, legal academics have been arguing for a broader legal education in which students learn 'law in context'.[176] Van Klink, De Vries and Bleeker, for example, advocate that legal education should aim to develop academically educated generalists, instead of legal specialists.[177] These authors state that in order for the students to be able to criticize the law, a broad education is necessary in which courses such as legal history, philosophy, or sociology are mandatory in addition to black letter law courses.[178] This is also argued by Appleby, Burdon and Reilly, who advocate that educators in legal education should teach their students to critically evaluate the assumptions of the law with the help of not only legal standards but also with standards stemming from external domains. In other words, in-depth knowledge of the law and general knowledge of other domains provide students with the tools to critically reflect on the law. Consequently, Appleby, Burdon and Reilly hold that intellectual breadth is a necessity in legal education, resulting in a call for the inclusion of, for example, legal theory in curricula.[179] Another way of broadening the knowledge and perspective of our students could be to develop a learning trajectory for broad development or to provide space in the curriculum, for instance a specified number of ECTS, that students are required to fill with

175 Bailin 1987, p. 28.

176 Appleby, Burdon and Reilly emphasize that law students need to have a global perspective and in-depth insight into society's ethical issues to be able to reflect critically on the law. See Appleby, Burdon and Reilly 2013, p. 363.

177 Van Klink, de Vries and Bleeker 2017, p. 6. This seems to differ from academics who advocate the ideal of the T-shaped lawyer, who is a generalist as well as a specialist. See, for example, Mak 2020, pp. 9-10, 25.

178 Van Klink de Vries and Bleeker 2017, p. 6. See also: Francot and Corrias 2016, p. 55. See also Appleby, Burdon and Reilly 2013, p. 363.

179 Appleby, Burdon & Reilly 2013, pp. 348, 360-361.

non-legal courses. To help students choose between available courses, a list with suggested preselected courses from other Departments could be provided.

While designing or redesigning a course, educators could support the aim of developing in-depth and broad knowledge by including literature from outside the legal domain or by developing assignments that require more than solely legal knowledge and skills. Inside the classroom, educators could emphasize the worth of in-depth and broad knowledge by letting the students practice with taking on multiple perspectives in addition to the legal perspective during instructional interventions. Furthermore, educators could contribute to a learning culture and learning environment that is supportive of intellectual breadth by modeling and by providing additional literature, news articles or other media that provide information from various domains. Also, educators could explicitly recognize the use of broad knowledge by complimenting or otherwise appreciating students who try to include external perspectives in their contributions.

No. 2 – Be open minded

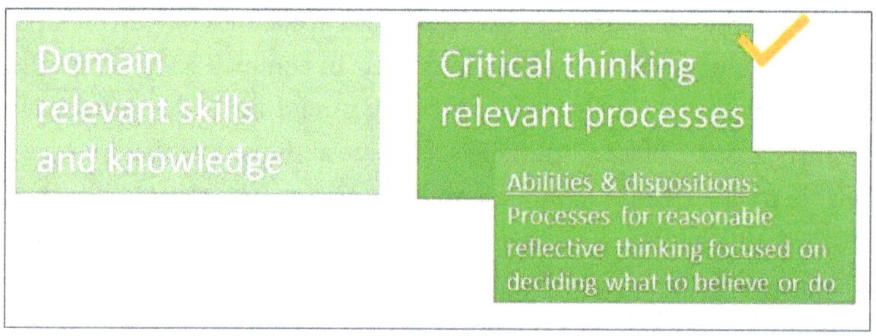

The second suggestion involves open-mindedness. Open-mindedness is a key disposition for the critical thinking process, especially in the information gathering phase where the critical thinker is required to remain alert to and open to alternatives and to seriously consider other points of view and, ultimately, to be willing to change their mind when evidence and reasons give cause to do so.[180] Being open-minded is not a passive, but an active enterprise: It requires conscious effort to not easily slip into a mindset with fixed, rigid opinions and beliefs but to continue to engage with other views. Furthermore, remaining open to other perspectives and the willingness to reconsider your own beliefs takes courage.

Diversity in student and teacher population could create an environment in which the development of open mindedness is stimulated. Such an environment challenges students to discuss their opinions with people of different backgrounds. During such discussions, students will need to remain open minded to (and mindful of) points of view other than

180 See Ennis 2015, pp. 32-33.

their own. Educators could instruct their students on the importance of open mindedness and give them feedback on the way they participate in the discussion. For educators in higher education, being open minded includes being open to our students' viewpoints. So, providing room in class for students to come up with and discuss alternative interpretations of issues or course content offers an opportunity for opening our minds to new or alternatives possibilities. At the same time, this shows our students the open-minded behavior we would like to see from them. Also, taking on a counter position in the case of group consensus during a discussion to stimulate the students to reconsider their viewpoints provides educators with another opportunity for optimizing student open mindedness.[181] In addition, it could support the students' development of the disposition of open mindedness to explicitly view and consider the value of every contribution made by the students without immediately shutting some down and judging them irrelevant, underdeveloped or unpractical. To practice this with students, thinking strategies such as the thinking routines from Project Zero's Making Thinking Visible – which are also recommended for scaffolding students' thinking –[182] could be used.

No. 3 – Delay judgment

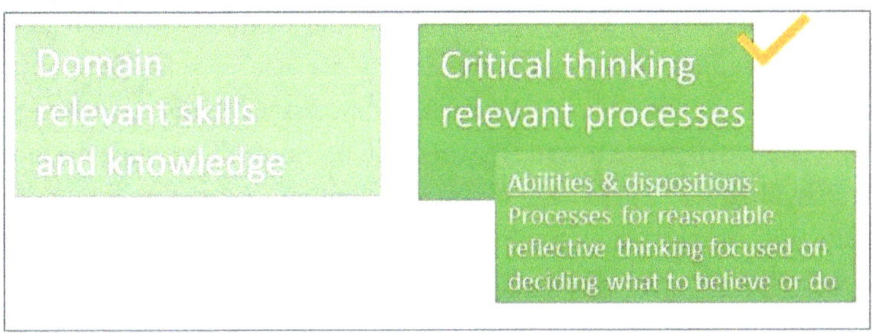

Suspending judgment is the third suggestion for incorporating critical thinking into ALE. After the information gathering stage, where open mindedness is of high importance, the inference making and decision making phases follow in the critical thinking process. It is in these stages that the delay of judgment is of the essence. This is recognizable in Ennis's emphasis on openness for alternatives – and thus, remaining in uncertainty – during this phase of the critical thinking process.[183] Dewey also thought that delaying judgment was at the heart of critical thinking and he defined it as postponing definite suggestions, not going with first impressions, and first thoroughly exploring the nature of the problem. Until the problem was thoroughly determined, the critical thinker had to remain in

181 See: Van Klink and De Vries 2013, p. 44.
182 Gunawardena & Wilson 2021, p. 3.
183 Ennis 1991, p. 7.

uncertainty.[184] Following Oakeshott, Van Klink and De Vries, too, argue that suspending judgment is important for academic education: They view it as a tranquil period of not-knowing during which no value judgment has to be made on the worth of information. Van Klink and De Vries describe this experience of 'not knowing' as a vital part of the learning process.[185] Van Klink adds that this phase will result in students realizing the fallibility of knowledge and the realization that all knowledge can be questioned.[186] The tranquility of the suspension stage does not therefore mean that it is without uncertainty or without action: It takes a constant considering of the information without immediately reaching for a fixed and certain answer.[187] According to De Vries, suspension of judgment is required for (self-)reflection and taking responsibility. He advocates that the university should offer a space where judgment can be delayed, in order for students to learn the law, learn to think like lawyers and become their own person.[188]

Delaying judgment is an endeavor that takes place *after* the information gathering is concluded: At this point, the critical thinker enters a stage in which they do not yet judge the available information. This means that during the inference making stage all possibilities of connections between the information gathered are still on the table and can be freely explored *until* the final judgment is made on what to believe or do. Important to note is that open mindedness (which is the state of mind during the information gathering) and delaying judgment appear to coincide. Thus, in practice, it is not possible to completely separate these two actions within the critical thinking process. Because the way the process works in practice is less structured than it is in theory, it may occur that while the judgment is delayed, the individual is still gathering – or at least finding – information that they take with them in the final decision-making. Especially in contemporary times, where (new) information awaits with every swipe on a screen or visit to a website, a complete halt of the search for information is not realistic in many instances. Nevertheless, I propose to clearly separate open mindedness and delaying judgment for the sake of initially teaching students to systematically take the steps of the critical thinking process in order for them to become critical thinkers. Later on in their education, the two could be less strictly separated. It would be a missed opportunity to capture open-mindedness and delaying judgment under the same umbrella, since the separation of concepts so clearly provides students with insight into what they are supposed to do at specific moments in the critical thinking process. In explanation, in the stage of gathering information the students are required to be open minded for information that provides other ideas or alternatives than their previous information. Only after halting the search for relevant information, do they

184 Dewey 1910, p. 74.
185 Van Klink & De Vries 2013, p. 44, De Vries 2021, pp. 75, 92.
186 Van Klink 2016, p. 24.
187 See also: Van Klink & De Vries 2013, p. 44.
188 De Vries 2021, p. 92-93.

start the process of valuing the information by finding inferences that lead to a judgment. During this stage, students are expected to remain open to other alternatives, such as other possible inferences and conclusions until all possible inferences are explored and valued. This suspension of judgment is then followed by a judgment on what to do or believe.

How can we include a space for open mindedness and the suspension of judgment in legal education? One route could be established by explicitly including the 'art of doubt' in our law schools. Ulrich Beck describes 'the art of reflexive doubt' as a liberating endeavor and as a starting point for relativism, tolerance and flexibility. It allows space for others and requires (re-)examination of one's own ideas and convictions. However, it is often accompanied by some discomfort and self-disillusion.[189] Practicing the art of doubt consists of continued questioning and it is therefore a strategy for learning how to manage uncertainty. This is because through constant questioning students become aware of their not-knowing and become used to the uncomfortable feeling of uncertainty. This might be the point where we could introduce a re-mystification of legal education: The art of doubt allows for the deliberate introduction of a level of uncertainty in specific parts of academic education, for example, by avoiding teaching and assessing for 'right' answers.[190] A number of legal academics call for a level of uncertainty in legal education in support of the development of student critical thinking. Van Klink and De Vries, for instance, suggest challenging students to question what is known in the legal domain and what the students themselves know, since they believe that this doubt will help students to be critical in assessing all knowledge claims and will help raise student awareness for the necessity of always assessing knowledge claims.[191] To confront students with uncertainty, Van Klink and De Vries propose reading difficult texts that the educator knows will not be completely understood by the students. This results in students experiencing intellectual uncertainty and raises an understanding that knowledge is the result of personal, active, effortful work.[192] In addition, Francot and Corrias hold that good academics are capable of self-authored judgment and have the ability to act, because they have insight into the knowledge, backgrounds and history of their domains and they are also aware of what is *not* yet known and what is uncertain in their domain. To educate students towards this goal, Francot and Corrias claim that legal education should make uncertainty manageable by offering tools that help students to select and order information.[193] Moreover, they argue that by connecting ongoing research and teaching, students learn that academic

189 See Beck 1997, pp. 162-163.

190 See: Ambrose et. al 2010, pp. 181.

191 Van Klink 2016, p. 22. Van Klink & De Vries 2013, p. 45.

192 Van Klink & De Vries 2013, p. 46.

193 Francot & Corrias 2016, pp. 54-55. This suggestion seems helpful in the information gathering phase and the inference making stage of the critical thinking process.

findings are part of an ongoing process and can be doubted or questioned.[194] Bailin, too, argues that students must become aware that knowledge is not static, but dynamic. She believes that educators should communicate that thinking and knowledge are creative and knowledge expands over time.[195] This will hopefully result in students taking knowledge seriously while understanding that knowledge claims are never absolute and must be questioned.[196] In the end, the goal is for the students to learn that uncertainty, questioning and doubt are part of an academic's life.[197] Even more so, they are inevitably part of an examined life in contemporary times. When we consider the ideas of the authors mentioned above, we see that all of them suggest that it is paramount for critical thinking that students learn to question – and thus doubt – the content of their domain. To do so, students need to understand the content and scope of their domain, the uncertainty that is part of the research process and they have to be aware of the effort that comes with creating knowledge. These are building blocks of the re-mystification of academic legal education.

Obviously, it is not the intention of a re-mystification of legal education to create unnecessary anxiety that paralyzes students and makes them incapable of learning, critical thinking, creative thinking and incapable of play and playfulness. Ambrose et al. suggest that educators in higher education make uncertainty relatively safe, by providing a level of support during the students' dealings with uncertainty, for example by explicitly explaining that critical thinking requires embracing complexity and resisting the pull of simplification and by clarifying that the goal of group discussions is not consensus, but a consideration and assessment of many points of view.[198]

An important skill of the art of doubt, which has already been mentioned earlier, is the skill to ask questions, such as clarifying questions. This skill is important for gathering information – where the critical thinker asks questions to find relevant information – and in the stages of inference making and decision making, where the critical thinker questions their own inferences and decisions. Open inquisitiveness – in other words, asking questions out of curiosity and without immediate judgment – is recommended.[199] This is especially the case in the information gathering stage: in cases where open inquisitiveness is employed, asking questions becomes a method of gathering information and gaining understanding of an issue, without judgment.[200]

194 Francot & Corrias 2016, pp. 57.
195 Bailin 1987, pp. 28-29.
196 Bailin 1987, p. 29.
197 Francot & Corrias 2016, p. 55.
198 Ambrose et. al 2010, pp. 180-181.
199 See, for example, Barnett 2015 p. 28
200 It is therefore also recommended to include the art of doubt in the information gathering stage of the critical thinking process. Here, it is a part of open mindedness.

Asking relevant questions should be a learning objective for ALE. Asking questions is in itself an important skill for critical thinkers as well as for creative thinkers (see chapter 5), since it helps stimulate curiosity and reflection.[201] For students to be able to ask the right questions and ask them effectively, practice and feedback are required. With this aim, educators could explain and model how an issue, problem, or opinion might be questioned. Dumitru believes that creating encounters with fields of Art positively influences the critical thinking dispositions of students, since Art's inquiry based curriculum promotes critical thinking development. Research shows that art students score better than students in other domains with regard to truth-seeking, maturity and open mindedness.[202] Consequently, encounters with art and methods used in art education could be of interest for educators in ALE.

After gaining understanding through asking questions openly, the questioning process may be followed by criticism. Criticizing is an important skill for legal students to develop. Francot and Van Klink describe legal criticism as questioning the results of a legal procedure or process, such as a court decision. In this situation, students could attempt to criticize the correctness or desirability of the court decision from a legal perspective.[203] This type of criticism consists of a judgment based on a chain of reasoning, which includes arguments in favor of and against the claim they are making, and arguments that invalidate the counter arguments.[204] However, receiving criticism or critical questions sometimes hinders inspiration. This situation threatens to occur when criticism is given with a lack of sensitivity, in a negative manner, without an effort to see the value of what is criticized, or with a focus on the past instead of on the future. In contrast, when criticism is the result of open inquisitiveness and wonder, it may stimulate improvements to the original idea, product or knowledge claim. This way, when a *gaze of wonder* lies at the basis of an educator's or peer's critical thinking and feedback – their criticism is transformed into positive, constructive feedback that is focused on the future. This *gaze of wonder* therefore provides a helpful tool for critical thinking and providing feedback for educators as well as for students. Wondering is the object of what Kegan calls 'the psychology of admiration' and linguistically stems from the Latin 'mirar'. It has two opposite sides, that – according to Kegan – are both important for human beings in contemporary times. On the one hand, 'wondering at', is related to concepts such as watching and reverencing; receptiveness; contemplation as an end in itself, and is the source of inspiration of the humanities. 'Wondering about', on the other hand, is linked to asking and reckoning; acting upon; a means to an end; analytic, and is the source of inspiration of the (natural) sciences. Despite,

201 See Adriansen 2010, p. 78. See also Almeida 2010, p. 89.
202 Dumitru 2019, p. 873.
203 Van Klink & Francot 2018, p. 2.
204 Van Klink & Francot 2018, p. 3.

or maybe because of, these differences, Kegan argues that the two sides of 'mirar' are two kinds of wisdom that could strengthen one another and good teaching is just this two-sided way of admiring, of wondering. An education that leans too much towards wondering about, will focus excessively on measurement and measurable teaching standards.[205] On the other hand, leaning too much toward *wondering at* also comes with pitfalls: It leaves room for deeply admiring any point of view without benchmarks that provide a basis for criticism. Kegan calls for individuals to remember to be the conscious master of science and for education to find a balance between wondering at and wondering about.[206] Based on the perils of legal education as described in the first chapter, it appears that legal education is now focused excessively on *wondering about*: and this research seeks to find a renewed balance by strengthening our skill to *wonder at*.

In an academic legal education where the art of doubt, asking questions and the *gaze of wonder* are part of the learning culture, curriculum, classroom and teaching method, students will practice how to remain open minded to alternatives; practice wondering at and being critical towards their own and another's opinion; are capable of openness to give new opinions or ideas the benefit of the doubt; are willing to be questioned by others; strive to be flexible in shifting positions if warranted, and exercise their ability to suspend judgment. A person who is trying to master these abilities is at the same time shaping their personality since the doubt of convictions, ideas, mind set and life choices are part of the process of personal growth. This results in dispositions that create space for critical thinking, creativity, collaboration and problem solving behavior.

No. 4 – Reward Courage

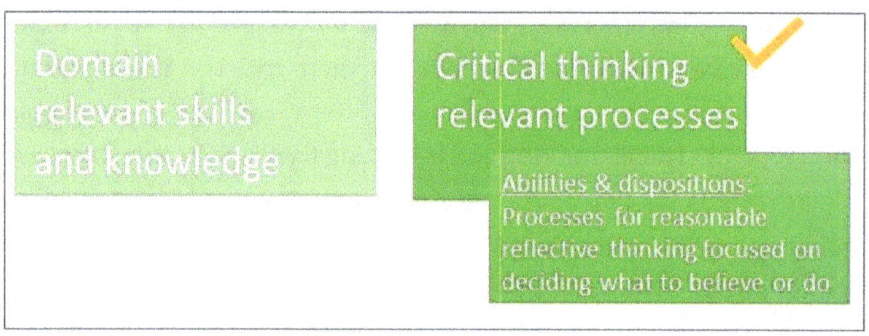

The proposal to reward courage is the fourth suggestion for integrating critical thinking into ALE. Swimming against the tide,[207] asking questions, remaining open to alternatives,

205 Kegan 1994, p. 8.
206 Kegan 1994, pp. 8-9.
207 Because of this, Barnett refers to having the courage to make up your own mind through critical thinking as an academic and intellectual value. See: Barnett 2015 p. 29.

suspending judgment and ultimately making judgments is a tension-filled endeavor. Especially decision making and judgment making in situations where the stakes are high, are a difficult and risky business. Judges make decisions in these kind of situations and are therefore, according to Van Domselaar and De Vries, in need of judicial courage.[208] Not only judges, but *all* academically educated legal professionals require courage. The reason for this is that, in the current landscape of the legal profession and general life in the late modern global society, choice is demanded of all academically educated legal professionals. Making a choice one way or the other and thereby taking responsibility based on examined judgments means that one has to stand by the choices one makes and acknowledge that one can be held accountable for the consequences of those decisions. However, decision-makers who are aware of this responsibility will probably also experience a sense of uncertainty or anxiety.

Consequently, it takes courage to be critical and make decisions. According to De Vries, courage is needed because at the moment a person – or legal professional – makes a decision, it is not clear if that decision is right or wrong, which results in a sense of uncertainty. Also, when that person has made a decision, others may express negative opinions in the form of criticism of that decision. This makes the decision-maker vulnerable.[209] Especially in the current context of 'social cancelling' and discussions that are only held in black-and-white, students might need support in being courageous, for example, though practicing coping techniques for dealing with harsh reactions.

Because of this, it is important for educators to be aware of the tension experienced by students when practicing their critical thinking skills and to understand that it takes courage for a student to speak up or to question their own beliefs. Consequently, creating a safe learning environment is a high priority. Educators could employ various techniques to support an environment where critical thinking can be developed by, first, establishing a relationship based on trust with their students. Furthermore, educators could develop a supportive environment of courage by using play and playfulness in their teaching style, by working in relatively small groups, by modeling the expected behavior and also by specifically complimenting students that take the risk and show critical thinking.

---

208 Van Domselaar 2015, p. 32 and De Vries 2021, p. 90.

209 De Vries 2021, p. 89.

No. 5 – Model desired behavior: attitudes and skills

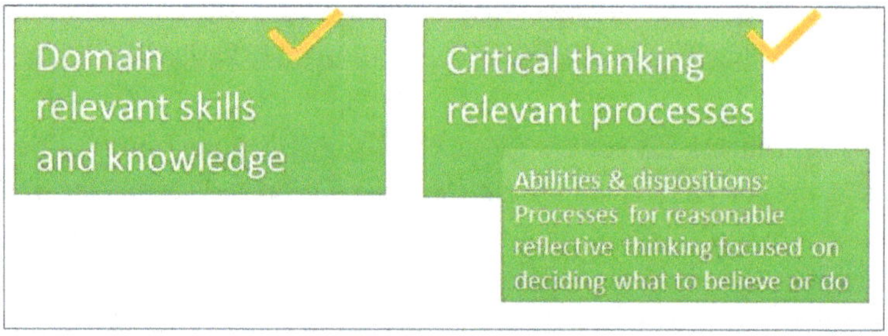

If educators in legal education wish for their students to learn critical thinking dispositions, skills and abilities, they could offer literature on the topic of critical thinking, that explains what critical thinking entails. Furthermore, they could construct opportunities for practice. An additional and very helpful instructional strategy would be for the educator to model the desired behavior.[210] Modeling starts with the belief that learning results from observation. It requires an educator to demonstrate the expected approach to thinking – for example, making inferences, developing an argument, making judgment, finding fallacies in a written passage – and the students to learn by observing their educator. In the case of critical thinking, which asks for complex cognitive skills, educators could model by verbalizing their thought process when they engage in critical thinking.[211] For instance, when an educator's goal is to teach their students to find fallacies in a written paper, they could start by reading aloud a paper and expressing the thoughts and thinking strategies they use while evaluating if the argument made in the paper is correct in the light of specific standards.

There exist various types of modeling, such as disposition modeling, task and performance modeling, meta cognitive modeling and student centered modeling. For legal education, all of these categories are of interest. In explanation, *disposition modeling* can be used for modeling personal and professional characteristics and strategies of thinking, including critical thinking. Moreover, *task and performance modeling* precedes practical tasks such as writing papers, performing an oral presentation or solving a case. Furthermore, in *meta cognitive modeling* educators verbally expresses their thought process (thinking-out-loud approach) when performing thinking strategies while, for instance, interpreting argumentations or making decisions. Finally, *student-centered modeling* is a way of creating a supportive learning environment and decreasing the educator-centeredness of the classroom by asking a student to demonstrate and verbally

210 Modeling is a strategy to support the development of student thinking, see: Ritchhart & Perkins 2008, p. 58.
211 Salisu & Ransom 2014, pp. 54-55.

explain their thought process.[212] In the case of modeling critical thinking, all of these types require the educator to verbally, explicitly explain the process of critical thinking, so that the students understand which steps they are required to take.

No. 6 – Make time

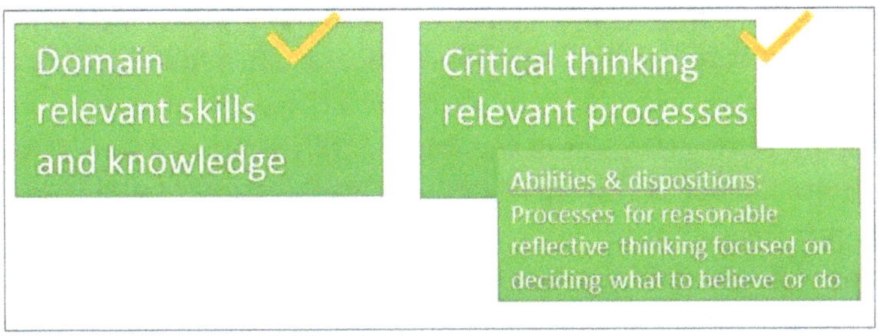

The sixth suggestion for integrating critical thinking into ALE is to make time. Developing critical thinking ability requires time and deceleration for practice, questioning, suspending judgment, exploring possibilities, thoughtful decision making, reflection and introspection to take place.[213] Unfortunately, time is often a scarce commodity in legal education as well as in the lives of our students. For example, because of the student loan system that was implemented in 2015, many current Dutch students hold part-time jobs and work two or more days a week in addition to their full-time study. One way or the other, this means that students have to split their time between work and study in addition to the time necessary for their social lives and family responsibilities. Also, students often feel that they are obligated to finish their Bachelor's degree within three years and their Master's in one or two years as well. Furthermore, due to the popular 8-8-4 approach in curricula, many Dutch law students have to grasp a course's content and need to work with that content within the timespan of only eight or four weeks.[214] Also, this 8-8-4 approach does not leave much breathing room for students (nor for educators) in between courses. Consequently, time for necessary mental and physical relaxation, reflection, integrating knowledge and skills, or further studying is lacking. Moreover, in my experience, it generally seems that during lectures, much attention goes to the explanation of the content, especially in first year courses. All of these circumstances do not allow for much time to elaborate on, discuss, reflect on or play with the material. It would be helpful for the development of critical thinking to find ways to make time.

212 Salisu & Ransom 2014, pp. 55-56.
213 See: De Vries 2021, p. 92.
214 Some universities use longer periods, for example 13 weeks instead of 8.

Not all of the circumstances described above can be changed at the hands of educators, who are often obliged to follow their national and institution's policies. If it is not possible to reduce our students' financial worries or expand the number of weeks a course consists of, then it is useful to make the most of the time that we have with our students. In their course design, educators might create time by using blended learning in order to flip the classroom. This would mean that students are encouraged to study the content at home by, for example, watching videos or listening to podcasts in addition to their preparation of the literature. During the contact hours between students and educators, more time can then be given to the active processing of and working with the learned content. Already, colleagues in legal education are experimenting with offering knowledge clips explaining core concepts that students watch at home in lieu of traditional lectures. The online learning that was a necessity during the quarantine time of the Covid-19 pandemic has accelerated the number of educators and students used to this way of teaching. Choosing for a 'flip the classroom' concept not only provides flexibility to students – who are able to choose at what moment to watch the clip, for example – but it also leaves time in class for a more in-depth and activated approach to the content. Additionally, educators can prepare for providing students thinking time, by incorporating extra time in their lesson plan. That way, there remains enough time for the students to engage in the selected instructional techniques – be it a group discussion, writing or judging of an argument or exploring the pros and cons of a specific perspective on a legal issue.

No. 7 – Create opportunities for practice and feedback, through appropriate instructional interventions, assignments and assessment

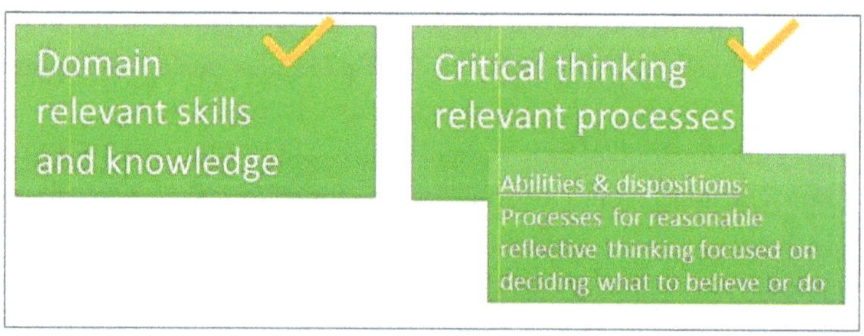

The seventh suggestion looks at the interventions, assignments and assessments that educators in legal education could construct to create opportunities for practice and feedback. Critical thinking is an acquired skill: You have to learn to do it, and as a consequence, it needs to be taught and practiced.[215] So, to develop critical thinking skills and dispositions, students need opportunities to practice and require regular feedback on

215 A claim Mulnix bases on Paul and Scriver's definition of critical thinking. Mulnix 2012, p. 465.

their performance. Moreover, students require the skills to deal with feedback and reflect on their learning process. This may all happen during class under instruction and guidance of an educator and in the company of peers. At the levels of course design and teaching method, interesting results for the teaching of critical thinking can be based on research by Abrami et al. This research shows that the development of generic critical thinking skills in students is supported by deliberately using the instructional interventions of dialogue and authentic/anchored instruction.[216] In addition to developing instructional strategies, the development and quality of a student's critical thinking can be tracked by choosing specific forms of assessment, including strategies for formative evaluation. In the following, both instructional interventions and appropriate assessment will be further explored.

First, instructional interventions can be used to support our students' critical thinking. As argued in the second chapter, this research calls for incorporating a broad variety of instructional interventions. Since dialogue is already an often used instructional technique in ALE, it seems that the desired variation in pedagogy is mostly to be found in forms of authentic/anchored instruction. Authentic/anchored instruction revolves around types of experiential learning and it often involves applied problem solving: Students are introduced to and confronted with real-life (but not exclusively professional) problems and issues. By reflecting on those issues and related ethics, for example with the help of structured thinking routines, student development is furthered. In addition, authentic/anchored instruction proves to be a way of providing a real and dynamic content in which students practice their critical thinking skills. In other words, it provides the context for the 'fusion'-approach of critical thinking (see for more information about this approach suggestion 9). Also, authentic/anchored instruction results in students being able to create their own knowledge, since it is no longer just the educator who is the authority that transfers knowledge, but the students who actively build up their knowledge through experiences that their educator has constructed. Now, instead of the educator's voice being dominant, the *student*'s voice becomes dominant – or at least louder – in the classroom.[217] Approaches to teaching that support this are *flipped classroom, Problem-Based Learning* and research projects.[218] Turning up the volume of the student's voice could also be supported by explicitly giving students positions of authority in class, for example by creating expert groups that share knowledge or through giving students the control over the topics to be discussed in class.[219] However broad the variety of instructional techniques will be, it is recommended to include collaborative learning techniques, for instance, by including

---

216 Abrami et al. 2015, p. 302. See Chapter Two for more information on these instructional interventions.
217 Cedrone 2013, pp. 825-826. See also Ritchhart & Church 2020, p. 10.
218 Gunawardena & Wilson 2021, p. 4.
219 Cedrone 2013, pp. 827-828. See also an experiment by De Vries in Van Klink & De Vries 2013, pp. 46-47.

opportunities for peer feedback on the learning process as well as on their written and oral products.[220] First, because collaborative learning techniques work really well for students in various levels of development.[221] Second, because collaboration between students automatically changes the educator's role into a supportive one: The educator has to facilitate and enable meaningful, challenging learning that students enjoy in their Zones of Proximal Development.[222] For example, the educator could select and construct authentic problems, related activities and challenges with care. This results in the student's voice becoming louder and in *active* learning.

Through instructional interventions, it is possible for students to repeatedly practice routes for (critical) thinking so that they develop thinking habits. For instance, within a role-play, students are able to practice how to make inferential connections between statements or they could explicitly practice how to recognize fallacies. Critical thinking and learning how to become a critical thinker are a process, not a product.[223] Therefore, repeatedly practicing critical thinking *within* the instructional intervention will help students to develop their critical thinking. This means two things. First, that *only* modeling critical thinking or showing examples of critical thinking, in for example literature, is not sufficient. According to Mulnix, skills training in critical thinking requires modeling, practice, providing feedback and some natural talent.[224] At the very least, students need to practice and practice often the skills and dispositions that are part of critical thinking. In this context it is important for educators and students to be aware of the fact that critical thinking is an effortful endeavor. Being able to think critically is not the result of a sudden 'eureka' experience, but the result of repeated practice by actively engaged students. Therefore, the repeated practice should be very deliberate, meaning that it will demand full concentration aimed at the improvement of critical thinking. Mulnix suggests that this focused practice can also be achieved by creating special exercises; graduated – scaffolded – practice, with exercises that gradually become more complex; close guidance and timely, specific feedback (and feed-forward) on the students efforts, progress and results.[225] The second thing stemming from the fact that the development of critical thinking is a process instead of a product, is that critical thinking ability should be regarded from a developmental point of view. This means that through practice and understanding,

220 Cedrone 2013, pp. 827-828.

221 If students are in the so-called instrumental developmental phase, they see others as sources of knowledge; in the third phase of socializing, the nearness of others provides the student with the opportunity to absorb the values of the group and in the self-authoring phase, students learn from the others how to balance points of view and value the process of understanding and reconciling areas of opposition. See Cedrone 2013, p. 827.

222 Cedrone 2013, pp. 827-828.

223 See Gunawardena & Wilson 2021, p. 3.

224 Mulnix 2012, pp. 474-475.

225 Mulnix 2012, p. 476.

students gain in competency with regard to critical thinking. More concretely, most students do not start their legal education in the highest stages of development. However, they *may* take steps towards the next stages during their studies. For example, students that go through an experience like a group project collaboration and discover the intricacies of a legal issue. Afterwards they practice their critical thinking skills by reflecting on the experience. This could have an effect on the students' development, such as a transformation towards the next stage of development, for example Kegan's self-authoring stage, or Kuhn's evaluative stage. This will open up new possibilities for that student's critical thinking, opportunities that were not possible on the lower stage of development. When viewing the development of critical thinking through this perspective, it becomes clear that the frustration and disappointment educators may sometimes feel with regard to their students' inability to think critically, are probably based on the educator's assumption that critical thinking skills and dispositions are a static product that you either do or do not have. However, as Gunawardena and Wilson have argued as well, critical thinking is a process that is built up through a careful scaffolding of a student's critical thinking development in education.[226] It is possible that a student who does not show the desired attitude for critical thinking is constrained by their developmental stage. This requires educators to make an effort to help these students along by offering experiences in their zone(s) of proximal development. These experiences will require students to practice with reflection and thinking routines that could become future thinking habits. When the educator is explicit in the use and practice of such thinking routines in the instructional techniques they use, students become aware of their cognitive activity while being critical, thus they will learn meta knowing skills.[227] Since these skills – which entail meta strategic knowing skills, meta cognitive knowing skills and epistemological knowing skills – are the intellectual skills most closely connected to critical thinking,[228] this will strengthen the students' development in critical thinking.

What kind of instructional interventions could be of interest for educators in ALE? There are many practical examples of instructional interventions that educators might employ. One is the use of the 'Making thinking visible' method which is created mainly for developing thinking dispositions[229] by Harvard's Project Zero's Visible Thinking.[230] This project has developed a large number of thinking routines for ingraining thinking habits. The starting point is that effective teaching of students' thinking – including critical thinking – does not start with theoretical instruction on thinking, but with providing

226 Gunawardena & Wilson 2021, pp. 8-9.

227 Pritchard 2009, p. 27. Meta knowing entails meta strategic knowing skills, meta cognitive knowing skills and epistemological knowing skills, See Kuhn 1999.

228 Kuhn 1999, p. 17.

229 See Ritchhart & Church 2020, p. 17.

230 See for more information: Visible Thinking | Project Zero (harvard.edu), last visited January 20th, 2022.

students with recurrent structures that scaffold[231] and support the students' thinking. Eventually, these structures become thinking routines.[232] Thinking routines are simple procedures that consist of only a few steps that are transferrable across contexts.[233] Consequently, these are available for use by students on all levels of education and in studying any kind of domain.[234] In addition to teaching thinking dispositions, Ritchhart and Church's research concludes that using the method of Making Thinking Visible also supports deep learning, student engagement and enables the student's voice to become dominant in the classroom.[235] To support educators in using thinking routines, the Visible Thinking Project has developed numerous thinking routines in their Toolbox, which I highly recommend colleagues in legal education to look up and give a try in their classes. Every thinking routine is aimed to develop a specific kind of thinking, for example, wondering and asking questions; making connections, or: considering different viewpoints. So an educator first has to pinpoint what kind of thinking they want their students to practice, based on which they can select a fitting thinking routine. Some examples of the developed thinking routines are See-Think-Wonder for exploring ideas, Circle of Viewpoints for digging deeper into ideas and Compass Points for examining propositions.[236]

In addition to the thinking routines that Project Zero has defined in the context of their project 'Making Thinking Visible', other instructional interventions are also possible for teaching students and make them practice with (critical) thinking and meta knowing skills. Mulnix, for example, suggests using argument maps in class to visualize chains of reasoning.[237] In my own course Introduction to Legal Philosophy I have worked with visualizing content and structuring the thinking of first year students by asking them to employ a Venn Diagram to show the differences and similarities between various theories.[238] Furthermore, Ogilvy and Holley propose a thinking routine called 'Talking aloud pairs' (TAPS), in which students discuss a problem in pairs: One student introduces and explains her solution, while her partner monitors the steps taken.[239] Sandel describes a thinking routine that could be explicitly used in legal education for the development of moral reasoning. The thinking routine is aimed at finding the underlying principles of a moral dilemma. The steps of this thinking routine are a Dilemma, an Initial conviction;

---

231 See also: Gunawardena & Wilson 2021, p. 3.
232 Ritchhart & Church 2020, p. xvii.
233 Ritchhart, Church & Morrison 2011, p. 45.
234 See: Ritchhart & Perkins 2008, p. 57.
235 Ritchhart & Church 2020, pp. 6-7.
236 See: PZ's Thinking Routines Toolbox | Project Zero (harvard.edu), last visited January 20th, 2022.
237 Mulnix 2012, p. 475.
238 See: Van Rossum 2021, pp. 186-187.
239 Ogilvy & Holley 1994, p. 346.

Reflection and confusion, in which the students explore multiple perspectives on the ethical dilemma, followed by a reconsideration.[240]

There are many instructional interventions supportive of critical thinking which focus on learning how to view an issue from various perspectives. In addition to the positive effect these kind of interventions have on students' critical thinking ability, they also add to the students' ability to empathize. Examples of these instructional interventions are role play, fieldtrips, ITAC Method, or reading and discussing literary novels. In role play, the educator encourages students to take on a role and to argue a position from the perspective of their character. Afterwards, the educator and students reflect on the role play and their experience. It is also possible to challenge the students' worldview by organizing fieldtrips that confront them with perspectives that they will not always experience themselves without prompting, such as visits to prisoners,[241] refugees, politicians, or artists. Van Klink, De Vries and Bleeker also describe a teaching method that emphasizes the importance of being able to take on multiple perspectives when they refer to Sokhi-Bulley's 'Thinking hat'-method and the ITAC method. These thinking routines aim at identifying and considering societal issues. Where, traditionally, legal students would use a step-by-step strategy starting with identifying the Issue, exploring the relevant Law, Applying the law and making Conclusions (ILAC), the ITAC method switches Law to Theory: Students identify the Issue, explore relevant Theory, Apply the theory and make Conclusions. This enables them to not just be critical from an internal perspective (Law), but to criticize the issue with an external, broader perspective (Theory). By switching the theory that is applied – from Kantian to Utilitarian, for instance – students are able to see the issue from a totally different perspective which could change their own conclusion or opinion. The inclusion of theory makes it possible for students to criticize the law based on external viewpoints, which supports their development of a critical attitude towards the law.[242] Furthermore, Machteld Vonk successfully experimented with engaging students in reading and discussing a literary novel. In her experience, the reading of literature created empathy, since students learn to take on the position of another person, namely the characters in the book. By doing so, they are better able to understand the complexity of problems and the interests of various parties. By reading literature, students imagine being in a situation that they will never encounter in real life. This successful experiment with an encounter with art and imagination to support student critical thinking abilities and dispositions provides inspiration for including other forms of art and culture in legal education, such as experiencing theater plays and additionally discussing the central

240 See: De Vries 2021, p. 95.

241 See, for instance, a fieldtrip described by Uygur that brought students in contact with prisoners in order for the students to develop empathy and see the law from the perspective of a prisoner. See: Van Klink 2016. See also Van Klink, De Vries and Bleeker 2017, p. 6.

242 Van Klink 2016, p. 26. Van Klink, De Vries and Bleeker 2017, p. 5.

issues and the personal experiences while viewing the play with the director and actors, visiting museums and discussing the artworks and the issues they depict with experts in the domain of art history. Not only might this support our students' critical thinking, but it also broadens their perception and their awareness of culture and history. In this context, Dumitru advocates that studying the Arts, Humanities and Culture is fundamental to developing critical thinking dispositions, as they enable the development of a person's character, such as one's ability to empathize.[243] Furthermore, these instructional interventions provide students who have never visited a museum or theater the opportunity to experience the value of such artistic expressions.

Above, types of instructional interventions relevant for critical thinking development have been explored. In addition, the following paragraph looks at how we could include types of assessment that support the development of critical thinking ability in ALE. With regard to assessment of critical thinking, it is important for students to make their thinking process visible, and not only the end result of their process of thought. In the case of summative assessment it may therefore be preferable to choose to assess in the form of essays, presentations, or open questions that also require a description of the thought process. This offers students some open space to question and discuss issues that have come up during the course. Assessing such an essay might be done based on, for example, the soundness of reasoning or the way the student considers various perspectives and comes to a decision with regard to the issue. Mathiasen and Andersen too suggest that educators in higher education assess with open-ended exam forms that are personally meaningful for the students.[244] However, the development of critical thinking ability especially requires formative assessment (which is now often called formative evaluation) which aims to change the educator's *and* students' perspectives from performing back to *learning*. Formative evaluation entails the opportunity for students to practice, gain feedback and learn, while educators make an effort to understand the student's learning.[245] This enables educators to monitor the progress of their students and scaffold their students' learning, with the goal of helping them take the next step in their learning process. It would be helpful for the development of our students if educators in legal education would find ways to include opportunities for formative evaluation in the curriculum. The thinking routines could be an effective tool for formative evaluation, since they are part of an effort to make thinking (and learning) *visible*. Therefore, it is a comprehensible expression of the students' understanding at a specific moment in time.[246] This offers the educator information about how to scaffold the student's further learning.

243 Dumitru 2019, p. 871.

244 Mathiasen & Andersen 2020, p. 48.

245 Ritchhart & Church 2020, p. 11.

246 See Ritchhart & Church 2020, p. 12.

No. 8 – Use play and playfulness

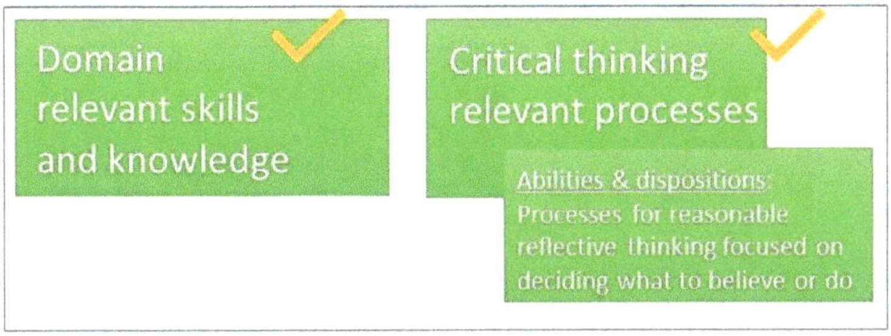

The eighth suggestion for incorporating critical thinking into ALE is using play and playfulness. The use of play and playfulness supports the achievement of learning goals, including learning goals regarding critical thinking. Critical thinking requires a level of imagination, since the student assesses an argument, situation or viewpoint and makes a judgment based on reasons that they have to construct themselves.[247] Reasoning involves inference making – seeking and making connections between assertions – and this is a creative endeavor. Both play and playfulness are important for creating an environment where one can do critical and imaginative work, where there is room for open mindedness, thinking of alternatives and suspending judgment. In this sense, Salen and Zimmerman describe play as 'free movement within a more rigid structure'.[248] In the rigid structure of the often formal environment of the university, the curriculum and its attainment goals and assessments, play and playfulness offer a free space of practice and experimenting. In such an environment – where taking risks is approached in a playful manner – it is easier to build up the courage to think critically.

Since play and playfulness are important for critical thinking, creative thinking and *Bildung* in general, a more detailed exploration of the concepts in the context of legal education is provided in the fifth chapter.

247 Bailin 1987, p. 25.
248 Glas et al. 2019, p. 16.

No. 9 – Emphasize the focus on the development of critical thinking development and critical thinking relevant processes

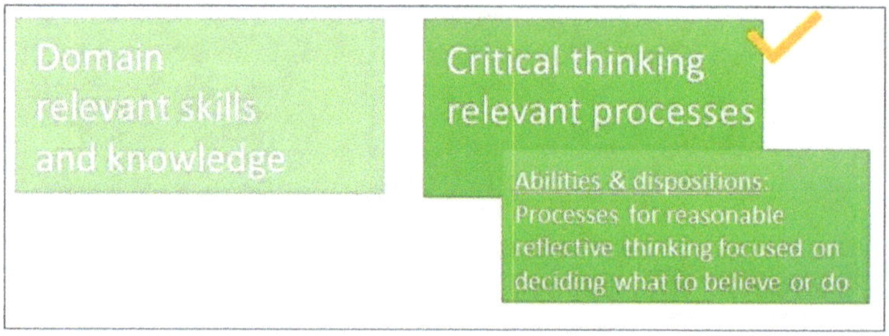

The ninth suggestion for incorporating critical thinking into ALE is to emphasize the focus on critical thinking development and on critical thinking relevant processes. At the moment, even though most educators will acknowledge its academic importance, critical thinking is often not explicitly explained and taught in legal education and there is no shared understanding of the concept and a shared strategy to support students in becoming critical thinkers is missing. A shared language of critical thinking alludes to conversation between educators, policy makers and students. Fortunately, we are able to change this situation and place more emphasis on critical thinking.

First, on the level of curriculum design, it is imperative that critical thinking is explicitly and in detail incorporated in the Bachelor's and Master's program's attainment goals, so that critical thinking becomes a clear aim of any academic legal education.[249] It has to be clarified what a Bachelor graduate and respectively a Master graduate is expected to be able to do with regard to critical thinking. Also, to make it more clear for students and educators what exactly is expected of the student at specific stages in their studies, it will be useful to explicitly decipher the level of the critical thinking skills and dispositions they need to be able to show at the end of every study year.[250] That way, their process of acquiring

249 See also: Adriansen 2010, p. 82.

250 Inspiration may be found in the Dublin descriptors (especially the dimension of making judgments) and the Framework for Qualifications of the European Higher Education Area, which recognizes eight qualification levels and explicated the learning outcomes of each, in three categories, including responsibility and critical thinking. However, *what exactly* is meant by critical thinking may still be further explicated and it is also only a broad description of what a *graduate* should be capable of: It does not describe what, for example, the level of critical thinking a first year student should be capable of. See Description of the eight EQF levels | Europass. See also: European Higher Education Area and Bologna Process (ehea.info). This is also the case with the current Dutch version which seems to be less detailed on the abilities one develops at every one of the Qualification Levels, but is still interesting: Hoger onderwijs | Nuffic. The Australian AQF Levels (Australian Qualifications Framework, AQF levels | Australian Qualifications Framework), explicates the level of critical thinking for various grades (for example Bachelor, Master, Doctoral) in the form of 10 levels. See Appleby, Burdon & Reilly 2013, p. 361.

critical thinking ability can be better scaffolded by their educators and students are able to provide themselves with self-feedback on the progression of their learning process. Additionally, having clear attainment goals for the first, second, and third year of the Bachelor program will provide the opportunity to develop fitting assessments throughout the curriculum, so that all courses in the curriculum are able to contribute in a logical way to the development of our students' critical thinking. This will all contribute to a specialized learning trajectory that focuses on developing critical thinking.

Secondly, educators can make a strategic choice – across the curriculum, per course or for each instructional form – for either a general, infusion, immersion or mixed approach (see below). This choice refers back to a discussion that is noticeable in the literature about whether the skills and dispositions required for critical thinking are generalizable across domains and fields. In other words, whether a legal professional who has developed skills and a fitting attitude for critical thinking within the domain of law is also able to utilize those skills in other domains, such as medicine, social sciences, economics, or philosophy. This is particularly relevant for the contemporary complex legal practice and civic life, in which the individual is required to understand and take a position in complex matters that transcend the legal domain. In this discussion, there are so-called specialists – also known as specifists – who argue that the skills and/or dispositions are domain specific and cannot be transferred across domains, and generalists. The latter group mainly holds that the skills and dispositions can be transferred across domains. Ennis can be regarded as a generalist.[251] A generalist would advocate that it is possible to teach critical thinking in generic courses that, for instance, solely focus on technical reasoning which includes argumentation structures, common fallacies, etc.[252] Paul and Scriver argue that, in principle, critical thinking *as a concept* is based on intellectual values such as clarity, consistency, fairness, accuracy, sound evidence and good reasons, which are not domain or subject specific.[253] However, employing critical thinking within a certain context – for example, in the legal context – demands domain specific knowledge.[254] This is also asserted by 'specifist' McPeck, who states that critical thinking is all about *thinking* and when a person thinks, they think about something specific.[255] Consequently, theorists who choose McPeck's line of thought argue that teaching critical thinking cannot be done without the context of a subject, field of domain.[256] To explain, to be able to critically assess, in other words 'to think about', legal reasoning, one is required to have knowledge of the law. There

251 Robinson 2011, p. 276. See also: Mason 2007, p. 341. See also: Gunawardena & Wilson 2021, p. 2.
252 See McPeck 1981, p. 14.
253 Mulnix 2012, p. 465. See also: www.criticalthinking.org/pages/defining-critical-thinking/766, last visited September 29th, 2021.
254 Facione 1990 p. 5.
255 McPeck 1981, pp. 3, 5.
256 McPeck 1990, p. 32. See also: Thayer-Bacon 2000, p. 57. See also Robinson 2011, p. 277 and Mason 2007, p. 340.

are also critical thinking theorists who seem to bridge the gap between the generalist and specialist view. Siegel, for example, is mainly a generalist, but differentiates between two components. While following Ennis on this issue with regard to the teachability of critical thinking, Siegel argues that *reason assessment* – which is part of critical thinking skills/abilities – is to a large extent generalizable, which means that it is not subject-specific. Of course, one needs to understand a particular domain or field in order to assess reasoning *within* that field, but the skills required for doing so, can be transferred to other domains as well.[257] With regard to the *critical spirit* – which is part of critical thinking dispositions – Siegel holds that these habits of mind, character traits and dispositions are completely transferrable to other fields: Once an individual has developed a critical spirit, they are able to use that spirit within any domain.[258] Mulnix seems to agree that critical thinking ability is partly generalizable, since she finds that although critical thinking depends on knowledge bound to specific domains, the skills necessary for critical thinking in one domain are the same as those needed in another. Especially the skill to recognize inferential relations – which Mulnix sees as the core of critical thinking – is transferrable across domains.[259] The dichotomy of viewpoints (generalists v. specifists) could be solved in two ways. The first places a 'relativist' position in between generalists and specifists, which holds that students can use their critical thinking *across* disciplines, but only *after* learning to be critical thinkers *within* a specific domain.[260] In other words, law students have to learn critical thinking skills and abilities within the legal domain and only after doing so, will they be able to employ their critical thinking abilities and dispositions in other domains such as economics, psychology or medicine. This relativist position can be recognized in Siegel's and Mulnix' approaches. The second way of bridging the gap between generalists and specifists calls for an 'infusion' between the generalists and specifists and sees the two standpoints as complementing instead of adversaries. Here, critical thinking is taught generically in the context of various disciplines.[261]

Based on these viewpoints, various educationalists gather that there are four approaches through which critical thinking can be taught in schools, universities and law schools, namely: the generic, infusion, immersion, or mixed approach.[262] The *general* approach entails teaching knowledge about critical thinking, critical thinking skills and dispositions in separate courses that aim at developing critical thinking. Because critical thinking is thought to be general and transferrable across disciplines, these courses would be the same for all students: It is irrelevant if they study law, criminology, medicine, philosophy

257 Siegel 1991, pp. 19, 23, 24.
258 Siegel 1991, p. 26.
259 Mulnix 2012, p. 470.
260 Robinson 2011, p. 277.
261 See: Robinson on Davies' infusion approach. Robinson 2011, p. 277.
262 Abrami et al. 2015, p. 281, Belaera et al. 2021, p. 2, Ennis 1989, p. 4.

or any other discipline. In an *infusion* approach, however, the disciplinary content *is* relevant: While studying legal subject matter, for example family law, students develop their critical thinking. Courses embracing this approach explicitly include critical thinking in their learning goals, and critical thinking is instructed explicitly in the context of the legal content. Conversely, this is not the case in the *immersion* approach. Here, the disciplinary content is important, and critical thinking is taught only implicitly in its context. This means that critical thinking is not explicitly instructed, nor is it part of the course's learning goals. Finally, the *mixed* approach combines the other three approaches: It entails teaching critical thinking separately in one or more general courses *and* teaching critical thinking either explicitly (infusion) or implicitly (immersion) in the context of subject matter during, for example, black letter law or jurisprudence courses.[263]

I argue that for ALE, it is most helpful to teach students critical thinking skills and dispositions in the context of legal content. Our students are often passionate about the law and about society, so their enthusiasm and engagement in these content related issues will support their engagement in and understanding of the components of critical thinking. At the same time, in order for them to truly *understand* what they are expected to do while thinking critically, students require knowledge of what critical thinking is[264] and need to be aware of the mental processes that critical thinking encompasses.[265] Consequently, I propose to include critical thinking awareness and training *in* legal courses, be it black letter law or jurisprudence courses, instead of teaching critical thinking in one or two separate courses that exclusively deal with 'critical thinking'. Additionally, since research shows that – although many educators opt for teaching critical thinking implicitly – it is best instructed explicitly through the *infusion* approach,[266] it is recommended to *explicitly* teach law students critical thinking in the context of legal subject matter and to include critical thinking in the learning goals of legal courses. This way, legal educators support their students' awareness and knowledge about what critical thinking *is* and help them train critical thinking skills and dispositions, in other words, the Critical Thinking Relevant Processes. This also gives students agency over their own learning process. It is therefore important that within legal courses, time is reserved for explaining and practicing critical thinking and for giving feedback on a student's critical thinking. Ideally, time could also be made for reading literature on critical thinking.[267]

263 Ennis 1989, pp. 4-5, Belaera et al. 2021, p. 2 and Abrami et al. 2015, pp. 281-282.

264 This requires knowledge of critical thinking theory, such as being aware of which types of fallacies may be apparent in reasoning. See Mulnix 2012, p. 475.

265 Mulnix 2012, p. 474.

266 Belaera et al. 2021, p. 10.

267 For example, literature that includes information on what critical thinking consists of, but also practical information and tools for reasoning, inference making, argumentation and recognizing or avoiding fallacies. See for example: Foresman, Fosl and Watson's *Critical thinking toolkit* (Foresman, Fosl & Watson 2017).

This implies that the critical thinking skills and dispositions that are part of a course's learning goals and that students have practiced with, need to be assessed.

Finally, to place emphasis on critical thinking in ALE, it could be helpful to use our language in a supportive way. According to Adriansen, educators – and students – in academic education should be more aware of the words they use, since the vocabulary that is used to describe the practices in the institution show its inclination. We might start a change in the way students regard critical thinking and their attitude towards their studies by consciously using language. For example, we could speak of the importance of learning to 'think like a lawyer' and immediately communicate that this important attribute of legal professionals actually includes a form of critical thinking,[268] since it is critical thinking applied to legal problems, which requires seeing things in perspective and solving real (legal) problems.[269]

No. 10 – Aim to develop the faculty of judgment

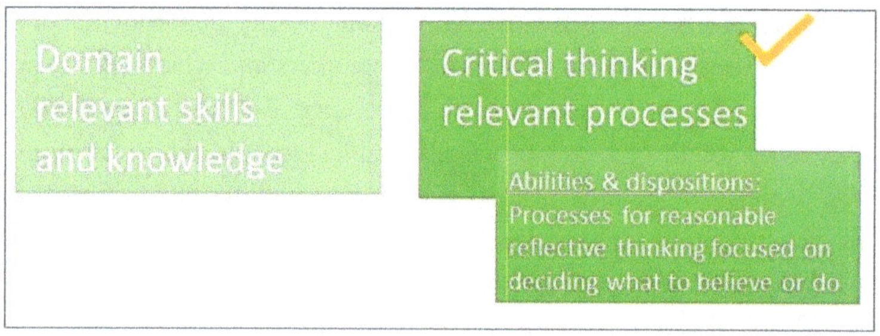

The tenth and final suggestion for incorporating critical thinking into ALE is to aim at developing the students' faculty of judgment. The critical thinking process is aimed at deciding what to believe or do.[270] Consequently, critical thinking is aimed at making a decision or judgment. It involves the ability to extract inferences (that hold between statements) from relevant information and base reasoned conclusions on these inferences. The critical thinker needs to provide an argumentation for their conclusion and is required to see through the flawed argumentations of others. Sometimes, making a judgment entails having the courage to go against the tide. As shown in this chapter, in order to be able to make such a judgment, the critical thinker requires Domain Relevant Skills and Critical Thinking Relevant Processes. The development of these components of critical

268 Holley & Ogilvy 1994, p. 343. See also Mudd 1983, p. 709.
269 Mudd 1983, pp.709-710.
270 See Ennis 1991, p. 7. Importantly, judging what to believe or do does not require the actual *doing*. This is part of *taking responsibility* and, therefore, falls under the scope of another element of *Bildung*: ACT responsibility (see chapter 5).

thinking is therefore paramount in legal education and educators in legal education can contribute to this by aiming at developing their students' faculty of judgment.

In accordance with Ennis's definition, Bailin and Battersby define critical thinking as the making of reasoned judgments. They describe that the critical thinker arrives at reasoned judgments through a dialectical process that involves comparing and weighing various positions and arguments that contend witheach other.[271] According to these authors, this might be practiced in educational settings through a community of inquiry, where reasons and arguments are exchanged. This exchange can be made even more worthwhile by challenging students to take on various roles, enabling them to view topics from multiple perspectives.[272] This kind of learning requires active students and student interaction and this can be stimulated by authentic/anchored instruction.[273] Bailin and Battersby suggest that educators can foster such a community of inquiry by modeling the expected attitudes and dispositions – in the words of these authors, 'virtues' – and by communicating explicit expectations between students and between educators and students.[274]

De Vries argues that playing an active part in the practice of law implies making decisions.[275] Indeed, not only judges, but also lawyers, public servants, tax advisors, notaries and legal academics regularly make judgments. In many of these cases where a decision has to be made, something is at stake. According to De Vries, students need to be able to deal with this reality of legal professionals.[276] It is therefore not surprising that Van Klink and De Vries advocate that the ultimate goal of legal education is to develop students' intellectual integrity to use their own faculty of judgment.[277] Van Klink's skeptical legal education aims for students to develop their faculty of judgment, which entails that students learn to make their own assessments of information. This assessment involves knowledge of how to interpret facts and rules (information); how to assess the information's relevance, and; the ability to understand which rules apply in specific situations and how to carry out the applicable rules.[278] Van Klink proposes to teach law students critical thinking through discussion and reflection, during which the students question the beliefs

271 Bailin & Battersby 2009, p. 1.
272 Bailin & Battersby 2015, pp. 371. Developing students' ability to approach topics from multiple perspectives is seen as crucial for critical thinking by other academics as well, such as Bal Sokhi-Bulley (See Sokhi-Bulley 2016, pp. 138-139).
273 Bailin & Battersby 2015, pp. 367, 371.
274 Bailin & Battersby 2015, pp. 371.
275 De Vries 2021, p. 89.
276 De Vries 2021, p. 89.
277 Van Klink & De Vries 2013, p. 42.
278 Van Klink 2016, pp. 19-20.

of the domain of law.[279] In other words, the students are invited to join in the conversation of the legal domain by critical questioning.

De Vries asserts that legal education should involve teaching students legal consciousness, which includes supporting the development of students' ability to make judgments, form opinions, take positions and to have courage.[280] Importantly, De Vries argues that decision making (coming to judgments) is not limited to applying rules to facts, but involves rational and moral reasoning.[281] With regard to the latter, the teaching of normative evaluation based either on ideas stemming from legal theory or an exploration of the moral basics of the law becomes part of legal education. In both instances, moral reasoning takes place within the boundaries of the legal domain: Students argue and decide based on perspectives on morality that form the foundation of law. In the end, students judge the morality of law based on perspectives from legal theory, since they understand how to interpret and use specific (legal) yardsticks, such as the rule of law, democracy of equality,[282] that are used when deciding what to do or believe in the context of law.

Nevertheless, if ALE aims not only at supporting the development of legal professionals, but also at the development of human beings able to contribute in contemporary society, our students are in need of developing the ability to think critically about themselves and their own values, since this supports their ACT responsibility (see chapter 5). This means that critical thinking transcends the domain of law. Only then are students able to develop personal, examined standards that function as their personal yardsticks when judging their own and another's choices, beliefs and values. To do so, students have to ask questions such as 'who am I?' and 'what do I find important as a human being, a citizen and legal academic?'. Searching for answers to these kind of questions is part of personal development and therefore part of *Bildung* and ACT responsibility. Moreover, it seems than the complexity of issues that legal professionals encounter – in which legal questions are intertwined with other complications, such as social, financial or medical issues – legal professionals are in need of broader standards to judge by than solely legal ones. Sometimes, well thought through personal standards could in these complex situations provide helpful decisions and answers. The Value and Knowledge education methodology (*Va*KE)[283] could provide some guidelines in the legal educator's endeavor to support their students' moral reasoning and value judging.

279 Van Klink 2016, pp. 30-32.
280 De Vries 2021, pp. 79-80.
281 De Vries 2021, pp. 80-81.
282 Van Klink & Francot 2018, p. 3.
283 See: Pnevmatikos, Christodoulou & Georgiadou 2019, p. 900.

This chapter aimed at exploring the concept of critical thinking as a part of contemporary *Bildung*. I started with an examination of the value and aim of critical thinking. This was followed by the search for a definition of critical thinking that could be helpful for educators in ALE. With Ennis's definition '*reasonable reflective thinking that is focused on deciding what to do or believe*' as a starting point, the critical thinking process and the necessary skills and abilities were mapped out. Based on these insights, the chapter proposed an initial model for incorporating critical thinking into ALE and provided ten suggestions for critical thinking in legal education. An exploration of each of the ten suggestions concluded this chapter. In the following chapter, the journey to understand what contemporary *Bildung* constists of continues with an exploration of the second element of *Bildung*, namely creative thinking.

4 The Spark of Creation. Teaching Creative Thinking in Academic Legal Education

"I am certain of nothing
but the holiness of the heart's affections,
and the truth of the Imagination."
- *John Keats*

Introduction

The previous chapter focused on the development of critical thinking, which is a rational and reasonable endeavor. Nevertheless, Keats's words remind us of the importance of sense and imagination for contemporary *Bildung* (see Chapter 2). Hence, in this chapter I suggest creative thinking - which requires sensibility and imagination - as a strategy for law students to manage uncertainty and to ultimately define and actively take their responsibility during their studies and in their future lives as global citizens. Consequently, this chapter explores how creativity and creative thinking may be taught in academic legal education (ALE) as a part of a student's personal development and *Bildung*. As has been noticed earlier in this research, managing uncertainty has become one of the most important skills needed in the 21st century.[1] For several reasons, creative thinking might be helpful and be a valuable addition to an individual's toolbox for managing uncertainty. First, creative thinking allows for seeing possibilities and opportunities. Individuals make choices based on the expected consequences. On the one hand, there are undesirable consequences, namely *risks*, which may evoke fear. On the other hand, there are desirable consequences, *opportunities* or *possibilities*, which trigger emotions such as excitement and enjoyment. Since fear may paralyze, it is often not a suitable advisor in moments of necessary choice and action. Seeing opportunities and possibilities alongside (and, in some cases, even instead of) the risk may support a person's choice-making ability as it helps with the selection between choice options and supports their ability to manage uncertainty. Furthermore, if there potentially are undesirable outcomes, a creative person is able think of possible solutions to counter those risks. Secondly, creative thinking

1 See Geldof 2011, pp. 18-19. See also: Nowotny 2016, p. xiii.

enables individuals to manage uncertainty, because the creative thought process itself is driven by a sense of curiosity with regard to the unknown. Since nothing embodies the unknown better than a state of uncertainty, creativity often thrives in uncertain times.[2] This is the case because everyday creativity highlights individual agency,[3] but also because creators shape the world[4] by addressing problems causing uncertainty by creating novel and valuable ideas or products that offer (temporary) reprieve from the unknown.[5] Also, similar to the critical thinking process, uncertainty has a central place in the creative thinking process. Creative thinking skills therefore enable a person to bear uncertainty, since they have become familiar with its presence. Consequently, teaching creative thinking in ALE could be a way to empower law students and to build their self-confidence in facing uncertainty.[6] The necessity for the improvement of law students' ability to cope with uncertainty during their academic education is highlighted by the alarming reports on the stress and pressure students experience.[7] The stress that students experience is

---

2 Nowotny 2016, p. vii. See also: Csikszentmihalyi 2013, p. 11.

3 Craft 2001, p. 54.

4 Jackson 2010, p. xii.

5 Nowotny argues that innovation (which is brought on by creativity) has become the focus of contemporary society in order to cope with the uncertainty of the future. See Nowotny 2016, p. 137.

6 See: Geldof 2011, p. 18. See on individual empowerment through creativity: Cropley 2001, pp. 1, 158. Jeffrey and Craft 2001, p. 6.

7 Stress can be seen as a symptom of the sense of uncertainty and is experienced when someone has the perception that a situation exceeds his or her personal resources to deal with issues (see Chacón-Cuberos et al. 2019, p. 2. See also Nowotny, who states that the balance between people's capabilities and the challenges they face conditions their well-being. Nowotny 2016, p. xiii). Whereas a certain amount of stress may have positive, stimulating effects, higher amounts can result in problems (see: Goldman & Wong 1997, p. 604). Unfortunately, stress-related problems are increasingly common in our students' lives. See for Dutch examples: https://www.nrc.nl/nieuws/2018/01/26/werkdruk-docent-en-student-enorm-a1590002 (2018) (last accessed 14 June 2018); https://www.rtlnieuws.nl/editienl/driekwartvan-studenten-is-uitgeput-aan-alle-kanten-werd-aan-me-getrokken (2017) (last accessed 13 June 2018); http://www.hogeronderwijs.nu/2014/04/steeds-meer-studenten-in-de-stress/ (2014) (last accessed 13 June 2018) and https://lsvb.nl/2013/03/29/psychische-klachten-bij-helft-studenten/ (2013) (last accessed 13 June 2018). Stress in the lives of university students, however, is not only a problem in the Netherlands, see for example https://adaa.org/finding-help/helping-others/college-students/facts (U.S.), https://www.spiegel.de/lebenundlernen/uni/stress-und-depression-im-studium-wo-studenten-hilfe-finden-a-1138904.html (Germany). Although data preceding 2019 showed that students already often experienced stress, the global health covid-19 crisis during 2020 and 2021 seems to have increased these problems. According to Dutch research called the 'Student Monitor' in 2021, 51% of the students in the Netherlands suffer from psychological symptoms because of stress such as emotional exhaustion. 12% of these students report that their symptoms are severe. 25% of the students report that they have had some kind of death wish or wanted to go to sleep and not wake up in the four weeks prior to the questionnaire. 80% of the responding students say that they experience loneliness (See: RIVM, Trimbos-instituut and GGD GHOR Nederland (2022), *Monitor Mentale gezondheid en Middelengebruik Studenten hoger onderwijs 2021. Deelrapport I. Mentale gezondheid van studenten in het hoger onderwijs*, pp. 12, 14. Available at: https://www.trimbos.nl/wp-content/uploads/2022/07/AF1955-Monitor-Studenten-Deelrapport-1-Mentale-gezondheid.pdf, Last visited November 27th 2022). For the international context, see, for example, www.bu.edu/articles/2022/mental-health-of-college-students-is-getting-worse/, last visited November 27th 2022.

reason for worry – and action – since the experience of *too much* stress may have severe physical and psychological consequences, such as reduced immune system functioning (resulting in health complaints), concentration problems, and diminished learning and memory functions.[8]

In the previous chapter, I proposed strengthening the focus on teaching critical thinking skills in legal education to support our students' and the future academically educated legal professional's ability to cope with uncertainty. This chapter adds that teaching creative thinking in legal education may enable our students to manage uncertainty and define and take their responsibility in contemporary life. How does creative thinking relate to critical thinking and what does creative ability add to critical thinking ability? Critical thinking and creative thinking are both processes of higher order thinking and, together, enable a person to seek solutions to identified problems. In both processes of thought uncertainty and doubt are a central presence. Moreover, the thinking processes share the necessity of abilities such as being open-minded, curious, skeptical, delaying judgment and asking questions. However, as seen in the third chapter, *critical thinking* aims at making decisions about what to do or believe in order for a person to become a self-authored thinker capable of shaping their own examined life. Furthermore, critical thinking is committed to reason and can be depicted as a linear, evaluative and selective process within a framework in which one deconstructs and works systematically.[9] In contrast, *creative thinking* is generally depicted as a process that transcends the framework: It can be described as imaginative, open to possibilities, generative, holistic, constructive, and open to serendipity.[10] When talking about being creative or thinking creatively, many characteristics and abilities come to mind. For example, *academics* describe creative thinking as being imaginative, original, curious and resourceful; able to make connections and able to make new combinations of incomplete data to view the world differently; able to value and employ feedback constructively; and able to represent and communicate ideas.[11] These creative attributes may contribute to the student's ability

8 Shaw, Peart & Fairhead 2017, pp. 442-443. See also: Pierceall & Keim 2007, p. 704.

9 See: Adriansen 2010, p. 69.

10 See: Adriansen 2010, p. 69. Critical thinking and creative thinking are not completely separate as being creative requires the ability to think critically, for example when identifying problems and when validating generated ideas. See Amabile 1996, pp. 94, 96.

11 Jackson specifically asked *academics* about their ideas on 'creativity' and creative people. See Jackson 2010, pp. xi-xii. This resonates with general descriptions of creativity and creative thinking, that agree that creative people view the world differently, are highly motivated, independent (non-conformists) and flexible, question assumptions and are able to experiment while bearing uncertainty and risk, see Cropley 2001, p. 60 and Lucas 2001, p. 38. Other traits that Dellas and Gaier linked to creative individuals in their research in 1970 were, for example, dominance, introversion, openness to stimuli, wide interests, self-acceptance, intuitiveness, social presence and poise, asocial attitude, concern for social norms, radicalism and rejection of external constraints. See Eysenck 2001, p. 212. In addition, creative people are said to prefer complexity to simplicity. See Eysenck 2001, p. 216.

to manage uncertainty and define and take their own responsibility in contemporary society.

This is the reason why not only critical thinking but also creative thinking skills are the distinguishing ability of contemporary academically educated legal professionals. However, currently, *critical thinking* – and not creative thinking – is often the main focus of the thinking skills that are taught in ALE.[12] Indeed, even though critical thinking could be further incorporated in legal education, it does gain more attention than creative thinking does. Critical thinking is also the skillset that academics name as the distinguishing element between an academic legal education and a vocational legal education.[13] Nevertheless, critical thinking and creative thinking complement one another: Both play their part in purposeful and effective thinking;[14] creative thinking requires critical thinking, and both thinking processes are needed for a person to take responsibility in contemporary life. I therefore advocate an academic legal education in which students are educated in both critical thinking and creative thinking.

Even though legal professionals may traditionally not be the first professional group that comes to mind when talking about creative thinking,[15] many lawyers are in dire need of creativity skills.[16] For example, legal professionals, such as lawyers or judges, need creative thinking skills when they try to solve multifaceted legal cases that concern people with complex issues in which, for instance, psychological, social and economic problems are intertwined with legal problems. Also, contemporary academically educated legal professionals are required to be able to go *beyond* their legal training and legal expertise, since other resources and parties (for example online legal databases, YouTube channels or even online legal advisers) provide traditional legal services to potential clients, such as explaining legal information and offering advice on legal matters. Therefore, new clients come to lawyers for *additional* or specialized advice, ideas and service. To be able to offer this, legal professionals will require creative thinking skills. Furthermore, in their professional capacity, a number of legal professionals face complex worldwide problems that transcend the legal domain, such as global health issues, refugee crises and environmental issues, that demand creative thinking skills. While attributing possible solutions to these problems, academically educated legal professionals help shape society

12 See: Adriansen 2010, p. 65.

13 Van Klink 2016, p. 15.

14 Paul & Elder 2019, pp. 5-7. Bailin 1987, pp. 23, 27.

15 Creativity is traditionally not advertised as a key characteristic of lawyers, who are probably more often seen as rule followers, risk-averse or skeptical. Nevertheless, there are customary activities of legal professionals that most definitely need a level of creativity, for example interpreting legal provisions in new ways and thinking of an original argument to win a case.

16 For instance, skills such as problem finding, problem solving, divergent thinking and collaborating. See on the needs in the legal field also DeStefano, M., *Legal Upheaval. A Guide To Creativity, Collaboration and Innovation in Law*, American Bar Association 2018.

through the (co-)*creation* of products such as legal judgments, legal provisions, (international) treaties and (international) contracts and, by doing so, provide legal certainty.[17] This requires them to deal with the complexity of these issues. For the aforementioned tasks, creative thinking is essential. Remarkably, the interest in creativity in law and legal education is not new: Fifty years ago, Yeamans asserted that creativity separates the *competent tradesman* from the *great lawyer*.[18] I argue that the 'great lawyer' of our time is a global citizen accomplished in the domain of law, who has an understanding of other domains, is capable of critical and creative thinking, and is capable of ACT responsibility, which enables them to make choices regarding their own responsibility and take actions accordingly. These great lawyers are able to deal with uncertainty and are capable of thinking of solutions that transcend the legal domain, and may offer new perspectives.

Creative thinking is therefore a necessary skill of the great lawyer in the 21st century. In addition, creative thinking is an important part of the *academic* attitude and skill that is closely connected to distinctive academic behavior, knowledge and skills. Abilities needed for creative thinking are also closely connected to abilities related to the educational notion of *Bildung*. To illustrate, creativity and creative thinking require both deep *and* broad knowledge and include skills such as problem finding and problem solving, critical thinking, autonomous (independent/self-authored) thinking, reflective doubt, and convergent and divergent thinking.[19] Subsequently, I argue that creative thinking ought to be taught explicitly in ALE. It enables students to become *academics* able to cope with uncertainty. In short, students trained in creative thinking will be better equipped to pinpoint problems and offer solutions in the conditions of contemporary society.

This chapter seeks an answer to the main question how educators in ALE can support the development of their students' creativity and creative thinking ability. To answer this question, various sub questions will come to the fore, such as: What are creativity and creative thinking? how does the creative thinking process work?, and how can we incorporate a focus on creative thinking into our law faculties, curricula and teaching in ALE? To answer these questions, the chapter first explores the theory of what creativity and creative thinking are. In this first part of the chapter, the history of creativity research and the definitions of creativity and creative thinking will be mapped out. Secondly, this chapter focuses on the creative process, with particular attention to research conducted by

17 See for further reading: Francot 2017, p. 98.

18 Yeamans 1971, p. 381.

19 Convergent thinking involves correctness, accuracy and speed, whereas divergent thinking sees to transformation, shifting perspective, seeing possibilities and finding multiple answers based on the same information. See Cropley 2001, pp. 1-2, 5. Furthermore, convergent thinking is explained in Albergaria Ameida, Teixeira-Dias & Medina 2010 (p. 88) as analytical, focused, judgmental, and detailed thinking, whereas divergent thinking is described as 'perceptual, imaginative, diffuse, free-flowing and associated'.

Teresa Amabile on this topic. While discovering the steps and conditions of the creative process, the way in which these theoretic concepts can be applied in the everyday practice of ALE will be examined. Thirdly, this chapter presents a model to explicitly create space for teaching creative thinking and creativity in ALE. This model has a similar structure to the model on incorporating critical thinking (chapter 3) and provides a total of eleven practical suggestions on the levels of (1) the learning culture and environment; (2) curriculum design; (3) course design, and; (4) teaching method and teaching style. The final part of the chapter elaborates on the practical suggestions that are provided to support and inspire educators in ALE.

CREATIVITY & CREATIVE THINKING

A short history of creativity

Creative thinking is the driving force of the creative process, which leads to creative *performance*, the generation of creative ideas or products.[20] It is therefore intimately linked to creativity. Whereas international scientific research on creativity in the field of psychology has been conducted since 1869,[21] philosophical interest in the concept of creativity has a much longer history and can be traced back to ancient Greece. From the classical antiquity throughout the Middle Ages and Renaissance, the predominant belief was that no human idea is ever truly new, since an external, higher power (for example a muse or a god) is believed to have given the idea to the human artist.[22] In contrast, from the late 18th century Romantic era onwards, creativity came to be understood as an *internal*

---

20 The difference between creative performance and creative thinking is that creative performance is observable and has measurable results, while creative thinking is not easily observable nor measurable, unless you measure the result. In that case one measures the performance that results from the act of creative thinking. See Baer and Kaufman 2012, p. 70. Asking someone to give a reflection on their mental process during a creative endeavor could be a way of 'visualizing' creative thinking.

21 See: Kekang 2017, p. 29.

22 For example, to indicate the process of getting an idea, Plato used the denominator 'inspiration'. This term shows the belief that human ideas are the result of divine inspiration or even divine possession of the human being. The experience of inspiration was seen as a holy one that was 'out of the senses', meaning that it was not physically experienced. It could be seen as a form of (temporary) mental madness. Plato (through the character of Socrates) explains inspiration in the Ion (See Plato, *Ion*, p. 10). Rothenberg & Hausman, pp. 31-33. See also Ryhammar & Brolin 1999, p. 260. See also Boden 1994, p. 1. This explanation of the birth of new ideas as an *external* process has existed over an extended period of time and is, for instance, noticeable in the Greek, Roman, and Christian traditions. Interestingly, contrary opinions were also apparent, for example, Aristotle did not view creativity as having a mysterious origin, but as a process linked to natural laws. See Rothenberg & Hausman 1976, p. 33. However, throughout the Middle Ages and the Renaissance, the 'external' idea of inspiration and creativity remained. See: Ryhammar & Brolin 1999, pp. 260-261. The belief that an idea is given by an external source may still be relevant today and is recognizable in, for example, art forms, such as the well-known song 'Inspiratie' (*inspiration*), sung by

human ability and attitude. During this time – in which the concept of *Bildung* also gained popularity – the senses, feeling and originality became important aspects of the individual's self-development. Creativity was seen as the capacity of the lone individual genius, who – unconstrained by their environment – *creates* ideas and works in a spontaneous process ruled by the senses. This view remained during the 19th century in which interest in creativity blossomed in the fields of psychology and educational studies.[23] In the 20th century, this curiosity remained and the scientific research into creativity gained momentum. Creativity expanded its relevance from the arts and aesthetics to the natural sciences and mathematics.[24] Interestingly, the scholarly work on the philosophy of creativity diminished in these times.[25] During the 20th century, the understanding that creativity stems from the *giftedness* of a specific individual,[26] slowly altered into a 'universalization' of creativity. Now, most theorists hold the opinion that every person has the ability to be creative to some degree in one or more domains and that creativity is a mindset and skill that can be trained.[27] This means that a person's creativity can be increased to some extent.[28] For educators, this implies that the creativity of students can be influenced and improved through careful guidance.

Mathilde Santing, in the Dutch-spoken musical 'Joe' with music and lyrics by Koen van Dijk and Ad van Dijk.

23 Ryhammar & Brolin 1999, pp. 260-261. See also Runco 2014, p. 326. See also Cropley 2004, p. 1. Very well-known is the research in creativity by Ellis Paul Torrance, who is sometimes referred to as the father of modern descriptions of creativity, since he developed the Torrance Tests of Creative Thinking in 1966. These tests are still relevant in the US for testing creativity. See Smith & Smith 2010, p. 252.

24 From the early 1950's renewed attention was given to creativity, starting with The Presidential Address of Guildford to the American Psychology Association in 1950. By most, this is seen as the landmark event that signaled the start of modern research on creativity. See Smith & Smith 2010, p. 252. Crucial in the development of theories, studies and policy on creativity was the launch of the first space satellite by the Russians in 1957, Sputnik. Although US scientists thought of Russian scientists as inferior, they still lost this first part of the Space Race. The reason given for this US failure was the absence of creativity and this was a problem in dire need of solving. In his speech, Guilford called for divergent thinking in addition to convergent thinking. The latter is important for intellectual ability, since is focuses on correctness, accuracy and speed. However, Guilford found that divergent thinking – which sees to transforming, shifting perspective, seeing possibilities and finding multiple answers based on the same information and the production of novelty – is also of the highest importance. Consequently, more emphasis was given to creativity in education. See Cropley 2001, pp. 1-2, 5.

25 Gaut argues that, during the second half of the 20th century (from the 1950s to 2000), there was little research conducted in the field of philosophy of creativity. See Gaut 2010, p. 1034.

26 See Craft 2001-A, p. 6. See also Jeffrey and Craft 2001, p. 1.

27 See Jeffrey and Craft 2001.

28 Amabile 1996, p. 82. See also Amabile 1983, p. 361. Even though someone's innate abilities in a domain are of importance for the level of creativity that can be achieved, it is possible to improve to some degree. According to Amabile, this improvement of their creativity is possible through independent playing with the domain or through guided formal or informal apprenticeship. See also on the possibility of developing creative ability De Bono 1992, pp. 30-31.

Defining creativity and creative thinking

The long history and the broad usage of the term *creativity* makes giving just one all-encompassing definition of the concept challenging.[29] In social psychology, many abilities and personality characteristics are attributed to creative individuals, some of which have already been mentioned in the introduction to this chapter. In addition to such personality traits, creative people need an eagerness to work diligently, the ability for deep involvement, freedom from external constraints and intellectual playfulness.[30] Thus, many things can be said about what creativity is and every scholar seems to have their own specification. However, there seems to be an overall agreement in the current descriptions of creativity that it is a *human* endeavor[31] which can take place in any domain[32] and involves the generation of something *novel* that has *value*.[33] Creative thinking is described in virtually the same way as creativity.[34] In the words of Lucas, creativity is not just an ability, but a *state of mind*.[35] This point of view seems to be shared by Craft, who explains that the core of everyday creativity is *possibility thinking*, which is central to an individual's adaptability

---

29 Various disciplines use their own term to explain the concept. For example, business economics speaks of entrepreneurship, while sociology uses the word innovation and psychology and pedagogics speak of creativity. See Ryhammar & Brolin 1999, p. 260.

30 Amabile 1996, pp. 82-83, 101-102. See also Amabile 1983, p. 362.

31 Creativity and creative thinking are both concepts in the human domain. A drawing made by a self-learning computer/AI, for example, is usually not considered a *creative* product. Many consider this denominator to be exclusive to *human* ideas and *human* products. Cropley described this standpoint as the view in which 'creative thinking is a bastion of human dignity'. In these times of increasing technologization and development of artificial intelligence, it might be one of the last domains exclusively reserved for humans. See Cropley 2008, p. 5.

32 The three characteristics (novelty, value and ethicality) of creativity concern the *artistic* creativity shown by, for example, painters, sculptors and composers, as well as the *scientific* creativity that natural scientists and philosophers show. Importantly, this means that creativity is not solely an attitude and skill reserved for artists, but also for other people tasked with creating something novel that is of value.

33 According to Ryhammar and Brolin, there seems to be general consensus on defining creativity as "a person's ability to produce new or original ideas, insights, restructurings, inventions, or artistic objects, which are accepted by experts as being of scientific, aesthetical, social, or technological value", see Ryhammar & Brolin 1999, p. 260. Generating novelty is often understood as creating something new (an idea or product) through synthesizing existing ideas. See Lucas 2001, p. 38, Kozbeld, Beghetto & Runco 2010 on research by Mednick (1962), p. 32, Adair, pp. 6-7, Boden 2001, p. 96, Welling 2007, p. 164. By 'value' can be understood that it has a use, of which the novelty is appropriate, for instance to solve the problem. See, for instance, Beghetto 2009, p. 2, Cropley 2001, p. 6 and Jahnke, Haertel & Wildt 2017, p. 88. See also De Bono 2007, p. 5 and Welling 2007, p. 164.

34 For example, Weinstein and Morton define creative thinking as *'the generation of ideas that are 1) unusual or original and 2) that have some standard of value'* (see Weinstein & Morton 2003, pp. 837-838), which is intimately linked to how creativity is defined by Amabile, namely *'the production of responses or works that are reliably assessed as creative by appropriate judges'* (see: Amabile). The connection between creative thinking and creativity is also stressed by Kekang, who considers creative thinking the core of the creative mind. See Kekang 2017, p. 29.

35 Which involves seeing, thinking and innovating, see Lucas 2001, p. 38.

and flexibility.[36] If we wish to *explicitly* embrace creativity in the curricula of law schools, this state of mind of possibility thinking should be fostered.

According to, for example, Kaufman and Beghetto, Craft, Cropley and Amabile,[37] there exists a continuum of creativity levels, from lower to higher levels of creativity.[38] An individual's level of creativity in any domain starts with the lowest level and may progress to the higher levels. In the light of this continuum, it is important to note that legal education does not have to train students predominantly for the highest level of creative thinking. In other words, not all law students need to be taught how to create 'Big-C'. Big-C creativity (or: sublime-C) is only attainable for great inventors and alters the set of symbolic rules and procedures of an existing knowledge domain, such as law. Added to that, for it to be called big-C creativity, the field (the group of peers working in the domain) needs to embrace the innovation as valuable for the domain.[39] Because it is not necessary to create on the level of big-C in order to be able to thrive in the uncertain circumstances of contemporary life, it seems not essential to focus on reaching big-C during an academic education in law. Also, it is not reasonable to attempt to train all students towards big-C when there are only so few individuals truly able to be successful in achieving greatness and legendary status in any domain, including law.

36 This 'possibility thinking' may be seen as an ability as well as a state of mind. Craft, pp. 49, 54. Liu and Noppe-Brandon also pose possibility thinking as a crucial ability. See Liu & Noppe-Brandon 2009.

37 Kaufman and Beghetto 2009. Cropley 2008, p. 10. Amabile 1996, p. 82. See also Amabile 1983, p. 361. Craft 2001, p. 46.

38 It is assumed that every individual with normal cognitive abilities can be creative to some degree on this scale of creativity, see Amabile 1996, p. 82. Individuals may function on various creativity levels in different domains (Amabile 1996, p. 82) For example, someone might be able to reach pro-C level in law, but will remain at little-C level in the domains of music and baking.

39 Csikszentmihalyi 2013, pp. 27-28. Kaufman & Beghetto 2009, p. 2. Big-C's impact on the domain is lasting and will often still be marveled at after the inventor's death, it becomes legendary, see Kaufman & Beghetto 2009, pp. 2, 8. Individuals that achieved big-C are, for instance, Einstein, Freud, Bach and Mozart. In the domain of law, one might think of Grotius (Hugo de Groot, 1583-1645), Willem Pompe (Dutch expert in criminal law, 1893-1968) or Ruth Bader Ginsberg (justice of the supreme court of the United States 1993-2020). Since it not only depends on the creative work (or idea) in itself, but also on the effect and value of the idea on the domain *and* the acknowledgement of its value and novelty by the field, only a select few are able to reach the big-C level of creativity. Furthermore, achieving the level of big-C often takes time. Indeed, the acknowledgement of having created big-C might only be given post mortem, which was the case for Vincent van Gogh, whose paintings barely sold during his lifetime but are now viewed as highly creative and innovative for their time.

After ruling out big-C creativity as an objective of legal education, based on the 'Four-C model',[40] the three levels of creativity that remain are mini-C,[41] little-C and pro-C.[42] All three are of interest for ALE. Mini-C is an important part of the learning process, since it involves the discovery of something new *to the individual* that adds something to their existing knowledge.[43] In legal education, for instance, mini-C occurs when law students read literature and discover concepts that are new for their personal understanding of the domain. In contrast to the subjectivity of mini-C, in the Four-C model, little-C concerns more objective forms of creativity.[44] Little-C can be achieved by every individual and involves creative experiences and expressions that people encounter in everyday life, such as adding notes or lyrics while singing an existing pop song or walking home using a new route.[45] This is the kind of creativity that Craft refers to as *possibility thinking*, which involves having knowledge relevant to the domain; active engagement through thought or intuition and; intentional action.[46] In the past twelve years as an educator in legal education, I have seen students experience little-C: From the trio of third-year students that discovered

---

40 Traditionally, only two levels of creativity were recognized: big-C and little-C. In this dichotomy between big-C and little-C creativity, all forms of creativity that cannot be called big-C, are little-C. Therefore, this dichotomy only differentiates between creative genius on the one hand, and everything else creative on the other. This makes it impossible to differentiate between a professional composer who composes well-written and novel music pieces for a living, but does not invent valuable and lasting changes in the domain of Music, and an amateur-enthusiast who improvises quite awful songs for family and friends: They would both be creating little-C. This is why Kaufman and Beghetto argue that this dichotomy between big-C and little-C lacks essential nuance. To make it possible to point out differences in 'little-C' creativity expressions, Kaufman and Beghetto divide all levels of creativity that are not big-C into, not one, but three categories, i.e. mini-C, little-C and pro-C. See Kozbelt, Beghetto & Runco 2010, p. 23. Kaufman & Beghetto 2009, p. 3. See on the dichotomy between little-C and big-C: Csikszentmihalyi 2013 (who mainly focuses on big-C).

41 Mini-C is a category of creativity that refers to very personal forms of creativity and is defined as 'the novel and personally meaningful interpretation of experiences, actions, and events'. It is a level of creativity in which an individual experiences something that is new for them personally. Mini-C is subjective, intra-personal, and often remains unexpressed (although children are known to express their mini-C experiences, 'mixing yellow and blue crayons result in a green color!'). It is therefore more or less a mental or internal experience of something new, solely from the perspective of the individual. See Kaufman & Beghetto 2009, p. 2.

42 See Kaufman & Beghetto 2009. Since the 'Four-C model' differentiates between mini-C, little-C and pro-C *within* the original 'little-C' category, Kaufman and Beghetto stress that 'little-C' in their model is not the same as the original definition of little-C (all 'everyday creativity'). The newly added categories help to make a distinction between subjective (mini-C) and objective creativity (little-C) and between little C, highly accomplished little-C (pro-C) and big-C creativity. See Kozbelt, Beghetto & Runco 2010, p. 24.

43 Kaufman & Beghetto 2009, p. 3. Mini-C occurs, for example, when a novice painter discovers how to blend yellow and blue crayons on paper to create the color green or a child that discovers that a flute can be used not only to whistle one note, but also to whistle a tune that exists of different notes of various lengths. These illustrations show that mini-C is a subjective and very personal category of creativity.

44 The novelty of the experience is not solely internal and therefore subjective to the individual. For instance, little-C will be apparent in the case of a trained recreational dancer who creates their own choreography to a pop song.

45 Kozbelt, Beghetto & Runco 2010, p. 23.

46 Craft 2001, p. 49.

a new argument to support their client's criminal case in the course Moot Court to the first year student in Introduction to Legal Philosophy, who spoke up and provided me and her classmates with a detailed description of why she thought that New Zealand's prime minister Arden's actions regarding the Covid-crisis made her a 'true prince' in terms of Machiavelli's *The Prince*. An example of a little-C experience in legal practice might be the lawyer who approaches and solves a problem in a different manner than usual. Finally, the second highest level of creativity is pro-C.[47] This is highly accomplished professional creativity[48] that requires expertise in a knowledge domain, motivation and performance that surpasses little-C creativity.[49] Different from little-C, pro-C in most cases requires formal training in the domain. It also requires approximately ten years of experience in the domain and cannot be achieved by all (which is the case for little-C).[50] Nevertheless, pro-C is not as exclusive as big-C, since certainly hundreds of people in any given domain may achieve pro-C.[51] It is possible to attain pro-C through 'formal apprenticeship' in an academic institution. Examples of legal professionals functioning on the level of pro-C are the academically educated legal professional who writes scientific articles that contribute to the legal domain, or the family law lawyer, notary or judge who is able to find new solutions in complex and multifaceted cases.

In short, all our students have the potential to be creative on a level in the continuum, in any domain and therefore, also in the legal domain. Furthermore, it is possible to *improve* their creativity in the domain of law (and in other domains). Therefore, as educators in law, we may take this opportunity to recognize and nurture our students' mini-C experiences of personal learning in the legal domain and help students develop those mini-C experiences into little-C creativity where they learn to think in possibilities. Also, we could support our students start building a foundation of knowledge, attitudes

47 Kaufman & Beghetto 2009, p. 5.

48 Kaufman and Beghetto describe it as 'effortful progression beyond little-C'.

49 Kozbelt, Beghetto & Runco 2010, p. 24.

50 Since pro-C requires a vast amount of knowledge, experts agree that approximately ten years (the actual length often depends on the complexity of the domain) of experience – exploring and experimenting – in the knowledge domain is necessary to achieve this level of creativity. See Kaufman & Beghetto 2009, p. 5.

51 Some people do not wish or are not able to continue their creative activity in a specific domain from little-C to pro-C. Nevertheless, for those able and willing, Kaufman and Beghetto describe the overall process of reaching the professional creativity level. According to them, every person starts with mini-C, with a personal, subjective discovery. From there, some people follow-up with a phase of play (experimenting) with their creativity in the domain. This leads to improvement and little-C creativity (objective creativity). After that, reaching pro-C through informal apprenticeship becomes a possibility, but this will take years of work. Most people who reach pro-C, however, progress from mini-C by beginning a formal apprenticeship (namely, an academic education) in the domain of choice. This supports their progress and makes it possible for some to reach pro-C in at least ten years' time. This second route is of interest for law schools. Furthermore, people are able to reach pro-C level in an area without it being their bread and butter and – vice versa – many professionals will never reach the creativity level required for pro-C in their own professional areas. For example, a person might have attained pro-C in guitar-playing, but primarily work as a lawyer where she only reaches little-C level. See Kaufman & Beghetto 2009, p. 5.

and skills that enables them to reach pro-C level later in their lives. Currently, the duration of an academic education in law consists (at least in the Netherlands) of only four years of study. This means that we will not be able to deliver novice legal professionals that are already capable of creativity on the level of pro-C at the completion of the Master's degree. However, in legal education, we could aim for laying the foundation that enables students to achieve pro-C in their futures, in an individual process of life-long learning.

In the previous section, the concepts of creativity and creative thinking were explored through a historical overview of the concepts that provided a preliminary definition of creativity as a human endeavor that generates something of value that is novel in the sense that it is new for the individual (mini-C and little C), their peers or their domain (pro-C and big-C). It has become clear that legal education could support their students' mini-C and little-C experiences in order for them to be capable of pro-C later in life. In the following section, the creative process and its components will be investigated further and, subsequently, the way in which this process may find a place within legal education will be explored.

The creative process and its components in legal education

One of the ways in which creative thinking may be incorporated in ALE is to focus on developing the traits and abilities that distinguish creative people. While doing so, it is helpful for students to practice the steps of a creative endeavor. To generate valuable and novel ideas, creators often go through a so-called creative process. From the second half of the 20th century onward, many experts in social psychology have presented their own theories on creativity and representations of the creative process.[52] Wallas's description of the creative process (1926), which is often regarded as a classic, inspired many theorists. His four stage-model consists of (1) preparation, (2) incubation, (3) illumination, and (4) verification.[53] In this model, Wallas not only included logical and conscious thinking (in stages 1 and 2) , but also subconscious thinking.[54] During the incubation period, a person suspends their conscious work on and thinking of the problem. They step away from the task at hand for a undefined length of time and focus on other things. Subconsciously, however, the problem simmers until, suddenly, seemingly out of nowhere,

52 These ideas are often in many ways similar, but at the same time there are slight (and also some significant) differences. This results in a vast number of studies and ideas on creativity and creative thinking. Well-known theorists in the field of creativity are, for example, Wallas, Guildford, Torrance, Csikszentmihalyi, Boden, Gardner, Simonton, Kaufman and Amabile.

53 In *The Art of Thought* (1926), Graham Wallas introduced the earliest creative thinking model (Wallas 1926, pp. 95-96) and, even though it is mainly focused on creativity as *giftedness* that is not attainable for all individuals, his work on creativity is still very influential. See Sadler-Smith 2015, p. 342.

54 Kekang 2017, pp. 34-35.

a solution bubbles up.[55] This moment of illumination after a period of conscious distance from the task at hand is often recognizable for artists and scientists. By combining conscious and subconscious processes in the description of creative thinking, Wallas's model captures the wonder of the creative process.

Although that mysterious experience of creative insight is beautiful, for educational practice, we require a practical step-by-step plan of the creative process, so that *every student* may be able to travel through the process. So, this chapter draws on Teresa Amabile's componential model of creativity. This model is very helpful and insightful for educators in legal education, since it consists of five steps and, importantly, also shows four underlying components, that describe what is needed to be able to 'walk through' the steps of the creative process. These components provide educators with practical guidelines on what to teach their students so that they are capable of creative thinking. The componential model of creativity is thus highly useful in legal education. Amabile's model involves an interpretation of the four so-called *P*'s that are traditionally identified in theories on creativity, namely *process*, *product*, *person (personality)* and *place*.[56] Amabile's componential model of creativity incorporates the development (and necessity) of personality traits and abilities required for creativity. It aims at producing creative work on the level of little-C. And although Kaufman and Beghetto signal that Amabile's componential model of creativity seems to be mainly focused on little-C creativity,[57] in my opinion, the model may also be applicable to forms of creativity on the level of pro-C, because professionals seeking to generate new ideas repeatedly go through the same creative process and conditions as described by Amabile. Furthermore, they require ample experience in little-C before being able to gain the level of pro-C. This makes the model helpful for at least two of the levels of creativity which may be fostered in ALE. Amabile's description of the creative process provides educators and students in legal education with a tool that brings clarity. The tool helps to understand the steps required to come up with new ideas and sheds a light on the skills and qualities that need honing during an academic legal education. However, I deem Amabile's description a little *too* straightforward in its logical, rational steps toward new ideas. It does not seem to explicitly capture the experience of 'unexplainable inspiration' that often accompanies the creation of something novel. Introducing Wallas's narrative of the incubation and illumination stages *within* the five stages described by Amabile enables a depiction of the creative process that embraces both its rational and mystical elements. Amabile herself specifically recognizes the stages theorized by Wallas as experiences that many creators recognize.[58] In the following, the

55 Cropley 2001, p. 41.

56 Every theory on creativity focuses on the description of creativity on one or more of these P's. See on the four (and, for some, six) P's Kozbelt, Beghetto & Runco 2010, pp. 24-25.

57 Kaufman & Beghetto 2009, p. 3.

58 Amabile 1996, p. 101.

steps and components of the creative process will be clarified[59] and directly applied to the context of legal education.

Stages and components of the creative process

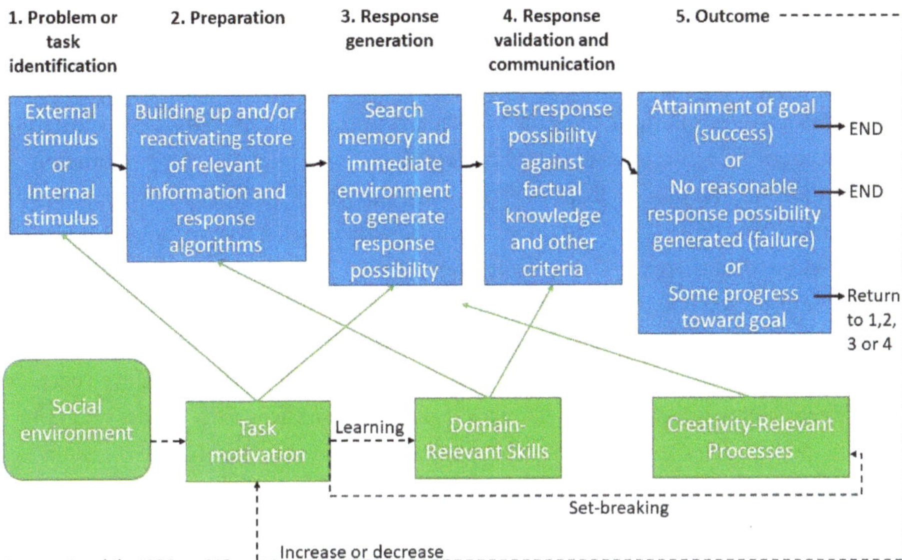

Source: Amabile 1996, p. 113.

As the image above shows, Amabile distinguishes five stages (indicated in blue) of the creative process. These steps will often occur in a linear fashion, but this does not exclude the possibility of going through the process in a non-linear order. For instance, it is entirely possible to leap from a latter to a former stage.[60] This process is fueled by creative thinking (especially in the third stage) and will result in a creative performance. In other words, the goal of the process is the production of a creative product.[61]

In chronological order, Amabile's stages of the creative process are: (1) problem and task identification, (2) preparation, (3) response generation, (4) response validation and communication and (5) outcome. In the first phase, a problem or task is recognized and defined. This might commence through an external stimulus (an assignment given by an educator or boss, for example) or through an internal stimulus (when individuals 'discover' a task or problem themselves, for example, because of their own curiosity).[62] During the

59 This explanation will have its basis in Amabile's componential model of creativity, with additions derived from other theories that are useful in the context of ALE.

60 Amabile 1996, p. 114.

61 See Baer and Kaufman 2012, p. 70.

62 This first stage is well-known in other descriptions of the creativity process as well, see for example Kozbelt, Beghetto & Runco 2010, pp. 30-31, and Craft 2001, p. 57.

second stage, the generation of novel ideas is prepared by building up or reactivating relevant information. This stage requires the acquisition of knowledge and the ability to remember already known concepts from one or more domains. Following the identification of a problem and the accumulation of appropriate knowledge, the third stage consists of response generation and involves the actual production of solutions and ideas in answer to the problem or task. Subsequently, the novel responses are tested and validated against factual knowledge of the appropriate domain(s) in the fourth stage. While doing so, the individual needs to communicate the ideas with actors in the relevant field (in the context of legal education, students, educators and perhaps legal professionals). After validation and communication, the process leads to an outcome, in other words, a creative product. This may for example be a solution to the problem, a work of art, a written document, an invented machine or a theory.[63] The response can then be judged a success, a failure, or partly successful. According to Amabile, the creative process ends in case of a success or definite failure. In case of the former, the problem is solved and further problematizing is unnecessary. In case of the latter, none of the responses can be validated and solve (parts of) the problem in any way. In my view, situations in which all the generated ideas do not account for *any* progress towards the goal at all must be quite rare. In most creative processes that do not conclude in a definite success, some progress towards the goal will have been made one way of the other. If so, the individual may go back to any of the earlier stages in the hope of gaining further progress towards a positive outcome.[64]

Anyone – so also legal professionals and law students – who aspires to take these five steps of the creative process, is – according to Amabile – in need of the four components that function as the fuel of the creative process (indicated in green in the image above),[65] one external component and three internal components. The external process that influences the creativity process is (i) the social environment. The three internal processes are (ii) task motivation, (iii) domain relevant skills, and (iv) creativity relevant processes. In the following, these four components will be further explored.

i Social Environment

The external component of the creative process is formed by the social environment.[66] This component centers specifically on one 'P' of creativity, namely on *Place*.[67] Amabile's

63 Cropley 2001, p. 6.
64 Amabile 1996, p. 113.
65 Amabile 2012, p. 1.
66 Amabile 2012, p. 2, Amabile 1996, pp. 114, 119-120.
67 Selecting the social environment as an element of creativity is based on the assumption that not just extraordinary, but also ordinary people can be creative, if their creativity is supported by their environment (Craft 2001-A, p. 2). This is a relatively new assumption in creativity research, because until the second half of the 20th century, only geniuses were viewed to be able to be creative. The social environment was not relevant to their 'success', but their innate talents and superiority were. Currently however, it is believed that

theory may be viewed as especially noteworthy because of its research on this element, although Amabile is certainly not alone in her interest, other social theorists attribute importance to the social environment for the creative thinking and creative performance of individuals as well.[68] It would be logical for educators in law schools to give special attention to the social environment, since it seems possible to create an environment that supports the creativity of law students.[69]

For creativity to thrive, the social environment has to offer opportunities for exploration, independent work, and support and valuing of originality.[70] In addition to Amabile, other researchers have also identified important characteristics for social environments that wish to nurture creativity. Adair proposes that such environments will have to value creativity and divergence, offer autonomy and create an environment in which judgment (or: evaluation) is suspended.[71] Specifically for educational settings, Belluigi states that a positive learning climate is key, it is important to be supportive and to encourage playfulness, experimenting and risk-taking.[72]

The most important role of the social environment within the creative process is its influence on task motivation (see next section).[73] By enhancing task motivation, the social environment at least supports the stages of the creativity process where *novelty* of the outcome is of the essence: Problem and task identification (stage one) and response generation (stage three). In other words, motivated people in supportive environments are better able to come up with new ideas to identified problems. Additionally, it is possible for the social environment to have an effect on other internal components of creativity as well as directly on the stages of creativity.[74] To illustrate, educators in legal education may further develop their students' domain relevant skills by organizing, for example, extra-

---

everyone, and not just people with an innate possibility for genius in a domain, has the ability to be creative and this ability may be given a chance to grow in creativity nurturing environments. Since it seems far easier to change an environment than it is to change a personality, this *P* had gotten much interest from educators.

68 From the 1980's and 1990's onwards, under the influence of social theory and system theory, this belief in the importance of the social environment gained the interest of creativity researchers, such as Csikszentmihalyi, Runco (See Runco 2014, p. 180), and Amabile. See Jeffrey and Craft 2001, p. 1. The importance of the social environment is also stressed by, for example, Cropley, who states that the sources of creative behavior are 'interactions between abilities and knowledge, personal properties, motivation and the properties of the surrounding social environment'. See Cropley, pp. 2-3. In addition, Amabile includes the social environment as a crucial component of the creative process. See Amabile, 1996, pp. 119-120. See also Amabile 1983, p. 358.

69 See also Amabile 1996, p. 203.

70 In contrast, an environment might also stifle creativity. See Amabile 1996, p. 120.

71 Adair 2007, pp. 90-91. See also Amabile's point that harsh criticism – in other words, judgment – blocks creativity: Amabile 2012, p. 2. Adaire's requisite for autonomy can be aligned with Amabile's 'independent work', whereas his 'valuing creativity and divergent thinking' matches Amabile's 'valuing of originality'.

72 Belluigi 2010, p. 47.

73 Amabile 1996, p. 115.

74 Amabile 1996, p. 115.

curricular workshops and masterclasses. At the same time, by offering courses in which complex problems are central that challenge students to find solutions transcending the legal domain, legal educators support their students' development of creativity relevant processes.

Our students are embedded in various social environments, such as the settings of work, leisure activities, family, friends and society at large. Educators in legal academic education are able to influence the students' social environment that involves the university, the legal faculty, the various departments and classrooms. Here, we are able to create an environment that is not averse, but instead supportive of creative thinking and will engage students, resulting in intrinsic task motivation. This entails open mindedness, which could entail, for instance, that educators (and students) value new ideas and originality and that they support divergent (or – as De Bono would say – lateral) thinking. Also, in support of a social environment that stimulates creativity, harsh criticism of new ideas and too much time pressure should be avoided, while autonomy, risk-taking and positive challenges need to be encouraged.[75] Another suggestion for fostering a social environment that stimulates creativity would be to embrace play and being playful in the academic educational setting (for example in teaching methods, teaching styles and assessments).

In addition to requirements in the *social* environment, Amabile suggests that creativity might also be positively influenced by the *physical* environment. By offering visual stimulation in the classroom, for example, creativity could be increased to some extent, provided that students know how to use the visual cues or are taught how to use them in class assignments.[76] Other research also shows that physical aspects of the environment are able to support creativity in individuals, for instance colors (showing a brief glimpse of green before the commencing with the creative task),[77] sounds (moderate 'white' noise, such as rain or the background noise of a cafe),[78] lighting (dim lighting or darkness)[79] or even the tidiness of the environment (a disordered environment increases creativity).[80] In other words, changing our now often orderly, sterile, silent, white painted, glass paneled, unimaginative classrooms into creative environments with supportive colors, furnishings, sounds and lighting may positively influence our students' creative ability (and our own). New technology, such as virtual reality might provide opportunities to create virtual spaces that inspire creativity or challenge students to be creative. The *virtual reality*

75 Amabile 2012, p. 2. See also Berg and Seeber who highlight in *The Slow Professor* the importance of timelessness for creativity in academic work and study. See Berg and Seeber 2016, p. 27.

76 Amabile 1996, p. 228.

77 Lichtenfeld, Elliot, Maier & Pekrun 2011, p. 791.

78 Mehta, Zhu & Cheema 2012, pp. 791, 795.

79 Steidle & Werth 2013, p. 76.

80 Vohs, Redden & Rahinel 2013, p. 1866.

courtroom developed by the Dutch project PleitVRij,[81] for instance, offers law students of several institutes the opportunity to practice their oral presentation skills together in a *virtual reality* setting that feels extraordinarily real.

This completes the exploration of the *external* component of the creative process, the social environment. The following three sections offer an in-depth description of the three *internal* components of the creative thinking process: task motivation, domain relevant skills and creativity relevant processes.

ii Task Motivation

Task motivation determines how a person approaches a task. This *internal* component of the creative process occurs within the individual who creates. Task motivation varies per task: A student may be very motivated to start a written assignment on the right to freedom of speech, but quite unmotivated for giving an oral commentary on Machiavelli's *The Prince*. According to Amabile, task motivation is especially needed for problem and task identification (stage one) and response generation (stage three). Moreover, task motivation has a positive influence on the learning process for acquiring domain relevant skills (see next section).

Especially relevant for task motivation, creativity *and* deep learning[82] is intrinsic motivation.[83] This is a state of deep involvement and playfulness which occurs, for example, when a person feels involvement, enjoyment, interest, curiosity, or perceives a challenge.[84] This brings to mind what Csikszentmihalyi describes as 'flow'.[85] As already noted in the

---

81 PleitVRij is a collaborative project of the Vrije Universiteit Amsterdam and the Rijksuniversiteit Groningen. The two institutions were joined by Utrecht University in 2021. In 2018 and in 2022, this innovative project was funded by the Ministry of Education, Culture and Science of the Netherlands. As a member of the project group, I have seen my students experience the life-like setting of the *virtual reality* courtroom and have noticed the difference between them practicing their plea in a 'normal', unimaginative classroom and in this realistic setting in *VR*. For more information on PleitVRij, see: www.surf.nl/pleitvrij.

82 Deep learning is the opposite of surface learning. According to Biggs, students that adopt a deep approach to learning enjoy and are interested in their academic task, search for the task's meaning and personalize the task, try to form hypotheses about the task and are able to integrate parts of the task into a coherent whole that they can connect to previous knowledge. See Biggs 1987, p. 15. Deep learning is driven by intrinsic motivation, see Biggs 2011, p. 61. Furthermore, deep learning depends on connecting new knowledge (previously unknown to the student) to already processed knowledge. Uncovering these connections and being aware of the importance of making links between old and new knowledge are important tasks for educators. See Biggs 2011, p. 67.

83 Baer and Kaufman 2012, p. 69.

84 Amabile 1996, p. 115, p. 131. See also Amabile 2012, p. 2.

85 Flow entails intense concentration, a loss of self-consciousness and a distorted sense of time. During 'flow' a person has an autotelic experience, which means that they are doing the activity because of its inherent enjoyability (for its own sake) and not because of any (external) benefit that the activity may have. Controlling one's attention or focus is of utmost importance for the ability to experience flow. Therefore, individuals with attention disorders generally find it difficult to experience flow. Csikszentmihalyi 2008, pp. 67, 71, 84-85. See also Gardner 1994, p. 144.

former section, intrinsic motivation may be increased by the environment, for example, by complimenting a novel idea or by providing opportunities for further exploration. In these ways, the environment may increase a person's motivation to persist in solving a problem or completing a task. In educational settings, intrinsic motivation may be supported when given tasks are (to a certain extent) open-ended and students have to find their own paths towards a solution.[86] If a student is innately interested in a topic or finds a task enjoyable, they will show more creativity.

However, intrinsic motivation is fragile and easily destroyed. For example, it might be damaged when a student expects to be evaluated.[87] Moreover, the level of intrinsic motivation (and creativity) will decrease when rewards, a form of extrinsic motivation, are offered to students *only if* they complete a task or study a topic. Baer and Kaufman (who base their argumentation on research conducted by Amabile) suggest that, if an educator wishes to use extrinsic motivation by, for example, offering bonus points or extra credits, she should not offer those as rewards, but only as circumstances that will make the task at hand more pleasurable. The bottom line here is that the reward should not be perceived as such by the students, otherwise their intrinsic motivation (and their creativity) will suffer.[88] Sometimes, the positive effects of using extrinsic motivation surpass the pain it causes. For example, if an educator in a Legal Skills course offers a reward for every written assignment a student hands in, the student will practice their skills more often (as long as the reward is offered). The short term consequence of this reward system is that the student will not be more (but, unfortunately, probably less) motivated to write legal articles for fun. However, in this particular situation, the aim is for the student to practice their writing skills as much as possible – quantity is of the essence. The loss of fun, intrinsic motivation and, yes, creativity, may be worth the development of the student's writing skills.[89] Fortunately, the increase of their skills in writing might help this student regain the lost intrinsic motivation after a while. In other words, the feeling of competency and accompanying self-confidence resulting from the acquired skill set may stimulate the student to use their skills for enjoyment in the future and – who knows? – this particular student might come to be a renowned legal publicist.

Amabile also proposes that it is to a certain extent possible to influence intrinsic motivation by using extrinsic motivation. In these cases, the extrinsic factors that are used for extrinsic motivation support the individual's sense of competence or enable their deeper involvement with the task itself without undermining their sense of self-determination. This might be done, for example, by offering a challenge that relates to

86 Amabile 1996, pp. 120, 133.
87 Baer & Kaufman 2012, p. 75. See also Amabile 1996, p. 120, Amabile 2012, p. 2 and Adair 2007, pp. 90-91.
88 Baer and Kaufman 2012, p. 81. See also Runco 2014, p. 183.
89 See also Baer and Kaufman 2012.

someone's interests. In this way, extrinsic factors may enhances intrinsic motivation and, thus, creativity.[90]

iii Domain Relevant Skills

Domain Relevant Skills (DRS) are the second internal component of creativity in Amabile's model.[91] Domain relevant skills have already been explored in the previous chapter, where DRS are presented as essential for critical thinking. Academics researching creative thinking hold that DRS are vital for creative thinking, as well. In explanation, if a person aspires to be creative in a domain, for example in law, then they require knowledge and skills that are central to that domain, otherwise they cannot know which problems need solving or which solutions will work within the context of that specific domain. Hence, deep knowledge is required for creative thinking. Furthermore, I agree with Boden's argument that in addition to expertise in a domain, *broad* knowledge is also prerequisite for creativity.[92] Having not only in-depth knowledge of one domain, but also broad knowledge of others is useful, since it supports identifying complex problems and provides a bigger toolbox that prepares for response generation (stage 2). Broad knowledge also enables the validation of the possible responses, because you need knowledge of all the domains you are working with to know that you are contributing something new and valuable (stage 4).[93] The more knowledge an individual has, the more connections between existing ideas they will be able to make (see next section).[94] Therefore, more new ideas might be generated. In legal education, this could be supported, by for instance, making it mandatory (or at least easier) for students to follow courses in other disciplines. This is especially relevant for law schools in the Netherlands, where – in contrast to legal education in, for example, the United States – students do not start with a broad, liberal education in an undergraduate degree, but start their studies immediately and specifically in the domain of law.[95]

iv Creativity Relevant Processes

The four components of the creative process are completed by Creativity Relevant Processes (CRP). To be called creative, responses to a problem or task cannot just be based on domain relevant skills and undertaken with task motivation. To be truly creative, the

90 Amabile 1996, p. 118.

91 The relevance of domain relevant skills for creativity is backed by other theories on creativity, see Cropley 2001, p. 19, Boden 2001, p. 95, Csikszentmihalyi 2013, pp. 88-90.

92 Boden 2001, p. 98. See also on the importance of broad knowledge Csikszentmihalyi 2013, p. 88.

93 See also Boden 2001, p. 98.

94 Amabile 1983, p. 363. See also Boden 2001, p. 96.

95 Stolker 2014, pp. 17-18.

response needs to be novel,[96] which is often linked to the element of surprise, the response has to have a level of unexpectedness.[97] To be able to generate such responses (stage 3), a person is in need of CRP. First, these CRP involve personality characteristics,[98] which refer to one of the 'P's of creativity, namely *person*.[99] According to Amabile,[100] the personality characteristics that are specific for creative people include, for instance, independence,[101] self-discipline,[102] the ability to delay gratification and perseverance when frustrated, and non-conformity in thinking.[103] Other theorists add characteristics such as openness to experience;[104] wide interests;[105] imagination;[106] originality and inventiveness;[107] humor and playfulness;[108] courage;[109] preference for complexity;[110] flexibility;[111] and tolerance of

96 The level of 'novelty' may differ: it does not necessarily have to be a new idea that changes the domain (big-C), but may also be a novelty that adds something valuable to the domain (pro-C) or an idea that is new to the creator (mini- of little-C).

97 Amabile 1983, p. 364.

98 Amabile 2001, p. 333. See also Amabile 2012, p. 2.

99 Personality characteristics (or personality traits) are not the same as a person's (creative) attitudes. Whereas the former remain relatively stable throughout an individual's life, the latter may vary per day, see Runco 2014, p. 185.

100 Amabile 1983, p. 365.

101 Other theorists speak of *autonomy*, which is intimately related to independence as a personality characteristic for creativity. See Cropley 2001, p. 60. In the same spirit, Craft (Craft 2001, p. 56) mentions self-determination and self-direction, for which – according to Runco – 'ego strength' is needed (Runco 2014, p. 185). Boden seems to agree with Runco, since she states that self-confidence is required for the self-critical expertise that lies at the heart of creativity (Boden 2001, p. 98). I prefer the use of the word 'self-authored thinking' to indicate the independence of thought.

102 Csikszentmihalyi, too, argues that determination and discipline are needed to gain the control of the mind (and focus) needed for flow. See Csikszentmihalyi 2008, p. 213.

103 Amabile 1983, p. 365. Eysenck and Barron also consider non-conformity a personality characteristic of creative individuals, see Cropley 2001, pp. 60, 64.

104 See Cropley on studies performed by Eysenck and Dellas & Gaier (Cropley 2001, pp. 59-60). See also Maslow 1976, p. 88. Sometimes this characteristic is described as 'being childlike' or 'being in touch with childhood' See Craft 2001, p. 48, see also Maslow 1976, p. 88.

105 See Cropley on Dellas & Gaier: Cropley 2001, p. 60.

106 Craft also proposes that being imaginative is a necessity for creativity (in her case, for little-C creativity), see Craft 2001, p. 58. Liu and Noppe-Brandon call for a renewed appreciation and nurturing of imagination (Liu & Noppe-Brandon 2009).

107 Craft refers to this in the terms of 'innovation'. See Craft 2001, p. 56.

108 Research by Graham, Sawyers & DeBord and a study by Isen, Daubman and Nowichi advocate play and playfulness as personality characteristics required for creativity. See Cropley 2001, p. 61.

109 To create something novel, often means going against the grain and defying conventions. To do so, one needs 'the courage to create', see Cropley 2001, p. 65. According to Csikszentmihalyi, courage (in this context, courage is for Csikszentmihalyi the same as resilience) an important virtue for mature coping with hardships. Courage helps to transform misfortune (or difficulty) into an enjoyable challenge. This transformational coping is a fruitful way for managing stress and stressful situations (including situations of chaos and uncertainty). See Csikszentmihalyi 2008, pp. 198-201.

110 See Cropley on a study conducted by Dacey and research by Shaughnessy & Manz and Barron & Harrington, Cropley 2001, pp. 60, 64. See also Eysenck 2001, p. 216.

111 Cropley describes flexibility as a necessary personality characteristic for creativity according to various studies conducted by Dellas and Gaier, Dacey, and Eysenck. See Cropley 2001, pp. 59-60.

ambiguity.[112] Second, in addition to a person's characteristics, the CRP involve work styles,[113] which may be developed by training. Work styles that enable creativity are, for instance, disciplined and diligent work.[114] Finally, CRP entails cognitive styles,[115] including negative capability and strong synthesizing ability. Additionally, Welling describes four mental operations that also seem part of cognitive styles relevant for what he calls 'creative cognition', namely application, analogy, combination (which seems similar to synthesizing) and abstraction.[116] This 'creative cognition' exists in a continuum of complexity, resulting in creative products that increase in creativity level: Application results in the lowest level of creativity, whereas abstraction results in high levels of creativity.[117] Similar to work styles, the cognitive styles might be included in the curriculum of legal education, since they are formed with training and experience. Cognitive styles are the ways in which a person gathers information from the world and sorts, organizes and recalls that information. It also includes the way in which a person copes with challenging situations.[118] In short, it might be described as 'the way in which a person thinks'. Cognitive styles that are linked to creativity are characterized by seeing and doing differently;[119] remembering accurately;[120] openness to new information; using wide categories; suspending judgment and keeping possibilities open; posing questions;[121] divergent thinking and convergent

---

112 See on studies conducted by Eysenck and Dacey, Cropley 2001, p. 60.

113 Amabile 2001, p. 333. See also Amabile 2012, p. 2.

114 Amabile 1983, p. 362.

115 Amabile 2001, p. 333. See also Amabile 2012, p. 2., Amabile 1996, p. 99.

116 Welling 2007, pp. 167-172.

117 Welling 2007, p. 167. Application means the application of an existing structure of rules in a normal context for these rules. Welling provides a legal example of a lawyer who tries to find the best way of fitting the details of a particular case within the existing structure of the law. By doing so, the lawyer applies legal rules in a specific case. The case is always slightly different, which turns the application into a (small) creative endeavor. See Welling 2007, p. 168. Analogy is one step further in the continuum of cognitive operations. It involves the transposition of an existing structure from its habitual context to a new context. See Welling 2007, p. 168. Following analogy in the continuum is combination generation, which is similar to what is called synthesizing ability or combinational creativity. It involves the combination of two or more concepts into a new idea. See Welling 2007, p. 169. Finally, the continuum is completed with abstraction discovery. This includes the discovery of, for example, patterns either in the concrete external world or in mental concepts. See Welling 2007, p. 170. Interestingly, these steps in the continuum of creative ability as described by Welling – which progress to more complicated and abstract ability and lead to a higher level of creativity – bear similarities with Bloom's taxonomy categories: (1) remember; (2) understand; (3) apply; (4) analyze; (5) evaluate, and; (6) create. Also, the continuum seems to be congruent with the developmental stages described by Kegan and Kuhn (see Chapter 1). It seems that the further a person has progressed on the developmental stages, the more innovative and creative they are able to be.

118 Cropley 2001, p. 43.

119 They perceive the world creatively, in other words, they view the world differently from others and approach/perform tasks in a different manner than other people. See Amabile 1996, pp. 88-89. Grant refers in this context to the experience of a *Vu ja de* (in contrast to a déjà vu), which means viewing something familiar with a new, fresh perspective that gives new insight. Grant 2017, p. 7.

120 Albergaria Ameida, Teixeira-Dias & Medina 2010, p. 88.

121 Liu & Noppe-Brandon 2009, p. 37. See also Albergaria Ameida, Teixeira-Dias & Medina 2010, p. 89.

thinking;[122] play and intellectual playfulness;[123] understanding complexities, and tolerance for discrepancies, incomplete information and ambiguous information.[124]

The ability to cope with uncertainty is – as said in the introduction to this chapter – one of the most important skills individuals, including academically educated legal professionals, may have in contemporary society where choices must always be made. As mentioned, one of the personality characteristics of creative people is that they tolerate, do not hide from, or even seek out uncertainty and ambiguity. Maslow, for instance, thought that creative people were relatively unafraid of the unknown and mysterious – and some creators are even drawn to it.[125] Moreover, according to Piirto, creative people have various core attitudes, two of which are the attitude of risk-taking and the attitude of tolerance for ambiguity.[126] Grant adds nuance to this idea by arguing that many creative people (or, in his words 'non-conformists') often struggle with uncertainty and fear and that they prefer to avoid risks. However, ultimately, they still *choose* to take the risk regardless of their perceived discomfort or even fear.[127] Creative thinking entails possibility thinking. Therefore, when confronted with moments of choice, creative individuals have the ability to think of opportunity and positive possibilities instead of only focusing on the possible risks. The anticipation of desirable opportunities as a consequence of a choice, results in positive feelings such as excitement. Nevertheless, creative people are by no means fearless or blind to risks. However, their innate courage, playfulness and independence allows for them to take a chance regardless of the risks. In ALE we could support these personality attributes by supporting the self-confidence and self-authored thinking of our students in the context of a safe, playful learning environment.

People able of creative thinking are 'possibility thinkers', capable of managing uncertainty. Hence, academically educated legal professionals need to learn ways of thinking that are productive for creativity. Fortunately, this is something that we are able to teach in legal academic education, for instance, by teaching the cognitive style of *negative capability*. John Keats, one of the Romantic Era's famous English poets, once

122 Albergaria Ameida, Teixeira-Dias & Medina 2010, p. 88.
123 See Russ 2003, pp. 292-293. See Jeffrey and Craft 2001, p. 9. See also Amabile 1983, p. 362.
124 Cropley 2001, p. 43, Lucas 2010, p. 39.
125 According to Maslow, self-actualizing creativity (SA-creativity), similar to little C-creativity, can be done by all. At the core of this SA-creativity are spontaneity and fearlessness. Individuals that show SA-creativity do not fear their own emotions and thoughts and have no fear of the judgment of others. See Maslow 1976, pp. 88-89.
126 Piirto 2011, pp. 27, 33.
127 Grant 2017, pp. 16-17.

described a poet's 'negative capability'[128] in a letter to his brothers[129] as the ability to experience ambivalence ('*being in uncertainties, mysteries and doubts*') without reaching for certainty ('*reaching after fact and reason*'). In other words, creative thinkers require the ability to be satisfied with incomplete or half-knowledge.[130] Keats suggested that this capability is found in creative artists (especially poets[131]). Li Ou notices that Keats's negative capability entails the belief that creative work (in the meaning of Keats, poetry) is characterized by its necessity for a 'full-scale human experience' that transcends clear facts and reason.[132] In the context of the lives of our students and legal professionals, this idea implies that a constant longing for certainty prevents them from having a *complete* experience.[133] This can also be recognized in the work of Maslow, who states that creative individuals search for truth without the need for certainty and are 'fully functioning people', because of their relative fearlessness.[134] So, by constantly reaching for certainty and not appreciating a situation of uncertainty, the individual limits the possibilities a given situation might hold. This diminishes their experience (and, probably, their creativeness). Since *complete* certainty is not attainable in life, it is of the highest importance for individuals to learn to tolerate and, indeed, *appreciate* uncertainty. This is what law students are in need of learning during their education, so that the worry and stress they experience in the face of current and future uncertainty may diminish. Many law students will not perceive uncertainty as natural or comfortable, so they will need to build their negative capability. During their academic education, students have the opportunity to practice with managing uncertainty by, for example, repeatedly going through creative processes. Experiencing the creative *process* provides a valuable appreciation for uncertainty, since it inevitably encompasses uncertainty:[135] At the end of every creative endeavor, there is a possibility of success or failure. By practicing with the stages of the

128 Keats: "*I had not a dispute but a disquisition with Dilke, on various subjects; several things dovetailed in my mind, & at once it struck me, what quality went to form a Man of Achievement especially in Literature & which Shakespeare possessed so enormously – I mean Negative Capability, that is when man is capable of being in uncertainties, Mysteries, doubts, without any irritable reaching after fact & reason – Coleridge, for instance, would let go by a fine isolated verisimilitude caught from the Penetralium of mystery, from being incapable of remaining content with half knowledge. This pursued through Volumes would perhaps take us no further than this, that with a great poet the sense of Beauty overcomes every other consideration, or rather obliterates all consideration*". See Ou, L., *Keats and Negative Capability*, London: Continuum 2009, p. 1.

129 Ou, L., *Keats and Negative Capability*, London: Continuum 2009, p. ix.

130 See Adair 2007, p. 93.

131 Keats regarded Shakespeare as a poet extraordinarily able to cope with the uncertainty of the creative process. See Adair 2007, p. 93.

132 Ou 2009, p. 2.

133 *Bildung* entails the complete (holistic) development of the individual's talents. This means that their reason and sensibility need to be developed equally. This could be done through creativity, which is a process that combines reason and sensibility.

134 Maslow 1976, p. 88.

135 For example, see Stolker, p. 342.

creative process, students get accustomed to the feeling of uncertainty. It also provides the opportunity to develop the necessary skills, knowledge and processes to deal with it, such as a playful attitude, delaying judgments and posing questions. Moreover, educators could introduce students to complexities and show why complexity offers an exciting challenge or even fun. Additionally, during lectures and while making assignments, students can be made aware of the inevitability of incomplete information and the worth of being open to new information and the possibility of multi-interpretable information. This may provide them with an appreciation for ambivalence.

In addition to teaching for negative capability, law schools may empower their students' creative thinking and creativity by teaching for a strong synthesizing ability. Maslow noted that creative people seem to have opposite personality traits: They are at the same time selfish *and* unselfish, thinkers *and* feelers, hard workers *and* players. However, they are able to merge these opposites into a logical, coherent synthesis.[136] According to Maslow, exactly this ability to unite separates is what distinguishes creative people from non-creative individuals.[137] Referring back to Yeamans, this might be the distinguishing ability of *great* lawyers.[138] Interestingly, the synthesizing ability to connect apparent opposites is also a part of *Bildung*. As explored in the second chapter, Schiller noted that by connecting the contrasting formal (reason) and sensuous (sensibility) drives, individuals are able to develop their whole human selves. In particular through playing with art, the human play drive was able to unify both reason and sensibility.[139] A novel idea coming from a combination of two seemingly unconnected 'old' ideas is regarded as unexpected and thus, *creative*. Creative people are able to make original connections that others do not,[140] which makes their ideas valuable, new and interesting.[141] The cognitive style required is the ability to unite disparate ideas: The farther apart the 'old' ideas are, the more original and creative the new connection.[142] Boden labels this type of creativity as 'combinational creativity'.[143] For legal professionals and law students to be able to do this, they need – as

136 Maslow 1976, p. 89.
137 Maslow 1976, p. 90.
138 Yeamans 1971, p. 381. See also Maslow 1976, p. 90.
139 Horlacher 2017, p. 17. Lechner 2003, p. 95. Beiser 2003, p. 96.
140 Lucas 2001, p. 38.
141 Boden 1994, p. 75.
142 Kozbeld, Beghetto & Runco 2010 on research by Mednick (1962), p. 32. See also Adair, pp. 6-7.
143 See Boden 2001, p. 96. The idea behind combinational creativity is that creating something out of nothing is impossible: new ideas are created by combining old ideas in unfamiliar ways. In addition to combinational creativity, Boden describes two other types of creativity, exploratory creativity and transformational creativity. These creativity types take time to develop, since the individual wielding them has to have an in-depth knowledge of the rules of the domain (conceptual space). In transformational creativity the rules of a domain are altered or broken, so that new ideas may be thought of that were previously impossible. This is a creativity type similar to big-C and requires knowledge, playfulness, judgment and self-discipline (Boden 2001, p. 97). Exploratory creativity is a type of creativity that does not require altering the rules of a domain (or transcending the domain), but it does often tweak the rules. It consists of an investigation of

Boden calls it – "a rich source of 'old' ideas". In other words, to make unexpected new connections between old ideas, having as much knowledge as possible is essential. Importantly, this not only entails facts, but rather many various types of knowledge, including knowledge of broader concepts.[144] Making connections also involves possibility thinking and connecting new knowledge and new experiences to prior knowledge.[145] In addition, individuals with this strong synthesizing ability can think in analogies.[146] They are able to make many sorts of different *and* new associations: They can associate similar ideas (more obvious associates), but also understand more distant analogies and find remote associates.[147] This is called 'mental flexibility'[148] and requires the cognitive styles of using wide categories, suspending judgment, remembering accurately and intellectual playfulness. Without a rich source of knowledge, seeing analogies between separate ideas is impossible, and mental flexibility diminishes.[149]

Educators in ALE may be able to support their students in their journey to learn how to make novel connections across domains by including a focus on the development of this ability in their course design and teaching methods. For instance, by offering in-depth knowledge of the legal domain relevant to their course *and* by prescribing literature from different domains that students are then asked to connect with the legal literature. An instructional intervention that could be used in class for practicing making connections as well, is the technique of 'forced associations'.[150] In assignments during class, students are explicitly challenged to find connections between seemingly unrelated concepts of the legal domain and of other domains, such as philosophy, sociology, visual arts, literature etc. Also, students may be encouraged to play with possible combinations of ideas, material

---

the possibilities within the domain. For both types of creativity, deep knowledge is needed of the domain so that the creator is able to play with those rules. Therefore, these types of creativity might be taught to graduate students, but not to freshman students. In order to nurture exploratory and transitional creativity, educators could discuss with their students that the rules of the legal domain *might* be subject to change (maybe even change brought on by the student) and that legal thinking is just one kind of thinking. Furthermore, implicit knowledge of the domain should always be reflected upon and made explicit knowledge. That way, students are offered room to play with the rules of the domain. According to Boden, educators who are willing to teach exploratory and transformative creativity have a challenge ahead of them: They need not only extensive knowledge, but also openness, flexible minds, and self-confidence. See Boden 2001, pp. 100-101.

144 Boden 2001, p. 96.

145 Liu & Noppe-Brandon 2009, p. 37. See also Adair 2007, pp. 6-7.

146 Adair 2007, pp. 6-7.

147 Boden 1994, p. 76. See also Boden 2001, p. 96. The more associations a person relatively has for a concept, the more creative that individual is, since they are able to make more connections. These connections might, for example, be based on function, sound or color. See Kozbeld, Beghetto & Runco 2010 on research by Mednick (1962), p. 32.

148 Boden 2001, p. 96.

149 Boden strongly argues that knowledge is the foundation of all creativity, be it combinational, exploratory or transformational creativity. See Boden 2001, pp. 95-96, 102.

150 Baer and Kaufman 2012, pp. 42-43.

and information. This will help them to come up with creative responses,[151] because the openness of play and a playful spirit supports finding new combinations and therefore encourages the construction of new responses/solutions to problems.

Creative Thinking in Academic Legal Education

Academically educated lawyers are not just required to be creative in the sense that they cleverly find novel arguments to support their clients' cases in court. More importantly, they need to be creative thinkers able to transcend the boundaries of the legal domain and find answers to complex and often multidisciplinary problems, often in collaboration with team members from different backgrounds and disciplines.[152] Hence, law students are in need of appropriate tools. It is the task of ALE to support law students by developing these tools, which include creativity and creative thinking. However, we do face challenges in the messy day-to-day practice of our educational endeavor. For example, in educational institutions such as universities, cultures or learning environments often linger that are sadly uncreative, for instance, the marketized university is an organization focused on effective time management, swift results, and assessments.[153] Moreover, I find that the

151 Jeffrey and Craft 2001, p. 9. See also Craft 2001, p. 58.

152 This is not just the case for lawyers, but for all academics, according to Nygaard, Courtney & Holtham 2010, p. 2.

153 See Chapter 1. Lucas makes a similar observation with regard to (primary) schools in the UK. See Lucas 2001, p. 35.

sheer number of enrolling law students may present a hurdle for educators attempting to teach creativity and creative thinking. Creativity requires time and teaching creativity requires individual attention for the process of every student, enough time to evaluate the student's progress and learning outcomes *and* time for educators to design their courses and lessons. However, in the past years, my teams (consisting of five to seven educators) and I have had the pleasure (but also the challenge) of teaching our 8-week courses to up to 800 students at a time. Although educators in, for instance, Philosophy, Mathematics or Language faculties might find these numbers simply mind-blowing, for Dutch colleagues in ALE, this is not exceptional. It is not even the highest number of first year students enrolling in a law faculty, which can climb up to 1200 students or more. This number of students and the relatively small number of educators (who often have many other tasks as well) makes individualized teaching tough. An additional task here is organizing guidance for novice, talented educators, whom law faculties regularly employ on short term contracts solely focused on teaching. These colleagues find themselves in the predicament of having to be flexible, open minded and knowledgeable while still trying to discover the craft of teaching, and studying the contents of the courses they will teach.

It has become clear that understanding creativity and creative thinking *and* being able to teach both to law students is not an easy task. Amabile's componential model of creativity provides a helpful understanding of the steps of creativity and what is required to take those steps towards creative outcomes. The previous section of this chapter has also shown that insights from creativity research may be directly applied to legal education. Yet, although I genuinely appreciate the clear analyses given by Amabile and other creativity theorists, these seem to fall short when it comes to the messy daily process of creativity and teaching creativity in law schools. Amabile's five stages of the creative process is quite clear-cut.[154] However, it is not desirable for legal educators to solely work with students in a structure that might be perceived as a straightjacket. This dampens the autonomy and creativity of students as well as educators. Also, the apparent straight path from finding a problem towards its solution might not completely do justice to the uncertainty of the act of creation. Creative people have experiences of randomness and inspiration, which point to a process that does not always consist of logical and chronological steps. So, to make the theory applicable for the daily context of legal education some amendments are required. Importantly, flexibility is needed in the way in which creative thinking and creativity may be given a place in legal education. Preserving the possibility of experiencing the creative process in different ways than described by

154 Amabile herself argues that, for performing more complex tasks (which would be the goal for academically educated legal professionals), there may be all kinds of loops and jumps possible between the stages of the creative process (Amabile 1996, p. 97). The described process therefore only offers limited insight and guidelines.

Amabile offers flexibility and leaves room for necessary uncertainty. This provides students with a chance to practice with uncertainty, which may offer them unexpected inspiration. Still, a romantic, but chaotic teaching of creativity in law schools is not useable. Fortunately, the theories on creativity offer us guidelines from which to start our search for a model for incorporating creativity in ALE. In the following, such a model will be proposed.

A Model for Integrating Creative Thinking into Academic Legal Education

The four components as described by Amabile will be especially helpful in drawing a model for integrating creative thinking into ALE. To remind us, the four components that drive the creative process are the social environment; task motivation; domain relevant skills and knowledge, and; creativity relevant processes. This means that if educators in ALE wish to support the development of their students' creative ability, they could do so by aiming for the presence and/or development of these components. While thinking of the initial model for integrating creativity into ALE as will be provided in the following, it may be helpful to keep the steps and components of the creative process in mind:

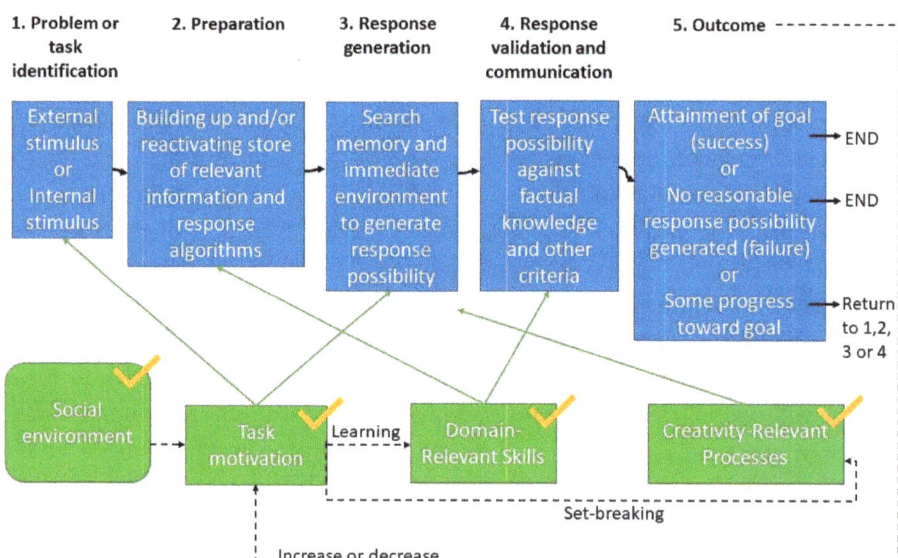

Source: Amabile 1996, p. 113.

The following initial outline of a model for creativity and creative thinking in legal education is meant to provide inspiration for educators. Just as is the case for the model for critical thinking as proposed in the previous chapter, the model for creative thinking is meant as a constant work-in-progress, explicitly open to further additions, suggestions and ideas. Since not all educators in law might view themselves as creative people, it may help if the tools offered to them are practical and applicable for all. Therefore, this version of the model involves eleven practical suggestions for educators in legal education who wish to incorporate creative thinking in their teaching. These suggestions are structured around the four levels educators in academic law schools influence, namely 1) the learning culture and environment; 2) curriculum design; 3) the course design, and; 4) their teaching method and teaching style. The model below shows which of these levels each of the eleven suggestions effect. Below the chart, the suggestions are further explored in detail. To show which component of the creative thinking process is (or which components are) supported by each suggestion, this will be indicated by yellow check marks at the start of the description of each suggestion. This model may serve as an evolving tool box for educators in search of some practical ideas on incorporating creativity and creative thinking in legal education.

Initial Model for Integrating Creative Thinking into Academic Legal Education

	I want to improve on the level of → **You can ↓**	**Learning Culture & Environment**	**Curriculum Design**	**Course Design**	**Teaching Method & Teaching Style**
1	Aim to develop deep and broad knowledge		•	•	•
2	Be open minded	•			•
3	Delay Judgment	•			•
4	Reward courage			•	•
5	Model desired behavior and attitudes				•
6	Make time	•	•	•	•
7	Create opportunities for practice and feedback, through appropriate instructional interventions, assignments and assessment.			•	•
8	Use play and playfulness	•	•	•	•

Initial Model for Integrating Creative Thinking into Academic Legal Education

	I want to improve on the level of → You can ↓	Learning Culture & Environment	Curriculum Design	Course Design	Teaching Method & Teaching Style
9	Add a focus on the development of creativity relevant processes	•	•	•	•
10	Use the physical environment	•			•
11	Encourage creative group work			•	•

No. 1 – Aim to develop deep and broad knowledge

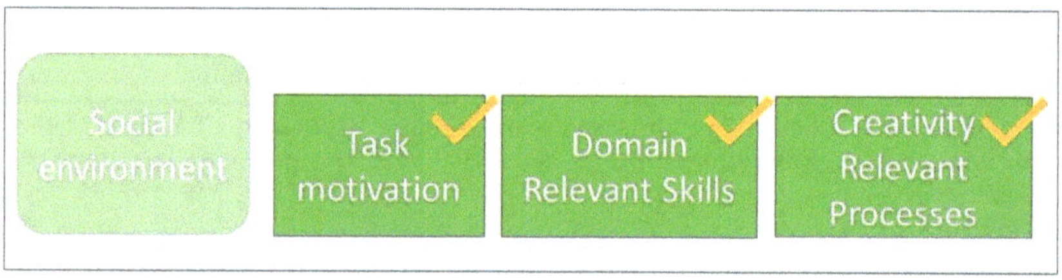

The first suggestion to integrate creative thinking into ALE is to aim for developing deep and broad knowledge. The better a person is able to make connections between apparent disparate concepts, the more creative they are able to be. This requires a vast amount of deep and broad knowledge that that person is able to remember accurately. Additionally, students who feel competent because they are able to understand the complexities of the domain – because of their vast source of deep and broad knowledge – will be more intrinsically motivated and engaged. So, law schools aspiring to teach for creative ability would be wise to offer their students a chance of studying legal issues in-depth as well studying the content of other domains. To support this, law schools might include mandatory courses in other domains on their curricula or challenge educators to develop legal courses that also include understanding of concepts from other domains. For further ideas on aiming for broad and in depth knowledge, see suggestion no. 1 in the previous chapter.

No. 2 – Be open minded

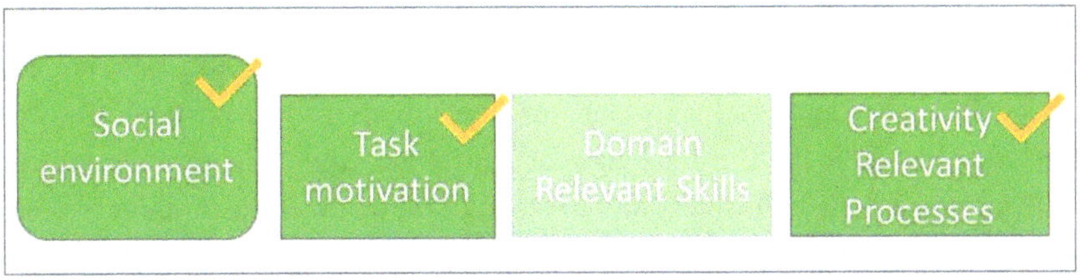

Being open minded is the second suggestion for stimulating creative thinking development in ALE. Educators are able to influence their students' understanding of the learning material and their support is important for students' creative self-efficacy and intellectual risk-taking.[155] Research shows that most educators in primary education embrace the idea that creativity should be fostered in education. However, it also shows that at the same time, educators do not embrace student behavior that is linked to creativity, such as boldness, unconventionality, longing for originality and independent decision making.[156] Conversely, educators like 'nice' students that are punctual, obedient, polite, and have openness for others' (read, the educator's) ideas. However, those are not per definition the traits that express creative thinking and creativity.[157] According to Beghetto, educators may dismiss unexpected ideas out of a desire for certainty: Sometimes they feel insecure about their own knowledge of the content, about going 'off script' and adding to possible confusion in the classroom or they do not dare to 'waste' the limited time available by discussing something unexpected while prescribed learning material remains untouched.[158] Additionally, Runco argues that in contrast to inexperienced educators (junior educators), more experienced educators in general seem to be less inclined to flexible thinking, since they are prone to follow the routines they have developed over the years.[159] This, too, may lead to dismissal of unexpected responses from students. However, repetitiously (softly) dismissing (almost) all unexpected and potentially creative ideas of students (for example by saying 'we will discuss this later' or 'interesting idea, however, it is not relevant now') may cause harm. Students might stop trying to come up with their own answers and will instead conform to what they now know to be the key to study success: Finding out what the educator wants to hear and repeating or imitating the answers the educator has

155 Beghetto 2009, p. 4.
156 Eysenck 2001 (pp. 212-213) lists some of the socially negative personality characteristics that creative students might show as were researched by Welsh in 1975. Amongst other descriptions, creative students are depicted as unstable, irresponsible, uncontrolled, rebellious and tactless. At the same time, creative individuals were also described as original, adventurous, refined, tolerant, flexible and interesting.
157 Cropley 2001, p. 137. See also Runco 2014, p. 173.
158 Beghetto 2009, p. 3.
159 Runco 2014, p. 180.

given.[160] Although these studies focused on educator and student behavior in primary schools, the findings are also relevant in the setting of higher education: Educators often appreciate punctual students that commit to deadlines and not only listen to, but also implement feedback. Students that arrive late or constantly introduce off-topic ideas are by many regarded as difficult. The challenge for educators, junior and senior educators alike, is to be aware of their inflexibility and to let go of the reins a little in order to create some flexibility (and invite a level of uncertainty). By being open minded and by valuing divergent thinking and originality, we encourage our students' creativity.

No. 3 – Delay Judgment

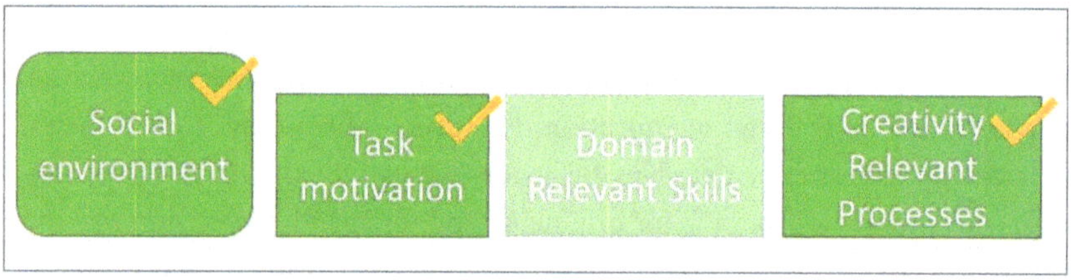

The third suggestion for incorporating creative thinking into ALE, is to try to delay judgement. Although the ability to think critically is an essential part of creative thinking and creativity, for instance, in the stages of problem identification (stage one) and during the validation of a possible solution (stage four), criticism and judgment are not always fruitful. If a student expects to be judged or if a student expects a critical audience, their creativity decreases.[161] As noted before in this chapter, Adair and Amabile both point out that the expectation of judgment or evaluation and harsh criticism may harm an individual's intrinsic motivation and their creativity. This is also stressed by Runco, who warns against using 'squelchers', evaluative phrases used by educators that might squelch creative thinking in students. For example, an educator who says "this is never going to work" or "you have to be serious" might unknowingly limit the student's creativity.[162] These insights are especially relevant for educators in Academia, where criticality is encouraged as part of the academic culture.[163]

To foster creativity, it is important to create an environment in which judgment is suspended.[164] Not only will the delay of judgments provide *time* for curiosity and possibility thinking,[165] it is also fitting for a creativity-stimulating environment where intrinsic

160 Beghetto 2009, p. 4.
161 Baer & Kaufman 2012, p. 75
162 Runco 2014, p. 183.
163 Adriansen 2010, p. 66.
164 Adair 2007, pp. 90-91.
165 Menkel-Meadow 2001, p. 122.

motivation is required. If ideas, which could potentially be good or even great, are criticized prematurely, the criticism will destroy the student's motivation and prevent them from generating new ideas in the future. Also, delaying judgment in the form of feedback ensures that educators do not unwittingly promote to students that stereotypical answers and solutions are best.[166] This, however, might not be natural for contemporary universities, where criticality and summative assessment are part of the culture. By no means do I mean to suggest eliminating any evaluation, feedback or assessment. Assessments are crucial for tracking the students' progress and qualitative feedback on creative work and ideas should eventually be given, since this helps students to be able to better validate the ideas they generate.[167] To make it feel less like an evaluation, peer feedback could be included. In 1971, Yeamans already pleaded for creative peer evaluation instead of critical peer evaluation in law schools based on Torrance's research findings.[168] Another way of making students aware of space for mistakes and growth might be to incorporate formative evaluation or to include the value of the process in the summative assessment. For example, students might be given points for their perseverance, courage, and personal growth instead of only validating the outcome.

If an educator wishes to encourage the creative thinking of their students, an important technique might be borrowed from the performing arts, especially from improv theater. When on stage, the guideline is to respond to every move, idea or thing that is given to you by your co-actor with "yes, and…". So, regardless of what your co-actor starts doing, crying, laughing, cooking, or snowboarding, you always agree with the idea and build upon it with a new one of your own. This response leads to new ideas and ultimately results in pleasurable and surprising scenes on stage. Technically, by not shutting a suggestion down, judgment is suspended or even eliminated from the situation. This provides space to explore the idea that is given and search for possibilities to make the most out of the idea. In contrast, if you shut your colleague's idea down immediately, not only will the audience notice a disconnect between the two actors on stage, but of greater concern, your co-actor will no longer be motivated to give you another proposal, which deprives the two of you of numerous possibly brilliant scenes. The strategy of building upon a team member's suggestions is also used in corporate brainstorming. However, for educators within a university context, the practical use of this approach might at first feel a little unnatural, since it seems opposite to our ingrained first reaction, which is to approach new ideas with an attitude of criticality. Where a critic initially searches for problems, flaws and doubt,[169] the creative approach is to react with an exploration of the

166 Cropley 2011, p. 151.
167 Lucas 2001, p. 39.
168 Yeamans 1971, p. 392.
169 See Weinfeld and Morton 2002, p. 838.

possible value of the idea. Nevertheless, if educators in ALE are willing to experiment with this creative approach, they may respond with "yes, and…" in various ways. First, in the relation between educator and student, for example, during a one-on-one talk about a student's thesis manuscript. In their role as supervisor, the educator could ask about the student's ideas by exploring them through the use of the "yes, and…" method. Secondly, in the collaboration between students, the educator could ask students to come up with problems and/or solutions to problems and instruct them to react to contributions with a "yes, and…" response. Finally, it is a usable tool in the relation between students with the material. While reading texts on law or philosophy of law, instead of asking for critique on the ideas offered by the author, an educator might ask 'how would you further enhance this theory?'.

No. 4 – Reward Courage

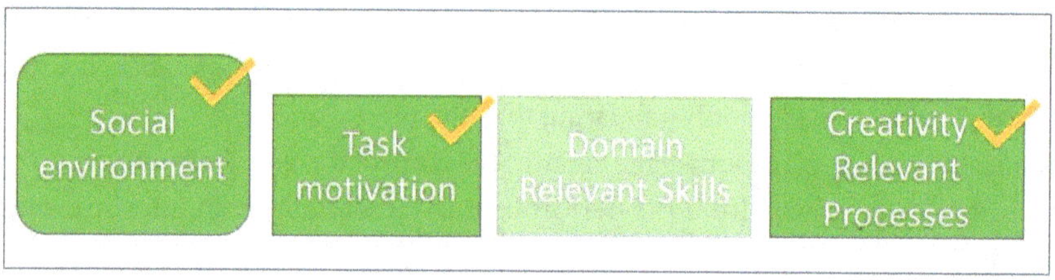

Rewarding courage is the fourth suggestion for stimulating creative thinking development in academic law schools. Students avoiding intellectual risk-taking is an undesirable outcome for an academic legal education. Therefore, courage shown by students in class, for instance through an unexpected contribution to the discussion, or an eccentric way of interpreting an assignment may be rewarded, by complimenting the behavior in class or even by including courage, divergent thinking or risk-taking in learning goals, assessment matrixes and assessment criteria.

Also, the mini- and little-C moments that our students experience have to be expressed and acknowledged in order for creative thinking to be nurtured. For educators, this takes some courage, an in-depth understanding of the subject[170] and a willingness to experience some uncertainty. Stimulating creative thinking, be it mini-C or little-C, also entails that educators recognize and support the students' creative experiences. A German study on how educators in higher education recognize creativity in students suggests that this is possible in a spectrum of six facets (which could become part of a course's learning goals): self-reflective learning; independent learning; showing curiosity and motivation; producing something; showing multi-perspectives and reaching for original, entirely new

170 Beghetto 2009, p. 3.

ideas.[171] It seems clear that the level of creativity in the facets are part of a continuum, from a low level (self-reflective learning) to higher (creating novel things) which correspond with the levels mini-C and little C of the four-C model.[172] By recognizing these signs of creativity, educators are able to provide support by, for example, complimenting the work a student has done so far or asking follow-up questions. Complimenting and asking follow-up questions are also ways to show students that the courage to think differently and to come up with new ideas is appreciated.

Obstructive factors on this matter that we see ourselves confronted with in legal education are the limited time that is reserved for lectures and classes, the vast number of students that take part in a working group (sometimes up to 45 students) and the fact that there is differentiation in the level of understanding between the students. This makes it harder for educators in legal education to support and acknowledge the contribution of creative students. However, it might be helpful to construct courses with the aforementioned 'six facets of creativity' in mind, for instance by including the facets in the learning goals. In that case, the educator's effort is backed by the course design.

No. 5 – Model desired behavior and attitudes

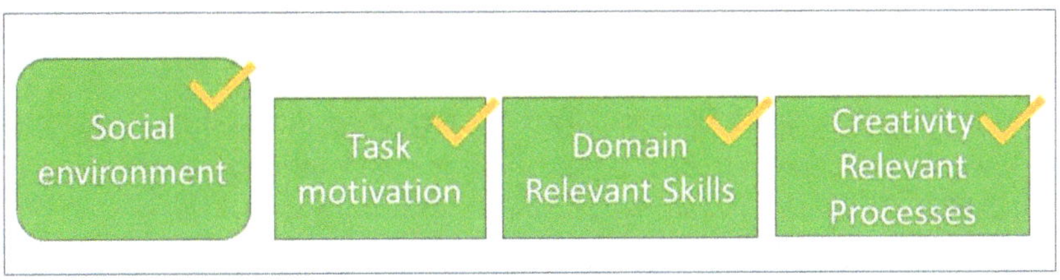

The fifth suggestion for incorporating creative thinking in ALE is to model the desired creative behavior and attitudes. A student's creativity can emerge in a climate where the educator takes on the role of coach or mentor who encourages the student's intrinsic motivation.[173] Educators can support student learning – and specifically their development of creativity – in various ways, one of which is by modeling the necessary conditions, attitudes and skills in their teaching style, for example, by treating students as equals and autonomous individuals, by being enthusiastic, lecturing dynamically and by expecting excellence.[174] Furthermore, research on primary schools shows that students whose

171 Jahnke 2017, pp. 90-91.

172 Jahnke 2017, p. 94. See on the four-C model Kaufman & Beghetto 2009.

173 Nygaard, Courtney & Holt 2014, p. 8. See also on the changing role of educators in higher education Cropley 2001, p. 168. See also Runco 2014, p. 182.

174 Research conducted by Chambers in 1975 showed that facilitating factors for student creative development in the teaching style are that the educator treated the students as individuals, encouraged student autonomy, served as a role model, was also available outside of college hours, made clear that excellence was expected

educator is intrinsically motivated towards work, see themselves as more motivated and competent as well. According to Amabile, this means that intrinsic motivation and student creativity can be enhanced by the attitude the educator models,[175] which can be classified as disposition modeling.[176] In my experience, disposition modeling is effective in higher education as well. For example, I have experienced that many students mirror behavior such as politeness, listening to others and a positive attitude. Modeling characteristics and attitudes crucial for creativity might therefore be effective when attempting to teach creativity to our students. This way, the educator shows what is expected of the students. So, when teaching a group of students writing skills, the educator may explain how they go through the creative process themselves when writing articles. Educators could also model negative capability by deliberately including moments of uncertainty in class, for example by making students the directors of the meeting or by explicitly acknowledging student questions the educator is not able to answer and demonstrating curiosity. By explicitly combining knowledge from different fields to come up with a new argument, for example, educators could model strong synthesizing ability. Educators could also more implicitly model desired behavior. For example, they might approach their subject in new ways, for example in combination with the visual arts, performing arts, sociology or mathematics to show unexpected combinations or use a combination of visual and auditory stimuli[177] to show that written language is only one way of getting your point across. Other important behavior for creativity that educators could model are an attitude of respect towards students and colleagues;[178] having broad interests; playfulness and humor, and flexibility.[179]

---

and achievable, enthusiastic, treated students as equals, gave immediate reward for creative student behavior (or work), gave lectures in an interesting and dynamic way and was also excellent when communicating individually with students. See Amabile 1996, p. 208.

175 Amabile 1996, p. 204. Amabile describes that research suggests that (in this case, primary school) educators of students that develop their creativity are described by classroom observers as, for example, more likable, more enthusiastic and more interested in the children. See Amabile 1996, p. 205. This seems to hint that there are certain attitudes or characteristics that educators require for supporting the development of creativity in students. Craft also states that an educator who models expertise and creative approaches stimulates young individuals that are new in a domain. See Craft 2006, p. 23.

176 Salisu & Ransom 2014, p. 55.

177 Lucas 2001, p. 40.

178 Lucas 2001, p. 40.

179 Runco 2014, p. 182.

No. 6 – Make time

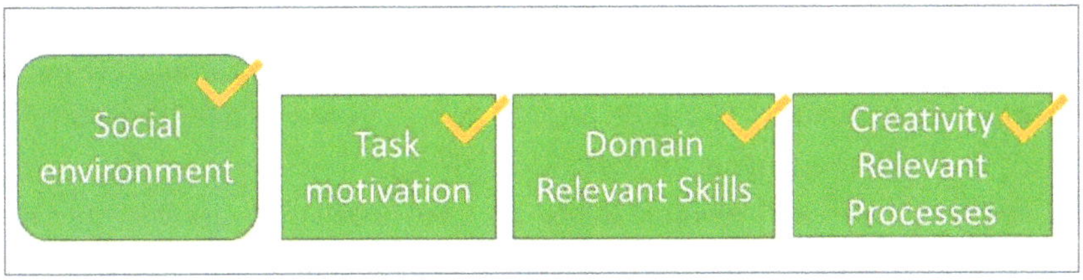

As is the case for critical thinking, creativity and creative thinking require time. Making time is therefore the sixth suggestion for incorporating creative thinking in legal education. To support creative thinking, educators might want to include time for error in their course design. In order for them to be creative, students require time to go through a creative process and discard ideas at the end of the process and start anew if needed. They need to learn that failure is an option and that it means starting over or going back a few steps without that being a problem. So, sufficient time for experimenting is required in the case of, for example, writing a paper, making a poster presentation, or finding a solution to a problem. However, currently, educators and students often only have limited time. Blended learning and a flipped classroom concept may give educators more time in contact hours to support their students' creative approach to the content. Also, a course design may include some flexibility to provide for time. In this way, stress with negative consequences may be avoided, such as stress that students perceive because of unnecessary strict time-limits.[180] Of course, deadlines and being able to meet them is part of an academic education, since legal professionals will also face strict deadlines in their professional lives, but exclusively focusing on deadlines in law school is not necessary nor fruitful. Educators may also make time in their chosen method of teaching, for example by making a clear selection of the content and the instructional interventions they employ.

No. 7 – Create appropriate assignments and assessments and stimulating instructional interventions

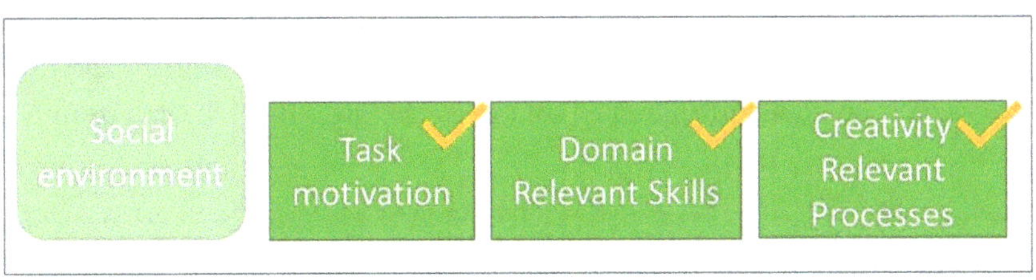

180 Lucas 2001, p. 39.

When designing a course that, amongst other learning goals, aims at teaching creativity and creative thinking, it is imperative to take into account some requirements of assignments and assessments that makes them appropriate for training and evaluating creativity. For example, the task has to be meaningful[181] and has to offer some level of complexity. It is also important to let students know that they are asked for creative responses. For the latter, it may be helpful to provide open ended tasks, ask questions that do not have clear cut answers and to challenge the students to connect unexpected ideas to solve tasks or problems. It is also possible to let students find their own problems (stage one of the creative process) instead of always offering the problem.[182] This touches on another vital aspect of assignments, assessments and instructional interventions that are appropriate for creativity: If possible, they have to provide room for the autonomy of the student. In the words of Craft, it is important that the students have 'decision making authority', which could make them more inclined to take risks (on their own conditions).[183] Furthermore, Belluigi and Amabile both stress that *formative* (instead of summative) assessment/evaluation with positive feedback is supportive for student creativity.[184] If students feels evaluated or judged on the task they are doing (for example, in the context of summative assessment), they will be less able to generate creative responses to the task.[185] However, it is possible to create some room for creativity (and autonomy) in written, summative exams. For example, one could include a question that offers the students a choice: They can either discuss and problematize the ideal state of Plato or Marx's ideal state. The students may choose whichever they like (or understand) best and problematize the chosen ideal state in the way they see fit. Another possibility is to provide an open ended task, for instance to write a free essay on any topic discussed in the course and connect that topic with a current societal problem.

Many aspects of the legal profession are specifically verbal, with a focus on the written and spoken word. Written assignments and assessments are therefore a natural part of an academic legal education for educators as well as for students. Nonetheless, to provide room for creativity, it might be helpful to include non-verbal tasks as part of instructional interventions, assessments or assignments. For example, students may be challenged to make posters, mind maps, mood boards, visualizations, storyboards,[186] or (non-verbal) videos. These tasks are probably beyond the students' comfort zone, which makes sure that they do not rely on 'standard' ingrained solutions. This gives them the opportunity to

181 Craft speaks of 'authenticity of the task', which means that an assignment needs to be relevant and authentic to the expert (the educator). See Craft 2006, p. 23.

182 Runco 2014, p. 186.

183 Craft 2006, p. 24.

184 Belluigi 2010, p. 47. The importance of positive, constructive feedback on creativity is also mentioned by Amabile. See Amabile 1996, p. 209.

185 Amabile 1996, p. 197.

186 Gow 2000, p. 32.

step outside their comfort zone which increases their chance for developing novelty.[187] For educators, it is imperative to keep in mind that, when evaluating as student's (creative) work, it is advisable not to penalize the student for immediate outcomes that are unsuccessful or penalties for mistakes, since those are not failures,[188] but part of the creative process the students are discovering.

Introducing them to models of creativity (such as Amabile's model) could support our students' early development of creative ability. By explaining the process of creativity and practicing the steps of the process in working groups, students learn to use it as a tool for creativity and creative thinking. However, later in life, or perhaps already in the Master's phase of their legal education, students have to be encouraged to break free of the constraints such a model of the creative process provides.[189]

No. 8 – Use play, playfulness and humor

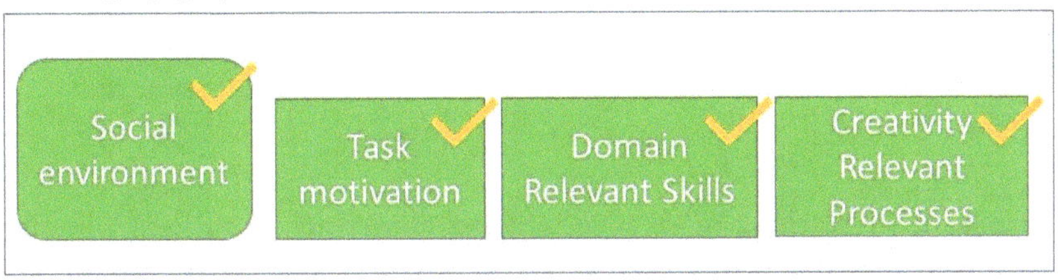

The eighth suggestion for developing creative thinking in ALE is to make use of play, playfulness and humor. Research shows that play and playfulness can positively influence creative ability.[190] In a playful learning culture and learning environment, students may discover that mistakes are normal steps towards the understanding of concepts and new ideas. Play and playfulness can positively influence the students' intrinsic motivation and, thus, task motivation. Educators could incorporate play activities in their course designs, such as serious games in the form of role play (with or without IT) or guests. In their teaching methods, educators may incorporate play by, for example, challenging students with a problem that they need to solve, for which they will have to experiment with combining ideas from various domains. The idea here is that the more the students are enabled to play around with ideas, the more they will come up with unusual connections. Moreover, students can be challenged to engage in play activities such as quizzes, creating quizzes themselves, making collages or mood boards based on legal problems, or by role

187 Runco 2014, p. 176.
188 Jackson 2010, p. xv.
189 Amabile 1996, p. 197.
190 Belluigi 2010, p. 47. See also Russ 2003, p. 292. See also Amabile 1996, pp. 225, 229. Amabile refers to (among others) Piaget, Lieberman and Sutton-Smith who describe the importance of play for novelty, flexibility and creativity.

playing legal cases. All these activities and, actually, *all* classroom activities could be done in a playful, lighthearted spirit which expresses itself in, for example, humor. The suggestion of using play and playfulness is central to all four components of creativity *and* important for critical thinking and *Bildung* (see chapters 2 and 3), student engagement and student learning. A detailed description of play and playfulness and their use in legal education (specifically on the level of teaching method and teaching style) can therefore be found in the sixth chapter, which also includes several practical examples in its appendix.

No. 9 – Add a focus on the development of creativity relevant processes

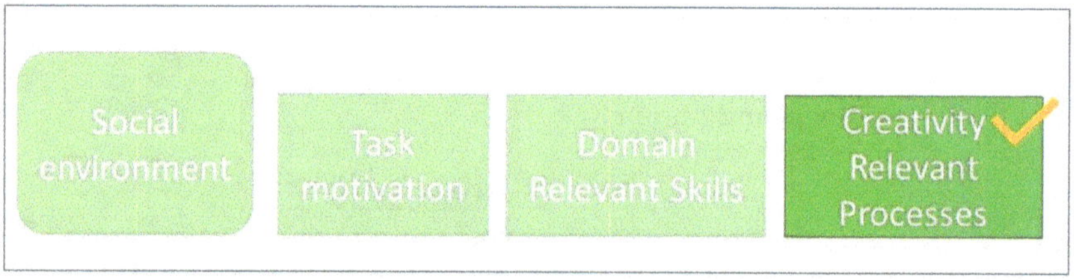

If we aim to take the teaching of creative thinking and creativity in legal education seriously, a focus on developing creativity relevant processes (CRP) is of the essence. This could entail changes in the attainment objectives of the curricula of our Bachelor's and Master's programs as well as adjustments to the learning goals of individual courses. A suggestion could be to focus on supporting students in the development of a personal *CRP toolbox*, which includes at least training in negative capability and synthesizing ability. For negative capability we could consider a re-mystification of legal education, which entails leaving room for uncertainty. To do so, it is important to note which kinds of uncertainty are desirable (for example, uncertainty on the specific questions asked in exams, unannounced instructional interventions during working groups, open ended assignments) and which are not (for instance, uncertainty on the reliability of online assessment tools such as TestVision or on the attainment objectives of the curriculum).

To make sure that students practice their synthesizing ability and develop a toolbox for making new connections, educators could use various techniques and activities, including forced associations;[191] mind mapping;[192] use of analogy;[193] brainstorming;[194] imagination; thought experiments; examination of opposites, and metaphorical thinking.[195]

No. 10 – Use the physical environment

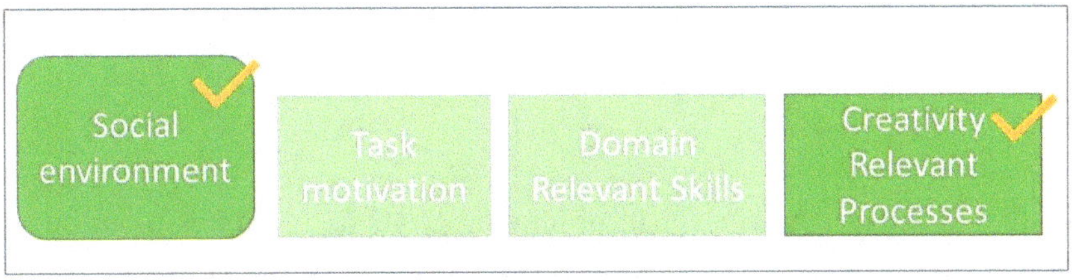

Using the physical environment effectively to support the students' development of creative thinking is the tenth suggestion to be discussed in this chapter. Creativity research has shown that the physical environment may positively influence an individual's creativity. The sound, colors, tidiness and lighting of a place may support creativity (see earlier in this chapter). Universities (or their architects and interior designers on the verge of constructing new buildings or remodeling existing ones) may take those insights into account. In case the institution is not able to adjust the physical environment, law faculties and educators may take it upon themselves to make small changes with effects on the creativity of students and staff. Classrooms and offices could rather simply be outfitted with (second hand) lamps, rugs, paintings, relaxing study chairs and community tables. It is also possible to include domain relevant items in a room, such as posters that provide relevant visual content, robes, timelines etc. Also, instead of 'clean desk-policies', clutter and personal items could be permitted in the offices of the faculty staff. A first step here would be to make educators aware of the effects the physical environment has on the creative ability of their students, so that they can try to influence the environment accordingly.

191 Baer and Kaufman 2012, pp. 42-43.

192 Mindmapping includes delaying judgment, idea generation and group work. See Runco 2014, p. 188. See als: Gow 2000, p. 32.

193 Based on research by De Bono, Menkel-Meadow summarizes twelve formal techniques to enhance creativity including use of analogy, transfer of concepts/ideas across disciplines, and challenging assumptions, brainstorming, and visualization. See: Menkel-Meadow 2001, p. 123.

194 Cropley 2001, pp. 138-139.

195 Gow 2000, p. 32.

No. 11 – Encourage creative group work

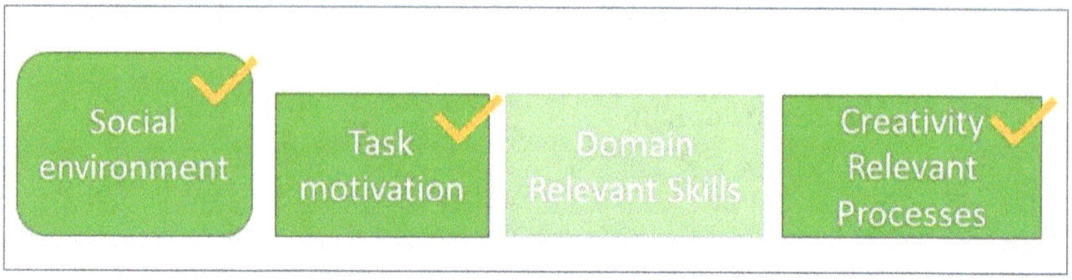

The eleventh and final suggestion for incorporating creativity in ALE is to encourage creative group work. Working creatively with others is said to be one of the 21st century skills.[196] Here, creativity becomes a social activity: Problems are tackled in a heteronomous team lacking hierarchy that, in optimal circumstances, consists of many members that meet regularly. According to Nygaard, Courtney and Holtham new members of the team are welcomed with open arms, because of their fresh ideas and new perspectives. Interestingly, working in a group may have a positive influence on an individual's intrinsic motivation.[197] Still, Amabile cautiously concluded based on her research that it might be the case that people working on a problem as a group may generate less novel ideas to solve that problem than if they were trying to solve it individually.[198] However, I find that the quantity of the ideas is not always of the highest importance. It might also be that together, people are able to come to qualitative and useable ideas more quickly and an early selection of ideas is not always undesirable, especially when time is of the essence. Also, collaboration is an indissoluble part of the lives of many professionals working in the legal domain. Learning how to work with others is therefore an important skill in addition to the contribution collaborative work may have on creativity.

Educators in legal education are able to encourage creative group work by incorporating forms of collaboration into their course design. Developing a (legal) solution to a societal problem as a group during the course might be an assignment that supports students' collaboration skills. Other possibilities for assessments that include teamwork are: group research projects, essays or presentations. However, it is important to provide students with guidelines, supervision, and feedback on how they collaborate. Based on my experience in courses that work with collaboration (i.e. Legal Skills and Moot Court), I see that students are often assumed to be adequate at working with team members. Unfortunately, this is not always the case and this results in frustration, disappointment or downright animosity between group members. The ultimate consequences of these

196 Piirto describes that working creatively with others is one of the 21st century skills, together with creative thinking and implementing innovation. See Piita 2011, p. 1.

197 Nygaard, Courtney & Holtham 2010, p. 5.

198 Amabile 1996, p. 197.

feelings are students continuing alone, dropping out of the course or getting inferior results. For this reason, sufficient guidance is necessary. Piirto proposes the attitude of group trust as one of the core attitudes connected to creative thinking.[199] In the context of collaboration in law school courses, this trust in the group may also include trust between the individual team members and in the supervisor (the educator).

This chapter's aim was to explore creative thinking as a part of *Bildung* in ALE. After defining the concept and delving into the stages and components of the creative thinking process, an initial model for integrating creative thinking in legal education was offered. With the discussion of the eleven practical suggestions that are part of the model, this chapter has come to its conclusion. The following chapter explores the third element of contemporary *Bildung* that is of interest for educators in legal education – responsibility.

199 Piirto 2011, p. 39.

5 History Has Its Eyes on You. Introducing ACT Responsibility in Academic Legal Education

"What kind of a man must one be if he is allowed to put his hand on the wheel of history?"
– *Max Weber*[1]

Introduction

The question Max Weber considers – to what kind of person would we entrust responsibility for the future? – is just as relevant today as it was more than a hundred years ago. In this chapter, I propose ACT responsibility as the ability that allows academic legal professionals to 'put their hands on the wheel of history' and influence the current and future society. The chapter examines the possibility of 'responsibility' as a mode of dealing with the difficulty of solving complex and globalized problems and the accompanying social sense of uncertainty. According to Jonsen, responsibility today has become a move forward into the unknown.[2] This can be interpreted in two ways. On the one hand, it has become much more difficult both to attribute and to take responsibility for one's choices in these times of abundant choice opportunities with unknown consequences and complex, globalized problems. This renders the locus of responsibility uncertain and daunting for the time being. This, in its turn, may lead to constant worry, the shunning of uncertainty, or negative feelings towards a call for taking responsibility. The scope of the responsibility may simply seem too overwhelming. On the other hand, responsibility provides a way of diminishing the unknown. In this context, Davis suggests that an important function of responsibility is to end uncertainty, because by attributing or taking responsibility, the potential mistrust that people place in each other might be alleviated.[3] In specific situations, this idea appears correct. In private law, for example, liability is a well-known form of responsibility that provides a level of certainty about the future conduct of others. For

1 Max Weber in his lecture Politics as a Vocation. See Weber 1919, p. 115.
2 Davis 2001, p. 6. Based on Jonsen in Responsibility in Modern Religious Ethics, p. 30. The move into the unknown includes that in contemporary society, we are led only by general rules and values, which we have to give content to ourselves.
3 Davis 2001, p. 4.

instance, by knowing that the salesman of a new laptop is *responsible* for selling well functioning devices, the client is able to trust in the quality of the obtained product. If the product has an unfortunate malfunction, the salesman is *liable* and the customer may trust in satisfactory client service. In addition to responsibility's function to provide some trust in others, or at least in a level of certainty about others' future behavior, identifying and taking personal responsibility could empower the individual, because the individual gains some certainty about their own position and ability to contribute to (a small portion of) the solution of complex problems. Although I do not concur that all uncertainty can be (or should be) ended, responsibility does offer a strategy for managing uncertainty. By defining, attributing, and taking responsibility it becomes more clear who is to solve problems and how. This is relevant for all citizens in contemporary global society, who all face complex problems. As members of the global society, legal professionals are confronted with complex challenges, too. In this situation, their personal, vocational and collective responsibility offers them a mode of conduct.

In the face of the current and approaching global complex problems – such as environmental and societal challenges – the ability to define, attribute and take responsibility is helpful for all global citizens, and also for academically educated citizens including academically educated lawyers. By more explicitly supporting the development of a sense of responsibility in students, academic law schools in the Netherlands could live up to their mission of supporting the development of their students' sense of societal responsibility, which is allocated to them in the Higher Education and Scientific Research Act (Dutch: *Wet op het Hoger Onderwijs en Wetenschappelijk Onderzoek*).[4] This mission is probably shared by educators in academic institutions beyond the Dutch borders as well, since the United Nations 17 Sustainable Development Goals for 2030[5] are dedicated to describing the principles of societal and environmental responsibility.[6] Bearing the UN Sustainable Development Goals in mind, it can be argued that responsibility is essential for *all* citizens of the global community and *everyone* should strive to contribute within the scope of their power to the welfare of humanity and sustainability. If this is something we aim for, a focus on responsibility needs to be realized in all areas of education in a way

4 A mission statement of higher education has been formulated in the Dutch Higher Education and Scientific Research Act (Wet op het Hoger Onderwijs en Wetenschappelijk Onderzoek), art. 1.3, section 5 (translated from Dutch by the author): '*institutions of higher education will also include a focus on the personal development of their students and the furthering of their student's sense of societal responsibility* (…)'.

5 The 17 UN Sustainability goals are: 1) No poverty; 2) Zero hunger; 3) Good health and well-being; 4) Quality Education; 5) Gender Equality; 6) Clean water and sanitation; 7) Affordable and clean energy; 8) Decent work and economic growth; 9) Industry, innovation and infrastructure; 10) reduced inequalities; 11) Sustainable cities and communities; 12) Responsible consumption and production; 13) Climate action; 14) Life below water; 15) Life on land; 16) Peace, justice and strong institutions, and 17) Partnership for the goals.

6 See for the UN's 17 Sustainable Development Goals: https://sdgs.un.org/goals, last visited October 1st, 2022.

befitting the students and the aim of the specific area of education. In the context of this research on *academic* education, I specifically explore the responsibility of academically educated legal professionals and seek strategies to incorporate a focus on such a responsibility in academic legal education (ALE).

I advocate that academics have a specific kind of responsibility to contribute to a solution of contemporary problems and to the welfare of humanity and the environment. In other words, they have a specific responsibility to pursue justice, human well-being and sustainability. This responsibility is rooted in the fact that academically educated citizens have been given time to study at a university and to gain deep understanding in one or more knowledge domains, to gather scientific insights, to become adept in critical thinking skills, to develop the ability to distinguish between fact and fiction and to become able to conduct their own research to find truth or at least to debunk fiction sold as factual truth. These abilities provide academics with a crucial set of skills and insights for a society flooded by unfiltered information and dealing with immense problems, such as climate change, wild life extinction, irresponsible exploitation of natural resources, increasing poverty and inequality, mass migration due to wars, violence or famine and renewed tension in international politics. Spreading their insights and contributing to society by actively using their academic skills is part of an academic's responsibility. In addition to these specific traits and abilities of academics, *legal* academics have not only gained deep insight into aspects of the law, but may also hold important key roles in society, for example, in the judiciary, legislation, administration or (international) politics. This enables them to actively and positively influence social development, which touches the lives of fellow global citizens and the environment. In their roles as criminal prosecutors, national policy makers, notaries, corporate lawyers, diplomats, NGO-employees, researchers, educators or judges and lawyers in legal fields such as criminal law, private law, tax law, family law, migration law, European law and international law, academically educated legal professionals can make a difference – or can at least seek to make a difference. Their ability to influence current developments lends them great power and with that power comes great responsibility. Therefore, academically educated legal professionals have to be aware of their responsibility and to be able to identify the scope of their own responsibility by reflecting on their societal roles as an academic, legal professional and citizen. Based on their self-authored identification of their own responsibility, academically educated legal professionals are required to be able take responsibility and take action.

Instead of Kant's University of Reason, Humboldt's University of Culture or the University of Excellence as criticized by Readings (see chapter 1), I advocate that the university that befits our time is a University of Responsibility. Consequently, I propose responsibility as the unifying principle of the contemporary University's disciplines and as the legitimizing idea of the university. Within this University, the *Bildung* of students is paramount. In the second chapter, a renewed interpretation of *Bildung* is offered to counter the current state of affairs in ALE in which a focus on the training of vocational skills has eclipsed legal education's academic component. In this renewed interpretation of *Bildung*, center stage is given to the abilities for critical thinking (chapter 3), creative thinking (chapter 4) and responsibility (this chapter). A route for developing these abilities is the use of playfulness and play with, for example, art and culture (chapter 6). Responsibility is a crucial element of this understanding of *Bildung* and seems to be both its reason and aim. Individuals take responsibility for their character and life choices by developing themselves in a perpetual *Bildung* process. At the same time, a person's *gebildete* character gives content to the way they *describe* their responsibility and the way they *take* responsibility. *Bildung* leads to a more defined picture and practice of one's responsibility. In explanation, *Bildung*'s inward dimension encompasses self-examination: Individuals take the responsibility to develop themselves and their talents and define their values and aims. Furthermore, the outward dimension of *Bildung* allows a person to be aware of their environment and the locus of their responsibility. In relation to their environment, individuals define their responsibility and are enabled to take responsibility. Components of this interpretation of *Bildung* that have already been further considered in previous chapters are critical thinking and creative thinking. These components culminate in a person's ability to define and take their responsibility for themselves and for their social and natural environment. This chapter explores responsibility as a vital part of the proposed interpretation of *Bildung* – which constitutes the academic component of a legal education – that commences during a student's academic education in law.

This research is aimed at finding ways to support the academic development of law students which includes their development into citizens and legal professionals able to function well in the complexity of contemporary society. It starts from the premise that educators in legal education can contribute to this goal. The required abilities of law students include an awareness of responsibility; the ability to identify their own responsibility and to take that responsibility; the capability to make self-authored decisions in the process of accumulating knowledge – for example *what* information to examine and *how* to study it; the ability to create a well deliberated position in life, and; being able to understand and solve complex problems that require insight beyond the legal domain by thinking critically and creatively.

This chapter seeks an answer to the overarching question how responsibility may be incorporated into ALE. To acquire an optimal interpretation of responsibility, this chapter draws on ideas on responsibility from various disciplines, such as philosophy, sociology and psychology. By doing so, I aim to show that this culminates in an understanding of responsibility that does justice to contemporary complexity. In order to answer this chapter's overarching question, I try to answer the following sub questions: What is responsibility?; What does the kind of responsibility required in contemporary times of academically educated legal professionals entail?, and In which way can legal educators create space for the development of this specific type of responsibility? To answer these questions and to gain a better understanding of the notion, this chapter starts with an overview of the history of conceptions of responsibility. This is followed by a classification of different types of responsibility that authors throughout history but especially in the last two centuries have described (among others P.F. Strawson, Wallace, Frankfurt, Young, Go, Weber, Levinas, Bauman, Jonas and Koehn as they have developed specific interpretations of responsibility). Then, the kind of responsibility that I propose as crucial for contemporary academically educated legal professionals – ACT responsibility – will be explored, followed by ideas on including and teaching this kind of responsibility in the context of ALE.

WHAT IS RESPONSIBILITY?

A history of responsibility

Because of its tradition in Christianity, Judaic theology and Kantian philosophy, responsibility is deeply ingrained in the thinking and social practices of the Western world.[7] However, what is meant by 'responsibility' depends on the context in which the concept is used. Responsibility might therefore be called a multi-contextual concept. Indeed, many thinkers have interpreted responsibility in just as many ways depending on their context and aim.[8] From Davis's point of view, responsibility has some ability to end distrust in others and end uncertainty. If that is the case, it is not surprising that the concept has held the interest of scholars throughout history. Another reason for the abundance of scholarly interest in responsibility, which indeed spans many domains and disciplines, is that responsibility can be viewed from many perspectives, such as legal and political analysis (for example, through punishment, the government holds individuals accountable and the state is held accountable by its citizens for its policies), moral theory (individuals consider the consequences of their actions – are their actions good or bad? – and consider the criteria that move them in their decision making), and social theory (in what way a person has ordered their values into an autonomous character and how civilization is structured),[9] or indeed, how uncertainty can be dealt with.

Nevertheless, the use of the specific noun 'responsibility' in philosophy is relatively new. According to McKeon, the philosophical treatment of the word only dates back to

7 Matravers 2007, p. 4.
8 See also Kaila 2007, p. 32.
9 McKeon calls these perspectives 'dimensions of responsibility': an external dimension (legal and political), internal dimension (moral and ethical) and a comprehensive/reciprocal dimension (social and cultural). See McKeon 1957, p. 5.

1859.[10] The noun probably made its entrance into the English language around the end of the 18th century from the domain of political debate. Murray's *Oxford English Dictionary* records that the noun made its first appearance in American letters with Alexander Hamilton's use of it in *The Federalist*.[11] This makes the noun 'responsibility' relatively young. Still, as a verb and in the adjective form the concept is known to have been used starting from the 13th century in France, around the 15th century in Germany and from the 16th century onward in the UK. It is most likely that the use of the adjectives 'responsibilité' and 'verantworten' derived from legal expressions in court that were used to establish innocence. Outside the court of law, 'responsible' became to mean 'the ability to respond' which established moral integrity.[12] In the Netherlands, the verb 'verantworde' – in current Dutch 'verantwoorden' – was used from around the 14th century mostly in legal contexts. The adjective 'verantwoordelijk' (accountable) dates back to the late 17th century. The earliest Dutch uses of 'verantwoorden' (in early Dutch) meant response or defense in the court of law. The addition of *ant* – which can be translated to *against* – in the word 'verantwoorden' shows that it included a retort against, for example, an accusation. Later uses of 'verantwoorden' in the Dutch language had the meaning of 'reacting to a question' and derived from the French 'répondre' and the Latin 'respondere'/'respondeo'.[13]

However, even if the exact, and Latin based,[14] noun 'responsibility' was not yet used, we can trace conceptions of responsibility back to ancient Greece. Koehn holds that there must have been an implicit concept of ethical responsibility in ancient Greek philosophy, because words that could be (loosely) interpreted as 'responsibility' were used, such as 'causality', 'task' and 'duty taken upon oneself'.[15] Davis argues that, in ancient Greece, responsibility was often seen as 'blameworthiness', in the sense that an individual was responsible for something if the blame could be placed upon their shoulders.[16] On closer inspection of Plato's ideal state, it is clear that Plato placed the responsibility for this state in the hands of a small group of philosopher kings, who excelled at the virtue of wisdom – in addition to the virtues of courage and temperance. Since these outstanding people were able to exit the proverbial platonic cave and *see* the light of truth (the Forms) the fate of the state could be entrusted to them as they could not be corrupted. This allocation of responsibility for the state to incorruptible philosopher kings provides a level of certainty

10 McKeon 1957, p. 6. See also: Davis 2001, p. 2 and Williams 2006.

11 Lerner 2011, p. 32. McKeon 1957, p. 8. See also Williams 2006 and Kaila 2007, p. 32.

12 Davis 2001, p. 2.

13 *Etymologisch woordenboek van het Nederlands*, https://www.etymologie.nl, last visited July 30th 2022. See also: See Lucas, J.R. (1995), 'Why did you do it?', in: *Responsibility*, Oxford: Oxford University Press 1995, p. 2.

14 Koehn 2019, p. 61.

15 Koehn 2019, p. 62.

16 Davis 2001, p. x.

to the people.[17] Additionally, according to Koehn, Plato's dialogues show an interpretation of responsibility which he calls 'Socratic Dialogical Responsibility' which he finds extremely relevant for contemporary problems. Key points of this 'Socratic Dialogical Responsibility' are a lifelong commitment to conversing with others (and ourselves) and taking care to avoid wrongdoing.[18]

Aristotle, too, wrote about what can now be viewed as 'responsibility'. For example, Aristotle holds that adult agents are responsible for their 'coming to be'. This means that individuals are held responsible for their character traits and their 'developed character'. The excellence of a character develops and shows itself in a person's emotions and in their voluntary actions.[19] Actions require a person to make a choice and to contemplate things that are within their power.[20] Aristotle regards human beings as different from other species because they are 'controlling origins' of action, which means that they can instigate – or decide to initiate – change (in other words, an *action*[21]) and do these things from reasoning.[22] In short, the controlling agent – the human being – has power since they can be the cause of an action. Aristotle speaks of a *voluntary* action when the action has an internal cause within the agent, namely if it stems from desire, decision or thought.[23] If the action was voluntary (the action was based on an internal cause), the agent is responsible for that action.[24] According to Aristotle, human agents are responsible for their virtuous as well as their vicious actions, in the sense that virtuous actions lead to being praised, whereas vicious actions result in being blamed.[25] In Aristotelian terms, blameworthiness of – responsibility for – an action requires an (1) epistemic and (2) control condition. In other words, (1) the effects of an action must have been foreseen and (2) the agent must have been in control of the action.[26] Davis argues that Aristotle does not view responsibility as a virtue.[27] In other words, it is not the golden mean – the desirable middle ground – between two vices. According to Davis, this means that Aristotle did not speak of a *moral*

17 Davis 2001, p. 5.
18 Koehn 2019, p. 69.
19 Cooper 2013, pp. 271, 307.
20 *Ethica Nichomachea*, 1112a30, in Aristotle 1999, p. 86.
21 Müller 2015, p. 9.
22 Müller 2015, pp. 5, 7. See also Cooper 2013, p. 273.
23 Cooper 2013, pp. 274, 276.
24 Cooper 2013, p. 275.
25 Cooper 2013, p. 267.
26 Vargas 2013, 'Responsible Agency', in: *Building Better Beings: A Theory of Moral Responsibility*, Oxford: Oxford University Press, p. 3.
27 According to Nielsen, Aristotle sees a *virtue* as a state concerned with decision (the process of deciding the golden mean). Decision itself requires the faculty of will, which belongs to Reason. Reasonable agents who have taken voluntary action are capable of blame and praise. In this sense, responsibility seems to be the consequence of decision (of a virtuous process) but is not a virtue in itself. See Nielsen 2016, p. 232.

responsibility.[28] Cooper concurs that the responsibility described by Aristotle is not a moral responsibility (it does not necessitate a free will, for example), but rather is merely a *causal* responsibility.[29] This seems to be the case because Aristotle hold agents responsible for what they *do voluntarily* and 'voluntarily' does not necessitate a human free will. It only requires that the action had its originating source within the agent, resulting in the person being subject to either praise or blame.[30]

After Aristotle and building upon insights from Stoics such as Zeno and Critias[31], responsibility came to mean 'duty'. In this meaning, it became part of Roman law, which stated that justice meant rendering every man his *due*.[32] In the Middle Ages – and still in the Christian tradition – it was also seen as specifically responsible behavior to obey the rules laid out in the testament(s). This 'responding to a duty' became the individual's responsibility.[33] For example, Augustine thought that God gave human beings a free will (*voluntas*) and freedom of choice. Because they could have chosen otherwise (and *better*), blame befell sinners who did not believe in God or who did not live according to the theological virtues.[34] It can be said that choosing to be virtuous and belief in God was the Christian's duty for which one could be held accountable. Nevertheless, the Catholic tradition to reverence mother Mary and the saints shows that responsibility for destiny, happy events or sorrow could in some cases be externalized and the practice of confession also served as a method for individuals to be relieved of their responsibility-as-duty.[35]

Since conceptions of the self (depictions of human beings) are central to how human responsibility is understood, interpretations of the responsibility concept have developed

---

28 Davis 2001, p. *x*. Lucas, however, points out that it might be possible to regard Aristotle's *phronesis* as an equivalent of responsibility. See Lucas, J.R. (1995), 'Beyond Responsibility', in: *Responsibility*, Oxford: Oxford University Press 1995, p. 1. Nevertheless, as indicated by Nielsen, it seems that phronesis has more to do with the process of decision making than with the actual responsibility for the action that follows the decision-making process. Only after an agent takes action is it possible to respond with either praise or blame. Thus, it seems that responsibility can be regarded as a consequence of the action following decision-making which leads to *phronesis*. See Nielsen 2016, p. 232.

29 Cooper 2013, pp. 267, 271.

30 *Ethica Nichomachea* 1109b30, in Aristotle 1999, p. 79. See also Müller 2015, p. 14, Nielsen 2016, p. 234; McKeon 1957, p. 11.

31 See Davis 2001, p. 5.

32 Zeno the Stoic was the first to describe the concepts of accountability and causal imputation (concepts related to responsibility) as 'duty'. Stoics saw duty as a universal term applicable to plants, animals and human action and the cosmos. Whereas the Greeks used the concept of 'justice' to describe virtues, the laws and the relationship between virtue and the laws (for example, Plato's ideal state is *just* when the philosopher kings – with their distinguishing virtue of wisdom – reign over the two other social classes – which are defined by the virtues courage and temperance), Zeno used the term 'duty'. See McKeon 1957, pp. 12-13.

33 Davis 2001, p. 13.

34 Couenhoven 2016, pp. 254-255.

35 See on the function of confession with regard to responsibility: Weber 2001 (original 1930), p. 216, note 149. See also Giddens 1976, p. xii: In the life of Catholics, a cycle of sin, repentance (during confession) and forgiveness continued to provide believers with hope for God's salvation and eternal life. This hope was non-existent in the life of Puritans. Weber 2001 (original 1930), pp. 62, 71.

along with new insights into human nature that were explored in historical eras such as the Renaissance in the 15th century (man as a central individual), the Reformation in the 16th century (the individual stands alone before God to account for his faithful life) and the Enlightenment in the 17th and 18th century.[36] From the Enlightenment onward, rational human beings are mostly viewed as creatures able to control nature through reason. Constantly evolving technology brought a sense of control over nature and control over what was formerly seen as destiny, resulting in unprecedented responsibilities for human beings.[37] For example, individuals might now be held responsible for the success of harvests, the prevention of floods or the perfect health of newborn babies. These events and situations could no longer be entirely externalized to an outward force, since human technology could influence their coming about. Moreover, starting from the Enlightenment, human beings were regarded as autonomous and were attributed a free will. This depiction of the human being has had consequences for criminal law. The codification of the Dutch penal code in 1886, for example, was founded in the context of the so-called 'Classical School' (*Klassieke Richting)* which has its roots in the work of *lumières* such as Cesare Beccaria's *Dei delitti e delle pene* and Kant's views on retribution as the aim of punishment and individual freedom from state interference.[38] According to Kant, individuals are capable of being held personally responsible for their beliefs and actions. He regarded the Enlightenment as a cognitive liberation process that entailed that individuals use their own *ratio* without the guidance of another, be it a statesman, the Church, or another human being or institution.[39] In this context, Kant called upon individuals to think for themselves ('*sapere aude!*').[40] As Kant wrote in his 1784 essay *Was ist Aufklärung?*, this autonomous thinking would herald the exit of mankind from its self-incurred immaturity.[41] Kant's individual ethics are deontological: A person's actions are *good* when they are in accordance with a moral duty or normative law (a categorical imperative) and wrong if they are not.[42] Since individuals are free agents capable of identifying and living according to these rational[43] moral duties, a person is responsible and can be held accountable if they fail to live in accordance with their moral duties.[44] Kant refers to this personal responsibility

36 Davis 2001, p. 3. See also on the duration of the Enlightenment era Oz-Salzberger 2014, p. 33.

37 Davis 2001, p. 4.

38 See Kelk 2005, p. 20. De Jong 2009, pp. 61, 68. See also Oz-Salzberger 2014, p. 38.

39 Oz-Salzberger 2014, pp. 32, 36.

40 Kant 1784.

41 Kant 1784. Oz-Salzberger 2014, pp. 32, 36.

42 Wilson 2014, pp. 447-448.

43 The content of rationality is moral: Through Kant's rational universalizability test, moral duties are identified. These duties are therefore in accordance with reason. See Williams 2006.

44 Note that Kant's moral duties and responsibility for living in accordance with the categorical imperatives is a more complex concept of responsibility than the earlier discussed 'responsibility-as-duty' (or 'simple' responsibility) in the context of, for example, Christian faith. In the latter, the duties are provided by an external authority and need merely to be followed. In Kant's theory, the moral agent is required to identify

as 'imputation' (*Zurechnung*); a past action (the *deed*) is imputed to the responsible - and thus accountable - agent (the *free* cause of the deed) who is then not only seen as the natural cause, but also the author of the action.[45] Imputation shows that the agent is morally responsible for their actions, that they can be held to account.[46] In criminal law, this responsibility for past actions results in a system of absolutist retribution: According to Kant, the responsible party - the offender - has to be punished equally to their criminal deed.[47] In the footsteps of Kant and under the influence of the 'Classical School' (*Klassieke Richting*), retribution is still an important aim of punishment in Dutch criminal law.[48]

Halfway through the 19th century, *personal* responsibility became more important under the influence of capitalism. In this view, the poor were held responsible for their own poverty.[49] During these times, capitalism turned responsibility into a virtue of public life (and not solely a topic of scholarly debate).[50] According to Max Weber (1864-1920), capitalism - which was boosted by the lingering aftermath of Christian sects' ideologies - stimulated the idea that people were individually responsible for their own possessions and well-being.[51] A reputation of responsibility was required, in the sense of respectability

---

the moral duties on their own (through universalizing maxims). For the distinction between simple and complex responsibility, see Davis 2001, p. 6, see also Davis 1999, p. 30.

45 Blöser 2015, pp. 184-185. See also Williams 2006.

46 Matravers 2007, p. 4.

47 Kant 1998.

48 Koenraadt 2004, p. 157. See also: Nagel 1999, pp. 69-70.

49 Interestingly, this individualizing tendency can also be recognized in criminal and criminological ideas in the second half of the 19th century. See Nagel 1999, p. 71.

50 Davis 2001, p. 3.

51 According to Weber, Christian Puritan sects - Methodism, Baptism, Pietism and especially Calvinism - that developed since the Reformation (16th century) created fertile ground for individualism and capitalism (which is, in the words of Weber, the rational organization of formally free labor. See Weber 1930, p. xxxiv). These sects prescribed a way of life that was rationalized and methodological. It combined a frugal life style with an impulse for the accumulation of wealth, based on an ultimate principle of predestination. Members of these sects believed that God had created all, that his plan was already laid out and could not be changed (Weber 1930, p. 56, Giddens 1976, pp. xi, xii). In this determined world, almost everyone was destined for damnation and only a few chosen individuals would ultimately receive salvation. However, no one could be certain if they were one of the *chosen* few and - because of His almightiness - it was impossible to influence God's decision through, for example, good deeds (Weber 1930, pp. 58-60, 65). In the end, this meant that it was every man for himself; the individual was destined to suffer uncertainty through life and then face God's decision (either salvation of damnation) on his own. Consequently, Weber argues that this ontology must have resulted in 'a feeling of unprecedented inner loneliness of the single individual' (Weber 1930, p. 60). To deal with this situation, two rules for living were of importance in the individual protestant ethic. One, it was every Christian's absolute duty to consider himself *chosen* (this showed faith in God) and, two, in order to deal with the uncertainty - and for the greater glory of God - they had to partake in intense worldly activity. In other words, they had to do their duty, live moderately (an act of self-control) and work diligently (Weber 1930, pp. 66-67, 69, 72). Work was considered a *Calling* from God (recognizable in the German noun Be*ruf* and the Dutch be*roep*) and became in itself an aim of life (Weber 1930, pp. 105-106). The possessions the individual gained through work, he held for the glory of God (Weber 1930, p. 114). If you worked hard and had (financial) success, this must be a blessing from God and *might* just mean that you are one of the *chosen*. Consequently, success in business is God's will for some people and a sign of His

or reliability.[52] In explanation, to convince others in the capitalistic society of your creditworthiness, so that they might give or lend you money to further your endeavors, you had to show your respectability – and thus responsibility – in other aspects of life as well.[53]

However, the capitalistic system *seemed* to crumble during the crisis of the Great Depression in 1929. In the United States, this led to the New Deal in 1933. The New Deal signaled the start of welfarism in which the responsibility for the good of the people (the good of all) was allocated to the State, which was entrusted with managing social policy.[54] In other words, the welfare of individuals in the sense of housing, work, health and education was seen as a collective responsibility shared by the members of the community and not by individual agents.[55] In these times, criminal behavior was regarded as the result of bad socialization. Criminal offenders were believed to be capable of rehabilitation through therapy, better schooling or sufficient housing, which were all the responsibility of the State.[56] This early 20th century move towards a 'therapeutic idea of responsibility'[57] does not depart from the premise that people are free to choose their actions, but held that factors external to the agent cause their behavior, such as their biology or social environment. The authority (the State) becomes responsible for intervening in the lives of

---

grace. These people must therefore find and explore further business opportunities for the greater glory of God, while remaining averse to luxury and frivolous matters. In other words, their accumulated wealth was meant for the glory of God and should hence be invested in new business opportunities or used for the welfare of the community (Weber 1930, pp. 104, 108-109, 115-116. Weber 1904, p. 322). This, of course, encourages the mindset and work ethos that is needed in capitalism; business owners had religious and ethical reason for exploring business opportunities and accumulating wealth, while poor laborers were motivated to work because it pleased God and was now considered not only necessary to fulfill their basic needs, but also because it is their divine Calling. The Puritan belief also justified the inequality of the distribution of wealth between bourgeois business owners and laborers: It was God's will to bless only some individuals (Weber 1930, pp. 120-121). According to Weber, the religious roots of the capitalist work ethos disappeared during the 19th century in which people worked hard to gain as much money as they could and viewed their work as a life calling without linking that calling to a deity (Weber 1930, p. 124. Weber 1904, p. 321).

52 Davis 1999, p. 45.

53 In 1904, Weber described (based on a field trip in a rural area in America) that becoming a member of a Puritan congregation was an intelligent way for aspiring businessmen to ensure their business of patronage *and* to be able to apply for credit. By presenting their certificate of membership of a congregation, a man showed his personal moral qualification, since one could only become a member of the sect after exhaustive tests. Possible future customers or business partners then knew, based on the fact that this person belonged to a congregation, that he could be trusted. By showing his congregation membership, the individual proved beyond doubt that he was qualified as a trustworthy businessman and proved his creditworthiness. This custom supported the development of the middle class. Weber 1904, pp. 303, 305, 308, 310, 312. See also Davis 2001, p. 2. See Weber 1930, pp. 114-115.

54 Matravers 2007, p. 5.

55 Young 2013, p. 9. See also Lippmann 1949, pp. 35-37.

56 Matravers 2007, p. 5.

57 See with regard to the distinction of classical responsibility and therapeutic responsibility: Davis 2001, p. 274.

its citizens at crucial moments, so that they are deterred from future criminal acts.[58] The belief that individuals are subjected to external factors is also recognizable in the development of the 'Modern School' (*Moderne Richting*) in Dutch criminal law in the first decades of the 20th century.[59] Inspired by insights from the upcoming science of criminology, lawyers and scientists departing from the *Moderne Richting*, focused on the offender and their circumstances instead of solely on the criminal act committed.[60] In the words of Buruma, 'individuals became a problem and object of state policy'.[61] An example of the influence of the *Moderne Richting* on the *Klassieke Richting* can be seen in the implementation of the measure to place an offender under a hospital order, namely the *Terbeschikkingstelling van de regering* (TBR, now: TBS) in 1928.[62] Since offenders were thought to have committed the criminal act because of their faulty biology or their unfortunate social circumstances, they were seen as not responsible for these actions and could not be held to account. Thus, wrongdoers were not blameworthy and did not require retributive punishment,[63] but rather therapy to help change their future behavior.

From the second half of the 20th century, responsibility once again became more and more important as a virtue in public life.[64] It also became a much discussed concept in scholarly literature. Whereas the debate on responsibility in the 18th and 19th century was held in the context of politics – for instance in discussions of the principles of representative government and how the government/state was responsible for its citizens – in the 20th century, the discussion turned to a more *individual* responsibility. In these times, many philosophers in the scholarly debate on individual *moral responsibility* seem to have focused on questions regarding free will and determinism.[65] The main concern here is that *if* causal determinism is true and all events are fixed, free will and responsibility may become impossible since individuals would have no control over their choices and actions. Compatibilists such as P.F. Strawson, R.J. Wallace and H. Frankfurt tried to harmonize determinism and responsibility by arguing that even if determinism is true, free will – or, at least, responsibility – is possible. These compatibilist attempts are often based on a redefinition of freedom. For example, compatibilists redefine 'freedom' as 'not being under compulsion', 'having the ability to *do* otherwise' or 'free to do an action for reasons of your own'.[66] On the other hand, incompatibilists such as Galen Strawson (son of the above mentioned compatibilist P.F. Strawson) argued that determinism turns free will and

58 Davis 2001, p. 274.
59 Van der Wolf 2013, par. 3.3.
60 Nagel 1999, p. 70. See also De Jong 2009, p. 68. Kelk 2005, pp. 21-22.
61 Buruma 1999, p. 14.
62 See: Van der Wolf 2015, par. 53.3.1. See also Koenraadt 2004, p. 163.
63 See Vincent 2015, p. 481. See Koenraadt 2004, p. 157. See also Kelk 2005, p. 23.
64 Davis 2001, p. 1.
65 Williams 2006.
66 See, for example, Frankfurt 1969, pp. 829-831.

responsibility into an impossible fantasy.[67] Galen Strawson's view that individuals cannot be morally responsible for what they do since they did not make themselves (the so-called 'basic argument'[68]) recalls the assumption of thinkers within the *Moderne Richting* who found that individuals are powerlessly subjected to their environment and biology.

The philosophical interest in *individual* (moral) responsibility finds its counterpart in the context of social policy. Indeed, in the 1970s, a shift occurred from welfarism to individualism, in which responsibility was no longer seen as a task of the state, but that of *individuals*. The Thatcher administration in the UK (1979) and the Reagan administration in the US (1980) put individual responsibility in the spotlight.[69] This change of perspective led to another depiction of poor people: They were seen as having caused their own situation by their behavior or capabilities and were therefore held responsible for their own misfortune.[70] The shift in thinking about responsibility resulted in reforms in social policies with regard to social security. For example, recipients of state funding were expected to do something in return or could only apply for state support for a limited number of years.[71] Another development that marked the new perspective was the tough attitude towards crime and wrongdoers.[72] The shift from state responsibility to personal responsibility was also noticeable in the language used: People that infringed the law were depicted as predators and evil.[73] The societal conviction that individuals are personally responsible for their lives remained during the last decades of the 20th century. In our modern world, the Greek interpretation of responsibility as blameworthiness is replaced by responsibility as the '*ability to respond*' to the question, why did you do that? This also fits the etymological basis of the Dutch word 'verantwoorden', the German 'Verantwortung', the Anglo-Saxon 'responsible' and the French 'responsible', which all mean response-able.[74] At the end of the 20th century and the beginning of the 21th century other types of responsibility, such as collective responsibility, social responsibility and corporate responsibility became more popular in the scientific, political and public discussions of responsibility.[75] In the following, these various kinds of responsibility will be further explored, so that the responsibility of academically educated legal professionals might be clearly identified within the discussions of responsibility.

67 G. Strawson 2008, pp. 16-17.
68 G. Strawson 2008, p. 1.
69 Matravers 2007, p. 6.
70 Young 2013, p. 3.
71 Young 2013, pp. 7-8.
72 Matravers 2007, p. 8.
73 See Matravers 2007, p. 9.
74 Davis 2001, p. 5.
75 See Williams 2006.

Defining responsibility

As can already be surmised from its long history and its constant transformation and many reinterpretations,[76] defining one fixed conception of responsibility that fits any context is not an easy task, nor does it seem necessary. When speaking of responsibility, people often implicitly or explicitly refer to some *kind* of responsibility within a specific context, such as social responsibility, moral responsibility, legal responsibility (liability/accountability), political responsibility,[77] corporate responsibility[78] or collective responsibility. All these responsibilities have a different meaning and content, they might refer to a different person or entity who is responsible, aim at other things for which that person or entity is responsible or hold someone responsible for past or future actions and occurrences. With the aim of developing a conception of responsibility to be used in the context of ALE, an understanding of the main interpretations of responsibility is required. Therefore, even though it is not an exhaustive overview of *all* possible interpretations of responsibility, the visual that will be constructed step-by-step in the following sections aspires to provide some insight into the main categories of responsibility. As a result, this Four-Axis graph functions as a tool to develop a grounded conception of the responsibility of academically educated legal professionals.

76 See Davis 2001, p. ix. See also Williams 2006. See also: Kaila 2007, p. 32.

77 See White 2017, p. 139. According to Davis, political responsibility includes remaining vigilant and keeping yourself informed. See Davis 2001, p. 17.

78 See White 2017, p. 134.

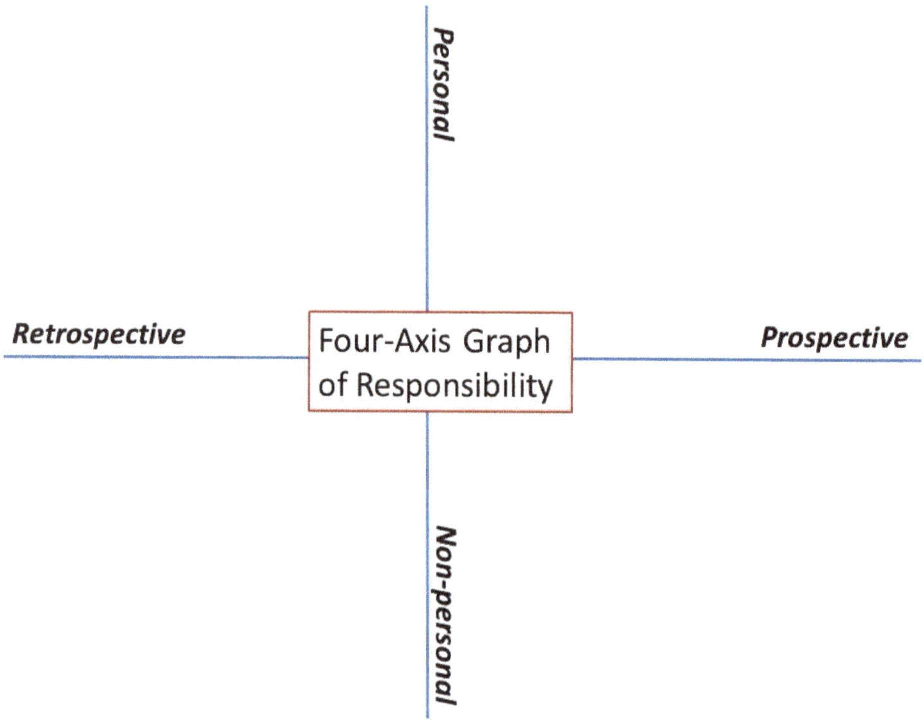

The horizontal axis of the graph above differentiates between the retrospective and prospective focus of a conception of responsibility. The key question here is where the focus of the responsibility lies. If the focus is on an action, omission or event in the *past*, the responsibility is retrospective. In the case of prospective responsibility, the allocated responsibility focuses on the *future*, the thing for which somebody is responsible lies in the future.[79] It does not have to do with past actions but is, for example, a responsibility to perform certain behavior, actions or duties *in the future*.

The vertical axis of the graph shows the distinction between non-personal responsibility and personal responsibility. Non-personal responsibility looks at the responsibilities that transcend the individual: It may concern collective responsibilities of a group of people, a society, or a government. Even though these might consist of many individuals, the responsibility ascribed to these entities is not of an individual nature. Personal responsibility, on the other hand, looks at the responsibility of single *individuals*. Based on Max Weber's *vocation* lectures,[80] Davis distinguishes two types – although 'levels' might be

79 Zimmerman 1988, p. 2.

80 In *Politics as a Vocation*, Weber describes the qualities of the political leader, who should have passion for a cause, a sense of responsibility and a sense of proportion. Weber 1919, pp. 95, 115, 126.

a more appropriate term – of responsibility within personal responsibility, namely simple responsibility and reflexive or complex responsibility. Simple responsibility is similar to the earlier mentioned responsibility in the context of the religious traditions and refers to the responsibility individuals have to do their duty and to be obedient, in other words, it is the responsibility-as-duty conception.[81] In this interpretation of responsibility, a person acts well when they are conscientious, dutiful, reliable, trustworthy or prudent; they need to abide by the rules and behave as expected.[82] The rule follower is responsible for fulfilling their duty through their actions, but not for the consequences of the action. After all, the rule or duty was given by an authority who would be responsible for the whole picture – including the consequences of the rule.[83] Simple responsibility could provide a leader (and all community members) with a level of certainty or predictability as to the conduct of the people.[84] Interestingly, simple responsibility looks at both past behavior with regard to a person's duty (an individual is responsible for past actions) *and* future behavior (future actions of the individual are under the obligation of their duty). Consequently, simple responsibility – or responsibility-as-duty – is located on both the retrospective and prospective Axis. Nevertheless, simple responsibility is not what this research aims for as an ability to be achieved by law students in their journey toward becoming academically educated legal professionals. First of all, because its scope too broad; it is a responsibility that can also be attributed to small children or even animals. For example, a dog might be seen as doing its duty – and thus acting responsibly – if it follows the commands of its owner. Secondly, in addition to its scope being too broad, simple responsibility (responsibility-as-duty) is also too narrow, it limits responsibility to merely following rules. Instead of limiting responsibility to only abiding by a deity's or leader's rules, contemporary times require law students to be capable of self-authored decision making and of defining their own more encompassing responsibility. Fortunately, in current society, simple responsibility is met with criticism[85] and is not the dominant interpretation of responsibility.[86]

---

81 Davis shows the link between so-called simple responsibility (responsibility-as-duty) and religion by describing that Adam and Eve were thrown out of Eden for not fulfilling their duty (responsibility) as prescribed to them by God. To explain, God forbade Adam and Eve to eat from the apple tree. Abiding by this rule therefore became their duty, or in other words, Adam and Eve's (simple) responsibility. However, in spite of the rule, both took a bite. As a consequence of breaking God's rule, and thus for not taking their simple responsibility, both were thrown out of Eden as punishment. See Davis 2001, p. 5. For living outside the Garden of Eden, or rather, for a life that is self-authored, it seems that simple responsibility necessarily needs to transform into a far more complex form of responsibility that transcends duty.

82 Davis 2001, p. 6.

83 Weber 1919, p. 126.

84 Davis 2001, p. 11.

85 Lucas, for example, criticizes the duty-interpretation as being boring or even cold. See Lucas (1995) 'Beyond Responsibility', in: *Responsibility*, Oxford: Oxford University Press 1995, p. 2.

86 See also Davis 1999, p. 30.

Most current interpretations of individual responsibility seem to share that the ability to shoulder responsibility is specifically *human*.[87] This has not always necessarily been the case, as history shows that in earlier times, animals were sometimes to a certain extent held responsible for their deeds.[88] Up until the 18th century, trials of animals are known to have occurred in Europe.[89] For example, in 1474, a pig was hanged by order of the bishop of Lausanne as punishment for devouring a baby that was sleeping in its crib and, in 1621, the law faculty of the University of Leipsic sentenced a cow to be killed on a barren stretch of land after pushing a woman, which caused her death.[90] In his famous study of animal trials, Evans shows many similar examples of animal convictions throughout history, many of which involved pigs and swine, but also rats, insects, dogs, donkeys and cows.[91] Nevertheless, in contemporary western societies, responsibility is usually not attributed to animals or children. Adults, too, are not always seen as capable of taking (moral and legal) responsibility or of accountability, for example, in case of actions done by someone with a severe mental disability or an offence committed during an acute psychosis or under the strain of extreme emotion. In these cases, the person might be seen as the cause of the action – they might have causal responsibility – but are not held to account – they are not blameworthy. Nevertheless, in 'normal' circumstances, adults are seen as being capable of shouldering responsibility. This conception of responsibility is more complex than mere 'simple' responsibility. According to Heidbrink, true responsibilities differ from duties (and laws) because they are unspecified obligations based on loose liabilities and open rules of action performed by an active actor. This requires situational knowledge, a degree of common sense and moral judgment.[92] Such a description is rather similar to what Davis outlines as complex or reflexive responsibility based on Weber's consequentialist theory of responsibility.[93] These ideas of responsibility might define the current perspective on responsibility more accurately than 'simple responsibility'. In reflexive responsibility, a person is taking responsibility when they are willing to think of the consequences of their actions, have a sense of when to consult their conscience, are able to change plans when

87 See for example Fischer & Ravizza 1993, p. 4. Importantly, *causal* responsibility might also be attributed to animals or children. See Fischer and Ravizza 1993, p. 5.

88 Most researchers agree that throughout history, animals were not attributed moral agency in the same sense as humans were attributed moral agency. However, there is some discussion in the literature about the reason for putting animals on trial. Some argue that the proceedings showed respect for God, who had created the animals and who might have been the driving force behind their actions. Others suggest that animal trials were important as they showed that justice was universal for all creation which included humans as well as animals. See Smith 2012, pp. 7-8.

89 See Smith 2012, pp. 5-6. Nagel even describes an animal trial (the trial of two dogs that were accused of tearing a thief into pieces) that took place much later, in 1974, in Glasgow. See Nagel (or. 1977) 1999, p. 66.

90 Evans 1906, pp. 41, 46.

91 See Evans 1906.

92 Heidbrink 2008, p. 11.

93 See Davis 1999, p. 35, 41.

the possible consequences of their actions might interfere with goals or commitments that they value highly and are willing to give a truthful explanation of their chosen actions.[94]

With help of the Four-Axis graph above, conceptions of responsibility can be categorized in four groups: retrospective non-personal responsibility (bottom left) retrospective personal responsibility (top left), prospective non-personal responsibility (bottom right) and prospective personal responsibility (top right). The positions on responsibility of the philosophers mentioned earlier in this chapter can be classified as follows:

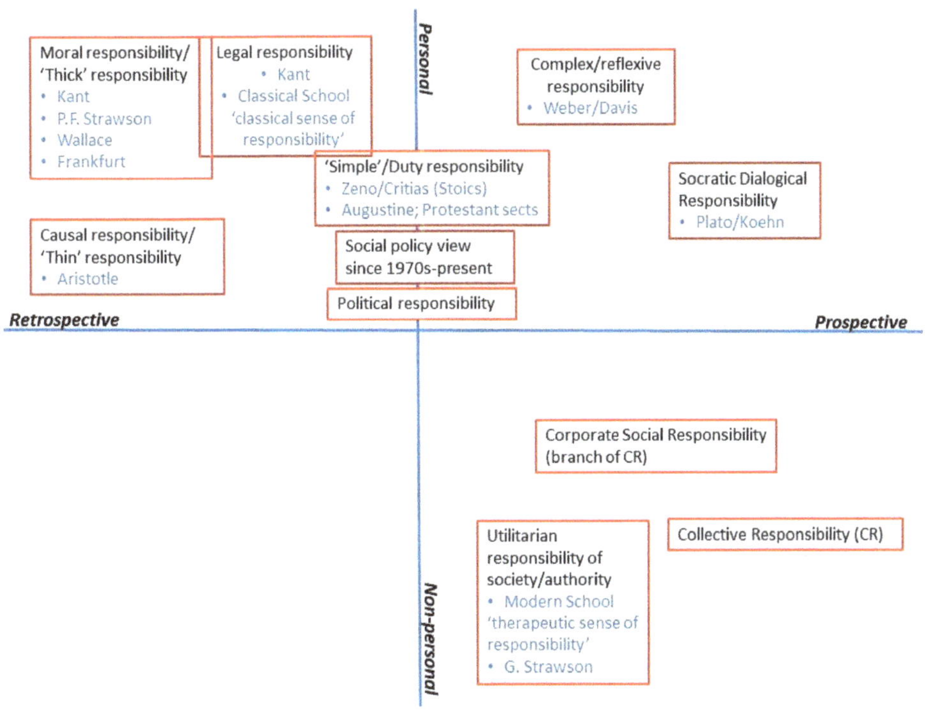

In the following, each of the four fields of the Four-Axis Graph will be further explored. By doing so, we gain clarity and insight into the many conceptions of responsibility. Based on that knowledge the kind of responsibility that befits academically educated legal professionals in contemporary times can be defined later on in this chapter.

94 Davis 2001, pp. 6-7. See also Weber 1919, p. 127.

Retrospective non-personal responsibility

First, retrospective non-personal responsibility (bottom left) looks at the responsibility of collectives, organizations, groups or societies for events, occurrences or actions in the near or distant past. Examples of this form of responsibility are the responsibility of the Dutch people for the trade in slaves in the 17th century or the responsibility of the Dutch State for war crimes in Rawagedeh, Indonesia in 1947.[95] Another form of retrospective non-personal responsibility might be what Janssen calls Corporate Historical Responsibility. This is a branch of Corporate Social Responsibility that looks at the responsibility of corporations for actions *in their historical past*; if they have collaborated in historical injustice, they are held responsible. These historical actions might, for instance, be the business's involvement in supporting the Apartheid Regime, the Third Reich or Slave trade.[96] Corporate Social Responsibility further includes the accountability of corporations for actions in the recent past,[97] such as the responsibility of fast-fashion corporations for having sold clothes sewed by workers in dangerous and inhumane working conditions.

Below, these types of retrospective non-personal responsibility are added to the Four-Axis Graph:

95 See Veraart, W.J. (2021), 'Klassiekers democratische rechtsstaat #21: De Toekomst en het Verleden', available at: www.nederlandrechtsstaat.nl/21-de-toekomst-en-het-verleden/, last visited August 30th 2022. See also: Immler, N.L. (2021), 'Het slavernijverleden als erfenis', available at: www.filosofie.nl/het-slavernijverleden-als-erfenis/, last visited August 30th 2022.

96 Janssen 2013, pp. 65-66, 69.

97 Janssen 2013, p. 69.

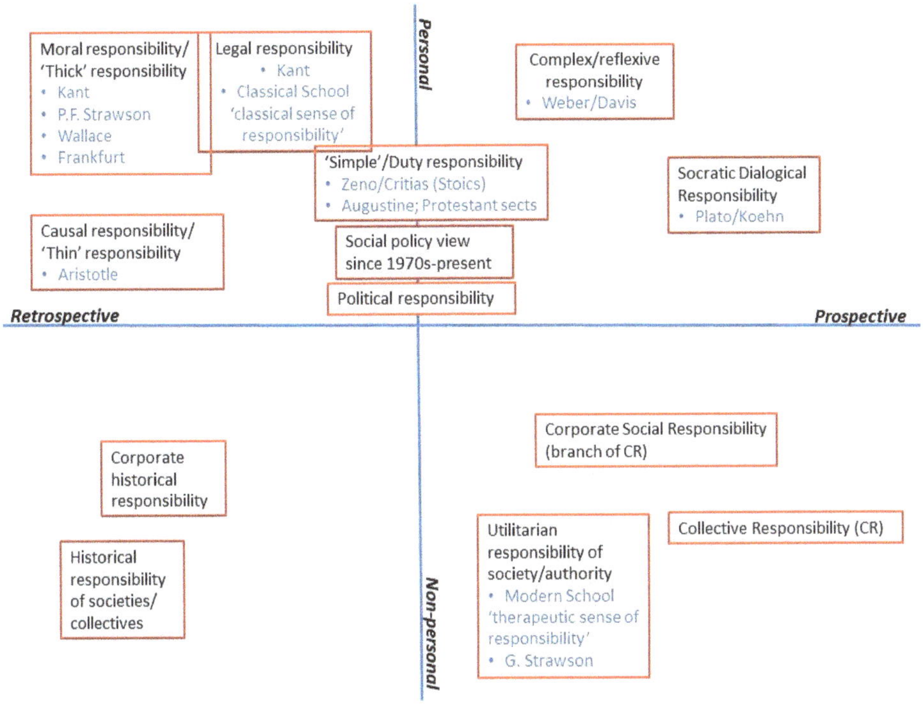

Retrospective personal responsibility

Second, the top left field in the Four-Axis Graph – which already includes the essential philosophers whose views on responsibility will be explored in the following – focuses on *retrospective personal responsibility*. This kind of responsibility entails that an individual (a person) is held responsible for an action, omission, event or occurrence in the past. For instance, a person who is held responsible for having driven through a red light and causing a severe car accident involving four vehicles. Examples of retrospective personal responsibility are moral responsibility, legal responsibility (responsibility in the context of law), or causal responsibility. These three kinds of retrospective personal responsibility will be further explicated in the following.

Moral responsibility will be the first kind of retrospective personal responsibility to be examined in this section. Cuypers regrets that *moral responsibility* has been specified in so many notions – such as appraisability, answerability, attributability, liability or accountability – that the content of the concept becomes blurred.[98] Hence, I start the explanation of the concept with just one description of moral responsibility and take that as a starting point to travel through three well-known descriptions within the philosophical

98 Cuypers 2019, p. 233.

debate on moral responsibility in the 20th century: P.F. Strawson's, R.J. Wallace's and H. Frankfurt's conceptions. To start, according to Johann Go, individual moral responsibility (which he calls 'thick responsibility') is the attribution of an action to an agent *and* accompanied by the appropriate moral response such as blame or praise.[99] In other words, it consists of an agent's action in the past and an appropriate response to that action. Peter F. Strawson (1919-2006) famously called these responses 'reactive attitudes'.[100] In the tradition of Hume – who emphasized how people judge and influence another's behavior through emotions that lead to moral conduct[101] – Strawson describes in his highly influential article *Freedom and Resentment* (1962) that human beings place high importance on the intentions and attitudes that other people express towards them; these attitudes characterize human relationships and are uniquely human.[102] Examples of such reactive attitudes are forgiveness, hurt feelings, love, hate, resentment, praise, blame or gratitude and they can be expressed in human practices such as punishment or reward.[103] In contrast to incompatibilist theories, Strawson thought that freedom (of will) was not necessary for these reactive attitudes to be appropriate. According to Strawson, pessimists – those saying that determinism is incompatible with free will – are of the opinion that punishment and moral condemnation are fair (just/appropriate) when there is moral guilt, which implies moral responsibility. Strawson continues that these theorists hold that, in its turn, moral responsibility implies freedom, indicating that indeterminism is true and thus the falsity of determinism.[104] Because of this, these libertarians claim that determinism is untrue and individuals can be held to account based on their free will. Other pessimists, though, conclude that – since determinism is true – *fair* moral condemnation is impossible.[105] However, Strawson disagrees with both. Instead, he points out that the reactive attitudes construe moral responsibility.[106] Hence, since human practices of excusing or exempting moral responsibility are not dependent on a free will, but are solely grounded in the human practice of reactive attitudes, Strawson's compatibilist theory argues that responsibility can still exist even if determinism is true.[107] Not metaphysical notions like free will, but the practical human practices of adopting reactive attitudes establish a person's responsibility.[108] With the reactive attitude, someone's action is *valued*. In the words of Zimmerman: the reaction *values* whether the thing you did was

99 Go 2020, p. 2. See also Fischer & Ravizza 1993, p. 4.
100 See Williams 2006.
101 See Williams 2006.
102 Strawson, 1974, pp. 5-6. Fischer & Ravizza 1993, p. 14.
103 Strawson, 1974, p. 4. Matravers 2007, p. 1.
104 Strawson 1974 (original 1962), p. 2. See also Fischer & Ravizza 1993, p. 10.
105 See also Fischer & Ravizza 1993, p. 10.
106 Matravers 2007, p. 34.
107 Matravers 2007, p. 34.
108 Cuypers 2019, p. 234. Fischer & Ravizza 1993, p. 16.

good or bad. If you receive a pro-attitude your behavior was good and if you receive a contra-attitude you did something bad.[109] According to Fischer and Ravizza, this Strawsonian conception of moral responsibility – in which the reactive attitudes alone construe responsibility – differs from 'moral ledger' accounts of moral responsibility,[110] in which moral responsibility is a theoretical objective judgment of the moral value of the agent *preceding* any reactive attitudes. In the moral ledger conception of moral responsibility – for example, Zimmerman's description of appraisability[111] – an 'account' of the agent's moral value is *theoretically* kept – a moral record or ledger – in which praise adds credit whereas blame subtracts credit and adds debit. Consequently, an agent is morally responsible for an action because the action is part of the agent's moral ledger *and* because it is appropriate to adopt a reactive attitude towards them.[112]

Similar to Strawson, R. Jay Wallace (1957-) – who according to Go describes a moral ledger account of responsibility[113] – holds that reactive attitudes provide the key to understanding what it exactly *is* to hold someone responsible.[114] In the opinion of Wallace, holding someone responsible is different from being morally responsible. Being morally responsible depends on the human practice of blame, guilt or resentment (moral reactive attitudes)[115] and not on metaphysical concepts such as free will. What Wallace argues is that only if someone is *fairly* held responsible, that person is morally responsible.[116] The normative question what makes the reactive attitude fair is therefore central to understanding when someone can be held responsible. Wallace advocates that the *fairness* of holding someone responsible through reactive attitudes or practices such as punishment

109 Zimmerman 2010, p. 103.

110 According to Cuypers, the Strawsonian conception and the moral ledger conception are dominant in current literature on the nature of moral responsibility, with the former being discussed the most. See Cuypers 2019, p. 233. Go, too, emphasizes the importance of the moral ledger account of responsibility in contemporary debates on moral responsibility. Different from Cuypers, Go seems to include Strawson's conception of responsibility in the tradition of moral ledger accounts. Go 2019, p. 5.

111 Cuyper 2019, p. 239. Zimmerman 1988, p. 38. In explanation of moral responsibility, Zimmerman offers three distinctions that he argues philosophers on moral responsibility often forget. These distinctions are 1) between appraisability (an agent deserves a type of moral judgment, which can be a private judgment) and liability (an agent deserves a certain type of *overt* treatment, such as punishment); 2) between two modes of appraisability, namely *direct* (the appraisability of the volition to act in itself) and *indirect* appraisability (appraisability of merely the consequences of the act); and 3) between culpability (a type of appraisability, namely *blameworthiness*) and wrongdoing. See Zimmerman 1988, pp. *x*, 4, 54.

112 Fischer & Ravizza 1993, pp. 16-17. Zimmerman speaks in this context of 'moral appraisability'. See Zimmerman 1988, p. 38. See also Cuypers 2019, p. 234.

113 Go 2019, p. 5. However, Matravers and Rossi & Warfield describe Wallace's conception as a 'reasons-responsive' account of responsibility (just as P.F. Strawson's). The confusion once again highlights the difficulty in understanding the subtle differences between conceptions of moral responsibility. See Matravers 2007, p. 34 and Rossi and Warfield 2016, p. 616.

114 Wallace 2002, p. 680.

115 See Cuypers 2019, p. 236.

116 Matravers describes this as 'an agent is morally responsible in so far as it is fair to hold him morally responsible'. See Matravers 2007, p. 35.

(which include the reactive attitude of blame) is not determined by the question if that person was *free* to do otherwise (or is in possession of a free will) but rather with if they can be said to have had *moral competence*. This moral competence consists of the 'general capacity to grasp moral reasons and the general capacity to guide one's conduct by the light of such a moral understanding'. Wallace shortens the description of these capacities into 'powers of reflective self-control'.[117] In short, Wallace holds that individuals are responsible for their actions when they are in the possession of these powers of reflective self-control. In such cases, the individual can be held responsible, because 1) they have violated a moral obligation that we accept[118] and 2) they have moral competence. Thus, the individual has violated moral obligations which results in moral reactive attitudes such as resentment, blame and guilt.[119] Without this moral competence, individuals could not have breached the moral obligation and cannot be blamed.[120] Importantly, Wallace distinguishes between two sorts of responsibility. First, an agent is *accountable* when they have the powers of self-control. Second, an agent is *blameworthy* when they are morale accountable *and* are appropriately blamed for violating moral obligations because they have intentionally violated these obligations.[121] Cuypers maintains that Wallace's idea of reflective self-control shows that his theory of moral responsibility combines the Strawsonian conception of responsibility with Kant's theory of moral agency.[122] Because it describes moral responsibility not in terms of freedom of will, but in the sense of psychological capacities,[123] Wallace's theory can co-exist with a possible determinism; it is a compatibilist theory, also called 'reasons-responsiveness' compatibilism.[124]

Harry Frankfurt (1929-2023) is yet another well-known compatibilist and became renowned because of the so-called 'Frankfurt cases'. Frankfurt distinguishes human beings from other creatures based on the structure of their will, which consist of first- *and* second order desires.[125] In explanation, a person can have first order desires – for example, I desire to eat a cookie and take a nap on the couch – and second order desires – I *want to desire* to eat a carrot and go to the gym. I *really want* – this is the second order desire – to be moved by a first order desire to go to the gym and eat vegetables instead of by the first order desire to eat cookies and sleep the day away. Second order desires are therefore

117 Wallace 2002, pp. 680-681.

118 Matravers 2007, p. 36.

119 Cuypers 2019, p. 236. See also Rossi and Warfield 2016, p. 615.

120 Matravers 2007, p. 36.

121 Rossi and Warfield 2016, p. 615.

122 Cuypers 2019, p. 235.

123 Matravers 2007, p. 37.

124 Matravers 2007, pp. 34-35. Rossi and Warfield 2016, p. 616.

125 See Frankfurt 1971, pp. 6-7. This depiction of human beings differs from P.F. Strawson's depiction. According to Frankfurt, for calling an entity a 'person', Strawson only requires that the entity has mental and physical abilities. However, Frankfurt argues that many non-human creatures can then be called 'persons', such as animals. He regards this a violation of our language. See Frankfurt 1971, p. 5.

desires *about desires*.[126] According to Frankfurt, agents are morally responsible when their first and second order desires correspond.[127] This involves some deliberation: The agent has to reflect on their first order desires, form a second order desire (formulate what they *really want their effective will to be*), and then act out of the first order desire they want their effective will to be.[128] Since responsibility is based on the hierarchical relationship between first- and second order desires, Frankfurt's theory can be called a 'hierarchical model of moral responsibility'.[129] Frankfurt continues by saying that second order desires are the reason people are capable of either enjoying or lacking free will. In other words, the control condition of moral responsibility – freedom of the will – is only apparent when an entity has the capability of corresponding the second order desire to the first order desires – the ability to deliberate. Just doing what you want (first order desire) is not freedom. Instead, Frankfurt describes that freedom is having the will (first order desire) you want (in other words, the first order desire selected by the second order desire). Consequently, Frankfurt holds that an agent's moral responsibility does not require 'the ability to do otherwise', since freedom does not mean 'being free to *do* whatever you want', but rather 'being free to *will* whatever you want'.[130] In his famous Frankfurt cases, Frankfurt debunks the notion of freedom as 'the ability to do otherwise' and being unfree as a person who 'could not have done differently'. This traditional interpretation results in the idea that when a person could not have done otherwise than they did, they are not responsible. In a number of case descriptions, Frankfurt shows various situations in which a person could not have done differently than they did, but intuitively we would still not decide that this individual was exempt from moral responsibility (even though they could not have done otherwise).[131] For instance, a situation in which Melik chose to study for his exam Introduction to Legal Philosophy out of his own accord (with corresponding first- and second order desires), while his mother would have forced him to do so if he had instead chosen to go to a party. Melik still performed his action (studying) out of his own accord, which – according to Frankfurt – makes his will *free* (and Melik morally responsible for his choice) even if, in practice, he *could not have done differently* (because his mother would have forced him to study instead of going to the party if he had chosen differently).

P.F. Strawson's, Wallace's and Frankfurt's theories on moral responsibility as discussed above are all examples of *compatibilism*: They seek space for moral responsibility in a

126 See Frankfurt 1971, pp. 6-7. Interestingly, this recalls what it means to lead an examined life, in which decisions and actions are carefully considered.

127 Because of this 'corresponding', Matravers and Fischer & Ravizza call Frankfurt's theory a 'mesh theory'. Matravers 2007, p. 28. Fischer & Ravizza 1993, p. 25.

128 If individuals only act based on first order desires without deliberation, they act 'wantonly', according to Frankfurt. See Frankfurt 1971, p. 11.

129 Fischer & Ravizza 1993, p. 25.

130 Frankfurt 1971, p. 19.

131 See Pink 2009, p. 140.

causally determined world. However, these theorists participate in a philosophical discussion on moral responsibility where the entire notion of responsibility sometimes seems threatened by causal determinism.[132] Even though most thinkers on moral responsibility in the 20th century are – just like the philosophers introduced – recognizable as compatibilists who believe that even if determinism is true, *moral* responsibility is possible, incompatibilists, such as the earlier mentioned G. Strawson, argue otherwise. G. Strawson aims to show with his 'basic argument' that (even) if determinism is true and all is preordained, moral responsibility for past actions is impossible. This is the case because an agent can only be truly morally responsible when they are the ultimate cause of the action. Since individuals did not make themselves – it was not an action they caused – they cannot be morally responsible.[133] This, of course, problematizes moral responsibility.

In sum, moral responsibility is a personal responsibility in which human individuals are held responsible if they did the deed or brought it about, knew the relevant facts surrounding their action (the cognition condition) *and* did the action 'freely' (the control condition).[134] As we have seen, the latter condition may be redefined by some compatibilists into 'based on reasons' or 'based on moral competence' or 'based on the capability of second order desires'. When these prerequisites are present, people can be held morally responsible for numerous things, mostly for their actions, but also for their beliefs, choices, character, events, occurrences and processes. Importantly, there might be excusing conditions in some circumstances. For instance, if the agent did not know the consequences of his action (ignorance) or when the agent was forced to act (coercion).[135] Since moral responsibility originates from the idea that an action follows from a person's own agency which they have in their power, an action can be attributed to a person if it is not the result of external factors (such as coercion, force) that are outside the control of the agent, but the action is in some way the result of a person's agency.[136] This results in a moral, retrospective personal responsibility which is a necessary condition for the individual deserving reactive attitudes.[137] The *moral* responsibility for a past action or omission makes these attitudes *justified*. Because of the presence of praise or blame, Go calls this responsibility 'thick' responsibility or the 'attributability conception of responsibility'.[138] In theories of moral responsibility the reason for the praise or blame – which are the consequences of a person's responsibility – is the action done by the actor (in the past). In merit-based responsibility this is called *desert*: the agent *deserves* the blame. In contrast, in

132 Matravers 2007, p. 21.
133 See G. Strawson 2008.
134 See for example Fischer & Ravizza 1993, p. 8.
135 Fischer & Ravizza 1993, p. 7.
136 Pink 2009, p. 130. See also Zheng 2019, p. 114.
137 Williams 2006.
138 Go 2019, p. 4.

consequential responsibility theories, the reactive attitudes are a means to an end: By blaming or praising an agent society aims to either prevent the behavior in the future or stimulate the agent to continue the behavior.

Moral responsibility overlaps to some extent with the earlier mentioned *legal responsibility*, since both the moral and legal systems are normative and include norms. In a society's political debate, some moral norms – which result in a person's moral responsibility – are considered of great importance, such as norms that prohibit murdering, stealing or counterfeiting. However, the moral system cannot enforce its norms in ways other than the distribution of moral blame. By embedding these norms in the legal system, they gain legal quality and can now be enforced.[139] For example, the moral norm that it is unacceptable that an agent severely (physically) hurts another person is also part of the legal normative system in the form of legislation that prohibits abuse (for instance, article 300 of the Dutch Criminal Code). If the human agent did assault someone and broke the law though their action or did otherwise not meet their legal obligation, they are *blameworthy* and can thus be legally held to account. Often this is done through punishment – as long as there are no excusing conditions.[140] After the punishment, the offender has sufficiently 'responded' and is ideally no longer (morally) blamed for the action.

The (im)possibility of moral responsibility has been much discussed and those who do argue that moral responsibility exists have interpreted it in many ways. The third example of retrospective personal responsibility, *causal responsibility*, is less controversial. Causal responsibility – as the term already suggests – looks at the causation of an event or occurrence.[141] Francot and De Vries describe this type of responsibility as 'the possibility to attribute an effect or consequence to an actor whose actions have caused the effect.'[142] Whereas moral and legal responsibility require physical and mental capacity, this is not the case with causal responsibility.[143] Also, similar to the earlier discussed 'simple responsibility' or 'responsibility-as-duty', it is not exclusively human. As Fischer and Ravizza explain, a human houseguest *and* a kitten might both be causally responsible for shattering your prized Waterford vase.[144] Zimmerman even argues that causal responsibility may even be ascribed to objects: A fire might be *caused* by a short-circuit.[145] For incompatibilists who hold that *moral* responsibility is impossible, causal responsibility could provide a solution to still hold someone responsible for the consequences of a past

139 Francot 2008, p. 97.
140 Hart 2008, p. 28.
141 Zimmerman 1988, p. 1.
142 Francot & De Vries 2011, p. 208.
143 Cane 2016, p. 280.
144 Fischer & Ravizza 1993, p. 5.
145 Zimmerman 1988, p. 1.

action. In the words of Go, this concerns 'thin responsibility', instead of a 'thick' responsibility. Here, a person is simply held responsible for an action, but without the normative reactive attitudes that are so central to moral responsibility.[146] In other words, if Jonathan broke a window he is held responsible because he *caused* the window to break, but he would not receive any moral blame. Interestingly, it seems that Aristotle describes a specific causal responsibility of human agents for the voluntary actions that they do,[147] which – contrary to other accounts of causal responsibility – can still result in either praise or blame. This is because Aristotle does not regard human autonomy, rationality or freedom as requirements for being the subject of blame or praise. The only necessity for these reactive attitudes is that the agent has *caused* the harm. If a person was the efficient *cause* of an action or change, they own that action. This means that they can be evaluated – through blame or praise – according to the standards that are being set for this action. If one has success in upholding the standard, one receives praise, and if not, blame. In this sense, Müller argues, blame and praise are tied to external quality standards, and not to moral standards.[148] Hence, we can still speak of a *causal* responsibility (and not of moral responsibility).

In the previous paragraphs, three common kinds of retrospective personal responsibility were explored: Moral responsibility, legal responsibility and causal responsibility. Recently, new accounts of retrospective personal responsibility, such as Johan Go's, can be noticed. Go's continuum threshold approach to responsibility separates thick responsibility (moral responsibility) from thin responsibility (causal responsibility).[149] It tries to preserve the notion of agency and responsibility while acknowledging the differences between people's backgrounds (their 'structure') which makes it harder for some people to make good choices than it is for others.[150] This way, Go aims to construct a theory of responsibility that is 'real'. With this denominator, Go means that his approach accepts that reality is flawed and people exist in unequal situations (their backgrounds or structures), which explains why some people find it harder to make the 'right' choices than others.[151] For instance, it is much harder for someone who has grown up in an environment where criminal behavior – such as drug dealing, stealing or physical violence – is normalized to not resort to these types of behavior than it would be for a person who has never been exposed to such an environment. In some conditions, these backgrounds might make it inappropriate to blame an agent for their conduct.[152] Go seeks a way to incorporate this

146 Go 2019, p. 9. See also Young 2011, p. 95.
147 Cooper 2-13, pp. 272-273.
148 See Müller 2015, p. 13.
149 Go 2019, p. 3.
150 Go 2019, pp. 1, 3.
151 Go 2019, p. 2.
152 Go 2019, p. 2.

notion in his continuum. Also, the question arises whether individuals or groups of individuals (the latter would be focused on retrospective non-personal responsibility) with challenging backgrounds should be held responsible in an equal manner to individuals who are in more fortunate positions.[153] As the title of the model suggests, the continuum-threshold-approach to responsibility consists of a continuum *and* it involves a two-step construction of assigning blame.[154] On the one end of the spectrum of responsibility, the continuum starts with a minimalist conception of responsibility:[155] A specific *causal* responsibility (thin responsibility). This is the so-called threshold and the first step of assigning blame: An individual must have caused an action or event *and* this action must not have originated from any force or coercion. However, the action does not have to be free from every internal or external influence. At the other end of the continuum is a perfectionist conception of responsibility: An action was done free from any internal and external constraints and the agent is fully blameworthy. Between the two ends of the continuum, the degree of blameworthiness of the action of an agent may vary. The evaluation of the degree of blameworthiness is the second step of assigning blame. This creates room for regarding one person as more – or less – responsible (in the sense of blameworthiness) than another based on, for example, their specific backgrounds.[156]

With Go's continuum-threshold-approach to responsibility added to moral responsibility, legal responsibility and causal responsibility, the previous paragraphs have mapped out four kinds of retrospective personal responsibility. When these conceptions of retrospective personal responsibility are added to the Four-Axis graph, they result in the following overview:

153 Go 2019, p. 4.

154 Go 2019, p. 10.

155 Go actually suggests that this threshold is not fixed; in consultation, a group of people may decide for themselves what the threshold is that they would like to use. Go 2011, p. 11.

156 Go 2021, p. 11.

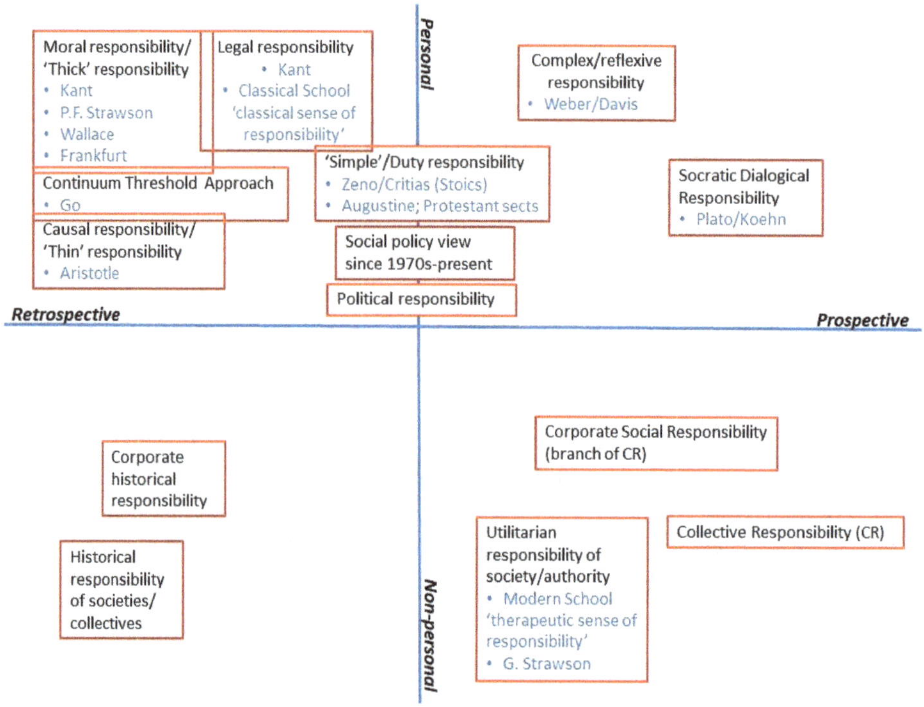

Prospective non-personal responsibility

In the previous sections, I explored the left side – the retrospective side – of the Four-Axis Graph, resulting in a description of retrospective non-personal responsibility and retrospective personal responsibility. In contrast to its left side, the Four-Axis Graph's right side looks at *prospective* responsibility. This ascribes a responsibility for the future.[157] The following paragraphs will map out two categories of prospective responsibility, since this responsibility can either be attributed to collectives, prospective non-personal responsibility, or to individuals, prospective personal responsibility. Importantly, personal prospective responsibilities may result from membership of a collective or group that has a non-personal prospective responsibility. For example, as a vocational group, *judges* have a shared responsibility for providing fair justice. For individual judges, this means making fair judgments in their own practice. In the following, three examples of prospective *non-personal* responsibility will be explored, namely 1) role responsibility of (vocational) groups, 2) collective responsibility and 3) corporate social responsibility.

157 Zimmerman 1988, p. 1.

The first example of prospective non-personal responsibility is role responsibility for collective (vocational) groups.[158] For example, as a vocational group, judges are responsible for fair justice and the vocational group of criminal law lawyers are responsible for providing any civilian who requires it with legal representation. Similarly – but outside the legal context – the vocational group of doctors are collectively responsible for accessible medical care for all members of society.

The second example of prospective non-personal responsibility is collective responsibility. There exist various conceptions of prospective non-personal responsibility, that will be discussed in the following. In general, collective responsibility does not see one individual agent as responsible but focuses on the social participation of all members of a group.[159] The group or collective has an intentional structure and this means that they have a kind of agency on their own, the collective is capable of intentional action.[160] Furthermore, in the words of Souffrant, collective responsibility is a shared responsibility taken by the group but delegated to its individual members.[161] Souffrant describes two models of collective responsibility that he thinks are fitting for contemporary society. The first is based on Goodin and looks at a collective commitment to achieve a specific outcome and is partly based on a commitment to help the most vulnerable of the group. In this endeavor, individual agents will also bear personal responsibility for their contribution to the outcome of the collective,[162] but it is primarily shared by all members of the collective.[163] The second model is rooted in John Locke's natural law in the state of nature with regard to obtaining property. This God-given law dictates not to destroy resources wantonly and leave enough of the same quality for others.[164] The idea of the collective responsibility based on this law is that society *and* collectives such as corporations should contribute to an effort to restore and revitalize the natural environments they destroy so that everything that lives can still thrive. Only in such an environment can individuals carve out their own individual lives.[165]

---

158 See, for instance, Lucas, 'The responsibilities of office', in: *Responsibility*, Oxford: Oxford University Press 1995, p. 1.

159 Souffrant 2013, pp. 149.

160 See Isaacs 2011, p. 53.

161 See Souffrant 2013, pp. 149, 165. According to Souffrant, a group in which an appointed leader shoulders the responsibility of the group cannot be called collective responsibility in this sense, it is still an individual responsibility. For a responsibility to be collective, it has to be shouldered by all through social participation. See Souffrant 2013 p. 149.

162 Goodin 1985, pp. 118, 134.

163 Goodin 1985, p. 136.

164 Locke 2003 (original 1689), Chapter V 'Of Property', under 31 and 33, pp. 113-114. See also Goodin 1985, p. 176.

165 Souffrant 2013, pp. 162-163.

At the moment, one of the most influential models of collective responsibility is Iris Young's Social Connections Model.[166] Instead of the so-called 'liability'-model[167] Young's model does not isolate the individual as a responsible agent – while someone else would not be seen as responsible, but looks at a model of shared responsibility. Importantly, it is a model that focuses on actions to be done in the future and it attempts to solve unjust background conditions[168] and therefore does not concern specific wrongdoings, like breaking a window, stealing a necklace or using plastic straws for drinking soda.[169] Instead, Young focuses on how to allocate responsibility *for addressing* and transforming structural injustice in society when each individual person cannot be held responsible for the cumulative effect of their specific actions.[170] Ultimately, Young argues that it is a people's collective responsibility to address social injustices: 'all those who contribute by their actions to structural processes with some unjust outcomes share responsibility for the injustice'.[171] However, Zheng argues that Young's model might provide a personal, moral responsibility anyway, one that connects ethics and politics, the individual and the collective, structure (a person's background conditions within society and life) and agency.[172] If that is the case, the model would include collective and personal responsibility.

Yet another kind of an even more encompassing collective responsibility is the collective responsibility of current generations for future generations (intergenerational equity). This is a responsibility for the existence of future generations and for their quality of life.[173] Because of technological advancements, human actions have gained the ability to destroy the earth or at least have impact for hundreds, if not thousands, of years (for instance, in the case of nuclear waste).[174] According to Postma, the possible magnitude of our impact results in an growing uncertainty and in increased responsibility.[175] Indeed, the temporal scope of this type of responsibility is vast: The responsibility extends not only to the lifetimes of our children and grandchildren, but also to those of all human beings that will be born in the following centuries.[176] Reasons for this responsibility are, for example, the concept of trusteeship – which obliges the current generation to care for the world since its forefathers bequeathed it to us with the intention of us passing it unharmed onto

166 Zheng 2019, p. 109. See also Go 2019, p. 6.

167 This 'liability model' refers to forms of retrospective personal responsibility, which are countered by Young's collective responsibility in the Social Connections Model.

168 Young holds that an individual cannot be blamed for their background (their 'social structure') that limits their options, see Go 2019, p. 6. See also Young 2011, p. 96.

169 Zheng 2019, p. 109.

170 Young 2011, p. 95.

171 Young 2011, p. 96. Go 2019, p. 6.

172 Zheng 2019, p. 110.

173 See Jonas 1984, p. 40.

174 Postma 2006, p. 19. Becchi 2011, pp. 79-80.

175 Postma 2006, p. 20.

176 Postma 2006, p. 19. See also UN Report of the Secretary-General 'Our Common Agenda' 2021, pp. 38-39.

the next generation;[177] the will of all the people(s) for humankind to survive[178], and a sense of (intergenerational) justice for the ones that will inherit the world as we leave it behind.[179] Goodin argues that the strongest reason for the current generation's responsibility for future generations is the vulnerability of these unborn generations. They are completely dependent upon us and the current generation can unilaterally decide to either help or harm the generations to come.[180] Therefore, we are obliged to protect them. However, critics argue that humans should not interfere with history and that by taking measures now, we limit the options of the generations to come. Gündling rejects this argument and states that humans *always* interfere in history even if they do not realize it, therefore the critics' argument is groundless.[181] In international politics and international law, the rights of future generations – and thus the collective obligations (responsibility) of current generations –[182] has gained recognition in the past century. In 1945, the *United Nations Charter* preamble specified its goal as to spare future generations the 'scourge of war'.[183] More than 40 years later, the UN Brundtland Report 'Our Common Future' (1987) formulated a leading definition[184] for sustainable development as the 'development that meets the needs of the present without compromising the ability of future generations to meet their own needs'.[185] Additionally, the Brundtland Report offered examples of human action that is hurtful for future generations, such as overexploiting natural resources (for instance, non-renewable fossil fuels and minerals, water and land), ill-considered large scale use of technology (resulting in, for example, the emission of toxic gases, settled agriculture and genetic manipulation) and actions that result in the loss of plant and animal species. These actions are hurtful, since they rapidly close the options of choice of future generations.[186] In this Report, the conservation of nature is described as a collective

177 See Goodin 1985, p. 174. In this sense, within the concept of trusteeship, the current generation would have an obligation towards the previous generations (the forefathers) as well as towards future generations.

178 Gründling 1990, p. 210.

179 Postma 2006, p. 19. See also Goodin 1985, p. 169.

180 Goodin 1985, p. 177.

181 Gründling 1990, p. 210.

182 Gründling 1990, p. 210.

183 The first sentences of the preamble to the UN Charter states: '*We the peoples of the United Nations, determined to save succeeding generations from the scourge of war, which twice in our lifetime has brought untold sorrow to mankind, and to reaffirm faith in fundamental human rights, in the dignity and worth of the human person, in the equal rights of men and women and of nations large and small, and to establish conditions under which justice and respect for the obligations arising from treaties and other sources of international law can be maintained, and to promote social progress and better standards of life in larger freedom (...)*'

184 See, for example, Postma 2006, p. 19.

185 UN Report of the World Commission on Environment and Development 'Our Common Future' 1987, Chapter 2, under 1.

186 UN Report of the World Commission on Environment and Development 'Our Common Future' 1987, Chapter 2, part 1, under 6, 7, 8, 12, 13 and 14. See also UN Report of the Secretary-General 'Our Common Agenda' 2021, p. 44.

moral obligation (responsibility) of current generations to other living beings and future human generations.[187] The obligation became a legal one in 1997, with the *UNESCO Declaration on the responsibility of the present generations towards the future generations.* The Declaration's first article provides the fundamental duty of current generations to fully safeguard the needs and interests of the present and future generations. The subsequent articles offer the basic principles of these needs and interests, such as the freedom of choice in political social and economic systems and freedom in culture and religion; the obligation to maintain and perpetuate humankind; the preservation of the earth and the protection of the environment; the preservation of cultural diversity and cultural heritage, and; peace.[188] Nevertheless, in 2021, the UN Report of the Secretary-General 'Our Common Agenda' stated that although the previous UN documents granted recognition to the need for a focus on the well-being of future generations, this recognition did not necessarily mean that meaningful steps to protect the future generations' interest had been taken. 'Our Common Agenda' aimed at long term thinking and proposed practical steps such as the establishment of a Special Envoy for Future Generations, Future Labs and a Declaration on Future Generations.[189]

The interest in prospective collective responsibility is not limited to international politics. In philosophy, humankind's collective responsibility for the preservation of the natural environment in the face of technological developments has gained more attention since 1984 due to, for example, Hans Jonas' well-known work *The Imperative of Responsibility.*[190] Hans Jonas (1903-1993) broadened the scope of collective responsibility by including responsibility for the environment and for animal life. Jonas was concerned about the consequences of the technological age. He criticized the western dichotomy between humans and nature that contributes to the exploitation of the natural environment. Also, Jonas criticized the western linear view of time – instead of a circular view – which results in the individual's lack of interest in the human race's and earth's future beyond their own limited lifespan.[191] Instead, Jonas argues that, since humans belong to the

187 UN Report of the World Commission on Environment and Development 'Our Common Future' 1987, Chapter 2, part 3, under 55. This moral obligation can also be noticed in Goodin 1985, p. 170.

188 UNESCO Declaration on the responsibility of the present generations towards the future generations 1997, articles 1, 2, 3, 4, 5, 7 and 9. The declaration can be found at portal.unesco.org/en/ev.php-URL_ID=13178&URL_DO=DO_PRINTPAGE&URL_SECTION=201.html, last visited September 30th 2022.

189 UN Report of the Secretary-General 'Our Common Agenda' 2021, pp. 44-45.

190 Strydom 1999, p. 65.

191 Vogel 2001, pp. 133, 143. These criticisms are also articulated by Somogyvári. According to Somogyvári, the western, modern view of time is linear. Rooted in the Christian faith and dissociated from nature, life is viewed as having a beginning and an end. In other words, life is finite. God gave nature to humans for their use and it will finally be destroyed at the end of time. So, nature only exists to serve mankind and is therefore subordinate to man (Somogyvári 2009, pp. 343, 348). As Weber already pointed out (as discussed earlier this chapter), within the Christian tradition, individuals are solely responsible for themselves. They do not necessarily concern themselves with earlier or future generations, nor is their concern directed at respecting

meaningful whole of nature, they have a responsibility towards it.[192] In addition to a responsibility for past actions that have damaged the environment, Jonas proposes a prospective (moral) responsibility transcending the direct interest of the human individual. This responsibility is focused on the preservation of nature and on securing future life on our planet.[193] Nature is vulnerable to our technological interventions and damage has already be done by humankind to the natural environment. Because we are the ones that have power over the environment through technology and the power of self-control in this matter, the responsibility for the planet's preservation is ours.[194] This is an ontological responsibility resulting in the imperative to 'act so that the effects of your action are compatible with the permanence of genuine human life'.[195] In *The Imperative of Responsibility* Jonas explains that this responsibility is primarily a collective one for the policy of states and international organizations.[196]

In addition to its recognition in philosophy, the realization of a need for human rights and sustainable development for the current and future generations is also recognizable in the domain of economics, where ecological economics made its entrance in 1994. In contrast to traditional economics, ecological economics calls for a change in the ideal of a successful economy, which is currently measured in economic growth (an increasing GDP) – which we can no longer sustain in the light of its negative impact on the natural environment and human equality. Instead, ecological economics proposes redefining a successful economy in terms of human well-being and sustainability.[197] However, in spite of its almost thirty-year existence, the call for an ecological economy has not been heard – or at least its message has not been heeded – on the national and international levels. We still mostly see the traditional – neoliberal and capitalist interpretation – of economic success being practiced. Nevertheless, change is forthcoming. In addition to the UN Reports, its 2030 goals and the UNESCO declaration, global crises have become more urgent and tangible in the past years. People directly feel and see the consequences of their personal and collective actions in the energy crisis; the covid-crisis; ocean and air pollution; climate change and the related change in local weather, the loss of biodiversity and the loss of animal species. Furthermore, there seems to be a growing awareness of the

nature and the preservation of it in itself (Somogyvári 2009, p. 349). However, throughout history, many cultures knew a *circular* (or cyclical) view of time, with nature leading the passing of time. According to Somogyvári, the many cycles of nature – winter, spring, summer and autumn, or night following day, or birth, growth, decline and death (and in some views, rebirth) – can be understood as forming a perpetual spiral (Somogyvári 2009, p. 344). In cyclical views of time, nature and humanity are a unity which makes humankind responsible for nature, the past *and* the future (Somogyvári 2009, p. 348).

192 Vogel 2001, p. 131.

193 Hoskins et al. 2011, p. 24.

194 Jonas 1984, pp. 6-8.

195 Jonas 1984, p. 11.

196 Jonas 1984, p. 12. See also Somogyvári 2009, p. 347.

197 See: Victor 2010, p. 244 and Constanza et al. 2015, pp. 87-89. See also Raworth 2017.

inequality between the global North and South. These circumstances might bring a crucial momentum for change upon us.

The third example of prospective non-personal responsibility to be discussed in this section is corporate social responsibility (CSR) which has been the subject of discussion among theorists since the second half of the 20th century.[198] CSR could be viewed as a branch of collective responsibility – or at least, in some theories corporate responsibilities might be included in 'collective responsibility'. CSR starts with the viewpoint that corporations have social responsibilities beyond their legal and economic obligations. These social responsibilities include a moral obligation to contribute to the greater good of society; and to be accountable for their actions.[199] According to Janssen, CSR is a strategy for corporations to maintain their right to exist in a society in the 'Age of Apology', where societies are reflecting on their dark pasts (which seems similar to the previously discussed retrospective Corporate Historical Responsibility).[200] This description corresponds with 'instrumental theories' of CSR, that hold that wealth creation is the ultimate goal of corporations and social activities are no more than instrumental to that goal. However, there are also three other categories of theories of CSR, namely 1) political theories, that emphasize the power of corporations within society and looks at how to use that power responsibly in politics; 2) integrative theories, that focus on how a corporation may integrate social demands because that is preeminent for the survival of the business itself, and 3) ethical theories, that are concerned with the ethical responsibilities (which are more important than any other demand on their business) corporations have towards society.[201] Also, Corporate Historical Responsibility (CHR) seems to have implications for the future in addition to its principal focus on the past. It demands specific future behavior from corporations that were involved in historical injustices. In explanation, CHR demands that corporations are committed to justice in the present and future in order for the (past) injustice to not happen again.[202]

After adding the kinds of responsibility as discussed in the previous section, the Four-Axis Graph appears as follows:

198 Garriga & Melé 2004, p. 51.
199 Souffrant 2013, p. 140.
200 Janssen 2013, pp. 64, 69.
201 Garriga & Melé 2004, pp. 52-53.
202 Janssen 2013, p. 70.

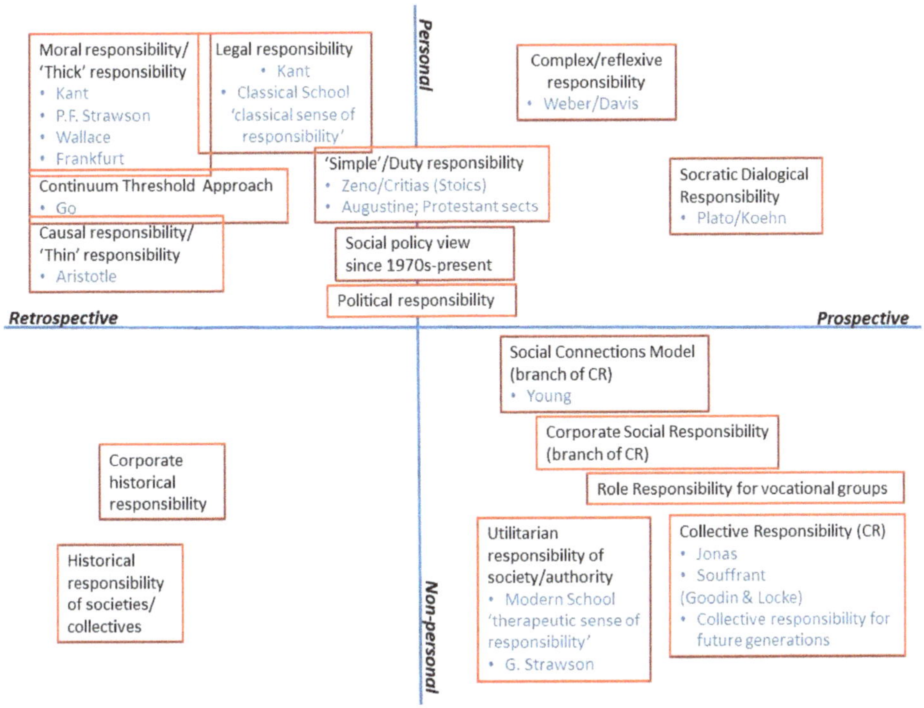

Prospective personal responsibility

After having mapped out retrospective non-personal, retrospective personal responsibility and prospective non-personal responsibility, the only part of the Four-Axis Graph that still needs exploring is its top right corner which shows personal prospective responsibility. This type of responsibility relates to the responsibilities of individual people in future conduct. Three examples of this kind of responsibility will be clarified, namely 1) individual role responsibility, 2) political responsibility and 3) responsibility for the other, society and the environment.

First, individuals may have personal prospective responsibilities stemming from their societal role or membership of a (vocational) group. This is individual role responsibility. According to May, role responsibilities are the responsibilities professionals have because they have voluntarily agreed to take on a certain set of tasks. By taking on the role, one accepts duties or obligations that they otherwise would not have had.[203] Often these duties are focused on future conduct to secure the well-being of others or in support of the aims or purposes of the organization in which the role-bearer operates.[204] For example,

203 May 1992, p. 131.
204 Hart 1968 p. 212, in: Cane 2016, p. 280.

individual Dutch lawyers are – in their professional role – bound to the professional rules of conduct set down by the Bar. If their individual conduct is in compliance with the rules this would support, for instance, the collective aim of providing legal aid and the goal of preserving the public's trust in the vocational group. According to Lucas, individual role responsibility requires the role bearers to have some authority or power to fulfill their duty.[205] In addition to its prospective focus, May holds that individual role responsibility also has a retrospective aspect. When a lawyer ignores their role obligations or fails to perform their role-related duties properly, then they are – in retrospect – accountable for the resulting damage.[206]

Secondly, political responsibility looks at the responsibility of politicians and political leaders in the context of their vocation. Max Weber describes in *Politics as a Vocation* his view of the political responsibility of a political leader by defining a leader's qualities and by contrasting the leader's conduct with the conduct of civil servants. The latter, according to Weber, should merely execute orders given by the superior authorities. They are responsible for acting upon their duty, but not for the consequences of their actions. This is what has been called by Davis 'simple responsibility' and is 'responsibility-as-duty'. The political leader, on the other hand, has an untransferable 'exclusive personal responsibility'.[207] The true leader is someone who is moved by an 'ethics of responsibility' (instead of solely by an ethics of absolute ends). According to Weber, this means the leader is aware in their heart and soul of a responsibility for the (foreseeable) consequences of their actions and is able to give an account of these consequences.[208] Even though the leader's responsibility is for the most part an internal process of deliberating and feeling the sense of responsibility of the consequences of your actions, Davis argues that Weber's account of responsibility is still *relational*, since the political leader has to make compromises with others and has an obligation to account for his action(s) towards his subjects.[209] This institutionalized moment of accountability is the true test of democratic leaders, so that the subjects are able find out if their current leaders are indeed better than their competition.[210] Some authors widen the scope of what political responsibility contains. May, for instance, defends a special political responsibility for philosophers as a vocational group to be careful in formulating critiques and new insights. Note that, here, political responsibility becomes a vocational responsibility.[211] Others seem to use 'political responsibility' in an Aristotelian manner, which gives the word a different content. For example, Wolff calls

205 Lucas 1995'The responsibilities of office', in: *Responsibility*, Oxford: Oxford University Press 1995, pp. 1-2.
206 May 1992, p. 131.
207 Weber 1919, pp. 95, 115, 126.
208 Weber 1919, pp. 120, 121, 127.
209 Davis 1999, p. 37.
210 Davis 1999, p. 33.
211 May 1992, p. 128.

what is mostly seen as the overarching concept 'social responsibility', '*political* responsibility'.[212] This seems a reference to all the responsibilities society members have in a *polis*. This may then include corporate social responsibility, political responsibility, legal responsibility and many other forms of responsibility. It would therefore be clearer to gather all these notions of responsibility under the overarching denominator 'social responsibility' and reserve the word 'political responsibility' for the responsibility of people – politicians – that are actively involved in politics.

The third example of prospective personal responsibility to be discussed here is personal responsibility for the other, society and the environment. In the 20th century, various philosophers have thought about a radical different ethics than was dominant in the context of the Western tradition of individualism, neo-liberalism and individual rights.[213] For instance, instead of individuals only being responsible for themselves, Levinas, Bauman and Koehn describe an ethics in which being human inherently means being responsible for another.[214] The addressees of this kind of responsibility, namely others (be it living others or others yet to be born) and the environment are largely the same as those of the earlier described collective responsibility for future generations. The goals of taking action for the common good, promoting human well-being and preserving the environment seem similar as well. However, in the context of *personal* responsibility, the individual has their own separate responsibility from that of the collective. In exploration of this kind of prospective personal responsibility, I draw on the work of Levinas and Koehn. To do justice to Levinas's description of philosophy, the following will stay close to his own theoretical terminology.

Emmanuel Levinas (1906-1995) is famous for his description of the asymmetric face-to-face relationship between the Self and the Other in which I have a primary responsibility for the Other.[215] Levinas describes that Western philosophy has conceptualized the individual subject (the Self, I) as having the tendency to totalize everything around him, which means that he makes everything a part of himself. For example, in order to live and – in the vocabulary of Levinas – 'enjoy' life, I drink water, soak up sunrays, eat fruits and vegetables and have pets. My approach to all these things is that I totalize them: I *use* them for myself – or, in other words, I reduce them to me.[216] This leads to my complacency.

212 Wolff 2011, p. 13.

213 Vogel 2001, p. 144.

214 Levinas, for example, criticizes western philosophy in which individualism has predominantly provided space for the individual and his egoism. This egocentric individual may use (totalize) others – which makes them part of himself and *neutralizes* them. Levinas 2012, pp. 37, 40.

215 Levinas 2012, p. 215. Duyndam & Poorthuis 2003, pp. 14, 21.

216 Keij 2021, p. 27. See also Duyndam & Poorthuis 2003, pp. 17-18. This egoism is an important prerequisite for responsibility, since it makes life worth living and this supports the development of the ability to empathize with an Other. So, in order for the Self to be able to care for the Other, he first has to care for himself. See Keij 2021, p. 28.

However, the Other is radically different from – and transcends – the Self,[217] in such a manner that the totalizing effect that I have on everything around me *cannot* and *should not* take place with regard to the Other.[218] In other words, I cannot and should not reduce him to a part of me. Instead, when the Other comes face-to-face with the Self, I see the Other in all his vulnerability and defenselessness.[219] This touches me.[220] Specifically, I am vulnerable (sensitive) to the vulnerability of the Other. Because of this, my state of complacency is interrupted and I become focused on the Other's interests.[221] The call of the Other invites me to care for him,[222] and even though I cannot refuse this primary responsibility,[223] I *can* choose *not* to take it.[224] However, this irresponsibility will be as hurtful for myself as the consequences might be for the Other.[225] Importantly, the Other invites me to take care of him, but how I take action is up to me. In this aspect, I am free in the way I give meaning to the responsibility.[226] In this relationship between the I and the Other, ethics is born and can be experienced (sensed); from the responsibility originates the normativity of, for instance, obligations that I have with regard to the Other.[227] Furthermore, the scope of the responsibility that I have for the Other is infinite. Hoskins et al. describe this as impossibly demanding, the responsibility goes beyond what is possible to do, beyond one's actions and their consequences and beyond what is voluntary and involuntary. It also is beyond legal norms.[228] In other words, it is an all-encompassing responsibility for the Other. According to Hoskins et al., there is great potential for societal interactions in this impossibility of the demand: It turns my focus on the interests of the Other and may even lead to self-sacrificing choices. Therefore, the impossible demand of the Other can inspire me to take political decisions in the interests of justice for others and the planet instead of in my self-interest.[229] Wolff, too, emphasizes such a political (social)[230]

217 Levinas 2012, pp. 28, 32, 35, 87. See also Duyndam & Poorthuis 2003, p. 15. The Other is also necessary for the I to Be, since I can only understand myself as an 'I' when I can juxtapose myself to the otherness of the Other. See Vogel 2001, p. 139.

218 Levinas 2012, pp. 28, 32, 41.

219 Levinas 2012, pp. 32, 213.

220 Levinas 2012, p. 260.

221 Levinas 2012, p. 46. Keij 2021, p. 30. Bernasconi 2018, pp. 97-98.

222 Levinas 2012, p. 214.

223 Levinas 2012, pp. 42, 211, 214.

224 Duyndam & Poorthuys 2003, pp. 22-23. Keij 2021, p. 31. See also Bernasconi 2018, p. 98.

225 Keij 2021, p. 31.

226 Levinas 2012, pp. 210, 218.

227 Levinas 2012, pp. 39, 41-42, 217. Bernasconi 2018, p. 96. See also Duyndam & Poorthuis 2003, pp. 13, 14, 53. See also Wolff 2011, p. 17. Importantly, the responsibility that I have for the Other is strictly *my* (no one else's) responsibility and is non-reciprocal. Bernasconi 2018, p. 96. See also Duyndam & Poorthuis 2003, p. 23.

228 Hoskins et al. 2011, p. 24. See also Bauman 2005-1, p. 52.

229 Hoskins et al. 2011, p. 22.

230 Wolff uses the denominator 'political' in a broader sense – namely beyond an interpretation that merely focuses on politicians (hence, 'political') – and refers to the term 'social'. Therefore, in Wolff's interpretation

dimension of Levinas's work.[231] However, Wolff also points out a possible lack of conception in Levinas's theory with regard to the individual's possibilities to mediate between the plurality of responsibilities within society, for how should I balance my responsibility for all others in society?[232] This is problematic, because when we redirect the focus from the one-on-one, asymmetric ethical face-to-face relation – in which I have an infinite responsibility for the vulnerable Other – to the level of society (the level politics and of the Third) – limitations to my responsibility for the sole Other become visible. In society, symmetrical relations between many equal subjects exist. Based on the idea that I have an infinite responsibility for the Other, this would seem to imply that I am wholly responsible for (and should offer my everything to) *each individual* Other. However, the sheer multitude of individuals that we encounter in society (from family members, neighbors, students and colleagues, to cashiers, librarians, homeless people and refugees) prevents us from being able to have infinite responsibility for every single Other. On this level, my prospective personal responsibility is therefore necessarily limited, but still existent.

Sociologist Zygmunt Bauman (1925-2017) draws heavily on the work of Levinas and especially on the description of the asymmetrical relationship between the I and the Other in his description of responsibility in our liquid modernity.[233] Following Levinas, Bauman argues that the individual has a unique, unconditional, nonreciprocal responsibility for the Other.[234] Ognjenovic surmises that Bauman finds the source of the individual's moral potential for being a responsible agent in the conviction that individuals are rational *and* emotional beings. The responsibility that follows is a responsibility for the dignity and well-being of others.[235] In his weakness and defenselessness (or vulnerability), the Other becomes an authority to whose command I listen before it is spoken.[236] The Other's silence or, at best, vague demand makes taking responsibility for the Other uncomfortably uncertain: I have to respond to the Other's demand, but will never know if I am interpreting the demand correctly. This results in feelings of ambiguity.[237] Furthermore, Bauman observes that in current society, individuals are burdened with a comprehensive individual responsibility for their choices and for their ultimate fate in life, be it one of limitless

---

'political' encompasses all human relationships. See Buddeberg 2012, p. 709.

231 Wolff 2011, p. 18.

232 See Buddeberg 2012, p. 710.

233 See, for example, Bauman 2005-1, pp. 48-53, 73.

234 Bauman 2005-1, pp. 51-52, 56, 74, 79. See also on nonreciprocal responsibility Ognjenovic 2010, p. 129.

235 Ognjenovic 2010, pp. 126-127. In *Postmodern Ethics*, Bauman describes how the moral potential of the individual – the potential to take (moral) responsibility for the other – can be realized. First, a person's innate moral potential must be explained to them. So, they come to understand the standards that they are able to meet, for example in the way they might take responsibility. Secondly, their environment has to de designed in such a way that individuals are supported in their effort to take moral action (to take responsibility). See Bauman 2005-1, p. 26.

236 Bauman 2005-1, pp. 73, 88.

237 Bauman 2005-1, pp. 20-21, 80.

success or bottomless failure.[238] In his *Postmodern Ethics*, Bauman contrasts *duties* – in other words, simple responsibility – with *responsibility*. Bauman argues that with regard to the former, everyone who has these duties becomes alike (heteronomous), whereas *responsibility* makes people into individuals (autonomous/self-authored). To explain, the duty to follow universal rules given by an authority – be it an institution of state or a vocational institution such as the Dutch Bar – turns people into rule abiding citizens, they become uniform. In contrast, individuals have to define and carry their own responsibility, which is indefinitely more difficult and complex.[239] This is the type of responsibility that Bauman says lies on the shoulders of individuals and which might feel too heavy to bear.[240] It is the responsibility to autonomously search for and choose rules that one wants to follow. According to Bauman, that requires flexibility, namely a readiness to change tactics on the fly, to leave commitments and loyalties if needed, and to pursue available opportunities instead of waiting for something that is in line with your established preference.[241] Bauman argues that this flexibility should be part of an academic curriculum.[242]

Like Levinas and Bauman, Koehn places prospective responsibility in a relational context.[243] Moreover, he finds that communication and performing actions for the good of all is elemental to taking responsibility. In explanation, Koehn advocates returning towards a Platonic interpretation of responsibility which he calls 'Socratic Dialogical Responsibility' (see also earlier this chapter). This is an individual responsibility[244] that requires individuals to be open to everyone's points of view. Everyone should be included in the dialogue, for they might say something worthwhile.[245] Furthermore, the Socratic Dialogical Responsibility requires a lifelong commitment to interpersonal communication and being careful to avoid wrongdoing. Following Koehn, this means at least two things. First, that individuals are required to actively engage with others in the community and with the environment. And, secondly, that they have to find and explore opportunities for themselves and for others to develop to support the common good.[246] According to Koehn, 'acting responsibly' equals leading a self-authored life, it means living a life shaped by the values you yourself have defined autonomously through reflection and conversations with

238 Bauman 2005-2, p. 305. Bauman 2007, pp. 3-4. Bauman & Donskis 2013, p. 100.

239 Bauman 2005-1, p. 54.

240 Bauman 2005-1, p. 20.

241 Bauman 2005-2, p. 305.

242 Bauman 2005-2, p. 316.

243 Levinas and Koehn are not alone in the assessment that responsibility is relational – in other words – that it is only possible (and only necessary) to take responsibility in relation to others. For example, Zygmunt Bauman and Gorana Ognjenovic also argue that responsibility is social – and thus relational. See and Ognjenovic 2010, pp. 125-126 and Bauman 2010, p. 99.

244 Koehn 2019, p. 75.

245 Koehn 2019, p. 72.

246 Koehn 2019, p. 69.

others.[247] Important for the ongoing dialogue between members of society and for responsible action is that people have to attempt to find common meanings of important concepts such as justice or courage.[248] Interestingly, the necessity for a connection with others and the requirement for self-development and the autonomous discovery of values is reminiscent of the self-authored thinking required for critical thinking and the constant self-development that is part of the inner dimension of *Bildung*.

Below, the theorists that were mapped out in the previous section have been added to the Four-Axis Graph. This results in the following overview with regard to all discussed conceptions of responsibility in this chapter:

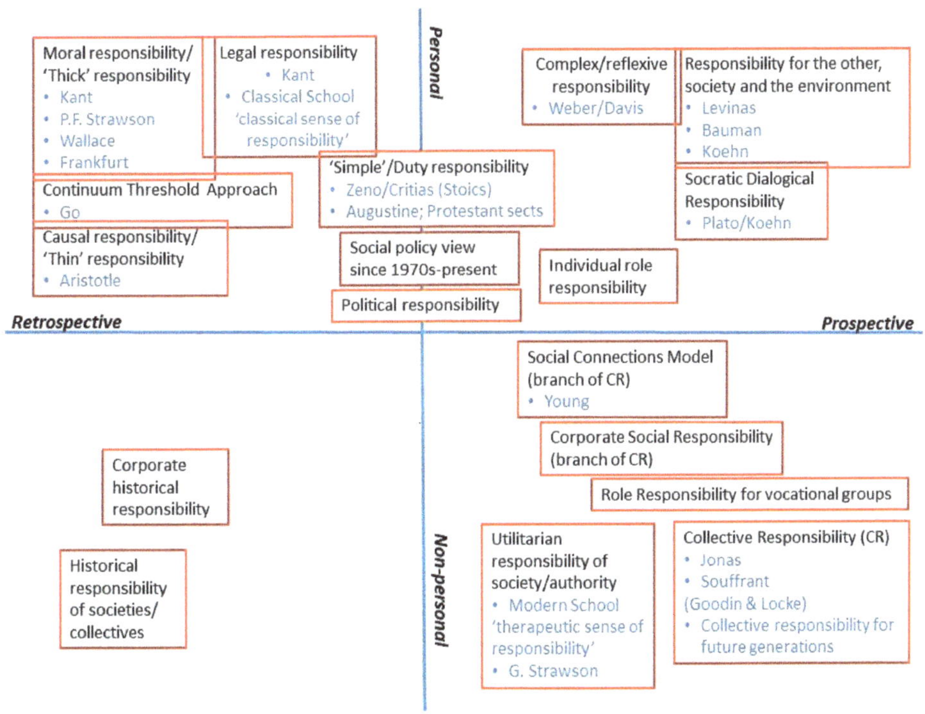

Defining responsibility in the context of academic legal education

Inspired by the many conceptions of responsibility that were explored earlier in this Chapter and visualized in the Four-Axis Graph above, the following section aims at defining a notion of responsibility for academically educated legal professionals and to

247 Koehn 2019, p. 72.
248 Koehn 2019, p. 68.

locate this notion of responsibility in the Four-Axis Graph. This notion of responsibility will be the one that law students can develop, so that they are able to utilize it in their futures as academically educated legal professionals.

So, the first aim is to describe an initial conception of responsibility relevant for contemporary academically educated legal professionals and the context in which they operate. This context is defined by a sense of uncertainty stemming from the complexity that is part of our globalized and technologized society. Individuals are subjected to a constant rush of choice opportunities and feel obliged to choose between these opportunities while knowing that every choice they make might have unknown, far-reaching consequences in both time and space. Contemporary legal professionals, such as lawyers, legal advisers, prosecutors or judges are not only confronted with these circumstances in their personal lives, but also find themselves confronted with complex problems in their professional capacity. To explain, judges, lawyers and prosecutors see themselves increasingly confronted with cases that involve multiple problems.[249] For example, cases in which someone is not only in debt and unemployed, but also in the middle of a messy divorce, on the brink of homelessness and suffering from depression. Such a situation consists of a combination of social, financial, medical, psychological and legal aspects. Finding a fitting answer, judgment or route of support for every individual problem demands the utmost – and certainly more than mere legal knowledge and skills – of academically educated legal professionals. To solve the problem and decide on a choice, they consider the whole of the situation and find fitting solutions by communicating effectively with all the involved professionals originating from other fields. This also demands a kind of choice making that is different from traditional 'simple' legal decisions and legal reasoning. Moreover, in times of existential global challenges, the further marketization of the legal profession and constant, increasing social change, legal professionals are required to redefine their vocation which also requires discovering new ways of thinking and acting. For example, in a world in which finding solutions for (global) complex problems becomes essential, professionals in the legal profession have to be able to understand and weigh, not only the legal, but *all* aspects of problems brought before them and they are required to communicate effectively with professionals working in

249 In the Netherlands, a pilot is being conducted to solve such multiple problems in a 'community court'. In such courts, there is more time for the judge to understand the circumstances of the accused and search for a sustainable solution. The idea of a community court is not new and stems from a New York example. See: www.rechtspraak.nl/Organisatie-en-contact/Organisatie/Raad-voor-de-rechtspraak/Kwaliteit-van-de-rechtspraak/innovatie-binnen-de-rechtspraak/MER/Paginas/multiproblemathiek-wijkrechtspraak.aspx, last visited October 30th 2022. See also: www.volkskrant.nl/nieuws-achtergrond/niet-alleen-het-delict-maar-ook-de-oorzaak-aanpakken-de-wijkrechter-blijft-definitief-in-rotterdam~b6581e7d/?referrer=https%3A%2F%2F, last visited November 28th 2022. For more information on the Community Court in New York, www.courtinnovation.org/programs/midtown-community-court/more-info, last visited November 3rd 2022.

other domains (for example child services, tax authorities, medical professionals, criminologists et cetera). Additionally, legal professionals are required to be able to shift focus from contributing to the market or the economy and seeing to the client's needs to seeing beyond these needs and aim for more abstract goals for which they share a responsibility, such as sustainability, human well-being and justice.[250]

Due to societal circumstances, a sense of uncertainty is bound to be experienced by all members of global society. However, if a person understands when, for whom and for what they are responsible and what that responsibility entails, these answers provide them with leading principles and a direction to pursue in their choices and consecutive actions. Also, defining one's own responsibility could ease the overwhelming experience of uncertainty in the face of current global challenges, because a person then has insight into what their individual contribution can *and cannot* be. As such, a clear understanding of responsibility provides limitations and an anchor, which would help with lessening the staggering experience of having an all-encompassing responsibility. Therefore, I propose such a responsibility for academically educated legal professionals, a responsibility that functions as a strategy for dealing with uncertainty and that offers individuals a mode of conduct.

Even though responsibility provides a strategy for managing uncertainty which is helpful in contemporary times, a question that could still be asked is *why* would academically educated legal professionals be responsible for anything at all? Various reasons can be thought of. First of all, the legal vocation in itself presupposes some responsibilities. For instance, academically educated legal professionals have the responsibility to interpret legal provisions and case law correctly and to solve (or prevent) legal problems, often through the distribution of responsibilities and liabilities.[251] Additionally, lawyers in Europe and members of the Dutch Bar have their own rules of conduct, which include their collective vocational responsibilities such as to see to the judicial protection of people that seek their help by defending their liberties and legal rights, that is, to see to the interests of their clients.[252] Secondly, as argued earlier, academically educated legal professionals have specific power – in the form of in-depth

250 Mak also notes the aims of pursuing sustainability, human well-being, social integration and social justice for academically educated legal professionals. See Mak 2017, pp. 17-18. This shift from solely focusing on economic growth towards aiming at human well-being and sustainability is also noticeable in the Economics subfield of ecological economics (as earlier discussed in the main text), that has been developing since the early 1990s, but currently seems to be gaining momentum. See Victor 2010, p. 244 and Constanza et al. 2015, pp. 87-89.

251 See also Francot & De Vries 2006, p. 9.

252 See, for example, the Dutch code of conduct for lawyers: https://regelgeving.advocatenorde.nl/content/gedragsregels-advocatuur, last visited October 2nd 2022, and for the European code of conduct for lawyers: https://regelgeving.advocatenorde.nl/content/gedragscode-voor-europese-advocaten, last visited October 2nd 2022.

knowledge in one or more knowledge domains, skills such as creative thinking and critical thinking, and their positions in society – which comes with the responsibility to use that power well and for the good of society. In our current global predicament, this could include using their power for the support of human well-being (including justice) and sustainability. This obligation – that is, to be responsible – also finds its source in a collective global commitment to (and need for) human rights and sustainability for the sake of the survival of humankind and for the sake of the planet and environment that sustain the human species. Based on these reasons, it can be said that academically educated legal professionals have a specific responsibility. In the following, the various aspects of this responsibility will be further explored.

ACT: three-stage-rocket responsibility

The conception of responsibility that I propose involves a three-stage-rocket responsibility containing Awareness, Choice and Taking action. In short, it is ACT responsibility. In the following, the first outline of this ACT responsibility will be further clarified by explaining these three components in more detail.

1 Awareness

First of all, every single academically educated legal professional – and law student – has to be **aware** of the fundamental responsibility that falls on them. As the green sections of the Four-Axis graph below shows, this primary responsibility of academically educated legal professionals is located on the right side of the Graph.

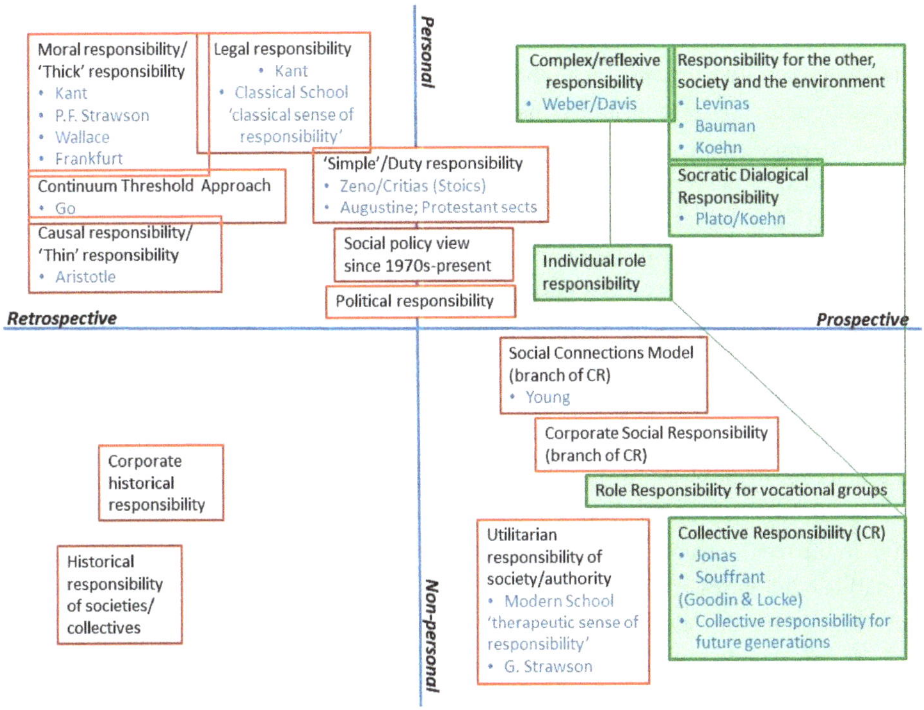

In other words, it is a prospective responsibility. This fundamental responsibility is both practical (as opposed to abstract) and social (as opposed to individual). In explanation, it is not a philosophical conception, because in this interpretation, responsibility is viewed as an agreement between persons that is essential to their co-existence. Simply put, no human is alone in this world, there are other humans and species with whom to interact. In contrast to a dominant view of individualism and rational neo-liberalism in western thought, this conception of responsibility touches those of Levinas,[253] Weber,[254] Bauman[255] and Koehn in their descriptions of individual responsibility. In accordance with these philosophers' thoughts on responsibility, the responsibility I refer to is a social phenomenon, entailing that it is a *relational* concept. This means that responsibility exists between humans. The individual experiences responsibility because of the existence of the Other. Levinas describes how individuals are sensitive to one another, which makes their relation possible. This is also recognizable in Bauman's description of responsibility. Similar to the call for more attention to the development of sensibility or feeling (which is

253 See also Hoskins et al. 2011, p. 23.
254 See Davis 1999, p. 43.
255 Bauman 2005-1, p. 35.

an important element of the *Bildung* concept as explicated in chapter 2) in the predominantly rational context of ALE, I propose a kind of responsibility in which individuals are sensitive towards each other's needs.

In addition to this responsibility that exists between humans, I suggest that the fundamental responsibility that academically educated legal professionals have to be aware of, consists of the responsibility that humans have for their natural environment as well. This is an addition to Levinas's and Bauman's relational responsibility that is based on a person's openness to the vulnerability of the *human* Other. Drawing on insights from Hoskins et al. and Jonas, I argue that the primary responsibility for academically educated legal professionals also includes the relation of human beings to nature, to other animal and plant species.[256] In their responsibility, individuals relate to other humans, to society at large and to other living creatures that for their survival depend on the planet that humans have the power to destroy.[257] On the personal level, an individual takes responsibility for themselves. In the relationship with others and the relation to society, the individual might attribute responsibility to the other(s) or take responsibility for the other(s). In the relationship with the other(s) and society at large, collaboration (which is relational) is often necessary to reach shared goals, such as preserving the environment and protecting human rights.[258] In the relationship between the human individual and nature, no responsibility can be externally attributed, so individual are required to take their own responsibility. In all four relationships one's responsibility is perceptible and relevant, since the responsibility is a response to somebody or something that implicitly or explicitly questions, calls to account or relies on you.

When applied to the context of academically educated legal professionals, their fundamental responsibility that they have to be aware of is thus located in these four relationships to (1) the self, (2) the other, (3) society and (4) the natural environment. So, on the personal level, (1) lawyers are responsible for their personal and professional development (their *Bildung*), their opinions and beliefs, their choices, their learning process, their actions and the consequences of these actions. With regard to others, (2) the academic legal professional is responsible for their client(s) and for the well-being of others – and especially the vulnerable, including those who cannot (yet) speak for themselves such as future generations. With regard to society, (3) academically educated legal professionals are responsible for furthering justice (which includes equality) for all members of society, and for the life and quality of life of future generations. With regard to the natural environment, (4) legal professionals have a responsibility to take part in an effort to contribute to preservation and protection of the environment. Recently, we have

256 Hoskins et al. 2011, p. 22.
257 Voget-Kleschin et al. 2019, p. 493.
258 Hoskins et al. 2011, p. 22.

seen examples of legal professionals taking this responsibility. For instance, in 2019, the Dutch Supreme Court ruled in favor of the Urgenda foundation in the groundbreaking case *Urgenda vs. the Netherlands*. The Supreme Court concluded that the Dutch government was required to reduce greenhouse gas emission by 25 percent in 2020 compared to its emissions in 1990, since a failure to meet this goal would result in a breach of human rights, specifically article 2 (right to life) and article 8 (right to respect for family life) of the ECHR.[259] Furthermore, on October 25th 2022, an administrative judge in France ruled that the license of the municipality of La Clusaz would not be extended. La Clusaz, which houses a ski resort, wanted to build an artificial lake in a nature reserve to ensure fake snow for ski enthusiasts in spite of above zero temperatures due to global warming. The judge concluded that the public interest in producing fake snow did not outweigh the public interest in preserving the natural environment.[260] In these cases, legal professionals took their responsibility as members of human kind, global citizens and legal professionals and used their expertise and skills to pursue sustainability. Inspired by these examples, other academically educated legal professionals could do the same in cases concerning sustainability and justice, such as the fight against poverty, the pursuit of equality or the protection of the environment.

The fundamental responsibility that academically educated legal professionals have to be aware of within ACT responsibility is a *prospective* – future oriented – responsibility. Even though retrospective responsibility is important in certain contexts, under current circumstances, the future requires most of our attention. In explanation, the moment of choice is focused on the future: You consider 'what should I choose to do' not 'what did I choose to do'. The fact that making choices is so difficult, is because we are taken aback by the possibilities or risks that our choices might have for the future. So, concern about the future – be it someone's own near future, the future of others or even that of future generations – seems to be the communal focus. Considering a prospective responsibility for academically educated legal professionals reflects this societal orientation on the future.

Also, inspired by Jonas, Levinas and Bauman – who all distinctively describe a prospective personal responsibility – I propose a prospective *personal* responsibility in addition to a *non-personal* responsibility for 21st century academically educated legal professionals. In stark contrast to the theories of responsibility for others and/or the natural environment as described by Jonas, Levinas and Koehn, mass societies are characterized by the shifting of responsibility.[261] The numerous others in a globalized

259 Supreme Court of the Netherlands, Urgenda vs. the State of the Netherlands, ECLI:NL:HR:2019:2006, December 20th 2019. See also Antronopoulos 2020, pp. 119-120.

260 See: https://www.trouw.nl/buitenland/franse-klimaatactivisten-verslaan-sneeuwkanonnen~b6c93a00, last visited October 28th 2022.

261 Somogyvári 2009, p. 350.

world, make individuals experience that they are alone even in crowded spaces and many shift – or escape – their responsibility. Darley and Latané investigated this phenomenon in the 1960s and called it 'diffusion of responsibility'. Shocked by a vicious murder on the streets of New York City where none of the 38 witnesses (who watched the crime happen from behind their apartment windows) intervened or even called the police, Darley and Latané conducted an experiment to find out what the reason for the bystanders' inaction could be.[262] They found that the reason for the failure of individuals to take responsibility (the so-called 'bystander effect') is not alienation, indifference or apathy for the suffering of others, but that people in crowded places – who do not have direct contact with one another – expect others to respond.[263] The knowledge that others are present to witness an event – others who might also respond – decreases the chance that an individual will take responsibility to act themselves.[264] The greater the crowd, the greater the diffusion of responsibility between the people present and the less individuals are inclined to take *personal* responsibility and act.[265] In other words, in a crowd, people – as individuals – are less likely to intervene. This does not mean, however, that in a crowd someone in need is less likely to get help than when only one individual witnesses that person's emergency. Recent research reasserts that the chance is high that at least *someone* in the crowd *will* help.[266] In an additional experiment, Latané and Darley also discovered that if others are present but act unconcerned or inactive in the face of a possible emergency, individuals are less likely to assume their responsibility and take action. Social norms dictating calmness and indifference, the risk of embarrassment and the idea that the present others *would* act if there truly was any danger, ensure that individuals fail to act.[267]

How does this relate to our current predicament? Mass societies, such as our global society, consist of many individuals and know only rare moments of contact between people.[268] Indeed, most people traveling through the social space are transfixed by the

262 Darley & Latané 1968, p. 377.

263 Interestingly, they also concluded that the subjects who failed to respond to the emergency (to take responsibility) in the experiment seemed to remain in a state of inaction because they *could not make a choice*. Because of this, they stayed in a situation of conflict which was reportedly expressed in sweating, trembling hands and nervousness. The ones who *did act*, however, did not experience these symptoms at the end of the experiment. They had resolved their state of conflict by taking responsibility. See Darley & Latané 1968, p. 382.

264 Latané & Darley 1968, p. 215.

265 Darley & Latané 1968, pp. 378, 380.

266 Philpot, Liebst, Levine, Bernasco and Lindegaard published research related to the hypothesis of the bystander effect. In this research, the question whether a victim of public aggression would receive help is investigated. In more than 90% of the 219 situations studied by these researchers at least one bystander stepped in. The more bystanders were present, the higher the changes of someone intervening. See Philpot, Liebst, Levine, Bernasco and Lindegaard 2020, pp. 67, 71.

267 Latané & Darley 1968, pp. 216, 220-221.

268 This is due to individualism and dissolving social bonds. See, for example, Bauman's description of cloakroom communities: Bauman 2000, pp. 95, 199-200.

personal universe provided by their mobile devices. In such a context, responsibility can become so diffused that is it almost unnoticeable for individuals. Bauman argues that people in contemporary society have all become global bystanders facing the personal challenge of identifying and taking responsibility. The knowledge of the pain others suffer – which one knows by merely swiping a finger across the screen – confronts the individual with the question if they should do something to stop it and if they could make a difference by taking action. Staying inactive and failing to take responsibility, however, might result in (vague) feelings of guilt.[269] Interestingly, Bauman analyzes that people try to reject their guilt through two new strategies since denying any knowledge of the wrongdoing is no longer an acceptable excuse in the age of information. First, people could try to dehumanize the sufferers or declare that these people brought the wrong upon themselves, so that the moral duty to take responsibility towards them disappears. Secondly, by convincing themselves that there is nothing they can do to help people try to escape their responsibility. Both strategies result in individual inactiveness.[270] According to Somogyvári, global bystanders in mass societies tend to wait for others to react to solve problems and will shift responsibilities to organizations and institutions and then just (in the best situation) follow the rules given by the institutions.[271] This shift from personal towards collective responsibility was described in 1999 by Strydom, who considered Hans Jonas to be one of the philosophers at the start of this transformation in the 1980s.[272] Recognizable in Jonas's theory is that collective responsibility for the environment and others in the present and future is distributed to authorities or institutions such as states, international organizations and (international) corporations.[273] However, when individuals merely follow the rules given to them by institutions, this can only be described as simple responsibility-as-duty. So, by following EU and national law, many people in the Netherlands no longer buy plastic straws and single-use plastic cutlery, but most of them will not have viewed this transition as part of their personal responsibility for future generations. In our global society, many people are not inclined to take responsibility for others that live in the same building as they do, let alone take responsibility for people living down the street, in another city, country or even in the future. The fact that many others look away, are inactive or even actively deny the existence of current global crises and disregard the necessity of sustainable development, could negatively influence the ability of individuals to take responsibility and act.

Nevertheless, similar to Bauman's idea that individual responsibility takes center stage in our liquid modernity, and in accordance with Levinas's and Jonas's descriptions of

269 Bauman 2010, p. 96.
270 Bauman 2010, pp. 97-98.
271 Somogyvári 2009, pp. 350-351.
272 Strydom 1999, p. 66.
273 See also Jonas 1984, p. 12.

personal responsibility, ACT responsibility starts from the basic principle that every individual has their own, personal part to play within the collective. This makes the responsibility for others, succeeding generations and nature *personal*. This individual responsibility may cause a person to alter their actions and personally contribute to the needs and interests of other entities. For example, someone might decide to drive an electric car and cook on an electric stove in order to diminish their own use of natural resources and to preserve the environment. This type of responsibility is part of prospective personal responsibility. I argue that in the second decade of the 21st century and beyond, another shift in focus is necessary following the shift noted by Strydom in 1999. Instead of selecting either personal or collective responsibility, we are in need of *both*. In our time, in which we are confronted with the manifestation of risks and action has to be taken, collective and individual responsibility are both essential, which is why they are both part of ACT responsibility.

In summary, the first component of ACT responsibility starts with the fundamental awareness of the primary prospective non-personal and personal responsibility for the self, others, society and the natural environment to pursue human well-being, justice and sustainability. Furthermore, this responsibility is expressed in four dimensions of responsibility located in the right part of the Four-Axis Graph (see below): 1) a collective responsibility as member of human kind; 2) a vocational responsibility for the whole vocational group of academically educated legal professionals; 3) a personal vocational responsibility for individual academically educated legal professionals, and; 4) a personal responsibility for yourself, others and the environment. In the following these four dimensions of responsibility will be further described.

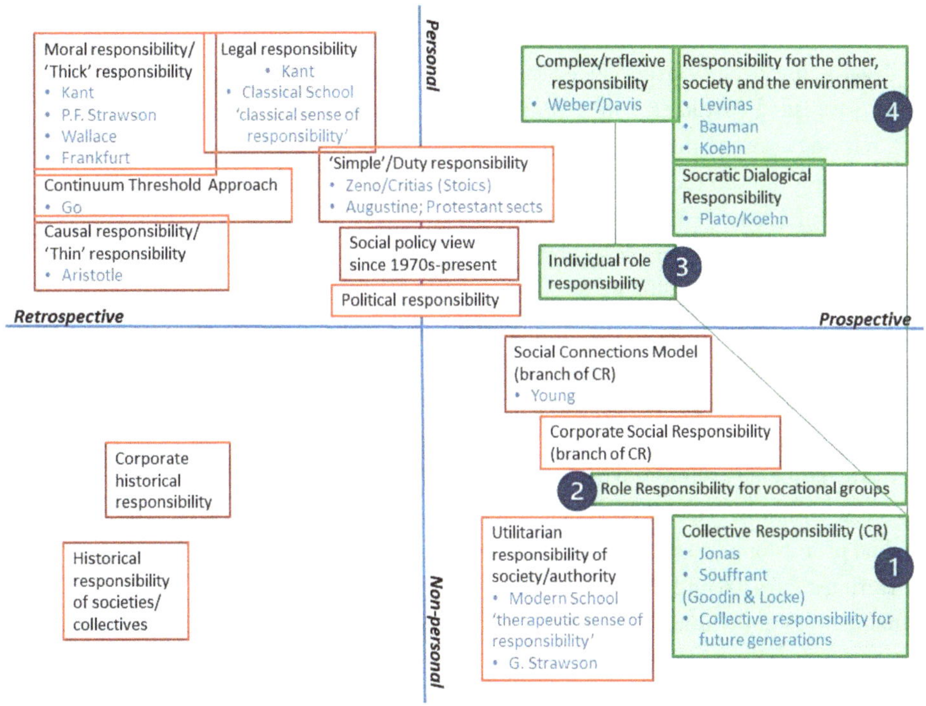

Firstly, academically educated legal professionals have, as members of humankind, a fundamental prospective *collective* responsibility to pursue local and global justice – for example by protecting human rights through fighting against poverty, protecting the vulnerable from exploitation and by striving for the realization of human equality. Moreover, this collective responsibility expands to the obligation to pursue sustainability so that future generations will be able enjoy to the earth's natural resources. Through technology, the human race has amassed great power over nature – and the ultimate power to destroy the earth. This destructive potential makes the collective responsibility for protection and preservation of the environment all the more pressing. This collective responsibility lies primarily with international institutions – such as the UN and the EU – and with the nation state. Legal professionals active on this level of law and policy making are able to contribute by developing (inter)national regulations and strategies to support, for instance, human rights, justice and sustainability.

Secondly, as a *vocational group*, academically educated legal professionals can be said to have a *collective* prospective responsibility for the pursuit of human well-being, justice and sustainability. Academically educated legal professionals have exclusive access to specific positions in society, such as judge, lawyer or criminal prosecutor. These positions come with essential societal responsibilities of the occupational group such as guaranteeing due process and ensuring a fair trial for every person. In addition, the vocational group has a shared responsibility to end some forms of uncertainty for individuals (for instance the – legal – uncertainty experienced by clients, suspects, fighting spouses seeking a divorce, dissatisfied customers, property sellers and buyers et cetera) by providing legal advice, relaying accurate information and by developing legal provisions and case law on – for example – the protection of customers and prenuptial agreements. Furthermore, legal professionals could play a role in conquering poverty in society by enabling the fair distribution of resources through legislation and case law.

Thirdly, as individual members of the vocational group, every academically educated legal professional has a prospective *individual* responsibility to personally contribute to the responsibilities of the occupational group. For example, the aforementioned *Urgenda vs. the Netherlands* case showed that individual legal professionals – in this case, the judges of the Dutch Supreme Court – are able to contribute to sustainability in their professional roles. As such they have offered an individual professional contribution to the occupational group's responsibility. The same holds true for other legal professionals who act as individual professionals to support the vocational group's responsibility by providing legal aid, ensuring a fair trial and due process, developing case law and legislation and so on.

Finally, every individual has a fundamental prospective personal responsibility for themselves, others and the environment. With regard to this personal responsibility, individuals are required to take responsibility for their personal choices in the complexity of today's living conditions. On this personal level, individuals can pursue (social) justice and sustainability. For example, a person might choose to donate to or even do voluntary work in a food bank, the Salvation Army, battered women shelter, recycling center, or an NGO focused on wildlife preservation or another organization that aims at justice, human well-being or sustainability.

To conclude, the idea of ACT responsibility is that, at their core, academically educated legal professional are **aware** of the aforementioned dimensions of their fundamental prospective, collective, role and personal responsibility. To develop this awareness, academically educated legal professional could seek, aim to understand and critically reflect upon information about the subjects that they have this responsibility for. However, as said before, this is an all-encompassing responsibility that might be experienced as a burden that is too heavy to bear. Therefore, the second part of ACT responsibility involves each person's own choice with regard to the responsibility/responsibilities they focus on.

2 Choice

The second component of the three-stage rocket responsibility involves **Choice**. As mentioned above, the first step op ACT responsibility, being aware of the fundamental and all-encompassing responsibility, can be overwhelming. This might result in uncertainty, anxiety or fear which, in turn, might lead to inaction or overburdened individuals who try to live up to the comprehensive fundamental responsibility. When confronted with such an extensive responsibility, it is necessary to make a selection to point out which responsibilities to take on – and which to pass on.[274] This selection – or choice – is a strategy to narrow down the all-encompassing responsibility. However, it is still not effortless or comfortable, since making choices remains to an extent uncertain. According to Bauman, only a limited number of choices – and often only trivial ones – can be clearly regarded as either good or bad. Unfortunately, most choices, and especially complex ones such as our choice of responsibility, are made between contradictory moral impulses and remain shrouded by uncertainty.[275] For example, the moral impulse to have responsibility solely for my own happiness or – at the other end of the spectrum – the moral impulse to have responsibility for the natural environment. Taken to their extremes, both impulses are undesirable because they lead to immoral consequences. In explanation, if I want to follow the moral impulse to only have responsibility for myself, I might lose myself in hedonism and forget about others and my relationship to them. On the other hand, if I follow the moral impulse to have responsibility for the natural environment to the extreme, I could glue myself to cultural heritage such as art works and in the process destroy these testaments of human creativity, craftmanship and thoughtfulness. This too, is undesirable.

274 The choice of which responsibility an individual takes on and which they will not take on might be one of the demanding, fundamental and principled choices Francot refers to. See Francot 2014, p. 202.

275 Bauman 2005, p. 11-12. See also Den Hertog 2008, p. 16.

So, no impulse is completely good, or completely bad and making a choice between two contradictory impulses therefore remains morally ambiguous, which makes selecting (choosing) your own responsibility uncertain and difficult. Nevertheless, through choice, every individual agent makes their responsibility distinct, defined and more bearable, because it becomes over-seeable and self-imposed. Furthermore, this element of ACT responsibility gives individuals ownership over their responsibility and makes every person's responsibility *their own*. During an academic legal education, students could practice how to make these self-authored choices regarding their own responsibility.

What becomes clear here is that, because of this element of choice, the notion of responsibility I suggest is – in the words of Weber and Davis – a *complex* responsibility. That is, it involves much more than performing a duty by following rules given by an external authority. In this sense, it transcends individual role responsibility and role responsibility of the vocational group of lawyers. While professional ethics are important, they are not sufficient for the responsibility necessary in the 21st century, since they simply entail following the rules given by an external authority. In the words of Bauman, in these liquid times 'one cannot be a true conformist'; 'following the rules, however scrupulously, does not save us from responsibility'.[276] Indeed, while being aware of their fundamental personal and collective responsibility, academically educated legal professionals – and law students – have to make choices in the way they define *their own* self-authored responsibility. These choices cannot be imposed on them by somebody else, since they are the result of every individual's personal deliberations and reflections on their knowledge, abilities, values and priorities. In other words, they are autonomous – or, self-authored.[277] In this sense, Bauman seems to have it right: Academically educated legal professionals should not – and, if they put ACT responsibility in practice, will not – be true conformists, because they will consider before making a choice whether to agree or not. Furthermore, this choice is adaptable, it follows a person's life-long learning process and requires constant reflection and deliberation. For example, when someone gains new knowledge that leads to change in their understanding of the world and their values, their choice of which responsibilities they want to bear and are able to bear may alter. So, the idea of ACT responsibility is that every academically educated legal professional should be able to define their responsibility, in their own contexts of life and work. This means that they are required to continuously reflect on their role(s), their knowledge, abilities, values and

276 Bauman 2005, p. 20.

277 Bauman argues that such a moral choice is not predictable, not utilitarian and cannot be rule-guided – as it would be in a simple responsibility or 'responsibility-as-duty'. This would be heteronomous instead of autonomous. The choices that are referred to here in ACT responsibility distinctively fit into Bauman's category of autonomous choice. See Bauman 2005, p. 11. In this research I mostly refer to these choices as being 'self-authored' and they are part of leading a self-authored life. 'Self-authoring' connects closely to the concept of autonomy, but highlight the self-directed authoring – writing – of one's own life, thinking and choices.

priorities. That self-formation is part of the inward dimension of *Bildung*, the self-reflection and self-development leads to contemplated, independent (life) choices. By making these choices on where their own responsibility lies within the all-encompassing responsibility for academically educated legal professionals, one defines their own self-authored responsibility. The individual decides (chooses) for what, for whom and to what extent they are responsible, which provides them with a level of agency. This choice-making involves critical and reflective thinking and creative thinking, as all are required for self-authoring the goals and accompanying rules of conduct and for changing these if needed. Therefore, it is a complex and dynamic responsibility.

3 Taking action

Following the definition of one's self-authored responsibility, is actually *taking* that responsibility by performing an action that corresponds with the choice. For that reason, **Taking action** is the final component of ACT responsibility. It involves the ability of the legal professional or law student to take congruent action based on the responsibility-choices that the individual has made for themselves. For example, after a lawyer in criminal law has made the choice to identify 'I provide legal aid to every person that needs it' as part of their own responsibility, they are expected to act accordingly, and actually offer legal aid to a person even if they dislike the criminal act they are accused of. Similarly, if the same lawyer chooses to include 'I reduce my use of natural resources such as natural gas as much as I can', they ideally take congruent action and, for instance, install solar panels and cook on an inductive stove. However, the lawyer might further refine their responsibility choices and set some boundaries. For instance, they might choose that although they find that their responsibility is to provide legal aid for everyone who needs it, they do not want to represent rapists. By making this choice, the lawyer narrows down their responsibility. By doing so, the lawyer not only has identified their responsibility (through choice), but has also taken their responsibility.

In these cases, the action is the result of a person's awareness of the all-encompassing responsibility and the personal choices they have made in shaping their own responsibility based on their knowledge, abilities, role(s), values and priorities. Precisely *because* you have made clear choices with regard to your self-authored responsibility, you are more predisposed to actually take action. This could be helpful in countering the 'diffusion of responsibility' phenomenon as described by Latané and Darley.

This final step of ACT responsibility relates to the outward dimension of *Bildung*. The actions of a person take place in society and they reflect the person's inner world. Davis describes Weber's idea of personhood as follows: Individuals gain personhood when they have stability or consistency of their inner connections with ultimate meanings or values of life which are directed towards goals which lead to accordance in goal oriented world-transforming action.[278] This is very close to not only what I have described here as the two final steps of ACT responsibility, but also to the *Bildung* concept. It looks at the inner development of a person and the ability to act correspondingly within society.

This three-stage-rocket ACT responsibility is at the same time a burden and a relief. It burdens academically educated legal professionals with the obligation to be aware of responsibility, to choose which responsibility is theirs and to act based on that responsibility. At the same time, by selecting their own responsibility individuals gain a defined and self-authored understanding of their responsibility. This provides boundaries to the all-encompassing responsibility and therefore brings some relief.

Teaching for ACT Responsibility in Academic Legal Education

In ACT responsibility, the difference between a vocational education in law and an academic legal education becomes visible. During the latter, students are ideally initiated into all the responsibility dimensions of ACT responsibility, namely non-personal and personal vocational responsibility, with both the collective responsibility as member of human kind and the personal responsibility for yourself, others and the environment as center of gravity. They are educated towards becoming critical and creative thinkers capable of defining their own complex responsibility (as is part of ACT responsibility) that transcends doing their duty and following vocational rules and regulations. Especially in legal theoretical courses, but also in black letter law courses – time for the development of this ACT responsibility could be provided. A vocational education in law has a different

278 Davis 1999, p. 37.

aim: The goal is for the students to become adept professionals. Naturally, in the time educators in vocational education have with their students, they focus on the role responsibility of the individual legal professional and the role responsibilities of the vocational group follows. Even though it would surely be desirable for students of a vocational legal education to also be mindful of other dimensions of responsibility in addition to the vocational dimensions, this is not essential for achieving the primary aim of a *vocational* education in law.

Teaching for ACT responsibility in ALE will provide law students with a strategy to cope with uncertainty. As will become clear in the following sections, critical and creative thinking skills are required for ACT responsibility; both thinking abilities are necessary to make choices in defining your own responsibility and to take congruent action. In explanation, to define what their personal responsibility is, students constantly have to critically reflect on what they find important, who they are, what their priorities are and they have to critically reflect on the information they acquire about the problems they encounter. Then, after they have outlined their personal responsibility, they need to find creative ways to solve the complex problem(s) and critically reflect on the ideas they come up with and the results they achieve. Since ACT responsibility includes critical thinking and creative thinking *and* involves the inward and outward dimensions of *Bildung*, it provides students with the tools, knowledge and skills to carry out their vocation as academically educated legal professionals and to lead their lives successfully in contemporary global society. The idea behind ACT responsibility is that students learn to be nuanced, critical and creative thinkers capable of making self-authored, well thought through decisions. These choices set boundaries for their responsibility and enable them to take action and have impact in society.

Educators in academic legal educators are able to take their prospective personal and role responsibility for supporting the development (of the sense of responsibility) of future generations of graduates in law. Since legal educators have an important role in shaping the culture of the profession,[279] it is possible for them to make a difference. However, at the moment, we generally educate law students in a traditional manner. We teach our students how to solve cases by applying legal rules that can be found in legal provisions and case law. From a traditional point of view, solving cases *according to the established legal rules* means the legal advisor, lawyer, prosecutor, or judge has taken their responsibility. Nevertheless, this is not what I describe as ACT responsibility, but seems rather similar to simple responsibility. As argued before, simple responsibility is not nearly enough for an academically educated person to be able to contribute to solving the complex problems of our globalized time. To better help our students to become able citizens of contemporary society, we have to aim at supporting the development of their ACT responsibility.

---

279 Appleby, Burton & Reilly 2013, p. 360.

Many educators in ALE would probably say that they already allocate responsibility to students for a number of things. For example, students in Academia are considered responsible for their own learning process, their personal and professional development and for being critically inclined towards themselves, others, information and the law. In addition to these responsibilities, the aim in law schools would primarily be to introduce students to the fundamental responsibility that falls on them and of which they have to be aware. Legal educators can gradually teach their students the ability to reflect upon and define their own responsibility with regard to their role as academically educated future legal professionals in the context of the contemporary global society. These responsibilities relate to the student's future legal vocation, their academic status and their lives as global citizens. *Bildung* and ACT responsibility are both processes of life-long learning, which is why it is not necessary for educators in legal educators to make sure that every student can define their responsibility perfectly and take congruent action at completion of their education in law. Still, we *could* aim at providing our students with information on the all-encompassing responsibility and the challenges of contemporary society, offering guidelines and strategies to develop their choice making ability and the ability for action (for example, by teaching them critical and creative thinking). This way, law graduates will be able to embark on their life-long learning journey with enough baggage for further development.

The next sections will delve into the question how educators in ALE could support their students' development of the three components of ACT responsibility. The aim is to provide preliminary ideas on how ACT responsibility could be integrated into ALE by making it a part of attainment goals and learning goals. Hence, preliminary learning goals that may be used in an individual course, in a specific learning trajectory or in overarching attainment goals for curricula – for each of the three elements of ACT responsibility will be proposed. This is followed by some practical suggestions for the teaching of awareness, choice making and taking action.

Teaching for responsibility-Awareness

With regard to developing a law student's responsibility-awareness, educators can aim to contribute to the student's awareness of the all-encompassing (and earlier described) responsibility. This requires the student to have knowledge and understanding of contemporary global challenges and an understanding of the necessity of pursuing sustainability and human well-being in the solution of these problems. Examples of relevant learning goals could be:

- The student is able to identify and outline main societal challenges;
- The student is able to search for and find relevant information on a societal theme, problem or dilemma;
- The student is able to judge if the gained information is credible;

- The student is able to understand the information and is able to link the new knowledge to earlier obtained knowledge;
- Based on the studied literature or other information source, the student is able to outline the main problem, main viewpoint and arguments;
- The student is able to pinpoint and explain the complexity of the problem/theme/dilemma;
- The student is able to identify fields of study that may be relevant for understanding the theme/problem/dilemma in more depth;
- The student is able to identity the responsibilities linked to the problem/theme/dilemma and is able to identify who bears this responsibility and for whom/what they have to take this responsibility.
- The student is able to describe the problem from multiple perspectives;
- The student is able to reflect critically on the information, the problem/theme/dilemma and the opinions related to it;
- The student is able to join an oral or a written discussion with peers on the theme and is able to make relevant, critical and creative contributions to the discussion;
- The student is able to find new information (such as news articles or academic articles) and identify it as belonging to a theme/problem/dilemma.

To help our students achieve these goals, educators in legal education will need to be conscious of their own responsibility as educators and are required to convey the vocational responsibilities of academically educated legal professionals to their students. Educators in ALE could aim at broadening their students' world by providing broad information on societal, professional and personal challenges and discussing world problems with students in their classrooms. This might be done by developing courses, for example, a course on private law or a course on legal philosophy, around important and relevant questions and by including literature on global challenges in the content of the course. Bain also suggests bringing together multiple disciplines within the course to answer the central questions.[280] Also, educators can include (some of) these learning goals in their courses and develop fitting learning activities. For instance, an educator might decide to let students watch documentaries about social and/or environmental problems such as poverty, inequality or the exploitation of workers in the clothing industry and prepare a group discussion or ask her students to write a paper on the topic. The educator could also invite guest speakers from various domains of study to talk with the students about global and societal challenges. Furthermore, educators could invite legal professionals, for instance judges, lawyers, notaries or policy makers to share their experiences in making decisions and acting in complex cases. Discussing complex legal cases with guest educators

280 See Bain 2021, pp. 31, 33.

such as judges or lawyers is especially relevant, but it can also be very helpful for students to discuss such cases among themselves and with their own educator. It is also possible to ask students to write a paper or present an oral presentation concerning a complex case and how they would solve the case if they had been involved as legal professionals. To train students in communicating with professionals originating from other (non-legal) fields, we can invite guest educators from other faculties, develop tasks in which students from various faculties need to work together, or ask law students to present their research findings (or teach an introductory class in law) to students that, for example, study medicine, philosophy, sociology, business, culture studies, finance or economics. Through frequent interaction, their effective communicative skills across disciplines evolves.

Teaching for Choice making

In the wake of developing the students' awareness of the fundamental responsibility of academically educated legal professionals, educators could organize specific moments during every student's Bachelor and Master program in which the student reflects on and makes choices regarding their own personal, professional and academic responsibility.

Possible learning goals that involve this choice making could be:

- The student is able to recognize and verbalize the demand(s) that societal challenges place upon them;
- The student is able to formulate their own values as human being, citizen, and academically educated legal professional;
- The student is able to formulate a realistic representation of their own knowledge and abilities;
- The student is able to contribute to a respectful discussion with peers on their responsibilities, values and priorities;
- The student is able to select and interpret the information and knowledge they need for making an informed decision;
- The student is able to delay their judgment for as long as needed to weigh all options before making a decision;
- The student is able to think of and formulate possible scenarios (for example, a worst case and a best case scenario) that could result from the choice that they are going to make;
- The student is able to weigh the interests involved in the choice;
- The student is able to make a decision after mindful consideration of their own knowledge, abilities, values and aims *and* the involved interests and possible future scenarios that may be the result of the choice;
- The student is able to explain their decision(s) and to provide arguments for the viewpoints or positions they have taken;

- The student is able to receive feedback on the position they have taken and – if warranted – is able to reconsider their point of view;
- The student is able to reflect and recognize if their new knowledge/understanding demands a change of their values and responsibilities and can make changes in these values and responsibilities accordingly;
- The student is able to formulate which contribution(s) they would like to make to others, society at large and the environment based on their knowledge, abilities, values and priorities;
- The student is able to describe how their strengths can help them achieve their goals and which aspects they need to develop further in order to achieve their goals;
- The student is able to describe their personal and professional responsibilities and can pinpoint for whom/what they are responsible and why;
- The student is aware that their self-authored responsibility may be subject to change in the future and is able to reconsider their choices when warranted.

To start their students' thinking process on their own responsibility, educators could start by discussing the far-reaching, all-encompassing responsibility of academically educated professionals with their students and to discuss why it is important to think about your responsibility/responsibilities as future members of the vocational group *and* as human beings living in contemporary society.

To be able to make choices regarding their own responsibility, students need time to reflect during their studies. This reflection concerns themselves, their opinions and beliefs. The thinking process may involve questions such as: who am I?; What drives me?; What are my values/convictions?; What do I think is *right*?; What moves me in decision making?; How can I contribute to change?; What do I want to change/what do I think needs changing?; Where lies my responsibility?; In which ways can I – as a legal professional – contribute to the lives of others and the planet? Pondering these questions results in self-knowledge and stimulates character forming (the inner dimension of *Bildung).*[281] In this sense, it involves a continuous questioning of the self. A student may start such an inner discussion on their own, and gain understanding in their strengths, values and priorities. However, in educational settings, it could also done with multiple students or in groups. That way, students can connect with others and question and learn from one another. This will sharpen every student's personal understanding. This is similar to what Koehn calls Socratic Dialogical Responsibility and is also part of outward *Bildung* since it looks at

281 An interesting example of a collection of responsibility-related questions used in educational settings that might inspire a list of our own (which would be focused on the specific situation of academic law students) can be found at: https://www.goodcharacter.com/middle_school/teaching-responsibility/, last visited November 1st 2022.

development within the context of society.[282] Since personality formation is a life-long process, it is recommendable to regularly revisit the questions and frequently reserve time during the student's education for such a reflection. As a method to teach students how to decide, educators could ask their students to make a decision tree which includes the possible courses of action and the possible consequences of the listed actions.[283]

Similar to critical thinking, defining one's own responsibility requires the ability to consider a problem, theme or dilemma from multiple perspectives. In addition to the methods as discussed in chapter 3, such as the thinking hats method or reading and discussing literature, this ability could be supported by developing a sensitivity to others.[284] The educator could stimulate students to make an effort in understanding someone else's plight, or someone else's points of view. For example, an educator could develop a course on legal aspects to societal problems and include a mandatory interview with a prisoner, a drug user, a homeless person, someone in financial trouble or a climate activist. In addition to the interview, the assignment could include a reflection on the insights the student has gained and the way this might have changed their view point. This might stimulate a sense of empathy[285] or at least an understanding of the challenges some people in our society face.

Moreover, in ALE, educators can integrate ACT responsibility's Choice making by including sustainability, human well-being, justice and responsibility as themes in their courses and discuss with the students how those themes relate to them and what current societal challenges mean to (and for) them. Or students could be asked to consider their (future) role as legal professionals and imagine what others (the general public, their bosses, companies or clients) might expect from them and to consider how those demands are similar (or dissimilar) to their own values. This might be in the form of an oral discussion, but of course it is also possible to ask the students to write a (short) paper, conduct interviews, start a role play, make a short film or documentary or create a collage

282 Koehn 2019, p. 73.

283 See for a similar example: Sternberg 2007, p. 34.

284 In addition to sensitivity being a part of critical thinking, its place here can be interpreted as a call for a somewhat Levinasian or Baumanian sense for the other. Furthermore, it is part of *Bildung*'s call for developing the ability of sense in addition to the development of reason.

285 Martha Nussbaum argues that 'thinking well' – by which she means critical thinking and reflection – is needed for democracies to be able to deal responsibly with globalized, complex problems. What is needed in addition to thinking well is empathy; the ability to imagine yourself in the other's shoes. According to Nussbaum, the survival of decent institutions can only be ensured through empathy. See Nussbaum 2016, p. 10. Furthermore, Nussbaum calls for academic educators to teach accountability and treat students as responsible agents. They are required to teach empathy, equality (in the sense that students view the other as a worthy human being), openness to error/weaknesses and an openness to uncertainty. The reason for these requirements of academic education is that these skills create a structure where people are able to stand against manipulation and will be able to maintain a healthy democracy. Nussbaum 2016, pp. 43-45.

or poem. These playful forms of reflection can be individual or group assignments and might provide new starting points for a discussion in class.

Teaching for Taking action

For ACT responsibility, it is not enough for students to be aware of the all-encompassing responsibility of academically educated legal professional and to have made choices with regard to what they consider their own responsibility. ACT responsibility requires the ability to actually take action. So, based on their self-authored choices regarding their responsibility, a law student has to be able to *take congruent action*. The action itself might take many forms, from helping an old lady who seems lost on the street, voluntary work in soup kitchens or animal shelters, to writing an opinion in a newspaper or on social media, joining a protest, starting a foundation, providing legal advice and avoiding the use of plastics. Regardless of the form of the action, law students require some support in how to take congruent action to their self-authored responsibility.

Below, some suggestions for learning goals for this component of ACT responsibility can be found:

- While deciding to take action, the student remains reflective and critical and identifies if the contemplated action is in correspondence with their self-authored responsibility;
- Through critical thinking and creative thinking, the student is able to determine which actions could and should follow their self-authored responsibility;
- The student is able to determine what it is necessary to do when performing the specific action;
- The student is able to act as a result of a contemplation on the possible consequences that concluded in a decision that they have sufficient reason to act;
- In the face of uncertainty about the possible consequences of an action, the student is able to determine if they have – or do not have – sufficient reason to act;
- The student is able to reflect on their past actions and reflect on whether their actions were congruent to their self-authored responsibility.

To be capable of actually *taking* responsibility – and thus take action – students need critical and creative thinking skills. Creative thinking and critical thinking are necessary for generating possible solutions and actions and for judging whether those actions are truly the most fitting. Ways to include these abilities in ALE have been proposed in chapters 3 and 4. In addition to these two skills, students require autonomy and power (influence) to be able to take action. This means that students need an amount of freedom (which they gain in ACT responsibility because of the self-authoring of the choice) and relevant knowledge and skills. Educators in legal education could support the development of abilities and knowledge that students need for taking actual action. This would provide the required power. During assignments or projects that concern taking action, it is important to offer the students an amount of autonomy. For example, law faculties could offer students opportunities to offer legal advice, to truly experience the problems others in society encounter through, for instance, internship with social work services, and to contribute to interdisciplinary (and international) think tanks of students to reflect on and find solutions for contemporary problems. Such activities could be rewarded with, for example, job offers, certificates, bonus points, or credits. In their law courses in all the years of the Bachelor's or Master's degree, educators might include overarching assignments that ask students to come up with (multidisciplined) solutions to actual problems in society. Ideally, these challenges would be formulated in consultation with professionals dealing with these problems, such as policy makers, first responders, social workers, the Dutch Bar or the Counsel of the Judiciary. In Moot Court courses that concern role play based on a legal case, educators may consider developing cases that hold multiple problems. For example, a case that concerns a client with familial, medical, social and financial problems. One of the learning goals of the course might then be that the student is able to deal with all aspects of the case.

To support their students' ability to take action, educators in ALE could also enable the development of their students' (personal) leadership qualities. For example, by using Sternberg's WICS system for leadership which is already utilized in Dutch primary education for gifted children. This model starts with the understanding that one can learn how to be a leader[286] and might also be interesting for our purposes in tertiary, academic education since it concerns many of the abilities ACT responsibility looks at. According to Sternberg, effective and creative leadership results from a combination of Wisdom, Intelligence, Creativity and these have to be Synthesized (in short, WICS).[287] The WICS system regards leadership as an activity in which one 'formulates, makes, and acts on decisions'.[288] As mentioned earlier, these leader activities seem to correspond to important components of ACT responsibility that have been explored in the previous sections of this chapter. Furthermore, Sternberg's Intelligence and Creativity partially overlaps with what has been explored in this research as critical thinking and creative thinking. Wisdom is described by Sternberg as mainly the decision to use your intelligence, creativity and knowledge for the common good. Moreover, wise people understand and can balance the interests of all involved parties. For our students, this translates into them being able to view a problem from many perspectives and being sensitive to the interests of others. Introducing students to a leadership system in, for example, extracurricular courses might

286 Sternberg 2007, p. 34. According to Sternberg, creative and effective leadership is not an innate trait, but can be learned during life.

287 Sternberg 2004, p. 108.

288 Sternberg 2007, p. 34.

be an interesting and worthwhile addition to our curricula to support law students in the ability to take action.

In conclusion, in search of a kind of responsibility befitting contemporary ALE and contemporary *Bildung*, we have traveled through many conceptions of responsibility. The structure of the Four-Axis Graph provided a way of pinpointing and visualizing the place and focus of the kind of responsibility educators in legal education could focus their efforts on. I have labeled this prospective personal, role and collective responsibility *ACT responsibility*, which is a complex responsibility that consists of awareness, choice making and taking action. For a person, and thus a student, to be capable of ACT responsibility, they require critical thinking and creative thinking ability. The suggestions mentioned above for incorporating ACT responsibility in ALE through, amongst others, attainment goals, learning goals, additions to the curriculum and supportive instructional interventions are meant as a first outline of what is possible for educators in ALE to do to support the development of their students' ACT responsibility.

While investigating *Bildung*, critical thinking, creative thinking and responsibility, I recurrently came across one specific approach for teaching and developing these elements of an academic legal education, namely through play and in a spirit of playfulness. Because such an approach could have a big impact in the teaching of educators in ALE, the following chapter offers a further exploration of both concepts and the way in which educators could incorporate play and playfulness into their teaching methods and teaching style.

6 ANYONE CAN WHISTLE. INTEGRATING PLAY AND PLAYFULNESS INTO ACADEMIC LEGAL EDUCATION*

"Play teaches people to be capable of living with others without control; it connects the experiences of vulnerability and surprise to curiosity and wonder, rather than to crippling anxiety."
– *Martha Nussbaum*[1]

INTRODUCTION

In the previous chapters, play and playfulness have recurrently come to the fore as ideal conditions in which to support the development of *Bildung*, ACT responsibility, critical thinking and creative thinking. In Nussbaum's citation above, too, play's importance for being able to deal with uncertainty – which is one of the most crucial abilities in contemporary life – is emphasized. Thus, in this chapter I explore play and playfulness as essential strategies for teaching critical thinking, creative thinking and ACT responsibility. Moreover, I advocate that 'anyone can whistle', which means that I am convinced that every educator who has an interest in experimenting with the suggestions offered in this research could integrate a play and playful approach in their teaching to support the student in achieving the learning goals. As argued in chapters 3 and 4, play and playfulness are important factors in the development of critical and creative thinking skills and dispositions. With regard to creativity, this is the case since play and playfulness positively influence the four crucial components of the creative process: the environment, individual task motivation, the development of domain relevant skills and the training of creativity relevant processes. As became clear in the initial models for integrating critical thinking and creative thinking in academic legal education (ALE) in chapters 3 and 4, educators could embed play and playfulness on all four levels that they influence in their universities:

---

* An earlier version of this chapter (and its appendix) was previously published in *Law and Method.* See Van Rossum, H.E. (2018-2), 'Time to Play: Integrating Play and Playfulness in Legal Philosophical Courses as Tools for Student Learning', in: *Law and Method. Special Issue on Active Learning and Teaching in Legal Education*, November 2018, pp. 1-19.

1 Nussbaum 2016, p. 101.

the learning culture and environment; curriculum design; course design, and; teaching method and teaching styles.

Although at first sight the use of play and playfulness in Academia might seem contra intuitive, I argue that they are not only useful, but even *belong* within the context of legal academic education. Indeed, in addition to their value for critical thinking and creativity, play and playfulness offer possibilities to engage students, support their ability for collaboration,[2] and enable educators to cultivate uncertainty in academic education, so that students learn how to cope with negative stress, uncertainty and ambiguity. This supports the development of the students' ACT responsibility.

Play has earned its reputation as a useful tool for learning and well-being in preschools, primary schools, and secondary schools[3] and has even entered some disciplines within higher education[4] but it has not yet found its way into law schools. The reason might be the serious and somewhat traditional nature of law and law schools whereas *play* and *playfulness* are often given a frivolous meaning. Therefore, legal academics might be hesitant to welcome play into academia as they argue – and rightfully so – that their work as legal professionals, researchers, and educators is of a very serious nature. However, the one-dimensional 'frivolous' interpretation of play overlooks its inherent seriousness.[5] I reckon that the premise that play is unproductive and thus useless or even embarrassing for (young) adults[6] is a serious misconception and, unfortunately, damaging for our students' academic development.[7] My mission here is to show that those ideas, which fit

2 Nørgård et al. 2017, p. 273.

3 The importance of play for learning in schools might be seen in, for instance, Sheridan 2011, p. 1. See also Tanis 2012, pp. 2-3. In addition, interesting in this context is, www.academicplay.com, last accessed June 15th 2018. The importance of play has also been recognized in Article 31 of the United Nations Convention on the Rights of the Child: '*1. States Parties recognize the right of the child to rest and leisure, to engage in play and recreational activities appropriate to the age of the child and to participate freely in cultural life and the arts. 2. States Parties shall respect and promote the right of the child to participate fully in cultural and artistic life and shall encourage the provision of appropriate and equal opportunities for cultural, artistic, recreational and leisure activity.*'

4 See James & Nerantzi 2019. See Tanis, 2012. See for a practical example in a course on music theory Berry 2015, pp. 45-68. See also: Nørgård et al. 2017, p. 273.

5 Huizinga stresses the serious aspect of play: '(...) all play, both of children and of grown-ups, can be performed in the most perfect seriousness'. See Huizinga 1980, p. 18. Caillois and Kerr and Apter agree on this point. According to them, human activity – and thus also play – can be performed in two distinct attitudes of mind, either serious (*telic, ludic*) or playful (*paratelic, paidia*). See Tanis 2012, pp. 44-46.

6 According to Van Vleet and Feeney, the conviction that play is not socially accepted in adulthood, since adults need to be productive, has resulted in a lack of research on play and playfulness in (young) adults. See Van Vleet and Feeney 2015, pp. 630-631.

7 For example, research by Proyer has found that playfulness in students has a positive influence on their academic performance, even though these students thought that they were less intelligent than their (less playful) peers. However, in this study, the playful students scored higher grades in a written exam and were more inclined to read additional (not mandatory) literature. Proyer 2011, pp. 464, 466-467.

seamlessly into the marketized university obsessed with productivity, are not part of the Academic spirit.

Play is valuable for and useable in ALE since it always has purpose and function.[8] In explanation, any play habitually has clearly described goals and challenges players to engage and collaborate.[9] Furthermore, play's purpose and function can be recognized in the seriousness that players often experience during play. Be it a game of chess or football or a theater play, to the player the game is all-encompassing, absorbing and is played fanatically.[10] Furthermore, research has found that play reduces stress and encourages problem-solving behavior.[11] Since stress-related problems are increasingly common in our students' lives,[12] and many students experience anxiety or fear of failure in their studies,[13] for example at the start of a new course or at the beginning of an exam, these effects of play are valuable for ALE. Also, play is believed to be a helpful way of learning empathy since a play-experience often requires working together in a non-threatening context.[14] Moreover, a playful attitude supports spontaneous learning, enables social interaction and collaboration, and furthers imagination.[15] Play and playfulness might, therefore, be integrated into legal education. Nevertheless, some research suggests that even though play and playfulness have the ability to increase student motivation, engagement, and enjoyment, those *external* motivational drivers do not necessarily result in deep learning and an excess of external motivation might even decrease intrinsic motivation.[16] Other research contradicts this perception and claims that deep learning occurs in the moment that students are carried away during play, when they experience *flow*.[17] Also, as seen in

8 Huizinga 1980, pp. 1, 5-6.

9 Huizinga 1980, p. 13; see also Thomas & Seely Brown 2011, p. 76.

10 Huizinga 1980, pp. 8, 10.

11 Tanis 2012, p. 51.

12 For example, https://www.nrc.nl/nieuws/2018/01/26/werkdruk-docent-en-student-enorm-a1590002 (2018) (last accessed June 14th 2018); https://www.rtlnieuws.nl/editienl/driekwart-van-studenten-is-uitgeput-aan-alle-kanten-werd-aan-me-getrokken (2017) (last accessed June 13th 2018); http://www.hogeronderwijs.nu/2014/04/steeds-meer-studenten-in-de-stress/ (2014) (last accessed June 13th 2018) and https://lsvb.nl/2013/03/29/psychische-klachten-bij-helft-studenten/ (2013)(last accessed June 13th 2018). See also: https://www.trimbos.nl/actueel/nieuws/hoger-onderwijs-moet-werk-maken-van-mentale-gezondheid-studenten/, (last accessed April 10th 2023) and https://www.rijksoverheid.nl/actueel/nieuws/2021/11/11/mentale-gezondheid-studenten-onder-druk, (last accessed April 10th 2023).

13 Fear of failure can be expressed in academic procrastination (students avoiding tasks, for example), self-handicapping (a cognitive strategy in which the student claims a hindrance that explains their failure which protects their self-esteem since it prevents them from being self-responsible for the failure) and learned helplessness (a student's personal perception that they have no control over the situation, which makes the student disengage from the start). Fear of failure is often connected to feelings of shame, for example, the shame of not living up to the standards set by the self or by others (family members, friends or teachers). See Choi 2021, pp. 2107-2110.

14 Nussbaum 2016, p. 99.

15 Nørgård et al. 2017, pp. 273-274.

16 Nørgård et al. 2017, p. 273.

17 Rice 2009, p. 96.

chapter 4, a momentarily lessening of intrinsic behavior by using incentives that focus on extrinsic motivation may be justified, for example in cases in which certain skills or specific behavior need to be trained.[18] In any case, playful learning supports creative thinking toward learning[19] and the acquiring of domain relevant skills. This may be a starting point for students to deepen their interest and engage in deep learning during or after class. Educators could help their students find ways to extend the play's effects on their intrinsic motivation by, for instance, engaging them in discussions on the play's (i.e., the course's) content.

In addition to the *usefulness* of play and playfulness in academic education as highlighted above, the concepts are truly more compatible with ALE than one might think. Research, higher education, and law share intrinsic features that play theorists attribute to play.[20] Moreover, many law schools already offer at least one form of play: Role-play in moot court courses. Also, it might be argued that play is inherent to law since role-play occurs during lawsuits[21] and legal reasoning and argumentation – fundamental parts of the legal profession – are in fact a game of skill and contest.[22] Philosophy (including legal philosophy), too, might be seen as play or a game, just as aspects of play can be noted in some of a university's traditions.[23] Consequently, using play and playfulness as tools for learning could be a natural way of teaching law.

In this chapter, I seek to provide an answer to the question how *play* and *playfulness* can be defined within the context of legal education and how these concepts could provide educators with tools to support student learning in the daily practice of legal courses. So, after a further exploration of their function in legal education, this chapter offers the first outlines of a definition of play and playfulness suited for ALE, drawing on the work of well-known play theorists and experts in learning theory such as Huizinga, Caillois, Lieberman, and Csikszentmihalyi. Secondly, the way in which play and playfulness might be integrated by adopting a playful approach to ALE with the use of game-based learning,

---

18 See Amabile 1996, p. 118.

19 Rice 2009, pp. 96-97.

20 All three have specific boundaries in time and space (see Huizinga 1980, pp. 10-11. Csikszentmihalyi & Bennett 1971, p. 46), are to a certain extent played voluntarily (see Huizinga 1980, p. 7. See also Csikszentmihalyi & Bennett 1971, pp. 45-46), are distinctly set apart from everyday life (see Huizinga 1980, pp. 8-9, 19, 21), promote the formation of social groupings (Huizinga 1980, pp. 12-13), and have the ability to captivate and engage the researcher, student, educator, or lawyer (Huizinga calls this captivation 'absorption', see Huizinga 1980, p. 13. See also Thomas & Seely Brown 2011, p. 76, Csikszentmihalyi & Bennett 1971, p. 47).

21 The players dress up in robes and play specific roles; see Huizinga 1980, p. 77.

22 See Huizinga 1980, pp. 76, 78. Wolthuis analyzed the play elements of (Dutch) parliamentary argumentation in Wolthuis 2007, pp. 12, 32.

23 See Huizinga 1980, pp. 152-156. Academia harbors traditions that include dressing-up by students (graduation) and professors (inaugural speeches) and studying in itself might fall within the definition of play as given by Huizinga. Research itself is a playful endeavor, where curiosity and inventiveness are of importance.

educational games and gamification will be explored. In addition, the appendix to this chapter specifically focuses on the level of teaching method and teaching style by sharing an overview of practical examples of instructional interventions that integrate play and playfulness into ALE. I have tested all of these examples in my own working groups. For a clear overview, these examples are divided into five main categories: (1) play with art; (2) role play; (3) physical play; (4) cooperative play with physical play artefacts, and; (5) online play activities.

By defining play and playfulness for legal education and by sharing practical examples of instructional interventions, I seek to inspire educators and contribute to innovation in and optimization of the theory of legal academic education and its practice.

Play and Playfulness

Using play and playfulness in legal education can be helpful for the students' understanding of our courses' content, for their preparation for (professional) life in contemporary times and for the development of their critical and creative thinking skills. Furthermore, by integrating play and playfulness in legal education students can be encouraged to engage in class, take part in deep and significant learning[24] and to develop themselves as human beings. Because of this, I suggest that incorporating play and playfulness in academic education is a way for educators to accomplish important objectives.

Firstly, play and playfulness are in themselves strategies for managing uncertainty and incorporating both in law schools provides a tension-filled yet relatively pleasurable and safe route for students to learn to deal with perpetual uncertainty.[25] The contemporary, globalized society with its many technological developments and its simultaneous distrust in science has led to an increase of possibilities of choice.[26] Not all possibilities can be realized and a selection needs to be made, although any choice might have unwanted, far-reaching consequences.[27] This turns decision making into a frightening endeavor, as uncertainty (the unknown) becomes a constant factor in everyday life. Francot describes moments in time in which uncertainty surfaces as moments in which it is difficult or even impossible to make a selection between options of choice. The reason for this difficulty or impossibility is often a lack of information, as the options of choice might be unclear or unknown and the consequences of the choice unforeseeable.[28] For some, the sense of

24 Nørgård et al. 2017, p. 276.

25 Ambrose et al. 2010, p. 48.

26 Beck 2007, p. 156. See also for further reading on this definition of late modernity, based on the social theories of Zygmunt Bauman and Ulrich Beck: Van Rossum 2018-1.

27 See Francot 2018, p. 90; see also: Francot 2014, p. 204.

28 Francot 2018, p. 98.

uncertainty may be experienced as chaos. To cope with chaos, they seek ways to organize the turmoil. Play may provide a useful strategy in this endeavor, since – according to Sicart – play is an activity between destruction and creation and between chaos and order.[29] In other words, play may bridge the gap between these extremes.[30] As future academically educated legal professionals,[31] our students need to learn how to deal with the uncertainty of unclear options of choice, not knowing which choices to make, the unknown consequences of the chosen action, and a feeling of a constant lack of crucial information. By including play and playfulness, we initiate a *re-mystification* of legal education, where students learn how to deal with choice and uncertainty as an inevitable part of life. The *re-mystification* of legal education entails the (re-)introduction of uncertainty, possibility, risk, and doubt within legal education. Instead of shielding students from uncertainty, it offers students a (relatively) safe place to practice dealing with these core elements of late modernity's society and encourages them to define, take and attribute responsibility within these circumstances.[32] Play inherently entails possibility, tension, and uncertainty,[33] but cultivates these by limiting the options of choice through the play's rules.[34] As such, play offers students a limited uncertainty within its boundaries, which gives students the opportunity to practice decision making within a learning environment that entails small-scale risks. It is the risk of playing that makes the play – makes learning, studying, and participating in class – exciting, enjoyable and inspires creativity,[35] especially if the play is performed with a playful attitude.[36]

Secondly, play and playfulness support student creativity. The imagination and outside-the-box thinking associated with playfulness are part of creativity relevant skills and will enable students and legal professionals to think of novel possibilities. Also, including play and playfulness in class stimulates intrinsic motivation and engages our students. This is essential to legal education as it positively influences student outcomes and study success and may facilitate deep learning and, thus, the development of domain relevant skills.[37]

---

29 Sicart 2014, pp. 3, 9.

30 This seems to correspond with Schiller's interpretation of the play drive that synthesizes between the extremes of the formal drive and sensuous drive.

31 Academically educated legal professionals need to be able to deal with uncertainty and risk as they are confronted with social, economic and technological developments that need normative regulation through law and are actively involved in legislating and deciding issues of uncertainty, such as questions of liability and responsibility. See Ambrus et al. 2017, p. 5.

32 *Re-mystification* is an attempt to counter the current corporatized and marketized attitude toward legal education, in which legal education seems to be regarded as a clear-cut product purchased by the student-consumer. See Van Rossum 2018-1, pp. 249-250, 255. See also Van Klink & De Vries 2016, p. 3.

33 Huizinga 1980, p. 11.

34 Csikszentmihalyi & Bennett 1971, p. 45.

35 Play enables creative thinking due to its ability to inspire fantasies and actions; see Biesty 2003, p. 46.

36 Tanis 2012, p. 46.

37 Zepke 2017, pp. 5-6; see also Rice 2009, p. 96.

Studies in engagement in higher education have shown that a student's feelings of emotional belonging are of importance for their engagement. Necessary for those feelings of belonging are, for instance, a sense of relevance in what is learned; a balance between choice, autonomy, risk, growth, and enjoyment; trust relationships with educators; and strong social networks.[38] Play and playfulness are able to offer most of these conditions, which are obviously also prerequisites for creativity.[39] Through play, a course's content can be presented to a student as a meaningful learning experience that highlights the course's relevance and value. During meaningful learning, students relate prior knowledge and skills to new content in a meaningful context.[40] By doing so, they construct new understanding as the meaningful learning experiences enable deep learning. Also, play's inherent uncertainty offers students a sense of risk within a safe and shared learning environment structured by rules, where they are free to make autonomous choices toward reaching the play's end. Moreover, with a playful attitude students are able to enjoy making those choices and playing around with the course's content.

Thirdly, play may be viewed as an activity that stimulates self-realization and makes us specifically *human*. Play is therefore an activity that supports *Bildung*. Play-theorist Huizinga reasoned that mankind (the *homo ludens*) is defined by play. According to Huizinga, play is inevitably part of western culture and has been a central part of the history of human society since at least the Roman Empire.[41] As previously described in the second chapter, Schiller found playing with art to be a part of an individual's *Bildung*, because playing (the play drive) enables the formal and sensuous drives to connect, thus uniting seemingly contrasting halves of the human personality.[42] The importance both Huizinga and Schiller allocate to play for humanity is also supported by Sicart, who states that play is essential for moral well-being and living a complete life, since it provides freedom to understand, practice and test conventions and habitual interpretations of the world.[43] As such, play supports contemplation of the world and our being in the world and provides a way of connecting with others.[44] Integrating play in law schools could therefore support our students' *Bildung*.

---

38 Zepke 2017, p. 5.

39 See the section on *creative relevant processes* in chapter 4.

40 Zurita et al. 2015, p. 2.

41 Huizinga 1980, pp. 173-194.

42 Horlacher 2017, p. 17. Lechner 2003, p. 95. Beiser 2003, p. 96.

43 Sicart 2014, pp. 5-6.

44 Sicart 2014, p. 1.

Definitions

If we are interested in using play and playfulness in our faculties and, ultimately, in our classrooms, we first need a definition of these two concepts. Sutton-Smith and Tanis have made it clear that a distinction has to be made between the concept of play and the concept of playfulness.[45] Even though that difference is not black-and-white and the concepts are often used interchangeably, in general terms, *play* refers to the activity or content of play whereas *playfulness* refers to the mental state of being lighthearted, which is often the case *during* play, but may also occur outside of play.[46] Providing a conceptualization of play and playfulness has proven difficult as scholars from many different disciplines have approached these concepts from various points of view.[47] To provide a starting point for the use of play and playfulness in legal education, I draw upon the insights of leading play theorists.

Play

Play can be understood as the activity or content of playing and manifests itself, for instance, in games.[48] Huizinga characterizes play as a free activity, consciously outside everyday life, unconnected with material interest and unserious (although players may be completely absorbed in the play), with its own boundaries of time and space, its own rules, holding tension and promoting the formation of social groupings that surround themselves with secrecy.[49] According to Huizinga and theorists following his tradition, play necessitates a so-called *magic circle*, which separates the world of the play (with its own rules) from everyday life (whose rules are suspended during play).[50] Caillois agrees with Huizinga that play is voluntary, separate, unproductive (a play – for example, gambling – may have material interests, but it does not *create* wealth or goods),[51] uncertain, and centered around precise rules.[52] However, Caillois contests the need for secrecy of social groups and adds a

---

45 See also Stenros 2015, p. 54.

46 Sutton-Smith 1997, p. 147; see also Tanis 2012, p. 7. See also Sicart 2014, p. 22.

47 Sutton-Smith 1997, p. 6; see also Tanis 2012, pp. 6-7.

48 Tanis 2012, p. 7. Apart from a critical redefinition of Huizinga's characteristics of play, Caillois offers a categorization of various games. Games are only one way for play to manifest itself, and according to Caillois, there are four categories of games: Games of competition and skill (*agon*), games of chance (*alea*), games of mimicry, and the experience of vertigo (*ilinx*). See Caillois 1961, pp. 12, 14-26; Tanis 2012, pp. 43-44; Csikszentmihalyi 2008, pp. 72-74. Sicart specifically states that games are not the same as play, they are only one way to play, whereas 'play' is a far more encompassing action and includes a way of human *being*. See Sicart 2014, p. 2.

49 Huizinga 1980, p. 13; Biesty 2003, p. 43.

50 See Ejsing-Duun 2014, p. 94.

51 Caillois 1961, p. 5.

52 Caillois 1961, p. 9.

new feature, namely, play as being *make-believe*.[53] In addition to the uncertainty of play as described by both play theorists, Csikszentmihalyi and Bennett explain that play is grounded in possibility, as play offers the player possibilities of choice within a playground limited by rules. In the end, the choice of action is voluntarily made by the individual player.[54] During deliberation between choices of action, the player might experience anxiety, especially since there are too many opportunities for action that are often incompatible.[55] However, play also offers the player the opportunity to be immensely absorbed and to enjoy *an optimal experience* and corresponding pleasure.[56] Play can improve an individual's problem-solving abilities and reduce stress.[57] According to some researchers, play also facilitates learning in adult life (e.g., in the workplace) and creativity.[58] Moreover, in correspondence with Huizinga's idea that play promotes social grouping, play is helpful in community building.[59]

Based on Huizinga's characteristics of play in combination with the additions and changes made by Caillois, Csikszentmihalyi, and Bennett, play in law schools can be defined through six features that are selected based on their functionality for legal education.

The first feature of play in ALE is limited freedom. Play as a voluntary activity[60] means that the player enters the play voluntarily and chooses options during the play of their own volition. Although the voluntary *joining* of play might sometimes be in question in the context of legal education,[61] as students will be confronted with a play constructed by their educator and are expected to participate and will be assessed, they are still free to choose between options provided *within* the play. Therefore, the free aspect of play is not annihilated, but merely limited by the students' choice to enroll in the Bachelor's or

53 See Caillois 1961, p. 7. According to Caillois, *rules* and *make-believe* preclude one-another because rules and make-believe both create an alternate reality for the player and these two features therefore show the same function of play. See: Tanis 2012, p. 43. Following this argument, however, leads us to the assumption that make-believe might also be understood as a part of the characteristics 'outside ordinary life' (Huizinga) and 'separate' (Caillois), as *make-believe* entails that something does not truly exist in ordinary life, but rather in a separated, fictional sphere, apart from ordinary life.

54 Csikszentmihalyi & Bennett 1971, pp. 45-46.

55 Csikszentmihalyi & Bennett 1971, pp. 45-46.

56 Csikszentmihalyi 2008, p. 71; Tanis 2012, p. 51. The features that describe *flow* or *an optimal experience* are very similar to those of play and playfulness.

57 See Tanis 2012, p. 51.

58 Tanis 2012, p. 54.

59 Tanis 2012, p. 54.

60 According to Huizinga, without this voluntary aspect, play will only be a task and will not be enjoyed. Huizinga 1980, p. 8; Csikszentmihalyi & Bennet 1971, p. 45; Caillois 1961, p. 9.

61 Sicart, too, criticizes Huizinga's idea of the mandatory voluntariness of play, since voluntariness does not define the play activity and it is also not necessary for joining in play: some might enter play based on of social pressure or the play may just happen to them without any conscious choice. See Sicart 2014, note 70 (to chapter 1), pp. 114-115.

Master's program and commitment to the corresponding learning process and accompanying rules of the playing field.[62]

Second, I emphasize that play in ALE always serves a purpose in achieving learning goals, in contrast to the classic conviction that play is an unproductive activity without material gain and is simply 'fun'.[63] I state that, although play might be inherently enjoyable and fun, in the context of legal education play always has at least an immaterial gain since it supports the development of contemporary *Bildung*, ACT responsibility, empathy, learning and the achievement of learning goals such as collaboration skills; critical and creative thinking ability; the development of presentation skills; remembering, understanding, and applying theoretical concepts; and the creation of solutions to contemporary problems.

Third, play in legal education is set consciously outside everyday life. In addition to the argument that studying at a university already is an activity consciously *outside* ordinary life, since the years in university constitute a transition period between high school and work, a classroom situation in itself stands apart from everyday life. There are additional rules of conduct which the educator and students abide by. The play we use as a tool for learning in our classrooms, too, is separate from ordinary life, as the play has its own rules and instructions that only concern the players, but not individuals outside the classroom. Role-play in our classrooms, for example, in moot court games or debates, creates such an alternate reality for its players. However, at the same time, we may imagine lowering the walls between the university and everyday life in our play, especially since the integration of play aims at developing, amongst others, creativity skills and *Bildung*, which both *need* a connection with others and society.

The fourth feature is that play has its own boundaries in time and place, which create a sense of order. In academic law schools, the secluded, marked playground is the university, its campus, lecture halls, or classrooms. This playing field has specific rules, not only rules of order within the university and its campus, but also rules of conduct in classrooms. As such, the classroom and the university are temporary worlds within the students' ordinary world. Students can be absorbed in these temporary worlds,[64] although in my experience, absorption is becoming more difficult for students with the distractions of the everyday world through smartphones and laptops that disenchant the play world.[65] Especially in the context of online education, educators need to be watchful of disengaging

62 The way in which an educator enables their students to learn is the consequence of that free choice that has showed the students' consent. See Biesty 2003, p. 45.

63 Huizinga 1980, pp. 2-4. The idea that play is merely an end in itself has also been contested by Biesty, who finds that through play, players might potentially develop new skills. Biesty states that play – even while it might be fun – has other ends as well, for instance, learning to take the role of the other and learning new skills. See Biesty 2003, pp. 43 and 45.

64 Huizinga 1980, p. 10.

65 Huizinga 1980, p. 21.

students who are unable to feel absorbed. For example, when universities were mandated to only offer online education during the 2020 and 2021 Covid-19 crisis, students experienced social isolation and struggled to remain engaged and motivated without the physical playground or the university. If play is used as a tool for learning in class, that play comes with its own rules that mark another playground. The demarcation of time is also rather specific; for example, the duration of a Bachelor's program is three years, a semester six months, a course eight weeks, and a class two or three hours. Within a class too, a play form is limited through time, for example, half an hour or 45 minutes.

Fifth, play always entails possibility, tension, and uncertainty.[66] It provides the player with many options of choice[67] in order to reach the play's goal. For instance, in the play of ALE, students are given many possibilities of choice during their Bachelor's program, such as optional courses, various study strategies, and internships. But even though students aim for success from the start, it will remain uncertain until the end of the play if their choices will have the desired outcome. Studying for a law degree at the university is a game of chance and skill: The student is not certain of success, but has the expectation that they might succeed. The same rings true for enrolling in a course and participating in a class and a play form within that classroom. Because of this tension, play holds the middle between anxiety – when there are too many potentially dangerous choices of action – and boredom – if there are too few choices of action.[68] The play is not interesting or exciting when it is failsafe and too easy to be perceived as a challenge. Also, according to Huizinga, this tension gives the play an ethical value, as it tests the students' skill, courage, and perseverance by demanding them to play the game of legal education in accordance with the corresponding rules.[69] However, I currently experience that many of my students attempt to avoid this risk of education and are afraid of failure: They seek order and stability.[70] Unfortunately, this is a counterproductive attitude in professional and civic life, which is situated in a playing field where options of choice are complex and uncertain, just as the possible outcomes of choice. Through practice in low(er)-risk play during class,

---

66 Huizinga 1980, pp. 10-11; Caillois 1961, p. 7.

67 Csikszentmihalyi & Bennett 1971, p. 45.

68 Csikszentmihalyi & Bennett 1971, pp. 45-46. See also on the tension that play entails between stress and non-stress Sutton-Smith 2003, p. 4. This view correlates with play's position between order (boredom, non-stress) and chaos (anxiety, stress). See Sicart 2014, pp. 3, 9.

69 Huizinga 1980, p. 11.

70 Reports on increasing student fear of failure, stress and anxiety can be found in newspaper articles, scientific publications and mental health research as well. See, for example, www.rtlnieuws.nl/nieuws/nederland/artikel/4919486/student-studie-leenstelsel-studieadvies-psychische-problemen (2019), last visited May 21st 2023, Giel et al. 2020 p. 123, Choi 2021, p. 2108 and RIVM, Trimbos-instituut and GGD GHOR Nederland (2022), *Monitor Mentale gezondheid en Middelengebruik Studenten hoger onderwijs 2021. Deelrapport I. Mentale gezondheid van studenten in het hoger onderwijs*, pp. 12, 14. Available at: https://www.trimbos.nl/wp-content/uploads/2022/07/AF1955-Monitor-Studenten-Deelrapport-1-Mentale-gezondheid.pdf, Last visited November 27th 2022).

legal educators are able to familiarize and train students in decision making and prepare them for their future field of work and their lives in contemporary society.

Finally, play in law schools promotes the formation of social grouping, because students share the withdrawing from everyday society and collectively accept the temporary order of the play.[71] Play within a classroom will often be a group activity that demands collaboration. Even if this is not the case, for example, in individual assignments, the fact that all classmates are simultaneously engaged in the challenge makes the activity a shared one. That shared experience creates social bonds, which are helpful for creating a safe learning environment.

To summarize, play within ALE can be described as a (1) partly voluntary activity that (2) enables achievement of learning goals, (3) is consciously separated from everyday life by rules and/or make-believe, (4) has its own boundaries in time and space, (5) entails possibility, tension, and uncertainty, and (6) promotes the formation of social grouping.

Playfulness

Playfulness is referred to as a state of mind, one that is associated with lightheartedness and fun.[72] Huizinga's definition of the *play spirit* is very much related to play's connection to uncertainty and tension as he states that it means 'to dare', 'to bear uncertainty', 'to take risk', and 'to endure tension'.[73] In addition to this characteristic of being able to manage uncertainty, Sicart argues that playfulness 're-ambiguates' the world, because the playful spirit is able to disrupt a (serious) context that is not created or intended for play without destroying it. In other words, approaching the serious contexts of Academia, higher education or legal practice with playfulness gives freedom to these contexts by making them more open to interpretation and wonder, and less clear cut. Playfulness disrupts the (serious) order by adding some ambiguity, making the context less explained.[74] Based on these ideas of Huizinga and Sicart, it may be argued that playfulness is an essential part of what was defined in chapter 4 as 'negative capability'. This is the cognitive style that entails the ability to experience ambivalence without reaching for certainty and that leads to a 'complete experience'.[75] Caillois describes two distinct mind-sets in which an individual can engage in play, for example, in various categories of games. The first mind-set is one of a serious nature, *ludus*, to which discipline, effort, and patience are central. The second is the playful mind-set of *paidia*, associated with words such as childlike, carefree, joyful, and spontaneous.[76] This differentiation of mind-sets in which play can be conducted is

71 Huizinga 1980, pp. 12-13.
72 Tanis 2012, p. 7.
73 Huizinga 1980, p. 132.
74 Sicart 2014, pp. 27-29.
75 See Ou 2009, p. 1.
76 Tanis 2012, p. 44.

also recognizable in the reversal theory as described by Kerr and Apter. These authors theorize that all human activity is done either in a *telic* or a *paratelic* state of mind. A *telic*, serious attitude is focused on purpose whereas the *paratelic*, playful attitude is defined as spontaneous, free, experimenting and fantasizing.[77]

More substantive research on the concept of playfulness has been conducted by Lieberman. According to her, playfulness is a state of mind that can be characterized by five components. First, physical spontaneity, seen in, for example, exaggerated movement, gestures, and facial expressions. Second, social spontaneity, recognizable when individuals interact with others, and third, cognitive spontaneity. The latter is expressed in curiosity, inventiveness (creativity), and imagination. According to Lieberman, playfulness also manifests joy, for instance, through enjoyment and a positive disposition toward life. Finally, the fifth component entails a sense of humor.[78]

Many of the characteristics associated with playfulness, such as creativity, imagination, experimenting and enjoyment, are highly valued in contemporary life. Moreover, a playful attitude as in being curious, free, and open to experimenting without being afraid of failure is helpful for learning. Having a playful state of mind reduces stress and anxiety, since an individual with a *telic* state of mind perceives arousal or excitement as anxiety, whereas someone with a *paratelic* attitude experiences these as pleasurable and enjoyable.[79]

This conceptualization of *playfulness* can be applied in ALE without much alteration. In this context, playfulness is a (1) lighthearted, joyful state of mind that (2) enables students and educators to bear uncertainty and entails (3) humor, joy, and/or carefreeness and (4) physical, social, and cognitive spontaneity. In practice, these forms of spontaneity are recognizable in physical movement and gestures, collaboration and group work, and curiosity, creativity and imagination.

At the moment, seriousness and goal orientation are often given center stage in legal education, but this solely *telic* attitude leads to anxiety when students encounter yet unknown challenges. Seriousness needs to be complemented by playfulness, *ludus* and *paidia* are both much needed mind-sets to be able to cope with any circumstance. Adopting a playful attitude is valuable for students, be it during a play activity in class or overall while considering their studying, development or futures. Being playful in class involves that the educator accepts and encourages mistakes as part of the learning process. This is helpful for creating a safe learning environment and a supportive learning culture. This

77 Tanis 2012, pp. 45-46. The playful mind-set, described here as *paidia* and 'paratelic' corresponds to what Suits calls 'the lusory attitude' (stemming from 'ludens'). See Nørgård et al. 2017, p. 274.

78 See Tanis's description of Lieberman's interpretation of playfulness in combination with Guirdard, Ferland, and Dutil's in Tanis 2012, pp. 8-9.

79 Tanis 2012, p. 46.

can be encouraged by the educator through humor, which helps reduce anxiety and stress, increase self-motivation and strengthen the bond between educator and students.[80]

It is necessary to alternate between playful and serious attitudes in class, although the play itself will always have a serious purpose, namely, to help students achieve learning goals. The inherent spontaneity of playfulness involves creativity, imagination, and collaboration, which are valuable and necessary skills and personality traits for legal professionals who face the challenges of contemporary society.[81]

INTEGRATING PLAY AND PLAYFULNESS INTO LEGAL EDUCATION: PLAYFUL APPROACH

How can educators integrate play and playfulness into their academic law school's learning culture and curriculum, and in their course design, teaching method and teaching style? Games may provide a safe space where play can take place and students are able to experiment playfully.[82] Recently, a move towards gamification or 'a gameful approach' through the use of game-based solutions can be noted in higher education.[83] *Gamification* is an umbrella term that is widely used in business, commerce and education. In that wide use, some researchers argue, the term has lost some of its depth and is now interpretated

80 Ardalan 2015, p. 71
81 See Van Rossum 2018-1.
82 Kapp 2012, p. xxi.
83 Nørgård et al. 2017, p. 273. See also James 2019, p. 7. See also Siemon and Eckardt 2017, p. 153.

as just 'using game mechanics to make activities more engaging and fun'.[84] This is somewhat different from the traditional definition of gamification as 'using game mechanics in non-game contexts'.[85] However, the term is interpreted even more broadly by Kapp who defines it in the context of learning as 'using game-based mechanics, aesthetics and game thinking to engage people (in our case: learners/students), motivate action, promote learning, and solve problems'.[86] At the moment, gamification is often inherently connected to new technology and IT-applications, such as computer games, virtual reality, apps, online quizzes et cetera. However, the use of technology is not a prerequisite for gamification or game-based learning. From a practical point of view, the game-based mechanics (or *building blocks*) used in gamification that are most often mentioned include inserting levels of accomplishment, the possibility of earning rewards such as awards or badges,[87] scores (including points or leaderboards) and time constraints.[88] Kapp adds other key elements (mechanics) such as challenge; engagement; storytelling; distributed practice; visualization of characters (for example, by using avatars); interactivity (through collaboration or competition); problem solving; feedback;[89] sense of control; autonomy, and; sense of mastery.[90] Marczewski presents six player-types, each with their own motivation, who can be engaged in a game if specific game elements are provided.[91] The most important goal of gamification is to increase student engagement, by gamifying the content of a course or lecture though adding game elements.[92] In addition to this intrinsic gamification (adding game elements and game thinking to gamify the content), *extrinsic* gamification is also a possibility. In this scenario, game elements can be added to the structure of a course or curriculum *without* editing the content.[93] This is the case, for example, when students earn a badge for every written essay they hand in, without it being a part of a more encompassing alteration of the course. In order to gamify ALE, game thinking is necessary, which means that designers of curricula, courses, and lectures are required to transform everyday experiences into a game that includes a story, competition or cooperation and exploration.[94] One way of gamifying legal education might be by incorporating so-called 'game based solutions'. According to Marczewski, there are five categories of game-based solutions: Playful Design, Gamification, Simulation, Serious

84 See for example Kevin Kruse's *forword* in Kapp 2012, p. xviii, and Karl Kapp in Kapp 2012, p. 10.
85 Nørgård et al. 2017, p. 273. See also Ejsing-Duun 2014, p. 92. Deterding et al. 2014, p. 5.
86 Kapp 2012, p. 10.
87 See, in addition to Kapp 2012, pp. 12-13, Ejsing-Duun 2014, p. 94.
88 Kapp 2012, pp. 11.
89 See also Ejsing-Duun 2014, p. 94.
90 Kapp 2012, pp. xviii, xxi, 8, 12-13.
91 Marczewski 2018, 108-112, 260. See Marczewski's website for a first outline: www.gamified.uk, last visited June 9th, 2021.
92 See: Ejsing-Duun 2014, p. 94. Kapp 2012, pp. 18. See also Rojas et al. 2013, p. 135.
93 Marczewski 2018, p. 56.
94 Kapp 2012, p. 11.

Game, and Game. These categories seem to exist in a spectrum from aesthetics, to structure and, ultimately, gameplay.[95] They also are part of a continuum of elements that are necessary for (or define) the categories. In explanation, the first category, *play design*, is defined by 'aesthetics' and only requires (1) game aesthetics. This is the case, for example, if a syllabus looks similar to the appealing instructions of a game (think, for example, of the beautiful and appealing instructions included in board games such as Catan, Ticket to Ride or Pandemic). The following two categories are more defined by 'structure': *gamification* requires game aesthetics and (2) game elements, for example, the online environment is attractively game-like and the course includes levels of achievement and badges. *Simulation* also requires (3) a virtual world (in addition to playful design and game elements, students, for example, tackle a fictional case that is based in reality, are given the role of lawyer and plead in a courtroom that includes competition, a client, judges and an audience). The final two categories of game-based solutions are most defined by 'gameplay', which means that there has to be a true *game*. Kapp summarizes Koster's interpretation of *game* as 'a system in which players engage in an abstract challenge, defined by rules, interactivity, and feedback, that results in a quantifiable outcome often eliciting an emotional reaction."[96] In the second edition of his *Theory of Fun*, Koster adds that games are essentially attractive patterns (systems) for the human brain: Good games exercise the brain and make sure that the learning is done before the player stops playing.[97] The fourth category of game-based solutions, *serious game*,[98] can be divided into the subcategories gameful simulations, teaching games, meaningful games or purpose games, and requires game aesthetics, game elements, a virtual world and (4) game play. Finally, *game*, requires not only all the other elements, but also *entertainment*.[99]

The reason for the rise of the popularity of 'gamification' in higher education is, among others, the availability of technology, such as mobile phones, laptops, tablets and Wi-Fi which makes student engagement easier for both educators and students.[100] In my experience, the use of gamification though online possibilities has increased due to the covid-19 crisis in which online education was the only option for educators to connect with students. Most (if not all) of us quickly learned at least the basics of applying online games in our Zoom/Teams/GoogleMeet-classrooms. For example, students can join (or make) quizzes on online response systems such as Kahoot!,[101] Mentimeter or Socrative while educators are able to collect and use the students' contributions in real-time and

95 Marczewski 2018, p. 60.
96 Kapp 2012, p. 7-9.
97 Koster 2014, pp. 14, 38, 46.
98 Serious games may also be interpreted as educational games, which involve using games to teach, see Nørgård et al. 2017, p. 273.
99 Marczewski 2018, pp. 49-50, 52-55.
100 Kapp 2012, p. xviii (*forword* by Kevin Kruse).
101 Campillo-Ferrer et. al 2020.

respond accordingly.[102] These platforms use a playful interface (playful design) that attracts and stimulates collaboration, concentration and engagement. They may even support student creativity when educators challenge their student to make their own quizzes.[103] Even though the popularity of gamification (or game-based solutions) seems on the rise, Kapp warns that gamification is not suitable for every learning situation and educators should choose and design wisely.[104]

The game approach as described above seems a valuable way of including play and playfulness in legal education. However, the denominator 'game' excludes some forms of play and playfulness that are valuable for legal education, especially when concerning *Bildung*, which is not solely focused on quantifiability of outcomes. In contrast, games always have quantifiable outcomes. In other words, it is clear when a player (learner) wins or loses a game, they either win the challenge or they do not.[105] By doing so, games offer certainty, as the scoreboard gives a certain outcome and end to the game. It provides a winner and/or loser and there is no room for interpretation or ambiguity. However, this is not the case in *play* and *playfulness*, which have no clearly defined end state.[106] Play and playfulness are therefore more versatile, more open[107] and more uncertain than games. They are also less focused on results, less limited to technology and have a broader aim than solely student engagement. So, play and playfulness are more encompassing,[108] but *include* the use of games.[109] Since they may provide a path for including play and playfulness in our faculties, I applaud the integration of game based solutions in legal education.[110] However, I prefer that those solutions be only *part* of a broader approach, a *playful approach* to ALE.

This playful approach can be inserted on all four levels as discussed in the previous chapter. Play and playfulness can be given a place in the learning culture and environment; curriculum design; course design, and; teaching method and teaching style. The learning culture may turn into that seemingly illusive magic circle where students and educators engage with a playful (lusory, paratelic, paidia) attitude. For this, the learning environment is required to be a safe space, where competence and contemporary *Bildung* is achieved by

102 Kapp 2012, p. 18. See also: Campillo-Ferrer et. al 2020 and Rahman et. al. 2018, p. 2.

103 Campillo-Ferrer et. al 2020, pp. 2-3.

104 Kapp 2012, p. 14.

105 See, for example Ejsing-Duun 2014, p. 94: *'[games have] clear objectives, a clear progression and clear evaluation criteria (...)'*. Even more in contrast with the foundations of *Bildung* is the *efficiency* that gamification is meant to achieve according to Siemon and Eckardt. See Siemon and Eckardt 2017, p. 153.

106 Kapp 2012, p. 8.

107 See also James 2019, p. 7 and Marczewski 2018, p. 24.

108 See also Sicart 2014, p. 2.

109 See also Siemon and Eckardt 2017, p. 155.

110 For example, by using game-based solutions, educators may be able to steer their students' learning towards a state of playfulness. See Ejsing-Duun 2014, p. 94.

experimenting, exploring and making mistakes.[111] With regard to curriculum design, play and playfulness might be incorporated in attainment goals, for example by integrating a more detailed description of problem solving which includes a playful mindset and the aim that students should be able to 'play with possibilities'. In addition, curricula might be gamified by adding game elements and game mechanisms (extrinsic gamification). On the level of course design, educators may also insert play and playfulness by the use of play activities and game-based solutions. In classroom situations, be it physical or online, educators can incorporate play and playfulness in their teaching method and teaching style. First and foremost, they can do so by adopting a playful attitude and, while modeling this attitude, encouraging their students to approach their studies playfully. Also, educators could incorporate play activities in which students play with the content of the course. In some cases, this may take the form of games, but other forms are possible as well. Such instructional interventions may be categorized in five main categories: (1) Play with art; (2) Role Play, (3) Physical Play; (4) Cooperative Play with physical play artefacts, and (5) Online play activities.

With the definition of play and playfulness for ALE and the introduction of a playful approach to ALE, this chapter is concluded. However, for educators interested in including play and playfulness in their teaching method and teaching style, the appendix to this chapter shares 19 examples of playful instructional interventions.

111 Nørgård et al. 2017, pp. 274-275.

Appendix to Chapter 6 – The Playful Approach to Academic Legal Education: 19 examples of instructional interventions

Visiting the classroom: practical examples of play & playfulness in legal education

This appendix to Chapter 6 focuses specifically on integrating play and playfulness *into the classroom*, into an educator's teaching method and teaching style. In other words, it focuses on the fourth level educators may influence: The teaching method and teaching style. In the past twelve years as an educator at the Vrije Universiteit Amsterdam, I have seen students entering courses and my (physical or online) classroom with very different attitudes and study approaches. Some students are excited and enthusiastically start reading any material they can get their hands on, while others desperately search for control by asking many questions (e.g., about the exam). In other students' eyes (mostly when it concerns my Introduction to Legal Philosophy course) I see mild panic, disinterest, or even dislike of the subject. The challenge for us educators is channeling these feelings toward attitudes that are helpful for academic learning and will prepare our students for their professional life. At this point, the value of 'play' and 'playfulness' for the practice of legal education comes to the fore. How can educators integrate play and playfulness into their classes to persuade their students to engage in class and embrace relative uncertainty?

In this appendix, I share some examples in which play and playfulness are incorporated into the classroom. I have tested these examples in courses I taught and coordinated: Introduction to Legal Philosophy, Introduction to Law and Moot Court. The freshman course 'Introduction to Legal Philosophy' is a mandatory, introductory course, consisting of seven weeks of lectures and working groups, followed by a written assessment containing open ended questions. The course content consists of, broadly defined, a chronological historical overview of the most influential western legal philosophers from Ancient Greece to the early 20th century. The central learning goals are for the students to recognize, explain, and apply the concepts central to theories that are part of the course's content and to note and explain the differences or similarities between the theories by answering limited-size essay questions. Introduction to Law is also a mandatory freshman introductory course, an initiation of new students into the domain of law. Therefore, all fields of law are broadly discussed in the seven-week course. The course is concluded by a written assessment with open questions and (up until 2021-2022) multiple choice questions. Moot Court is a semester-long mandatory legal-skills course for third-year students, who will be pleading their cases in the roles of lawyers and prosecutors, based on written legal documents. The course is focused on skills training, the development of the students' oral presentation skills, writing skills and feedback processing skills in particular. The course is concluded with a simulation trial were the students plead their client's case in a simulated courtroom. Here, they compete against another student who represents the opposite party.

For these three courses, I utilized and developed various play activities such as games of dice, quizzes, poetry slams, visualization assignments, role-play activities, and assignments on music. I introduced these activities always as a challenge and with a playful attitude, in the hope that the students would approach the assignments with the same mind-set. Initially, I categorized the examples in four categories: (1) Play with art; (2) Role Play, (3) Physical Play, and (4) Cooperative Play with physical play artefacts. Recently, I added a separate category for (5) Online play activities. These are mainly drawn from my experience in teaching Introduction to Legal Philosophy online during the covid-19 crisis.

Below, an overview shows the 19 examples and the category/categories of play that they belong to. In the following, the examples will be further explored. For each example, I will clarify the learning goals, the activity itself, the way in which the activity fits into the concepts of play and playfulness as described in Chapter 6, and the student and educator experience.

Categorizing 19 examples of the Playful approach to academic legal education

Category → Example ↓		Play with art	Role Play	Physical Play	Cooperative play with physical play artefacts	Online play and playful activities
1	Visualization	•			•	
2	Poetry Slam	•			•	
3	Reading and discussing poetry	•			•	
4	Musical timeline	•				
5	Song lyrics and the law	•				
6	Moot Court		•	•		
7	Tell Sell		•			
8	Debate		•	•	•	
9	Legal Adviser		•			
10	Cross the line			•		
11	Walk-around quiz			•	•	

Categorizing 19 examples of the Playful approach to academic legal education

Category → Example ↓	Play with art	Role Play	Physical Play	Cooperative play with physical play artefacts	Online play and playful activities
12 Catch ball			•	•	
13 30 seconds				•	
14 Group quiz with cards				•	
15 Play of Dice – philosopher edition				•	
16 Cooperative word cloud					•
17 Morality in tow					•
18 Tell Sell – Zoom edition		•			•
19 PleitVRij – Moot court in *Virtual Reality*		•	•	•	•

1 Visualization

In this playful activity, I wanted to challenge my students to visualize the theoretical content of the legal philosophical course, with the goal of recapping the course's content and better enabling the students to remember and explain it. I focused on imaging, imagination, and explanation. My subgoals were to acknowledge visually inclined students and to motivate students who were struggling with the conceptual nature of the course's content by introducing them to visualizing as a strategy of learning. I also wanted to combine legal education and philosophy with the Arts. The duration of this activity was 20 minutes at the beginning of class, and it was meant as a *warming up* and as a review of the content of previous classes.

Every student randomly received a small card with the name of a previously discussed philosopher. To engage students and to make them realize that they already had prior knowledge and understanding, they were given two minutes to write down as many keywords connected to that philosopher's theory as they could without checking their textbooks. Then, the students needed to find a (picture of a) work of art online that – according to them – portrayed (part of) that philosopher's ideas and write a short explanation on the theorist's ideas on the basis of that specific work of art. It could be a photo, building, painting, sculpture, or any other visual art form. The written explanation would later be presented by them to the colleague sitting next to them in approximately three minutes per person. Afterwards, all written explanations and the corresponding pictures of artworks were combined in a document that all students received as a reference book for studying.

This activity meets the requirements of play since it was (1) partly voluntary – there was no mandatory presence of students in class and they were free to roam the Internet searching for whatever image they found fitting for their small presentation to depict the philosopher. The students were also free to choose to portray whatever part of the theory that they found most important. Furthermore, the activity (2) was focused on achieving learning goals, namely, remembering and explaining the course's content. Also, the activity (3) was separate from everyday life since it had its own rules and instructions. I gave these instructions to the students on a handout, which included rules such as that they had to work with the philosopher they were given, were not allowed to open their books while searching for keywords, could only choose visual art forms to depict the theory, and had to follow the time frame for every step of the activity. The classroom gave the activity a (4) boundary of space while the instruction on how much time the students had to complete the assignment gave it its temporal boundary. Students perceived (5) a level of uncertainty, since the unlimited possibilities of online images provided them with many options. Finally, the activity led to a certain extent of (6) social grouping: Students occasionally helped each other to find pictures and spoke to one another during the mini presentations.

Many students seemed able to perform the activity in a playful manner: they took on the uncertainties of the assignment as a challenge and expressed the joyful and spontaneous mind-set by laughing together with their peers. At the same time, most students appeared to be quite serious in their effort of finding the right image, and in that, some seemed to take on a more serious, *telic* attitude.

In this activity, thinking of images that could be relevant for the content of a philosopher's theory proved difficult for some students. Unsure of themselves, these students needed some encouragement and suggestions from their peers and the educator. In the future, I would like for those still anxious and in a (too) serious mind-set to also get into the playful modus. An option could be to let these students get inspired through working with a partner. In the end, many students were able to find pictures of artworks that they could effectively link to their philosopher and some were able to rely on prior knowledge of art history while choosing their image. A few students did not obey the rule that they could not just include an image or a portrait of the philosopher. In future uses of the activity, that will need some additional explaining in advance, since imagining how an image connects to a philosophical concept is central to this exercise. Nevertheless, all students were engaged while searching online for options and explaining their personal choice and presenting and discussing their work of art. Accessing sources proved to be a challenge, since not all students brought their laptops to class. To help them, I brought fifteen quite random pictures of artworks, from which these students could choose. I enjoyed the students' engagement: They clearly put effort into executing the task in earnest, but at the same time displayed enthusiasm and enjoyment.

2 *Poetry Slam – Philosopher Speed Date*

This playful play activity was a poetry slam that I incorporated at the beginning of the final class of the Introduction to Legal Philosophy. It was meant as a review of the past seven weeks of legal philosophy. The learning goal was for students to remember and understand the content of the course in such a way that they could translate it into another context. My subgoals were creating an abstract of the course through collaboration; training students in public speaking; ensuring that the students enjoy the process; and enabling them to feel a personal connection to one or more theories.

Every student – or in larger classes, every student couple – chose their own small card with the name of an earlier discussed philosopher. I instructed them to 'choose the philosopher that they wanted to have a ten-minute face-to-face with'. Then, I gave the students written instructions and theatrically recited my own poem about Nietzsche (who was not included in the course) as an example. After that, the students had ten minutes to write down some keywords on the philosopher they had chosen, select the keywords that they found most important, and write a poem consisting of a minimum of eight and a maximum of 12 lines. They could use any literature (including the Internet) or inspiration that they thought they needed to write the poem, and they were free to ask the educator for help. Also, the poem could be in any form. After ten minutes of writing, the students worked with their neighbor for five minutes to critically reflect on both their poems' content and form. This step was not included in the classes where the students worked at the poem in couples from the start. Finally, the students presented their poems in chronological order (starting with the Sophists and Plato) to the tunes of classical music (for example, *Greensleeves* or Bach's *Air)* to make their performance more theatrical. In the end, the poems were collected and distributed among the participating students as a creative abstract of the content of the course.

This poetry slam was (1) partly voluntary, since the students voluntarily attend classes. The students could also choose their own philosopher, use any literature, and decide what kind of poem they found fitting or manageable, and therefore, had an additional sense of freedom. The activity (2) was focused on achieving learning goals and (3) was separate from everyday life through its rules, namely, the written instructions. Similar to the visualization activity, the (4) boundaries of space and time were the classroom and the amount of time given to the students to finish their poems. The many possible ways of writing a poem offered the students (5) a level of uncertainty. At the same time that uncertainty was limited by the content of the course (only the ideas of the philosophers central to the course could be chosen as an inspiration for a poem). Finally, (6) social grouping was a positive effect of this exercise. Not only were the students helping each other while practicing the poem with a partner, but they also listened, laughed together and applauded when every student performed their poem.

Most students approached this assignment in a playful manner – more so than during the visualizing activity. Students took the risk of reciting a self-written poem to their peers, which most engaged in with lighthearted humor, and many students became more open and expressed a spontaneity and creativity that I had not seen in previous lessons. During the recital I noticed a shared attention, appreciation, and enjoyment of all the poems presented.

The students' playful attitude resulted in a relaxed, carefree learning environment where they were experimenting with words and content and became creative. The reason for that playful state of mind was partly my own enthusiasm and the beautiful but somewhat clichéd (and therefore humorous) music that was the backdrop of the students' recital. The activity's success can probably also be explained by the fact that is was used in the final class. By that time the students had built up trust in themselves and each other and were familiar with my teaching methods. They understood that their efforts did not have to result in a perfect poem, and therefore, were more willing to take on the uncertainties related to the assignment. Nevertheless, a small number of students who were at first somewhat reluctant to write the poem remained. After some reassurance, they, too, began to work. Overall, most students seemed to enjoy creating their poems,[1] laughed during the recital, and became creative.[2] Moreover, their poems showed an understanding of the course's content. Especially in large groups, the length of the recital may be a challenge, with the risk of the listeners losing attention. To solve this problem, the assignment might be given to pairs or small groups.

3 *Reading and discussing poetry*

For the first lesson in Introduction to Legal Philosophy, I wanted the students to experience that (legal) philosophical thought can be found anywhere, and also in art forms such as poems. The goal of the activity was for the students to become engaged in talking about the poem and to discover that the overall theme of the course was already to be found there. Through follow-up questions I tried to encourage them to think of the content of the first lesson and to discover that the poem was multi-interpretable.

1 A small number of students experienced some stage fright, but were still able to read their poem aloud.

2 One couple even decided to choose their own accompanying music and created a rap about Machiavelli that they performed with much enthusiasm.

I gave all students a hand-out that included the poem (which was written in English) and five accompanying questions.[3] I then projected the poem in PowerPoint and continued to recite it in a theatrical way, while the students read along in silence. Afterwards, the students were asked to take five minutes to read the poem in small groups of two students. That way, they could help one another if there were any language-related problems and they were also able to discuss the meaning of the poem and come up with possible answers to the five questions. Then, every duo needed to partner up with another duo for two minutes, to compare possible answers and explain their ideas. Afterwards, a group discussion between all members of the working group took place in which there was room for various interpretations of the poem.

Again, the students 1) partly voluntarily joined this activity, since attending class was not mandatory. The goal of this activity was for the students to have a first introduction into the overall theme of the course, so it was 2) focused on achieving the learning goals. Since the activity was in the classroom on campus and came with its own instructions on the time frame and required collaborations, the activity was (3) separate from everyday life and (4) had its own boundaries of space and time. The students were asked to interpret the wordplay of the poet and their interpretation could vary. This brought some (5) uncertainty to the activity. By diving into the abstract poem with a partner and later discussing the interpretations with a group of four students, the assignment promoted (6) social bonding and group forming.

By dramatically reciting the poem as if it was a Shakespearean masterpiece, I tried to involve my students in a playful manner in the reading and discussing of the poem. The students were at least open to join in the assignment and showed curiosity in their attempt to make sense of the poem.

After communicating the activity's goal before handing out the assignment, all students joined in and read the poem with their partner. They did not show any hesitation or confusion over the fact that it was not a legal text but a poem. The reason for this might be that this was the first week of the course and they did not know what to expect and, thus, did not find it strange. Some found it difficult that the poem was in English, but sought help online or from classmates to understand the words. Some students went online to investigate the poet, discovered more about her background and tried to link that to their interpretation of the poem. The students were engaged in their discussions and most were very open in sharing their ideas in the final group discussion.

---

3 For example: Which problem is the poet referring to in this poem? Which point of view is recognizable on the balance between peace and justice? For what reason does the author come to this conclusion? Do you agree with the poet, and why?

4 Musical timeline

Introduction in Legal Philosophy is a historical overview of legal philosophy and it largely has a chronological build-up. From the second week onward, students travel from ancient Greece, the Roman Empire, the Middle Ages, to the Renaissance, Early Modernity and Modernity. With the goal of offering students auditory clues as well as visual ones (in the form of a timeline on the whiteboard) in order for them to experience the historical time we were 'visiting' each week, I decided to incorporate a musical timeline. At the start of every lesson and during the two breaks, I played music stemming from (mostly meaning 'composed in…') the appropriate time period we were discussing that moment.[4] The goal was for the students to gain a sense of historical chronology and events including artistic events, political and social events and I aimed at enriching their musical (and general) knowledge. For the musical timeline, I searched for appropriate music, bought a Bluetooth speaker (I find that the quality of the music should be as good as possible) and during class, I play the music via YouTube. Some students listened intently, others went to get a coffees or busied themselves with their phones while they subconsciously listened to the music. The musical timeline has therefore, for now, been a quite passive part of the lessons, although the music seems to inspire students. Those student reactions give reason to increase the use of music.

This activity was not as much focused on active *play*, but on creating a *playful* learning environment and learning culture where art is connected to legal theory and (legal) history. It was meant to inspire curiosity in students and to enjoy music within the classroom. Additionally, the musical timeline became something the students relied on during the course, in the sense that they knew what to expect in the structure of the lessons. True, some students were somewhat bemused by their 'arty teacher' and at times protested that they did not like the music (Medieval music was especially unpopular). I found these reactions honest, quite understandable and, frankly, they made me laugh. Other students admitted to knowing some pieces, told me that they regularly went to classical concerts with friends or their parents or shared that they had a musical talent themselves (some were even professional musicians in addition to their studies in law school!). On a number of occasions, I had the chance of discussing the connection between changes in music styles and historical (political, societal) change. One student was inspired enough to come up with a musical suggestion for the week on Machiavelli and suggested Tupac. The class went along with the idea, so the next week we were discussing and analyzing the lyrics of the rap-song to find connections between the song and the philosopher. Machiavelli seems to elicit inspiration, because in another group, a student

4 For instance, we listened to Josquin Duprez when discussing Machiavelli and Vivaldi and Bach when discussing Locke and Rousseau.

approached me and proudly told me he just went to a new opera (during the Amsterdam *Opera Forward Festival*) based on Machiavelli's life.

5 *Song lyrics and the law*

In many popular songs, legal themes are recognizable: Marriage, assault, divorce, and death are all represented in songs. I therefore presented freshman students Introduction to Law with seven lyrics to popular songs that were related to law or that described a legal case.[5] My goal was for the students to experience that legal cases are all around them. The other goal was for them to filter relevant legal information from a text and find the appropriate legal terminology and relevant legal provisions.

The activity took place as a review assignment at the start of the second week of Introduction to Law. In the previous week, the students had, among others, learned the difference between various fields of law (private law, public law); subjective rights and objective laws, and compulsory laws and supplementary laws. For the assignment, the students worked for fifteen minutes in small groups of two and could select two or three lyrics from the seven options I gave them on paper. All lyrics were accompanied by the same five questions that the students were required to answer, namely, what is the central legal problem/what is the case?; is this a case of private law or public law?; which legal provisions are appropriate here?; is this a case of compulsory or of supplementary laws?, and is the person in the song talking about subjective rights or about objective laws?

In this activity, the students – who (1) voluntarily joined class since – were asked to read lyrics and to interpret those within the legal framework. By answering the accompanying questions, the students reflected on the (2) learning goals of the previous week. In addition, the activity was (3) separate from everyday life and (4) had its own boundaries of time and space, for instance, it took place in the classroom on campus, the students were given fifteen minutes and needed to choose between the seven songs. It could happen that they chose a song that was difficult to interpret or that they would answer the questions incorrectly (for example, because they could not yet fathom the previous week's information). This might have brought some (5) uncertainty to the task. Finally, students worked together in pairs, which stimulated (6) social grouping.

I approached this assignment playfully, but observed that my students were seriously engaged in understanding the legal problem of the song and finding the legal solution. The fact that most songs were in Dutch helped the students' understanding and made them able to focus on the content of what was being said in the lyrics. Especially the rap-song by

5 The songs were *CD van jou, CD van mij* by Acda and De Munnik; *Zwart-Wit* by Frank Boeijen; *Ik leef niet meer voor jou* by Marco Borsato, *Alles hier is ook van jou* by Miss Montreal, *Drank en drugs* by Ronnie Flex and Lil' Kleine, *Hey Joe* by Jimmy Hendrix, and *Man Down* by Rihanna.

Ronnie Flex and Lil' Kleine, which is quite explicit, elicited hilarity and a few snorts. Some students (especially the ones that already had some experience and knowledge of the law) were motivated to solve as many songs as they could in the limited time. For that reason, the activity could be ideal for differentiation in class as well.

6 *Moot Court*

The third year course Moot Court takes twelve weeks and is focused on an elaborate role play. In groups of three, students receive a case that they will approach as either lawyers or prosecutors. They write legal documents based on the case and, ultimately, individually present their point of view in a simulated court. In this process, the students play the roles of opposing parties and collaborate in their own subgroups. Most of the time, they experience a sense of competition with regard to their opponents in court, which shows, for example, in their efforts of holding their arguments a secret from their adversaries. At the same time, they train their oral presentation skills in small scale training sessions of 3, 6 and 12 students. In those sessions the students learn to give each other honest and constructive feedback (including to the 'competition'). Most of the time, the students receive the case in a written document during an instruction by their supervisor, but my colleagues and I have also experimented in the civil law cases with presenting the case though actors who portrayed their clients, the claimant and defendant.

This simulation game ticks the boxes for a play activity. There is 1) limited freedom, since the students have chosen voluntarily to enroll in the Bachelor's degree of law and choose one of three areas of law for their case. The whole simulation is focused on students 2) obtaining the learning goals: in the process they learn how to write legal documents and how to present an oral presentation. They receive feedback on both. Since it is a game of make-believe, and the students truly consider themselves professional lawyers and prosecutors during the course, the activity is 3) separate from everyday life. It has 4) its own boundaries of space and time, the role play ending after the simulated session in court. The students experience some 5) uncertainty; even though there is a supervisor, they are thrown in the deep end and are expected to prepare the case quite independently. This means, for instance, that they need to find examples of legal documents themselves which they might use as templates for their own documents. Finally, 6) social grouping is stimulates, as the students collaborate in preparing their presentations and written documents.

There is a group of students that mostly feels excitement and sees this course as an opportunity to (finally) practice what they want to continue to do in their futures: plead cases before court. On the other hand, a number of students are anxious at the start of this mandatory course. Although they may choose the area of law they prefer, they sometimes find it difficult that they are paired up with two other students without having any say. Some students are scared of speaking in public, which often adds to their nervousness. However, the small scale of training sessions and personal guidance by their supervisor helps. Overall, students quickly immerse themselves in their case, establish their own (imaginary) company, including company stationary and create (if permitted) productions.

7 TellSell – *advertising philosophers*

As a review assignment, this activity's goal was to refresh the students' knowledge of the discussed philosophers of the previous weeks in Introduction to Legal Philosophy. An additional aim was for the students to become more invested in the philosophers, and thus, more invested in the content of the course. Similar to a known acting exercise that is often used as *warming-up*, the idea was for the students to take the role of salesman in a TV-show (in the Netherlands, one of these TV-shows is called *TellSell*) and present (sell) the philosopher as enthusiastically as possible to their co-players.

To start the group off with a playful example, I pitched Nietzsche in the role of a very excited salesman. This showed the students what the plan was and I hoped to model that they had to approach their philosopher with enthusiasm (even if they were not truly extremely interested in the philosopher's ideas). After the example and an instruction, the group of students was divided into smaller groups each consisting of three students. Every student was then appointed a philosopher that was discussed in the previous weeks (for instance, Kelsen, Radbruch, Plato, Aristoteles, Cicero, Augustine or Thomas Aquinas). Without consulting their literature, the students were required take two minutes to note eight key words relevant to this philosopher on a piece of paper or on their laptops. Additionally, they had to search for a picture (or painting or statue) of that philosopher online. Consequently, they were asked to write a very short enthusiastic sales pitch based on the eight key words in approximately 3 minutes. Afterwards, the students were required to pitch their philosopher in an oral presentation of one minute to their two team members.

In this role play the students (1) voluntarily joined the class and were provided with limited freedom, since they could create the pitch in any way they wanted, as long as it was one minute and focused on the philosopher. The assignment focused on (2) obtaining the learning goals, since it was a repetition of the content that students were required to understand. The classroom environment, limited time frames and instructions made the role-play (3) separate from everyday life and provided (4) boundaries in time and space. There was also some (5) uncertainty, since the students had to write their key words and pitch based of memory, which could be an incorrect description of the philosophy. Finally, the activity promoted (6) social grouping, since the students worked in small groups of three.

The students were open to the assignment and really attempted to sound like television-hosts presenting a new household-solution in their presentations. Most students were able to note the eight key words, although some had difficulties to distinguish between the philosophers or had forgotten (some of) the content of previous meetings. Interestingly, a number of students found it a challenge to focus on relevant information regarding the philosopher and these students noted words like, for example, 'Greece' or 'Middle Ages'. These were not necessarily incorrect, but not centered on the content of the philosopher's ideas. However, most students were able to write down eight relevant key words. There were students who found it hard to make a pitch based on the key words, and some did better than others in making the pitch a believable one. Nevertheless, the students worked individually – and together – on the assignment and were able to review the content of the course.

8 Debate

Another type of role play that I have experimented with in Introduction to Philosophy as well as in Introduction to Law, is debating. In debates, students are asked to take on the role of debater and present their arguments in favor of or against a premise. This means that they practice at being able to look at a situation from multiple (in this case, two) perspectives. Especially when they are asked to ague the opposite of their own conviction, students find themselves playing a role. The goal in both cases was for the students to learn about the content of the course, be it the contours of criminal law or the fundamental ideas of Kant or Utilitarianism. Additionally, I wanted the students to practice their argumentation skills, collaboration skills and oral presentation skills.

For the philosophy course, I gave my students a case on profitable organ trade which they had to debate as Kantians or Utilitarians. I divided the group into two sub groups, that were given their positions as Kantians of utilitarians. The students received the case and instructions on paper. Then, the students had 20 minutes to read the case (approximately 500 words) and work together to find arguments for the premise 'In these circumstances, buying a donor kidney from India is/is not acceptable'. Their arguments needed to be based on the relevant theory of Kant or Utilitarianism. They also had to construct a clear structure in which they wanted to present the arguments and appoint a presenter (or two presenters) for their team. Next, the classroom was physically restructured into a debate setting for the second half of the assignment. The students representing the group of Utilitarians were the first to present their arguments in a first term of five minutes. Likewise, the Kantians had five minutes to do the same for their arguments. Finally, each party had a minute for a response.

In the course Introduction to law, the students were presented with six premises related to traditional and current discussions in criminal law, such as 'It should be possible to give a perpetrator a higher sentence than would strictly be proportionate to his crime'. The students were divided into four teams in which they had to work together to find arguments. The groups were given their roles (pro or contra) for each of the two premises their group would be working on. Within the groups, they had to appoint two presenters per premise. Then, the students went to work for 15 minutes to find as many arguments as possible and they also were required to think of an effective structure to present these arguments in. They were encouraged to also think of counter-arguments for the second term (the response). After this phase, the debate began. The selected presenters of the group that were appointed to the 'pro-'role in the first premise started with a two minute term. The contra- group then followed with their own two minutes. Finally, both parties had a second term, in which they could respond to the first term of the adversary. The other premises and groups followed in the same structure.

The debate-activities involved limited freedom. Students (1) voluntarily joined the working group and could use any argument they could think of, as long as it fitted the instructions. The assignments were (2) focused on the learning goals, since the arguments were based on the students' required knowledge of Kant, Utilitarianism and criminal law. The debates took place in the classroom on campus, and the debate itself in a modified classroom. In addition, the activities had their own instructions and time limits, which made the debates (3) separate from everyday life and provided (4) boundaries of space and time. The students were able to make many choices in the way they structured and argued their point of view, they also did not know if their arguments would sway the other party. This added (5) uncertainty to the activity. Finally, (6) social grouping was supported, since the students worked together to find arguments.

In both examples of a classroom debate, the students were quickly engaged and deliberated together about which arguments were the strongest. From my perspective, it seemed that law students are quite open in preparing for and speaking during debates; they seem to have fun while thinking of arguments to win a case. This made these activities enjoyable for the students and their teacher.

9 *Legal adviser*

During the sixth lesson for Introduction to Law, which focused on administrative law, the first year students were given a case. Based on that case, they were asked to take the role of legal adviser and give advice to their client. The learning goals were for them to understand basic terms of administrative law and to be able to explain how citizens are protected by law within administrative law. Moreover, at the end of class, they were required to be able to solve a (simple) case.

The students were divided into groups of four to five students and were given a case with accompanying questions, including three questions for which they needed to take on the role of legal adviser and provide their client with legal advice in the matter. They had 15 minutes to answer the questions and write the advice.

Even though this role-play was not as elaborate as the previous examples, it was still an effective way of engaging the students in make-believe. The activity was, again, 1) partly voluntary, since the students were free to join (or skip) class. The goal of the activity was for the students to better understand administrative law, so it was 2) focused on the learning goals. The make-believe aspect of taking on a role as legal adviser 3) distinguished the play from everyday life and the provided time frame and the physical classroom added 4) boundaries of space and time. It was possible for the students to provide their client with incorrect of unclear advice, so this brought a sense of (5) uncertainty. The fact that they were engaging in the activity in groups of five or four students supported 6) social grouping.

This role-play was a small part of the overall activity (which consisted of more questions), but it is interesting to see how law students engage the moment they are asked to approach a case from a role that is relevant to their professional futures. Immediately they see it as a fun and interesting challenge and they seem to want to help their fictional client. All students were active and the students supported one another in their understanding.

10 Cross the Line

This example I used in the first class of the course Introduction to Legal Philosophy, and it was therefore meant as an immediate encounter with the upcoming teaching methods. The learning goal was for the students to understand the difference between thin and thick morality and to actively think of examples of both and test these. My subgoal was for them to literally get active and get up from their chairs. I also wanted them to act as a group, but still make individual decisions.

At the beginning of class I drew a line through the middle of the classroom with duct tape, which had the students wondering what would happen later in class. Halfway through the class, the subject of thick and thin morality was broached. All students received two post-its. In five minutes, they had to think of and write down a practical example of one rule of thin morality and one of thick morality – for example, the fictional rule that dating between colleagues is prohibited or the rule that every citizen should register as an organ donor. They gave their post-its to the educator, who selected the examples that the students would test together, on the basis of the examples' difficulty and diversity. Then, all students were asked to stand together in the middle of the room, right on the duct-taped line. The educator read a post-it aloud. The students then had to judge the example and cross the line to the left if they thought the example gave voice to thick morality and to the right if they thought it represented a rule of thin morality. The students *had* to make decisions, as it was not allowed to remain standing on the duct tape and they needed to be able to explain their choices. The educator asked some of the students to explain their decisions, which sometimes led to interesting discussions. This was repeated approximately five times.

In practice, *Cross the Line* was (1) partly voluntary, since the students voluntarily joined class, but at the same time the exercise was quite structured. Consequently, it was a little less free. The (2) learning goals as described earlier were central to the activity and the (3) rules that structured the task separated the activity from everyday life. I had deliberately chosen a more structured assignment for this very first activity in their first class. The (4) boundary of space consisted of the *play board* that was demarcated by the duct tape on the ground. The temporal boundary was not as clearly indicated as in other activities, since I did not give the students a time limit for their decision. However, I had planned a total duration of the activity of about fifteen minutes. In the assignment students (5) experienced some uncertainty since they had to publicly make their decisions without knowing if they were correct. The possibilities of action were limited to choosing either thick or thin morality. Since many students quickly understood the concepts of thick and thin morality, (6) social grouping arose where students helped or questioned each other. They also automatically tried to convince peers of their own convictions.

The physical movement of many students in a small amount of space resulted in a somewhat disorganized cluster every time the line needed to be crossed. That led to a playful attitude in which the students laughed and more spontaneously moved around one another.

Although the students seemed surprised that they needed to actively *move* during this exercise and at first stood up somewhat hesitantly, during the exercise they gained in enthusiasm and all participated. The students were laughing and engaged and often helped one another, without the educator's intervention. Therefore, this activity was a playful and active break during an otherwise immobile working group. Difficult examples in which some students could not choose a side led to discussions between the students that were helpful for a further understanding of the content.

11 Walk-around quiz

This activity is well-known by educators in primary education. However, I have experienced that many instructional interventions used in primary education can be employed in tertiary and academic education as well, including this one. Because of its popularity with students, I have used this playful activity on numerous occasions in both Introduction to Law and Introduction to Legal Philosophy. Here, I will describe the version that I used in the philosophical course.

I used this assignment in the very last working group, at the end of the course. The goal was for the students to have an opportunity to investigate one philosopher specifically and rehearse the content of the whole course with each other. The sub goal was for the students to end the course with a positive feeling and the belief that they had learned a lot. In total, the activity took 40 minutes. At the moment the students entered the classroom, I asked them to each choose a card with the name of a philosopher whom they wanted to investigate a little bit further. Then I explained what they were expected to do and why and I handed them instructions on paper together with two blank cards. In the first 10 minutes, the students were asked to formulate one difficult and one easy question about their philosopher and to note each of those on a card. On the back of the card they had to write the answer to the question. In the written instructions, they could find examples of an easy and a difficult question. Next, they were required to take four minutes (one minute per question) to check their questions and answers with their neighbor. In the meantime, I was walking around to read some of the questions to make sure that they were correct. After that, all of us could be relatively sure that all written cards held information that was correct. This meant that the physical part (the rehearsal) of the assignment could start. The students were asked to get up and walk through the classroom. While walking, they had to select a partner. Student A then asked Student B (while walking, or standing somewhere in the classroom); 'My philosopher is... Do you want an easy or difficult question?' Student B could then make a choice. For example, if the student was insecure about their understanding of St. Augustine, they could choose an easy question; if they answered it correctly, they would feel positive. The student could also prefer to be challenged and choose the difficult question. After the choice of a question, student A read their question aloud, followed by B, who would give the answer. If the given answer was not completely perfect, student A could give B a clue to make the answer better. B could than try to formulate a better answer. If that was still not a perfect answer, A was required to let B read the perfect answer to the question on the back of the card. Then, B could formulate their answer again. Finally, A would give B their card (which they had 'won' by giving a correct answer). Then, the roles switch and B would ask A if they wanted an easy or difficult question. After going through the questioning process again and A had obtained a card from B, the two would split up and find new partners, each with one new card in their possession. From there, the process had to be repeated as many times as possible during a time span of 15-20 minutes. The more people met and questions answered, the more the students had had the opportunity to practice and rehearse the content of the course.

There was no mandatory attendance, so the activity was (1) partly voluntary. In addition, the students were free to choose between the philosophers discussed during the course. By rehearsing the content, the activity is (2) focused on the learning goals. Especially during the physical part, the students engage in an activity that is (3) separate from everyday life: there are separate rules of conduct (the instructions) and there is a time frame of 20 minutes in which they need to partner up as much as possible to be able answer as many questions as they can. The time frame and the classroom provided (4) boundaries of space and time. While making the questions and answers, students may sense some (5) uncertainty when they wonder if their question is difficult enough, or if their written answer is correct. Also, while wandering through the classroom, the students could choose between a difficult or easy question, without knowing the question and with the risk of answering incorrectly. Finally, by partnering up with many colleagues, the students made connections with one another, which supports (6) social grouping.

During this playful activity, and especially during the physical part, students were active, laughed, had fun, and seemed to gain some confidence with regard to the content. In general, the activity is always a big hit, and students have asked if it was possible to do it more often, since they find the process enormously helpful. In truth, the students help each other and they discover that everyone struggles with some part of the content, or that those who do not, are willing to help others. Since the students can opt for an easy or difficult question, they are in charge of their sense of accomplishment. At the end of the activity, the students seem to have gained a positive disposition towards the course, each other and the upcoming exam.

12 Catch ball

This activity was played during the sixth week of Introduction to Law with a softshell (light) ball, the size of a football. The goal was for the students to practice with the content of the course in a playful manner. The activity was focused on knowledge and understanding.

Every student was given a number (from one to seven) that corresponded with the course's main themes (the weekly themes). Then, every student had 15 minutes to individually write down three questions relevant to their theme and to also prepare a brief answer to those questions. After this preparation phase, the physical phase could begin. The students helped by pushing all tables and chairs to the corners of the classroom, so that an empty center space remained. The students were asked to stand in a circle in that space. I threw the ball to the first student, which meant that this student had to ask the first question they had prepared. After stating the question, the student had to throw the ball to another student, who was then required to answer the posed question. If they did not know the answer, the ball could be tossed to another student. If, after throwing the ball twice, none of the students had answered the first student's question, the student who had posed the question was asked to give the answer themselves. If, however, the student who had caught the ball answered correctly, that student could then ask one of their own questions and throw the ball to the group member they wanted to answer the question. The goal for the group was to answer as many questions as possible in the space of 15 minutes. That way, they would have rehearsed most of the material of the course.

Just like the other instructional interventions as shared previously, this assignment was (1) partly voluntary, since the students voluntarily joined class. Also, they were free to formulate any (three) questions they could think of, as long as they were related to the theme they had been given. During the ball-play, they were free to throw the ball to any member of the group. Because of the fact that the themes were actually the weekly themes of the course, the questions were directly (2) related to the learning goals of the course. The time frames of 15 minutes and instruction as well as the act of tossing a ball at classmates (3) separated the activity from everyday life. The (4) boundaries of space were provided by the center space of the classroom which was cleared by removing the tables and chairs. The set time limits offered the boundaries of time. The fact that students were not sure which questions would be asked and if they would be appointed to answer, created some (5) uncertainty. The ball play in particular was a group activity which involved all students and it regularly led to shared laughs. In this sense, the activity (6) promoted social grouping.

Because of the physical activity that it required from the students, this was a really useful assignment as a warming-up at the start of class, but I can imagine that it may also work as a freshen-up half-way through a meeting. The ball that we used was very light and soft, which made it safe and humorous if someone (including the educator) was accidentally 'hit' by the ball. I noticed that students who had caught the ball but did not know the answer did not find it difficult to admit that and often, they were helped by their peers.

13 30 seconds

For the third week of the course Introduction to Law, I wanted the students to review the course's content of the previous weeks on the levels of knowledge and understanding in groups of four students. Furthermore, the goal was for the students to be active. The idea was that two teams consisting of two students compete against each other in a game of '30 seconds' (which in the 'non-legal' version is a popular board game). To do so, the students needed cards with each of five legal concepts that were discussed in the previous weeks (provided by the educator), a stopwatch and their literature (to check their answers if needed, after the activity).

The students were divided into groups of four that each was given a stack of cards (all with five legal concepts). Each group was then split into two teams (sub groups) of two students. The first team member of 'sub group 1' takes a card, without showing its contents to the other players. The stopwatch is set for 30 seconds by the players of the rivaling team. During the 30 seconds, the first team member describes the legal concepts on the card (without naming the concept), while their second team member tries to guess which concepts are being described. For each correctly guessed concept, the team receives a point. After 30 seconds, it is the turn of the second team to take a card. The game finished when all cards have been played. The team then add up the points they have received and the team with the most points wins. Mostly, this took approximately 10 minutes. After that, the groups of four were given five minutes to discuss and investigate the concepts that were not (or incorrectly) guessed.

In addition to this 30-seconds game (1) being (partly) voluntary, since the students were not obligated to come to class, the activity offered limited freedom as they were free (within the rules of the game) to describe to concepts in any way they expected their team member would guess the answer correctly. Because the concepts on the cards were part of (2) the learning goals, these were the focus of the game. The rules of the game, including the time limit of 30 seconds to describe all five concepts on the card and the instruction that they were not allowed to name (parts of) the concept itself made the game (3) separate from everyday life. Furthermore, the time frame of 30 seconds (4) provided a boundary of time, while the classroom added the boundary of space. For the student describing concepts, not-knowing which concepts were on the card they took from the stack brought (5) uncertainty and some tension. The same holds true for the students anticipating descriptions of concepts yet unknown. Because the duo's had to work together to gather points, the (6) formation of groups was promoted. Also, because the four students were playing together and laughing together the social bonding extended beyond the sub group of two.

30 seconds is a popular board game, which made explaining the rules during class easy. The students were engaged and tried to gather as many points as possible. During the activity, I saw students laughing and some fanatical facial expressions. The strict time limit of 30 seconds provides a tight time frame for describing the five concepts, so the students needed to be active and quick. This added to the overall energy-level during the rest of the class. My colleagues and I found this assignment to be helpful for the students' learning (of simple concepts) as it provides them with practice and immediate feedback and it also functioned as a great energizer.

14 Group Quiz with cards

This is a quiz activity that may take various forms. I have included it in Introduction to Law and Introduction to Legal Philosophy. The general idea is that every student receives a number of cards containing concepts or questions that they have to answer and then explain those to their group members. In this case, I will explain how the activity was used in the legal philosophical course.

This activity was employed in the second week of the course. Because of the early timing in the course, I aimed at engaging the students in an activity that was structured, focused on knowledge and not (yet) out of their comfort zones. In preparation, I made sixteen cards (per group of four students). Each card held a question regarding the content of the previous meeting. The students were divided into groups of four and each student received four cards. Then, all students had five minutes to prepare the answers to the questions individually and they were permitted to use their literature to do so. After this preparation, the students rejoined their sub group and they would present their questions and the answers they had found. Next, there was some time to discuss and perfect these answers within the team. After 10 minutes, the sub groups finished their discussion and the questions that were believed to be the most difficult were discussed with the whole class.

This activity included 1) limited freedom, since the students voluntarily joined class and were able to decide for themselves in which order they discussed the questions. The questions that the students answered and discussed 2) focused on the content and learning goals of the previous week. Also, the physical cards and the structure of the activity separated it from everyday life. In addition, the time frame of five minutes individual research and 10 minutes presentations and team discussion provided boundaries of time, while the boundary of space consisted of the physical classroom on campus. The 5) level of uncertainty was chosen to be quite low (for example, even though it might be possible to give incorrect answers to the questions, they were permitted to use literature to answer them), in order for the students to have some time to adjust to the course and gain a level of trust in their own abilities. Finally, the students worked together, which 6) supported social grouping.

The students dove into this activity and they were quickly engaged in answering and discussing the questions. A downside of formulating the questions as an educator surfaced in students trying to find certainty by making pictures of the cards, thinking that those were representative of the exam (which they were not, it involved questions for novices). This behavior seemed to be linked to a consumer-identity, which I would prefer to avoid in the future. Therefore, it might be possible to ask the students to think of questions themselves and answer these. This may be a way of supporting their sense of autonomy, prevent a false sense of certainty and avoid holding on to consumerism in Academia.

15 *Play of Dice – philosopher edition*

This play of dice is another cooperative activity that is quite popular amongst students. I employed this activity in the sixth week of Introduction to Legal Philosophy. Although it needs some preparation at the beginning of class, the results are often worth it. The goal was for the students to rehearse and discuss the content of the course in a playful manner. My subgoal was for the student to discover which parts of the theory they had forgotten (or missed or did not understand) and still needed to work on.

Required for this particular way of using dice in class are a number of normal dice (one per two students) and a pair of giant cubes (the size of a football). On all sides of the two big cubes (12 sides in total), I wrote the name of one of the philosophers as discussed during the course. So, there were a total of twelve names on the cubes. On the whiteboard, I wrote a scheme that showed to which part of a philosopher's theory the number on the small dice corresponded. For example, number 4 corresponded with 'morality/ethics' and number 6 with 'legal theory'. After instructing the students and explaining the scheme, we started the activity. First, the students formed pairs and each pair was given a small cube. Then, I asked one student to throw a big cube with philosophers. The philosopher that faced up, was to be discussed in a structured way, namely, first, one of the two students was required to throw the small cube. The number that it showed, was the part of the philosopher's theory that this student had to explain in one or two minutes to their partner. After that, another student was asked to toss a giant cube for a new philosopher and the process began again, but now, the other student would throw the small dice and explain part of that philosopher's theory. After 10 minutes, the students had talked about much of the course's content.

This activity was partly voluntary, since the students were not obligated to join class. They also had limited freedom, since *they* were the ones to roll the dice. During the play, the students were discussing the theories of all relevant philosophers and therefore, were 2) focused on the learning goals. The rules of the game 3) separated the activity from everyday life, especially the scheme made it clear that the normal numbers of the dice did not mean the same during the activity. 4) the classroom and the limited time for explanation provided the boundaries of space and time. Every time the dice rolled, the students had no idea which philosopher was going to be discussed and which part of that philosophy they would have to explain. This provided 5) a level of uncertainty. Sometimes, the student tasked with throwing the giant cube was cheered on, and the student-pairs were very focused on explaining the philosopher's theory to one another. By working with a partner 6) social grouping was promoted.

The students were engaged during this activity and the level of sound in the classroom reacted correspondingly. It was quite loud, but that told me that the students were discussing the content. Some pairs started to throw the cubes repeatedly, in order for them to discuss as much as possible about the philosopher in the two minutes they had. At first, some students were a bit shy (or a bit embarrassed) about tossing the giant cube but when approached with humor or a joke, they joined in.

Online education provides possibilities that are interesting to explore for educators in legal education. However, I found that one of the most important parts of the experience of play was difficult to copy in the online context, namely physical proximity that helps in collaboration. Also students are literally at a distance and that may be difficult – if not impossible – to bridge completely. However, digital solutions are available that support play activities in online education. In the following, I share short descriptions of online activities that involve play and playfulness. Some of these activities are versions of examples explained earlier that were adapted for the online context. For these examples, I will describe the learning goals, the activity itself and the experience of educators and students.

16 Cooperative Word cloud with Mentimeter

In this activity, students create a Word cloud in either Mentimeter or in Google Jamboard (in this example, I will focus on Mentimeter). The activity might be done in the context of a physical classroom, but may also be employed in online live education during, for example, a Zoom-meeting. I added this 20 minute activity as a review assignment to the third week of Introduction to Legal Philosophy. The goal was for the students to revisit the earlier discussed philosophers and to make them create a visualization of that content.

In preparation, I started a Menti (in mentimeter) for word clouds which consisted of five pages. Each page bore the name of one of the previously discussed philosophers (Radbruch, Kelsen, the Sophists, Plato and Aristotle). During class, the students were challenged to contribute two (sometimes three) key words per philosopher. This resulted in five online word clouds that held important key words for each philosopher. I then asked the students to take 5 minutes to discuss each word cloud with their neighbor(s) and to point out possible lack of clarity or faults in the word cloud. Finally, the parts that were perceived as the most difficult could be discussed within the whole group.

The students seemed to find this assignment insightful as they all enthusiastically engaged in adding to the word cloud and discussing the content. As an educator it was interesting to see (and to react to) which parts of the theory were selected by the students and if the students would be able to pinpoint flaws in the contribution of others. What also adds to the usefulness of word clouds, is the option in Mentimeter to save reactions. I was therefore able (if needed) to download the word clouds and provide them to the students as tools for learning.

17 *Morality in tow*

This activity is similar to the physical play example of *cross the line*. However, it was translated to the online context of Google Jamboard. The students were asked to take three minutes to write two virtual post-it notes and place them on the common Jamboard. One post-it was required to show an example of thick morality and the other an example of thin morality. After all students had contributed to the Jamboard and all examples were placed mixed-up all over the screen, I asked the students to move all examples of thick morality to the left side of the screen, and all examples of thin morality to the right. They were required to do so within two minutes. Finally, we discussed a selection of the examples in the group as a whole (in a Zoom-meeting).

Students no longer physically moved themselves over a line, but rather collaborated by moving each other's suggestions on thick and thin morality (which were typed on virtual post-its) over a line in the middle of the screen. Even though the physical version provided more buzz and contact between the students, in this version the students were still collaborating and came up with interesting examples. However, there it seems less playful, since there was less laughter.

18 *Tellsell Zoom*

This activity was a similar role play as the previously described TellSell-activity. However, the difference is the fact that this one was located in the online context of Zoom and Zoom break-out rooms. This also brought some changes in the instructions and organization of the play activity. I also added some changes in the content of the assignment, mainly because I realized that I wanted the students to be better able to compare the theories of the philosophers.

The working group was located in a Zoom-meeting. The students were divided into break-out rooms of four students. Each student was expected to individually prepare two philosophers, that they would ultimately present and discuss in the break-out room. After instructing the students and providing them with the written instructions, they went to their sub-group in the break-out rooms. There, the first step was for the students to decide which number each student would have (1, 2, 3 or 4). The numbers corresponded with a pair of philosophers. Next, the students had five minutes to individually prepare a sales pitch about the two philosophers. An additional requirement was for the students to add a difference and similarity between the philosophers at the end of the sales pitch. In their preparation, the students were welcome to use all their materials, notes, literature or other sources could be used. Then, the students rejoined their break-out room group (for example, by unmuting or turning on their cameras) and all students would present their pair of philosophers in one minute.

In a classroom environment, educators can quickly observe how all subgroups are performing and if there are students who have disengaged and who need to reconnect or additional explanation/attention. This is somewhat more difficult in an online setting such as Zoom. Even though I asked students for a report on their experience in the break-out sessions and sometimes joined in their sessions, it seemed less free, spontaneous and low key. At the same time, this loss of control for the educator might prove to be a wealth of autonomy for students.

19 PleitVRij – Moot court in virtual reality

From 2018 onward, together with colleagues from the Vrije Universiteit Amsterdam, the Rijksuniversiteit Groningen and the Universiteit Utrecht, I have experimented with play in *virtual reality*. Our students practice their skill in pleading within the context of a simulated *Virtual Reality* courtroom. In short, the goals of this innovative project, PleitVRij, are to provide the students with more opportunities to practice oral presenting and improvisation in a *realistic* setting and to add opportunities to gather feedback from a larger group of peers (from various institutes for higher education across the Netherlands). Therefore, PleitVRij offers students a *virtual* world that adds to their role play. Once a student wears the VR-goggles, they are completely immersed in the courtroom. Live in this courtroom, students meet a judge (who might be played by an educator or a student). They can then proceed to present their case before the judge and answer possible and unexpected questions the court asks. While the student is presenting, peers from their own institution and other institutions anywhere in the Netherlands that are connected to the project are able to observe in real time (if they are added to the session by the educator) and use an app to provide constructive feedback based on a number of assessment criteria. The students that have practiced may use this feedback to further develop their skills in oral presentation. In addition, the student has experienced pleading in a *realistic* setting, which is mostly only rarely possible in legal education.

Student reactions to this simulated role play were positive. In the written evaluation, they reported to find the *VR* environment realistic and feel that it enhances their experience during practicing and that the experience, the feedback and the observation of others will help them reflect upon and further develop their oral presentation skills. Especially after we were able to provide the group of students with more time for exchanging feedback and an additional moment of practicing their presentation immediately after receiving the feedback and filtering the most important suggestions, students experienced the worth of this type of practice. For educators, however, organizing these sessions is currently quite a complicated task, since all schedules must be aligned between the joining universities. Also, it takes a lot of supervision time for educators and technicians and only a limited number of students (only six per 90-minute session) are able to participate per session. Nevertheless, these are lessons we learn on our journey to seek ways to include technological innovations in legal education.

With the sharing of the previous 19 suggestions, this appendix to Chapter 6 – which focused on the integration of play and playfulness in ALE to further the development of *Bildung*, ACT responsibility, critical thinking and creative thinking – is concluded. By sharing these experiments in detail, I hope to encourage and invite colleagues in ALE to also seek for ways to integrate play and playfulness in their teaching method and teaching style.

Concluding Remarks – Go the Distance

"The greatest thing in this world is not so much where we stand as in what direction we are moving."
– *Johann Wolfgang von Goethe*

After a long journey, a place to rest may offer the adventurer a moment to consider how far they have come and an opportunity to make plans for the continuation of the journey. These concluding remarks are meant as such a moment, for educators in academic legal education (ALE) who may have become inspired to 'go the distance'. In the Introduction, the present concerns about whether ALE is still what we are looking for became the catalyst of our quest. These concerns exist because of the detrimental effect societal marketization has had on academic education and because contemporary society may demand other knowledge, skills and dispositions of its citizens and legal professionals than those that ALE traditionally focuses on. These circumstances gave reason for suggesting that ALE may need adjusting, and thus, we were sent on our way. We began our travels in search of the meaning of contemporary legal education's academic core and appropriate practical ideas and instructional interventions that educators could use in their everyday practice to contribute to the academic development of their students.

The main question that gave this research direction is:

How can educators in contemporary academic legal education contribute to the academic development of their students?

This question was answered in six chapters that each saw to the exploration of a part of the journey and sought the answers to essential sub questions.

The academic core of current legal education and student academic development

The main research question first led us to the subquestion what the academic core of an education, and especially a legal education, consists of. To understand what the academic core of any university education is, the first chapter explored the foundations of academia and traced its roots back to ancient Greece. It found that the values of our contemporary university are based on those of the first western university that was established in 1088, the University of Bologna. In contrast to the manner of teaching performed by the Church in the Middle Ages, the aim of academic education at this university was to develop as an individual thinker through debate and critical thinking. The key values of this first university were freedom of inquiry, and independence from ideology, state and social pressures. In the 19th century, the 'modern' university developed, which regarded intellectual inquiry as having its own intrinsic value since it was the product of Enlightenment. Fostering 'culture' – by which was meant the development of citizens through emancipation of the masses by conveying knowledge and through the pursuit of truth – was the aim that befitted the university of modernity. In this kind of university, for which the Humboldt University stood as prime example, the comprehensive development of the student was the ultimate goal which led to the preference for a broad education. For this, the humanities or liberal arts (for example, art, history and philosophy) were viewed as far more important than the natural sciences (such as medicine, biology or business studies). However, in the 20th century, this changed under the influence of, first, warfare and, then, marketization that both valued the practical usefulness of scientific research far more than they did the humanities.

This information gave rise to the sub question what the current circumstances are in which educators in academic law schools aim to contribute to their students' development and how these circumstances influence legal education's academic core. Here, we found that as a result of societal marketization, the university has become marketized as well. This means that, during the 20th century, the earlier values of the university seem to have largely been replaced by an economic rationality in which market values such as profit, effectiveness, efficiency, speed and measurability are given a central place. Therefore, corporatized universities aim at maximizing their output and increasing the speed in which they produce that output. The 'output' here are the fruits of research – such as articles, books or products – and graduating students. Unfortunately, this development ultimately results in undesired consequences, such as a damaging sense of urgency; a decrease in the quality of education offered at universities; burned-out staff and students, and; a one-dimensional university education.

These consequences are also felt in academic *legal* education, since this type of education takes place in the context of the marketized universities. Additionally, current ALE faces specific challenges. For example, there recently seems to have been a shift of focus within ALE towards the training of vocational skills at the expense of a broad education and at the expense of the development of academic abilities such as critical thinking and reflection. Because of this, there currently exists a disbalance between the vocational and academic components of legal education in which the vocational component is favored. Furthermore, educators in law schools seem to be mainly focused on the question of how teaching works, and less on how student learning works, even though the answers to the latter question may benefit the quality of our education greatly.

Knowledge of learning and developmental theory would be very helpful in scaffolding the academic development of our students. Also, in the context of the current circumstances of ALE, its traditional signature pedagogy, the Socratic Dialogue, may not be sufficient for engaging students, for in-depth learning and for supporting a full academic development.

However, despite having found Academia's historical roots and having noticed the detrimental effects of marketization on the university on its traditional values and aims, and although it had become clear that the vocational component of legal education was favored at the expense of its academic component, what 'academic' entailed remained unclear. So, to answer the subquestion what 'academic' development entails in contemporary times, the second chapter found inspiration in the 18th and 19th century educational ideal of *Bildung*. During this era, the meaning of the ideal for educational settings was the life-long self-formation of the individual – which meant the development of all one's talents, namely their reason *and* sensibility – in the context of and in connection with society. Developing both reason and sensibility (in contrast to the Enlightenment's sole focus on reason) was believed possible through the contemplation of art. Contrary to concerns that *Bildung*'s outward dimension can only result in law abiding, uncritical citizens, I have argued that *Bildung*'s core is the self-formation of the individual (the inward dimension). Therefore, *gebildete* individuals are critical citizens *par excellence*: They have in-depth knowledge about their society, but – because of their commitment to life-long development – remain open for other opinions and new insights that may necessitate change in society.

So what does this *Bildung* offer educators in law schools? By redefining *Bildung* for use in the current context of legal education, I offer a theoretical foundation for the academic core of legal education. Moreover, from this foundation sprout three components for a contemporary academic core of ALE. In explanation, in the redefinition of the educational ideal of *Bildung*, 'academic development' entails the development of ACT responsibility, which involves critical thinking and creative thinking. Through a playful approach to academic legal education, educators may support their students' development of these three components of contemporary *Bildung*, and thus contribute to the students' academic development.

With this, a preliminary answer to the subquestion what the academic development and the academic core of legal education consist of, is given: It comprises the redefinition of *Bildung* that entails ACT responsibility. This kind of responsibility that I suggest for academically educated legal professionals requires critical thinking ability and creative thinking ability. By further exploring critical thinking, creative thinking and responsibility, our understanding of what the academic core of legal education consists of becomes more complete. This offers us insight into what educators in ALE who want to support their students' academic development could aim to educate.

First, critical thinking is a way in which one can become a self-authored thinker and is only possible in higher developmental stages. In the third chapter, critical thinking in ALE is defined as '*reasonable reflective thinking that is focused on deciding what to do or believe*'. The critical thinking process – and thus critical thinking – requires domain relevant skills and knowledge (including broad and deep knowledge), and critical thinking relevant processes. Critical thinking processes entail abilities (such as analyzing arguments or judging the credibility of a source) and dispositions (such as trying to be well-informed or being open minded).

Secondly, creative thinking is often seen as a way of seeing opportunities or possibilities and is closely connected to academic work and *Bildung*. It requires deep and broad knowledge, and entails abilities such as problem finding, problem solving, critical thinking and convergent and divergent thinking. The definition of creative thinking presented in chapter 4 for use in ALE is that it is '*a human endeavor or state of mind, that can take place in any domain and involves the generation of something novel that has value.*' At the moment, most scholars share the opinion that creative thinking can be learned and developed. Also, many agree that there is a continuum of creativity levels that varies from mini-C and little-C, to pro-C and Big-C creativity. Amabile describes four components that support the creative thinking process and are therefore essential for supporting the development of creative thinking ability. These components are the social environment; task motivation; domain relevant skills and knowledge, and creativity relevant processes. These creativity relevant processes consist of personality characteristics (for example, independence, imagination and courage), work styles (for instance, disciplined work) and cognitive styles (amongst others, negative capability and strong synthesizing ability).

Thirdly, ACT responsibility is the three-stage rocket responsibility I have developed in this research for academically educated legal professionals. It consists of three components: Awareness, Choice and Taking action. In the first place, an academically educated legal professional has to be Aware of the fundamental, prospective – future oriented – personal and non-personal responsibility towards the self, the other, society and the natural environment to pursue human well-being, justice and sustainability. This fundamental responsibility is expressed in four dimensions of prospective responsibility, namely as a collective responsibility; a vocational responsibility for the whole vocational group of academically educated legal professionals; a personal vocational responsibility for individual academically educated legal professionals, and a personal responsibility. Secondly, ACT responsibility entails the ability to make a Choice, since every individual has to make their own decisions on which responsibilities to take on – and which not. By making a choice, which requires critical and creative thinking, a person narrows down the all-encompassing fundamental responsibility and takes ownership over their own responsibility. However, making these choices will not be easy, effortless or comfortable, as every choice demands selection, often without knowing all the possible consequences.

During the life-long learning (*Bildung*) process, the individual will continue to make choices regarding their responsibility and will be open to revise choices made earlier based on progressive insight. Finally, ACT responsibility involves the ability to Take action congruent with the self-authored responsibility-choices.

In ALE we aim to support our students' academic development in preparation for their future lives as academically educated legal professionals in contemporary society, which is defined by globalization, constant change, necessary choice, complexity and uncertainty. In the academic legal education that this research envisions, responsibility is a central theme in the form of ACT Responsibility which is not only the key component of contemporary *Bildung*, but is also essential for being able to deal with the current circumstances as an academically educated legal professional. This research therefore describes the foundations of an academic legal education located in a University of Responsibility.

How educators can support law students' academic development

Defining what 'the academic core of legal education' and 'academic development' entail in contemporary times, opened the path to inquire into the question how educators in ALE can support such an academic development of their students. This question fans out into various sub questions, such as: how can educators in ALE support students in their progression through the developmental stages?'; 'how can they support the learning of their students through the use of a variety of instructional interventions?'; 'how can educators support their students' development of critical thinking?'; 'how can they support their students' development of creative thinking?'; 'how can they support the development of their students' ACT responsibility?', and 'how can they use play and playfulness to support the academic development of their students?' The answers to these questions are formulated in chapters 1, 3, 4, 5 and 6.

First, with a further explanation of theories on learning, developmental stages and four categories of instructional interventions, the first chapter aimed to support and inspire educators in ALE in further evolving the education they offer. Most importantly, I encourage educators in legal education who are interested in contributing to the academic development of their students to explore the possibilities that stem from learning theory and developmental theory, to offer students assignments in their Zone of Proximal Development and to experiment with an arsenal of instructional interventions based on experiential learning theory.

For the integration of both critical thinking and creative thinking in ALE – which are essential for the development of ACT responsibility – the research presented two initial models. The practical suggestions the models offer to educators in ALE aim at improving the integration of critical thinking and creative thinking on four levels on which educators in legal education operate within the university: 1) the learning culture and – environment; 2) curriculum design; 3) the course design, and; 4) teaching method and teaching style. Below, the suggestions for the integration of critical and creative thinking in support of ACT responsibility are combined in one model. This results in a total of 13 practical suggestions spread over the four levels. In the final sections of chapters 3 and 4, these suggestions are further concretized.

Initial Model for Integrating Critical & Creative Thinking in Academic Legal Education

	I want to improve on the level of → You can ↓	Learning Culture & Environment	Curriculum Design	Course Design	Teaching Method & Teaching Style
1	Aim to develop deep and broad knowledge		•	•	•
2	Be open minded	•			•
3	Delay Judgment	•			•
4	Reward courage			•	•
5	Model desired behavior and attitudes				•
6	Make time	•	•	•	•
7	Create opportunities for practice and feedback, through appropriate instructional interventions, assignments and assessment.			•	•
8	Use play and playfulness	•	•	•	•
9	Emphasize the focus on the development of critical thinking and critical thinking relevant processes	•	•	•	•
10	Aim to develop the faculty of judgment		•	•	•
11	Add a focus on the development of creativity relevant processes	•	•	•	•
12	Use the physical environment	•			•
13	Encourage creative group work			•	•

In the final section of the fifth chapter, suggestions are offered that may help integrate the Awareness, Choice and Taking action of ACT responsibility into ALE by providing examples of possible learning goals that educators could include in curriculum design, course design and in their classrooms. Additionally, ACT responsibility as a whole, but especially Awareness could be conveyed through the overarching learning culture.

The final chapter and its appendix explore how educators in ALE could use play and playfulness to support the academic development of their students. Play and playfulness have been given additional attention as strategies for teaching ACT responsibility, critical thinking and creative thinking. The reason for this is that the importance of both concepts was repeatedly discovered throughout the research as important for *Bildung*, critical thinking and creative thinking *and* possible integrate on all four levels educators may influence: The learning climate; curriculum design; the course design, and teaching method and teaching style. After defining play and playfulness in the context of academic education, the appendix to the chapter aims to provide interested educators with inspiration on how to include play and playfulness in their teaching method and teaching style (level 4) by describing 19 examples of instructional interventions that are part of a playful approach to academic legal education.

To summarize, in this book I have argued that contemporary legal education's academic core – and thus the content of academic development – can be found in a reformulation of the 18th and 19th century educational ideal of *Bildung*. In this reinterpretation, *Bildung* consists of ACT responsibility, which necessitates critical thinking and creative thinking. Educators in ALE could support the academic development of their students by (further) integrating these three elements of *Bildung* in ALE. In the final sections of the third, fourth, fifth and sixth chapters, I have offered practical suggestions for educators in legal education on how to support the academic development of their students by integrating these elements. Furthermore, I advocate a focus on experiential learning theory as an theoretical basis for integrating a variety of instructional interventions and advise educators to approach their teaching and their development of their education with insight into the developmental stages of students. With that, they are able to pinpoint the 'zone of proximal development' of their students and offer experiences and assignments that will help them develop towards the following developmental stage. Finally, I advise educators to use play and playfulness in their teaching as these components are supportive of integrating critical and creative thinking on all levels educators might influence: The learning culture and environment, curriculum design, course design and teaching method and teaching style. At the end of these Concluding Remarks, the central theme of this research as described above is visualized in a 'visual of teaching for impact in academic legal education'.

Future research

Even though the main question to this research has been answered, the journey to further develop legal education and strengthen its academic core has only begun. The quest of educators in legal education who are interested in supporting the academic development of their students by integrating contemporary *Bildung* may continue on various paths. For example, the suggestions and models offered in this research may be even more elaborated on as educators in ALE might benefit from further concretization on how they may integrate contemporary *Bildung* into their own practice. This could, for instance, result in a specified rubrics for ACT responsibility. Such an elaboration could start with connecting the practice of ALE with insights from the field of educational science, with conversations between colleagues or by conducting and reflecting upon practical pilot projects. Moreover, it would be valuable to study what the effect of educating towards *Bildung* – in other words, educating for ACT responsibility, critical thinking and creative thinking as is proposed in this research – has on student and teacher experience and on the development of students. Another possibility for further study is to develop a strategy for the professional development of (novice) educators in ALE so that they have the options of acquiring relevant knowledge, training and collegial collaboration and feedback that supports the kind of education this research proposes.

Also, on a more fundamental level, it would be interesting to investigate how the kind of education this research envisions would in itself be able to deal with the uncertainty of the future. As part of contemporary society, ALE, too, is subject to accelerating change and faces an unknown future. The challenge for researchers in the field of philosophy of ALE is to investigate how legal education might be supported in becoming future-proof and develop a way in which ALE is capable of change and necessary adjustment without losing sight of its values and aims.

For now, however, my inquiry into the question '*how can educators in contemporary academic legal education contribute to the academic development of their students?*' comes to an end with the completion of the first phase of the journey. I hope that this research will provide my fellow educators in ALE with a useful and meaningful theoretical foundation for their educational efforts and that it has offered inspiration for further developing the education we offer law students. We all have an important role to play in the development of our students, since we are in a position to provide them with some guidance and support as they develop themselves towards becoming academically educated legal professionals and search for their place in the world. This challenges us, educators in ALE, to go the distance and define and take our own responsibility to develop legal education accordingly.

Visual of Teaching for Impact in Academic Legal Education

Literature

Abrami, P.C., Bernard, R.M., Borokhovski, E., Waddington, D.I, Wade, A., and Persson, T. (2015), 'Strategies for Teaching Students to Think Critically: A Meta-Analysis', in: *Review of Educational Research*, June 2015, vol. 85, no. 2, pp. 275-314.

Adair, J., *The Art of Creative Thinking. How to be Innovative and Develop Great Ideas*, London: Talbor Adair Press 2007.

Adriansen, H.K. (2010), 'How Criticality Affects Students' Creativity', in: Nygaard, C., Courtney, N. & Holtham, C., *Teaching Creativity - Creativity in Teaching (Learning in higher education series)*, Faringdon: Libri Publishing 2010, pp. 65-84.

Ahsmann, M.J.A.M. (2016), 'De juridische opleiding en de T-shaped lawyer: hoe leiden universiteiten goede juristen op?', in: *De Kwaliteit Binnen het Notariaat*, Stichting ter Bevordering der Notariële Wetenschap Amsterdam, Deventer: Wolters Kluwer 2016. Text available at: https://openaccess.leidenuniv.nl/bitstream/handle/1887/44686/DejuridischeopleidingendeT-shapedlawyer.pdf?sequence=1.

Albergaria Ameida, P., Teixeira-Dias, J.J., and Medina, J. (2010), 'Building a Culture of Creativity while Engaging Science Students in Questioning', in: Nygaard, C., Courtney, N. and Holtham, C., *Teaching Creativity - Creativity in Teaching (Learning in higher education series)*, Faringdon: Libri Publishing 2010, pp. 85-101.

Altbach, P.G., *The International Imperative in Higher Education*, Rotterdam: Sense Publishers 2013.

Amabile, T.M. (1983), 'The Social Psychology of Creativity: A componential Conceptualization', in: *Journal of Personality and Social Psychology*, vol. 45, No. 2, pp. 357-376. 1983

Amabile, T.M., *Creativity in Context. Update to the Social Psychology of Creativity*, Oxford: Westview Press 1996.

Amabile, T. (2001), 'Beyond Talent. John Irving and the Passionate Craft of Creativity', in: *American Psychologist*, vol. 56/4, pp. 333-336.

Amabile, T.M., *Componential Theory of Creativity*, working paper 2012, published in 2013 Encyclopedia of Management Theory (Eric H. Kessler, Ed.), Sage Publications, 2013.

Amani Smathers, R. (2014), 'The 21st Century T-shaped Lawyer', in: *Law Practice Magazine*, 2014, 40(4), pp. 34-39.

Ambrose, S.A., Bridges, M.W., DiPietro, M., Lovett, M.C., and Norman, M.K., *How Learning Works. 7 Research-Based Principles for Smart Teaching*, San Francisco: Jossey-Bass 2010.

Anderson, L.W., and Krathwohl, D.R. (eds.), *A Taxonomy for Learning, Teaching, and Assessing. A revision of Bloom's taxonomy of Educational Objectives*, New York: Longman 2001.

Anker, M., *The Ethics of Uncertainty. Aporetic Openings*, New York: Atropos Press 2009.

Antonopoulos, I. (2020), 'The future of climate policymaking in light of *Urgenda Foundation* v *the Netherlands*', in: *Environmental Law Review*, vol. 22, no. 2, pp. 199-124.

Appleby, G., Burdon, P., and Reilly, A. (2013), 'Critical Thinking in Legal Education: Our Journey', in: *Legal Education Review*, vol. 23, no. 2 (2013), pp. 345-378.

Ardalan, K. (2015), 'Using entertaining metaphors in the introduction of the case method in a case-based course', in: M. Li & Y. Zhao (Eds.). *Exploring learning & teaching in higher education*, Berlin-Heidelberg, Springer, pp. 69-96. Doi:10.1007/978-3-642-55352-3_3.

Aristotle, *Ethica. Ethica Nicomachea*, translated to Dutch, introduced and annotated by Christine Pannier and Jean Verhaeghe, Groningen: Historische Uitgeverij 1999.

Arum, R., and Roksa, J., *Academically Adrift. Limited Learning on College Campuses*, Chicago: The University of Chicago Press 2011.

Baer, J. and Kaufman, J.C., *Being Creative Inside and Outside the Classroom. How to Boost Your Students' Creativity – And Your Own*, Rotterdam: Sense Publishers 2012.

Bailin, S. (1987), 'Critical and Creative Thinking', in: *Informal Logic*, vol. IX1, Winter, pp. 23-30.

Bailin, S., and Battersby, M. (2009), 'Inquiry: A dialectical approach to teaching critical thinking', in: Rolita, J., (ed.), *Argument Cultures: Proceedings of OSSA 09*, CD-ROM, Windsor, ON: OSSA, pp. 1-10.

Bailin, S., and Battersby, M. (2016), 'Fostering the Virtues of Inquiry', in: *Topoi*, 35, pp. 367-374.

Bain, K., *Super Courses. The Future of Teaching and Learning*, Princeton NJ: Princeton University Press 2021.

Bammer, G., Smithson, M. and the Goolabri Group (2008), 'The Nature of Uncertainty', in: Bammer, G. and Smithson, M. (eds.), *Uncertainty and Risk. Multidisciplinary Perspectives*, London: Routledge 2008, pp. 289-303.

Barnett, R., *Higher Education: A Critical Business*, Bristol, PA USA: Society for Research into Higher Education and Open University Press 1997.

Barnett, R. (2011), 'The marketised university: defending the indefensible', in: Molesworth, M., Scullion, R., and Nixon, E., *The Marketisation of Higher Education and the Student as Consumer*, London: Routledge 2011, pp. 39-51.

Bauer, W. (2003), 'On the Relevance of *Bildung* for Democracy', in: *Educational Philosophy and Theory*, vol. 35, no. 2, pp. 211-225.

Bauman, Z. (1997), 'Universities: Old, New and Different', in: Smith and Webster (eds.), *The Postmodern University? Contested Visions of Higher Education in Society*, Buckingham: Society for Research into Higher Education & Open University Press 1997.

Bauman, Z. (2000), *Liquid Modernity*, Cambridge: Polity Press 2000.

Bauman, Z. (2005-1), *Postmodern Ethics*, Oxford: Blackwell Publishing 2005.

Bauman, Z. (2005-2), 'Education in Liquid Modernity', in: *The Review of Education, Pedagogy, and Cultural Studies*, vol. 27, no. 4, pp. 303-317.

Bauman, Z. (2005-3), *Liquid Life*, Cambridge: Polity Press 2005.

Bauman, Z., *Liquid Times. Living in an Age of Uncertainty*, Cambridge: Polity Press 2007.

Bauman, Z., *Does Ethics Have a Chance in a World of Consumers?*, Cambridge MA: Harvard University Press 2008.

Bauman, Z. (2010), 'Media, Bystanders, Actors', in: Ognjenovic, G. (ed.), *Responsibility in Context. Perspectives*, Dordrecht: Springer 2010, pp. 95-101.

Bauman, Z., *Collateral Damage. Social Inequalities in a Global Age*, Cambridge UK: Polity Press 2011.

Bauman, Z., and Donskins, L., *Moral Blindness. The Loss of Sensitivity in Liquid Modernity*, Cambridge: Polity Press 2013.

Becchi, P. (2011), 'Our Responsibility Towards Future Generations', in: Mathis, K. (ed.), *Efficiency, Sustainability, and Justice to Future Generations*, Dordrecht: Springer 2011, pp. 77-96.

Beck, U., *Risk Society. Towards a New Modernity*, London: Sage Publications 1992.

Beck, U., *The Reinvention of Politics. Rethinking Modernity in the Global Social Order*, Cambridge: Polity Press 1997.

Beck, U., *De wereldrisicomaatschappij. Op zoek naar verloren zekerheid*, Amsterdam: Wereldbibliotheek 2015.

Beghetto, R.A. (2009), 'In Search of the unexpected: Finding Creativity in the Micromoments of the classroom', in: *Psychology of Aesthetics, Creativity, and the arts*, vol. 3, no. 1, pp. 2-5.

Beiser, F.C., *The Romantic Imperative. The Concept of Early German Romanticism*, Cambridge MA: Harvard University Press 2003.

Belaera, L., Weinstein-Jones, Y., Ilie, S. and Baker, S.T. (2021), 'Critical thinking in practice: The priorities and practices of instructors teaching in higher education', in: *Thinking Skills and Creativity*, vol. 41, pp. 1-16.

Belluigi, D. (2010), 'Creating the Conditions for Creativity: Looking at Assessment in Fine Art Studio Practice', in: Nygaard, C., Courtney, N. & Holtham, C., *Teaching Creativity – Creativity in Teaching (Learning in higher education series)*, Faringdon: Libri Publishing 2010, pp. 47-63.

Berg, M., and Seeber, B.K., *The Slow Professor. Challenging the Culture of Speed in the Academy*, Toronto: University of Toronto Press 2016.

Bernasconi, R. (2018), 'Levinas, Social Vulnerability, and the Logic of South African Racism', in: *Suomen Antropologi*, vol. 43, no. 3, pp. 91-101.

Berry, W. (2015). Beyond survival: Using games to thrive in lecture. In: M. Li & Y. Zhao (Eds.). *Exploring learning &teaching in higher education* (pp. 45-68). New York, Springer.

Biesta, G.J.J., and Stams, G.J. (2000), 'Critical thinking and the question of critique: some lessons from deconstruction', in: *Studies in Philosophy and Education*, 20(1), pp. 57-74.

Biesta, G.J.J., *The Beautiful Risk of Education*, Boulder (CO, U.S.): Paradigm Publishers 2013.

Biesta, G.J.J., (2017), "Tussen reflexiviteit en vrijheid: 'Bildung' en 'Erziehung' als twee paradigma's voor persoonsvorming in het onderwijs", *Waardenwerk* 70/71, pp. 85-92.

Biesta, G.J.J. (2020), 'Risking ourselves in education: Qualification, Socialization, and Subjectification Revisited', in: *Educational Theory*, vol. 70, no. 1, pp. 89-104.

Biesty, P. (2003), 'Where is play?', in: Lytle, D.E. (Ed.), *Play and educational theory and practice*, Westport, Connecticut: Praeger Publishers, pp. 43-56.

Biggs, J.B., *Student Approaches to Learning and Studying*. Hawthorn, Victoria: Australian Council for Educational Research 1987.

Biggs, J.B., and Tang, C., *Teaching for Quality Learning at University. What the student does*, 4th edition, New York: Open University Press 2011.

Bloom, B.S. (ed.), Engelhart, M.D., Furst, E.J., Hill, W.H., & Krathwohl, D.R., *Taxonomy of Educational Objectives. The Classification of Educational Goals*, London: Longmans, Green and Co LTD 1956.

Blöser, C. (2015), 'Degrees of Responsibility in Kant's Practical Philosophy', in: *Kantian Review*, vol. 20, no. 2, pp. 183-209.

Boden, M.A., *Dimensions of Creativity*, Cambridge MA: MIT Press 1994.

Boden, M.A. (2001), 'Creativity and Knowledge', in Craft, A., Jeffrey, B. & Leibling, M. (eds.), *Creativity in education*, London: Continuum 2001, pp. 95-102.

Boden, M.A., *The Creative Mind. Myths and mechanisms* (second edition), London: Routledge 2004.

Bok, D., *Universities in the Marketplace. The commercialization of higher education*, Princeton NJ: Princeton University Press 2003.

Bono, E. de, *How To Have Creative Ideas. 61 exercises tot develop the mind*, London: Vermilion 2007.

Bono, E. de, *Serious Creativity. Using the power of lateral thinking to create new ideas*, New York: HarperCollins Publishers 1992.

Bosch-Boesjes, J.E. (2005), 'Wat maakt een goed jurist?', in: Brouwer (ed.), *Wat maakt een goed jurist? Over de academische vorming en het recht*. Den Haag: Boom Juridische Uitgevers 2005, pp. 25-28.

Boutellier, H., *De Veiligheidsutopie. Hedendaags onbehagen en verlangen rond misdaad en straf*, Den Haag: Boom Juridische uitgevers 2005.

Bowell, T., and Kemp, G., *Critical Thinking: a concise guide*, 3rd edition, London: Routledge 2010.

Brouwer, J.G (2005)., 'Pensez par vous-même!', in: Brouwer (ed.), *Wat maakt een goed jurist? Over de academische vorming en het recht*. Den Haag: Boom Juridische Uitgevers 2005, pp. 1-12.

Brown, W.J. (1909). Jurisprudence and legal education. *Columbia Law Review*, 9(3), 238-242.

Buchholz, S. et al. (2009), 'Life courses in the globalization process: the development of social inequalities in modern societies', in: *European Sociological Review*, vol. 25, no. 1, pp. 53-71.

Buddeberg, E. (2012), 'Ernst Wolff, Political Responsibility for a Globalised World. After Levinas' Humanism', in: *Ethical Theory and Moral Practice*, vol. 15, no. 5, pp. 709-710.

Buruma, Y. (1999), 'Inleiding: Een strafrechtelijke ideeëngeschiedenis van de 20ste eeuw', in: Buruma, Y. (ed.), *100 jaar strafrecht. Klassieke teksten van de twintigste eeuw'*, Amsterdam: Amsterdam University Press 1999, pp. 11-46.

Burris, J.L, Brechting E.H., Slasman, J. and Carlson, C.R. (2009), 'Factors associated with the psychological well-being and distress of university students', in: *Journal of American College Health*, vol. 57 no. 5, pp. 536-543.

Caillois, R., *Man, play and games*, New York: The Free Press of Glencoe 1961.

Campillo-Ferrer, J., Miralles-Martínez, P., and Sánchez-Ibáñez, R. (2020), 'Gamification in Higher Education: Impact on Student Motivation and the Acquisition of Social and Civic Key Competencies', in: *Sustainability*, 12, 4822.

Cane, P. (2016), 'Role Responsibility', *The Journal of Ethics*, vol. 20, no. 1/3, Special Issue on Responsibility, pp. 279-298.

Caviglioli, O., Odijk, D., Bruinen, I. & van Rossum, L. (eds.), *Dubbel Coderen: De kracht van woord + beeld in je les*, Vlissingen: Bazalt Educatieve Uitgaven 2021.

Cedrone, M.J. (2013), 'The Developmental Path of the Lawyer', in: *Capital University Law Review*, vol. 41, pp. 779-835.

Chacón-Cuberos, R., Olmedo-Moreno, E.M., Lara-Sánchez, A.J., Zurita-Ortega, F. & Castro-Sánchez and M. (2019), 'Basic psychological needs, emotional regulation and academic stress in university students: a structural model according to branch of knowledge', in: *Studies in Higher Education*, DOI: 10.1080/03075079.2019.1686610.

Choi, B. (2021), 'I'm Afraid of not succeeding in learning: introducing an instrument to measure higher education students' fear of failure in learning', *Studies in Higher Education*, vol. 46, no. 11, pp. 2107-2121.

Collini, S., *What are universities for?*, London: Penguin Books 2012.

Collini, S., *Speaking of Universities*, London: Verso 2018.

Constanza, R., Cumberland, J.H., Daly, H., Goodland, R., Norgaard, R.B., Kubiszewski, I. and Franco, C., *An Introduction to Ecological Economics*, second edition, London: CRS Press 2015.

Cooper, J.M. (2014), 'Aristotelian Responsibility', in: *Oxford Studies in Ancient Philosophy*, 45, pp. 265-312.

Corrias, L.D.A. (2016), 'Populism in a constitutional key: constituent power, popular sovereignty and constitutional identity', *European Constitutional Law Review*, vol. 12, no. 1, pp. 6-26.

Couenhoven, J. (2016), 'Augustine of Hippo', in: Timpe, K., Griffith, M., and Levy, N., *The Routledge Companion to Free Will*, London: Routledge 2016.

Cownie, F., *Legal Academics. Culture and Identities*, Oxford UK: Hart Publishing 2004.

Craft, A. (2001), 'Little c Creativity', in: Craft, A., Jeffrey, B. and Leibling, M. (eds.), *Creativity in education*, London: Continuum 2001, pp. 45-61.

Craft, A. (2001-A), *An analysis of research and literature on creativity in education*, report prepared for the Qualifications and Curriculum Authority, March 2001.

Craft, A., Jeffrey, B. and Leibling, M. (eds.), *Creativity in education*, London: Continuum 2001.

Craft, A. (2006), 'Creativity in schools', in: Jackson, N., Oliver, M., Shaw, M., and Wisdom, J. (eds), *Developing creativity in higher education. An imaginative curriculum*, London: Routledge 2006, pp. 19-28.

Cropley, A.J., *Creativity in education and in learning. A guide for educators and educators*, London: Kogan Page 2001.

Csikszentmihalyi, M. and Bennett, S. (1971). An exploratory model of play. *American Anthropologist*, New Series, 73(1), 45-58.

Csikszentmihalyi, M., *Flow. The psychology of optimal experience*, New York: Harper Perennial 2008.

Csikszentmihalyi, M., *Creativity. The psychology of discovery and invention*, New York: Harper Perennial 2013.

Cuypers, S.E. (2019), 'The Strawsonian and Ledger Conception of Moral Responsibility', in: *Ideas y Valores*, vol. 68, no. 171, pp. 231-249.

Daly, H. (2013), 'A further critique of growth economics', in: *Ecological Economics*, 88, pp. 20-24.

Darley, J.M., and Latané, B. (1968), 'Bystander Intervention in Emergencies: Diffusion of Responsibility', in: *Journal of Personality and Social Psychology*, vol. 8, no. 4, pp. 377-383.

Davies, M., and Barnett, R., 'Introduction', in: Davies, M., & Barnett, R., *The Palgrave Handbook of Critical Thinking in Higher Education*, New York: Palgrave MacMillan 2015.

Davis, W. (1999), 'Max Weber on Religion and Political Responsibility', in: *Religion*, vol. 29 (1999), pp. 29-60.

Davis, W. (2001a), 'Introduction', in: Davis, W. (ed.), *Taking Responsibility. Comparative Perspectives*, Charlottesville: University Press of Virginia 2001.

Davis, W. (2001b), 'Afterword', in: Davis, W. (ed.), *Taking Responsibility. Comparative Perspectives*, Charlottesville: University Press of Virginia 2001.

Deterding, S., Dixon, D., Khaled, R. and Nacke, L. (2014), 'Du game design au gamefulness: définir la gamification', in: *Sciences du jeu*, vol. 2, 2014, pp. 1-19.

Dewey, J., *How We Think. A restatement of the relation of reflective thinking to the educative process*, Lexington: D.C. Heath & Company 1933.

Domselaar, I. van (2015), 'Moral Quality in Adjudication: On Judicial Virtues and Civic Friendship', in: *Netherlands Journal of Legal Philosophy*, vol. 44, no. 1, 2015, pp. 24-46.

Donoghue, F., *The Last Professors. The corporate university and the fate of the humanities*, New York: Fordham University Press 2018.

Dumitru, D. (2019), 'Creating meaning. The importance of Arts, Humanities and Culture for critical thinking development', in: *Studies in Higher Education*, vol. 44, no. 5, pp. 870-879.

Duyndam, J. and Poorthuis, M., *Levinas*, Amersfoort: Lemniscaat 2003.

Ejsing-Duun, S. and Karoff, H.S. (2014), 'Gamification of a higher education course: what's the fun in that? In: I C. Busch (red.), *Proceedings of the 8th European Conference on Game Based Learning*, Academic Conferences and Publishing International Limited 2014, pp. 92-98.

Elmose, S. and Roth, W.M. (2005), 'Allgemeinbildung: readiness for living in risk society', in: *Journal of Curriculum Studies*, 2005:37(1), pp. 11-34.

Ennis, R.H. (1962), 'A Concept of *Critical Thinking*. A Proposed Basis for Research in the Teaching and Evaluation of Critical Thinking Ability', in: *Harvard Educational Review*, vol. 32, no. 1, pp. 81-111.

Ennis, R.H. (1987), 'A Taxonomy of Critical Thinking Dispositions and Abilities', in: Baron, J.B., and Sternberg, R.J. (eds.), *Teaching Thinking Skills. Theory and Practice*, New York: W.H. Freeman and Company 1987, pp. 9-26.

Ennis, R.H. (1989), 'Critical Thinking and Subject Specificity: Clarification and Needed Research', in: *Educational Researcher*, April 1989, vol. 18, no. 3, pp. 4-10.

Ennis, R.H. (1990), 'The Extent to Which Critical Thinking is Subject-Specific', in: *Educational Researcher*, MAY 1990, pp. 13-16.

Ennis, R.H. (1991), 'Critical Thinking: A Streamlined Conception', in: *Teaching Philosophy*, 14:1, March 1991, pp. 5-24.

Ennis, R.H., *Critical Thinking*, Upper Saddle River: Prentice-Hall 1996.

Ennis, R.H. (1996), 'Critical Thinking Dispositions: Their Nature and Assessability', in: *Informal Logic*, Vol. 18, Nos. 2 & 3, pp. 165-182.

Ennis, R.H. (2011a), 'Critical Thinking: Reflection and Perspective Part I', in: *Inquiry: Critical Thinking Across the Disciplines*, Spring 2011, vol. 26, no. 1, pp. 4-18.

Ennis, R.H. (2011b), 'Critical Thinking: Reflection and Perspective Part II', in: *Inquiry: Critical Thinking Across the Disciplines*, Summer 2011, vol. 26, no. 2, pp. 5-19.

Ennis, R.H. (2015), 'Critical Thinking: A Streamlined Conception', in: Davies, M., and Barnett, R., *The Palgrave Handbook of Critical Thinking in Higher Education*, New York: Palgrave MacMillan 2015, pp. 31-47.

Ennis, R.H. (2016), 'Definition: A Three-Dimensional Analysis with Bearing on Key Concepts', in: *OSSA Conference Archive*, 105, pp. 1-19.

Evans, E.P., *The Criminal Prosecution and Capital Punishment of Animals*, London: William Heinemann 1906.

Eysenck, H.J., 'The Measurement of Creativity', in: Boden, M.A., *Dimensions of Creativity*, Cambridge MA: MIT Press 1994, p. 212.

Facione, P.A., *Critical Thinking: A Statement of Expert Consensus for Purposes of Educational Assessment and Instruction* (The Delphi Report), Millbrae, CA USA: California Academic Press 1990.

Fischer, D.M., and Ravizza, M. (1993), 'Introduction', in: Fischer, D.M., and Ravizza, M. (eds.), *Perspectives on Moral Responsibility*, Ithaca/London: Cornell University Press, pp. 1-41.

Francot, L.M.A. and Vries, U.R.M.T. de (2006), 'Legal Education Re-Enchanted', in: *European Journal of Legal Education*, vol. 3, no. 1, pp. 3-20.

Francot-Timmermans, L.M.A., *Normativity's Re-Entry. Niklas Luhmann's Social Systems Theory: Society and the Law*, Nijmegen: Wolf Publishers 2008.

Francot, L.M.A. and Vries, U.R.M.T. de (2011), 'Justice Unbound. Responsibility in the Second Modernity', in: De Vries, U.R.M.T., & Francot L.M.A. (eds.), *Law's Environment: Critical Legal Perspectives*, The Hague: Eleven International Publishers, pp. 201-220.

Francot, L.M.A. (2014), 'Dealing with Complexity, Facing Uncertainty. Morality and Ethics in a Complex Society', in: *Archiv für Rechts- und Sozialphilosophie*, vol. 100, no. 2, 2014, pp. 201-2018.

Francot, L.M.A. and Corrias, L.D.A. (2016), 'Re-Bildung: an ideal reconsidered for legal education', in: Van Klink & De Vries (eds.), *Academic Learning in Law. Theoretical Positions, Teaching Experiments and Learning Experiences*, Cheltenham: Edward Elgar 2016, pp. 35-57.

Francot, L. and Mommers, S. (2017), 'Picking up the pace – legal slowness and the authority of the judiciary in the acceleration society (a Dutch case study)', in: *International Journal of the Legal Profession*, 2017:24(3), pp. 275-293.

Francot, L.M.A. (2018), 'Suspended in Gaffa: legal slowness in the acceleration society', in: Corrias, L.D.A. and Francot, L.M.A. (eds.), *Temporal Boundaries of Law and Politics*, Routledge Glasshouse 2018.

Frankfurt, H.G. (1969), 'Alternate Possibilities and Moral Responsibility', in: *The Journal of Philosophy*, vol. 66, no. 23, pp. 829-839.

Frankfurt, H.G. (1971), 'Freedom of the Will and the Concept of a Person', in: *The Journal of Philosophy*, vol. 68, no. 1, pp. 5-20.

Foresman, G.A., Fosl, P.S., and Watson J.C., *The Critical Thinking Toolkit*, Chichester, West Sussex, UK: Wiley Blackwell 2017.

Gardner, H., 'The Creator's Patterns', in: Boden, M.A., *Dimensions of Creativity*, Cambridge MA: MIT Press 1994, pp. 143-158.

Garriga, E. and Melé, D. (2004), 'Corporate Social Responsibility Theories: Mapping the Territory', in: *Journal of Business Ethics*, vol. 53, pp. 51-71.

Gaut, B. (2010), 'The Philosophy of Creativity', in: *Philosophy Compass*, vol. 5, no. 12, pp. 1034-1046.

Geldof, D., *Onzekerheid. Over leven in de risicomaatschappij*, Den Haag: Acco 2011.

Giddens, A. (1976), 'Introduction', in: Weber, M. (originally translated in 1930), *The Protestant Ethic and the Spirit of Capitalism*, London: Routledge 2001, pp. vii-xxiii.

Giel, L.I.S., Noordzij, G., Noordegraaf-Eelens, L and Denktaş, S. (2020), 'Fear of failure: a polynomial regression analysis of the joint impact of the perceived learnig environment and personal achievement goal orientation', in: *Anxiety, Stress & Coping*, vol 33, no. 2, pp. 123-139.

Giesinger, J. (2012), 'Liberal Education/Bildung: arguments For and Against', seminar at the Katholieke Universiteit Leuven, October 17th 2012, text available at http://www.erziehungsphilosophie.ch/vortraege/Giesinger_Bildung_Leuven.pdf.

Glas, R., Lammes, S., de Lange, M., Raessens, J. and De Vries, I. (2019), 'The Playful Citizen: An Introduction', in: *The Playful Citizen. Civic Engagement in a Mediatized Culture*, Amsterdam: Amsterdam University Press 2019.

Grant, A., *Originals. How non-conformists move the world*, New York: Penguin Books 2017.

Go, J.J. (2019), 'Structure, choice, and responsibility', in: *Ethics & Behavior*, vol. 30, no. 3, pp. 230-246.

Goldman C.S., and Wong, E.H. (1997), 'Stress and the college student', in: *Education*, 117(4), pp. 604-612.

Goodin, R.E., *Protecting the Vulnerable. A Reanalysis of Our Social Responsibilities*, Chicago: The University of Chicago Press 1985.

Gow, G. (2000), 'Understanding and teaching creativity', in: *Tech Directions*, January, pp. 32-34.

Gunawardena, M., and Wilson, K. (2021), 'Scaffolding students' critical thinking: A process not an end game', in: *Thinking Skills and Creativity*, vol. 4, pp. 2-10.

Gündling, L. (1990), 'Our Responsibility to Future Generations', in: *The American Journal of International Law*, vol. 84, no. 1, pp. 207-212.

Gur-Ze'ev, I. (2002), '*Bildung* and Critical Theory in the Face of Postmodern Education', in: *Journal of Philosophy of Education*, vol. 36, no. 3, pp. 391-408.

Halliday, T.C. and Osinsky, P. (2006), 'Globalization of law', in: *Annual Review of Sociology*, vol. 32, pp. 448-470.

Hart, H.L.A., *Punishment and Responsibility*, 2nd edition, Oxford: Oxford University Press 2008.

Heidbrink, L. (2008), 'The Limits of Responsibility in the Age of Globalisation', *Working papers of the Center for Responsibility Research*, Paper 5. Available at: www.responsibility-research.de/9.html, last visited August 29th 2022.

Hertog, L. den (2008), 'Weergave van hoofdgedachten uit *Postmodern Ethics*', in: Den Hertog, L., Francot, L.M.A. and De Vries, U.R.M.T. (red.), *Rechtsfilosofische Oefeningen: Zygmunt Bauman: onzekere verantwoordelijkheid*, Nijmegen: Wolf Legal Publishers 2008, pp. 13-24.

Hildebrandt, M. (June 24th 2011), *Oordeelsvorming door mens en machine: heuristieken, algoritmes en legitimatie*. Symposium Juridische Argumentatie.

Horlacher, R. (2004), Bildung – *a construction of a history of philosophy of education*. Studies in Philosophy and Education, 23:2004, pp. 409-426.

Horlacher, R., *The educated Subject and the German Concept of* Bildung. *A Comparative Cultural History*, London/New York: Routledge 2017.

Hoskins, T.K., Martin, B. and Humphries, M. (2011), 'The Power of Relational Responsibility', in: *Electronic Journal of Business Ethics and Organizational Studies*, vol. 16, no. 2, pp. 22-27.

Huijer, M. (2015), 'Bildung, de tandeloze tijger', in: *Trouw*, 4 oktober 2015. www.trouw.nl/nieuws/bildung-de-tandeloze-tijger~b36460f0/, last visited: December 31st 2021.

Huizinga, J. (1980). *Homo ludens. A study of the play-element in culture*. London U.K., Routledge & Kegan Paul. (Edition first published in 1949).

Humboldt, W. von, *Bildung des Menschen in Schule und Universität*, Grundlagen und Grundfragen der Erziehung, Heidelberg: Quelle & Meyer Verlag 1964.

Humboldt, W. von, 'On the spirit and the organizational framework of intellectual institutions in Berlin', in: *Reports and Documents. University Reform in Germany*, Minerva, January 1970, Volume 8, Issue 1-4, pp. 242-267. (https://doi.org/10.1007/BF01553214).

Isaacs, T., *Moral Responsibility in Collective Contexts*, Oxford: Oxford University Press 2011.

Izak, M., Kostera, M. and Zawadzki, M. (2017), 'The Future of University Education', in: Izak et al. (eds.), *The Future of University Education*, London: Palgrave Critical University Studies 2017, pp. 1-16.

Jackson, N., Oliver, M., Shaw, M., and Wisdom, J. (eds), *Developing creativity in higher education. An imaginative curriculum*, London: Routledge 2006, pp. 19-28.

Jackson, N. (2010), 'Forword', in: Nygaard, C., Courtney, N. and Holtham, C., *Teaching Creativity – Creativity in Teaching (Learning in higher education series)*, Faringdon: Libri Publishing 2010, pp. ix-xix.

Jahnke, I., Haertel, T., Wildt, J. (2017), 'Educators' conceptions of student creativity in higher education', in: *Innovations in Education and Teaching International*, vol. 54, no. 1, DOI: 10.1080/14703297.2015.1088396, pp. 87-95.

James, A. (2019), 'Making a Case for the Playful University', in: James, A., and Nerantzi, C. (eds.), *The Power of Play in Higher Education. Creativity in Tertiary Learning*, Palgrave Macmillan 2019, pp. 1-19.

James, A., and Nerantzi, C. (eds.), *The Power of Play in Higher Education. Creativity in Tertiary Learning*, Palgrave Macmillan 2019.

Janssen, C.I. (2013), 'Corporate Historical Responsibility (CHR): Addressing a Corporate Past of Forced Labor at Volkswagen', in: *Journal of Applied Communication Research*, vol. 41, no. 1, pp. 64-83.

Jeffrey, B., and Craft, A. (2001), 'The universalization of creativity', in: Craft, A., Jeffrey, B. and Leibling, M. (eds.), Creativity in education, London: Continuum 2001, pp. 1-13.

Jonas, H., *The Imperative of Responsibility. In Search of an Ethics for the Technological Age*, Chicago: The University of Chicago Press 1984.

Jong, F. de, *Daad-Schuld. Bijdrage aan een strafrechtelijke handelingsleer met bijzondere aandacht voor de normativering van het delictsbestanddeel opzet*, Den Haag: Boom Juridische Uitgevers 2009.

Kant, I. (1784), *Wat is Verlichting?*, originally published in 1784, translated to Dutch, introduced and annotated by B. Delfgaauw, Kampen: Kok Agora 1988, pp. 59-71.

Kant, I. (1998), *Metaphysik der Sitten*, 2, par. 49, in: Weischedel, W. (ed.), Frankfurt a.M., 1977 (1956). Translated to Dutch by P.C. Westerman in: *Rechtsfilosofie. Teksten*, Assen: Van Gorcum/ Open Universiteit, 1998, pp. 182-184.

Kant, I. (1803), *On Education/Über Pädagogik*, trans. Annette Churton, introduction by Caroline A.F. Rhys Davids, Boston MA: D.C. Heath & Co 1900.

Kant, I. (1798), 'The conflict of the faculties', translated by Mary J. Gregor and Robert Anchor, in: *Religion and Rational Theology*, Allen W. Wood and George Di Giovanni (eds.), Cambridge: Cambridge University Press 1996, pp. 233-327.

Kapp, K.M. *The Gamification of learning and instruction. Game-based methods and strategies for training and education*, San Francisco: Pfeiffer 2012.

Karlsohn, Th., 'Bildung, Emotion and Thought' (2018), in: Bengtsen, S.S.E. and Barnett, R. (eds.), *The Thinking University. Debating Higher Education: Philosophical Perspectives 1*, New York: Springer 2018, pp. 103-118. (https://doi.org/10.1007/978-3-319-77667-5).

Kaufman, J.C. and Beghetto, R.A. (2009), 'Beyond Big and Little: The Four C Model of Creativity', in: *Review of General Psychology*, vol. 13:1, pp. 1-12.

Kaufman, J.C. and Sternberg, R.J. (eds.), *The Cambridge Handbook of Creativity*, New York: Cambridge University Press 2010.

Keats, J., 'Ode on a Grecian Urn', in: Keats, J., *The Complete Poems of John Keats* (Introduction, glossary and Notes by Paul Wright), Ware (UK): Wordsworth Editions Limited, 2001, pp. 221-222.

Kegan, R., *In Over Our Heads. The Mental Demands of Modern Life*, Cambridge, Massachusetts: Harvard University Press 1994.

Keij, J., *Tijd als kwetsbaarheid in de filosofie van Levinas*, Amsterdam: Boom 2021.

Kekang, H., *A Theory of Creative Thinking. Construction and Verification of the Dual Circulation Model*, Springer 2017.

Kelk, C., *Studieboek materieel strafrecht*, Deventer: Kluwer 2005.

Kellner, D. (2002), 'Theorizing globalization', in: *Sociological Theory*, vol. 20, no. 3, pp. 285-286.

Kelly-Weeder, S., 'Binge drinking and disordered eating in college students' (2011), in: *Journal of the American Academy of Nurse Practitioners*, 23 (2011), pp. 33-41.

Klink, B.M.J. van (2012). 'Waarom zouden we ons aan de wet houden? Een pleidooi voor versterking van het staatsgezag', in: Jansen, T., Van den Brink G. and R. Kneyber, R. (eds.), *Gezagsdragers. De publieke zaak op zoek naar haar verdedigers*, Amsterdam: Boom, pp. 263-276.

Klink, B.M.J. van (2023), 'Critical Thinking in Academic Legal Education. A Liberal Conception', in: *Law and Method*, August 2023, DOI: 10.5553/REM/.000076.

Klink, B.M.J. van, and Vries, U.R.M.T. de (2013), 'Skeptical Legal Education. How to Develop a Critical Attitude?', in: *Law and Method*, vol. 3, no. 2, pp. 37-52.

Klink, B.M.J. van, and Vries, U.R.M.T. de (2016). 'Introduction: re-thinking academic legal education', in: Van Klink & De Vries (eds.), *Academic Learning in Law. Theoretical Positions, Teaching Experiments and Learning Experiences*, Cheltenham: Edward Elgar 2016, pp. 1-11.

Van Klink, B.M.J. van, 'Knowledge and aphasia: what is the use of skeptical legal education?', in: Van Klink & De Vries (eds.), *Academic Learning in Law. Theoretical Positions, Teaching Experiments and Learning Experiences*, Cheltenham: Edward Elgar 2016, pp. 15-34.

Klink, B.M.J. van, Vries, U.R.M.T. de, and Bleeker, T. (2017), 'Recht in Context. Naar een bredere academische vorming van juristen', in: *Nederlands Juristenblad*, vol 92, no. 14, pp. 916-922.

Klink, B.M.J. van, and Francot, L.M.A. (2019), 'Critical Writing Skills in Legal Education', in: *Law and Method. Special issue on active learning and teaching in legal education*, pp. 54-68.

Knigge, G., 'Academisch gehalte', in: Brouwer (ed.), *Wat maakt een goed jurist? Over de academische vorming en het recht*. Den Haag: Boom Juridische Uitgevers 2005, pp. 71-74.

Koehn, D., *Toward a New (Old) Theory of Responsibility: Moving beyond Accountability*, Cham, Switzerland: Springer 2019.

Koenraadt, F., 'Historische wortels en recente ontwikkelingen', in: Koenraadt, F., Mooij, A.W.M. and Van Mulbregt, J.M.L. (red.), *De persoon van de verdachte. De rapportage pro justitia vanuit het Pieter Baan Centrum*, 3rd edition, Deventer: Kluwer 2004, pp. 155-181.

Kolb, D.A., *Experiential Learning. Experience as the source of learning and development*, second edition, Upper Sadle River (New Jersey): Pearson Education, Inc. 2015.

Koster, R., *A Theory of Fun for Game Design*, second edition, Sebastopol, CA: O'Reilly Media 2014.

Kronman, A.T., *The Lost Lawyer. Failing Ideals of the Legal Profession*, Cambridge MA: Harvard University Press 1995.

Kozbelt, A., Beghetto, R.A., and Runco, M.A., 'Theories of Creativity', in: Kaufman, J.C. and Sternberg, R.J. (eds.), *The Cambridge Handbook of Creativity*, Cambridge: Cambridge University Press 2010, pp. 20-47.

Kuhn, D. (1999), 'A Developmental Model of Critical Thinking', in: *Educational Researcher*, March 1999, vol. 28, no. 2, pp. 16-25, 46.

Latané, B., and Darley, J.M. (1968), 'Group Inhibition of Bystander Intervention in Emergencies', in: *Journal of Personality and Social Psychology*, vol. 10, no.3, pp. 215-221.

Lechner, D., *'Bildung macht Frei!' Humanistische en realistische vorming in Duitsland 1600-1860*, Amsterdam: Aksant (Dissertation Rijksuniversiteit Groningen) 2003.

Lerner, R. (2001), "The American Founders' Responsibility", in: Davis, W. (ed.), *Taking Responsibility. Comparative Perspectives*, Charlottesville: University Press of Virginia 2001.

Levinas, E., *Totaliteit en Oneindigheid*, Amsterdam: Boom 2012.

Lichtenfeld, S., Elliot, A.J., Maier, M.A. and Pekrun, R. (2012), 'Fertile Green: Green Facilitates Creative Performance', in: *Personality and Social Psychology Bulletin 38* (6), pp. 784-797.

Lippmann, W. (1949), 'The Permanent New Deal', in: Rozwenc, E. (ed.) New *Deal – Revolution or Evolution*, Boston, D.C.: Heath and Company 1949, pp. 34-44.

Liu, E., and Noppe-Brandon, S., *Imagination first. Unlocking the power of possibility*, San Francisco: Jossey-Bass 2009.

Locke, J., *Two Treatises of Government and A Letter Concerning Toleration* (or. 1689), edited and introduction by Ian Shapiro, Binghamton (NY): Yale University 2003.

Lucas, B., 'Creative Teaching, Teaching Creativity and Creative Learning', in: Craft, A., Jeffrey, B. and Leibling, M. (eds.), *Creativity in education*, London: Continuum 2001, pp. 35-44.

Lucas, J.R., *Responsibility*, Oxford: Oxford University Press 1995.

Mak, E., *The T-Shaped Lawyer and Beyond. Rethinking legal professionalism and legal education for contemporary times*, Den Haag: Eleven International Publishing 2017.

Mak, E. (2020), 'Het gezag van juristen; een normatieve reflectie', in: Berlee, A. et al., *De toekomst van de jurist, de jurist van de toekomst*, Deventer: Wolters Kluwer 2020, pp. 9-34.

Maringe, F., 'Affordances and Constraints in a Transforming Higher Education Environment', in: Molesworth, M., Scullion, R., and Nixon, E., *The Marketisation of Higher Education and the Student as Consumer*, London: Routledge 2011, p. 142-154.

Marczewski, A., *Gamification. Even Ninja Monkeys Like To Play. Unicorn Edition*, Gamified UK 2018.

Martin, E., *Changing academic work: developing the learning university*, Buckingham: SRHE & Open university 1999, p. 97.

Maslow, A.H., 'Creativity in self-actualizing people', in: Rothenberg, A. and Hausman, C.R. (eds.), *The Creativity Question*, Durham: Duke University Press 1976, pp. 86-92.

Mason, M. (2007), 'Critical Thinking and Learning', in: *Educational Philosophy and Theory*, vol. 39, no. 4, pp. 339-349.

Masschelein, J., and Ricken, N. (2003), 'Do We (Still) Need the Concept of *Bildung*?', in: Educational Philosophy and Theory, vol. 35, no. 2, pp. 139-154.

Mathiasen, H. and Andersen, H.L. (2020), 'Development of Critical Thinking in Higher Education. A didactic approach to the challenge of developing students' critical thinking skills', in: *Journal of European Education*, 10 (1-2), pp. 38-52.

Matravers, M., *Responsibility and Justice*, Cambridge, UK: Polity Press 2007.

May, L., *Sharing Responsibility*, Chicago: Chicago University Press 1992.

McDonough, S. (2013). Learning to think like a teacher-educator. In: Brandenburg, R. and Wilson, J.Z., (Eds.). *Pedagogies for the future: Leading quality. Learning and teaching in higher education* (pp. 61-72). Rotterdam, Sense Publishers.

McKeon, R. (1957), 'The Development and the Significance of the Concept of Responsibility', in: *Revue Internationals de Philosophie*, vol. 11, no. 39 (1), pp. 2-32.

McPeck, J.E., *Critical Thinking and Education*, Oxford: Martin Robertson 1981.

McPeck, J.E., *Teaching Critical Thinking. Dialogue and Dialectic*, New York: Routledge 1990.

Menkel-Meadow, C. (2001), 'Aha? Is Creativity Possible in Legal Problem Solving and Teachable in Legal Education?', in: *Harvard Negotiation Law Review*, vol. 6:87, pp. 97-144.

Mehta, R., Zhu, R., and Cheema, A., (2012) 'Is Noise Always Bad? Exploring the Effects of Ambient Noise on Creative Cognition', in: *Journal of Consumer Research*, Vol. 39, No. 4, pp. 784-799.

Moran, S., 'The roles of creativity in society', in: Kaufman, J.C. and Sternberg, R.J. (eds.), *The Cambridge Handbook of Creativity*, New York: Cambridge University Press 2010, pp. 74-90.

Mudd, J. (1983), 'Thinking Critically About "Thinking Like a Lawyer"', *Journal of Legal Education*, December 1983; vol. 33, no. 4, pp. 704-711.

Müller, J. (2015), 'Aristotle on Agency and Responsibility in the *Eudemian Ethics*', in: *Phronesis*, vol. 60, no. 2, pp. 206-251.

Mummery, J., 'Students' beliefs regarding philosophical study and their development as critical thinkers', in: Brandenburg, R. and Wilson, J.Z. (eds.), *Pedagogies for the Future: Leading Quality Learning and Teaching in Higher Education*, Rotterdam: Sense Publishers 2013, pp. 99-110.

Mulnix, M.J. (2012), 'Thinking Critically about Critical Thinking', in: *Educational Philosophy and Theory*, vol. 44, no. 5, pp. 464-479.

Nagel, W.H. (1999/1977), 'Het strafrecht en de onmens', in: *100 jaar strafrecht. Klassieke teksten van de twintigste eeuw*', Amsterdam: Amsterdam University Press 1999, pp. 59-81.

Nielsen, K.M. (2016), 'Aristotle', in: Timpe, K., Griffith, M. and Levy, N., *The Routledge Companion to Free Will*, London: Routledge 2016.

Nietzsche, F., *Anti-education. On the future of Our Educational Institutions*, Translated by Damion Searls and with an introduction and notes by Paul Reitter and Chad Wellmon (eds.), New York: New York Review Books 2016.

Nixon, E., Scullion, R., and Hearn R., 'Her majesty the student: marketized higher education and the narcissistic (dis)satisfactions of the student-consumer' (2018), in: *Studies in Higher Education*, vol. 43:6, pp. 927-943.

Nowotny, H., *The Cunning of Uncertainty*, Cambridge: Polity Press 2016.

Nørgård, R., Toft-Nielsen, C. and Whitton, N. (2017), 'Playful learning in higher education: Developing a signature pedagogy', in: *International Journal of Play*, 6(3), pp. 272-282.

Nussbaum, M.C., *Not For Profit. Why democracy needs the humanities*, Princeton NJ: Princeton University Press 2016.

Nygaard, C., Courtney, N. and Holtham, C., *Teaching Creativity – Creativity in Teaching (Learning in higher education series)*, Faringdon: Libri Publishing 2010.

Oelker, J. (2013), 'Bildung': Ein Schutz vor 'Standards'?, Vortrag im Institut für Erziehungswissenschaft der Universität Zürich December 17th 2013, text available at: http://www.ife.uzh.ch/research/emeriti/oelkersjuergen/vortraegeprofoelkers/vortraege2013/Bildung_IfE.pdf, pp. 1-18.

Ogilvy, J.P., and Holley, D. (1994), 'Critical Thinking and the Law', in: *International Journal of the Legal Profession*, vol. 1, no. 3, pp. 343-367.

Ognjenovic, G. (2010), 'Moral Responsibility for Others: Why Does the "Being for" Always Precede the "Being with"', in: Ognjenovic, G. (ed.), *Responsibility in Context. Perspectives*, Dordrecht: Springer 2010, pp. 125-139.

Ou, L., *Keats and Negative Capability*, London: Continuum International Publishing Group 2009.

Oz-Salzberger, F. (2014), 'Enlightenment, National Enlightenments, and Translation', in: Garrett, A., *The Routledge Companion to Eighteenth Century Philosophy*, pp. 31-61.

Paul, R., and Elder, L., *The Nature and Functions of Critical & Creative Thinking*, 3rd edition, New York: Rowman & Littlefield 2012.

Paul, R., and Elder, L., *The Miniature Guide to Critical Thinking. Concepts and Tools*, 8th edition, New York: Rowman & Littlefield 2020.

Philpot, R., Liebst, L.S., Levine, M., Bernasco, W. and Lindegaard, M. (2020), 'Would I Be Helped? Cross-National CCTV Footage Shows That Intervenmtion Is the Norm in Public Conflicts', in: *American Psychologist*, vol. 75, no. 1, pp. 66-75.

Pierceall, E.A. and Keim, M.A. (2007), 'Stress and Coping Strategies Among Community College Students', in: *Community College Journal of Research and Practice*, vol. 31, no. 9, pp. 703-712.

Piirto, J., *Creativity for 21st Century Skills. How to Embed Creativity into the Curriculum*, Rotterdam: Sense Publishers 2011.

Pink, Th. (2009), 'Power and moral responsibility', in: *Philosophical Explorations*, 12:2, pp. 127-149.

Plato, *Ion*, translated to English by B. Jowett, The Project Gutenberg e-book, 1999 (most recently updated January 16th, 2013).

Ploeg, P. van der (2019). *Kritisch denken in burgerschapsvorming, Bildung en beroepsonderwijs: Opmaat voor visievorming NRO Werkplaats Democratisering van Kritisch Denken*. Rijksuniversiteit Groningen.

Pnevmatikos, D., Christodoulou, P., and Georgiadou, T. (2019), 'Promoting critical thinking in higher education through the values *and* knowledge education (V*a*KE) method', in: *Studies in Higher Education*, 44:5, pp. 892-901.

Pogge, T., *World Poverty and Human Rights. Cosmopolitan Responsibilities and Reforms*, Cambridge: Polity Press 2002.

Postma, D.W., *Why Care for Nature? In Search of an Ethical Framework for Environmental Responsibility and Education*, Dordrecht: Springer 2006.

Prange, K. (2004), '*Bildung*: a paradigm regained', in: *European Educational Research Journal*, Volume 3, Number 2, 2004, p. 501-509.

Prettejohn, E., *Beauty and Art 1750-2000*, Oxford: Oxford University Press 2005.

Pritchard, A., *Ways of Learning. Learning theories and learning styles in the classroom*, second edition, New York: Routledge 2009.

Proyer, R.T. (2011), 'Being playful and smart? The relations of adult playfulness with psychometric and self-estimated intelligence and academic performance', in: *Learning and Individual Differences*, 21, pp. 463-467.

Raber, J., *Progressivism's Aesthetic Education. The Bildungsroman and the American School, 1890-1920*, Cham, Switzerland: Palgrave Macmillan/Springer International 2018.

Rahman, R.A., Ahmad, S. and Rabaah Hashim, U. (2018), 'The effectiveness of gamification technique for higher education students engagement in polytech Muadzam Shah Pahang, Malaysia', in: *International Journal of Educational Technology in Higher Education*, 15:41, pp. 1-16.

Raworth, K., *Donuteconomie. In zeven stappen naar een economie voor de 21e eeuw*. Amsterdam: Nieuw Amsterdam 2017.

Readings, B., *The University in Ruins*, Cambridge MA: Harvard University Press 1996.

Reese, W.J. (2001), 'The Origins of Progressive Education', in: *History of Education Quarterly*, vol. 41 no. 1, pp. 1-24.

Rhodes, C. (2017), 'Academic Freedom in de Corporate University: Squandering Our Inheritance?', in: Izak et al. (eds.), *The Future of University Education*, London: Palgrave Critical University Studies 2017, pp. 19-38.

Rice, L. (2009). 'Playful Learning', in: *Journal for Education in the Built Environment*, 4(2), pp. 94-108.

Ritchhart, R., and Perkins, D. (2008), 'Making Thinking Visible', in: *Educational Leadership*, vol. 65, no. 5, pp. 57-61.

Ritchhart, R., Church, M., and Morrison, K., *Making Thinking Visible. How to Promote Engagement, Understanding and Independence for all learners*, San Francisco: Jossey-Bass 2011.

Ritchhart, R., and Church, M., *The Power of Making Thinking Visible. Practices to Engage and Empower All Learners*, San Francisco: Jossey-Bass 2020.

Robinson, S.R. (2011), 'Teaching logic and teaching critical thinking: revisiting McPeck', in: *Higher Education Research & Development*, vol. 30, no. 3, June 2011, pp. 275-287.

Rochette, A., *Teaching and Learning in Canadian Legal Education: An Empirical Exploration*, dissertation McGill University 2010.

Rojas, D., Kapralos, B. and Dubrowski, A. (2013), 'The missing Piece in the Gamification Puzzle', in: *Gamification*, October 2-4, pp. 135-138.

Rolfe, G., *The University in Dissent. Scholarship in the corporate university*, London: Routledge 2013.

Rossi, B, and Warfield, T.A. (2016), 'The Relationship between Moral Responsibility and Freedom', in: Timpe, K., Griffith, M. and Levy, N., *The Routledge Companion to Free Will*, London: Routledge 2016, pp. 612-622.

Rossum, W. van (2016), 'Visuals for a critical legal profession', in: Van Klink, B.M.J. and De Vries U.R.M.T. (eds.), *Academic Learning in Law. Theoretical Positions, Teaching Experiments and Learning Experiences*, Cheltenham: Edward Elgar 2016, pp. 160-179.

Rossum, H.E. van (2018-1), 'Lawyers, law schools and social change – defining the challenges of academic legal education in the late modernity', in: *International Journal of the Legal Profession*, 2018:25(3), pp. 245-260.

Rossum, H.E. van (2018-2), 'Time to Play: Integrating Play and Playfulness in Legal Philosophical Courses as Tools for Student Learning', in: *Law and Method. Special Issue on Active Learning and Teaching in Legal Education*, November 2018, pp. 1-19.

Rossum, H.E. van (2021), 'Dual Coding – a practical example in academic legal education', in: Caviglioli, O., Odijk, D., Bruinen, I. & van Rossum, L. (eds.), *Dubbel Coderen: De kracht van woord + beeld in je les*, Vlissingen: Bazalt Educatieve Uitgaven, pp. 186-187.

Rothenberg, A. & Hausman, C.R. (eds.), *The Creativity Question*, Durham: Duke University Press 1976.

Runco, M.A., *Creativity. Theories and Themes: Research, Development, and Practice* (second edition), https://doi.org/10.1016/B978-0-12-410512-6.00006-0, Cambridge (MA): Academic Press 2014, pp. 171-204.

Russ, S.W. (2003), 'Play and Creativity: developmental issues', in: *Scandinavian Journal of Educational Research*, vol. 47, no. 3, pp. 291-303.

Ryhammar, L. and Brolin, C. (1999), 'Creativity Research: historical considerations and main lines of development', in: *Scandinavian Journal of Educational Research*, vol. 43:3, pp. 259-273.

Salisu, A. and Ransom, E.N. (2014), 'The role of modeling towards impacting quality education', in: *International Letters of Social and Humanistic Sciences*, vol. 32, pp. 54-61.

Sadler-Smith, E. (2015), 'Wallas' Four-Stage Model of the Creative Process: More Than Meets the Eye?', in: *Creativity Research Journal*, 27(4), pp. 342-352.

Schiller, F. von, *Letters on the Aesthetical Education of Man*, first published in this translation in the Harvard Classics 1909 by Charles W. Eliot (ed.), Grindl Press 2015.

Scott Fruehwald, E., *How to Teach Lawyers, Judges, and Law Students Critical Thinking. Millions Saw the Apple Fall, but Newton asked Why*, (ISBN 9798608999987) 2020.

Sheridan, M.D. (revised by Howard, J. and Alderson, D.), *Play in early childhood. From birth to six years* (3rd edn.), New York: Routledge 2011.

Shulman, L.S. (2005), 'Signature pedagogies for the professions', in: *Daedalus*, Summer 2005, pp. 52-59.

Sicart, M., *Play Matters*, Cambridge MA: MIT Press 2014.

Siegel, H. (1991), 'The generalizability of Critical Thinking', in: *Educational Philosophy and Theory*, vol. 23, no. 1, pp. 18-30.

Siemon, D. and Eckhardt, L. (2017), 'Gamification of Teaching in Higher Education', in: Stieglitz, S., Lattemann, C., Robra-Bissantz, S., Zarnekow, R. and Brockmann, T. (eds.), *Gamification. Using Game Elements in Serious Contexts*, Springer 2017.

Smagorinsky, P. (2018), 'Deconflating the ZPD and instructional scaffolding: Retranslating and reconceiving the zone of proximal development as the zone of next development', in: *Learning, Culture and Social Interaction*, 16 (2018), pp. 70-75.

Smith, J.K, and Smith, L.F. (2010), 'Educational Creativity', in: Kaufman, J.C. and Sternberg, R.J. (eds.), *The Cambridge Handbook of Creativity*, New York: Cambridge University Press 2010, pp. 250-264.

Smith, K.K., *Governing Animals: Animal Welfare and Liberal State*, Oxford: Oxford University Press 2012.

Smithson, M., Bammer, G. and the Goolabri Group (2018), 'Coping and Managing under Uncertainty', in: Bammer, G. and Smithson, M. (eds.), *Uncertainty and Risk. Multidisciplinary Perspectives*, London: Routledge 2008, pp. 321-333.

Smits, J.M. (2014), 'Three Models of Legal Education and a Plea for Differentiation'. In: *China-EU Law Journal* 3 (2014), pp. 55-63; Maastricht European Private Law Institute Working Paper 2013/12. Available at https://ssrn.com/abstract=2335635 (http://dx.doi.org/10.2139/ssrn.2335635).

Sokhi-Bulley, B. (2016), 'Learning Law Differently: the importance of theory and methodology', in: Van Klink, B.M.J. and De Vries, U.R.M.T. (eds.), *Academic Learning in Law. Theoretical Positions, Teaching Experiments and Learning Experiences*, Cheltenham, U.K.: Elgar Publishing 2016, pp. 121-141.

Somogyvári, M. (2009), 'Time and Responsibility', in: *World Futures*, 65:5-6, pp. 342-355.

Souffrant, E.M., *Identity, Political Freedom, and Collective Responsibility. The Pillars and Foundations of Global Ethics*, New York: Palgrave MacMillan 2013.

Stegehuis, G. and Rammelt, C. (2022), 'Groei is een klimaatkiller en bevordert ons welzijn allang niet meer', in: *Trouw*, 2 May 2022.

Steidle, A. and Werth, L. (2013), 'Freedom from constraints: Darkness and dim illumination promote creativity', in: *Journal of Environmental Psychology*, 35, pp. 67-80.

Stenros, J. (2015), *Play, playfulness and games. A constructionist ludology approach*, Tampere: Tampere University Press 2015.

Sternberg, R.J. (2004), 'WICS: A Model of Educational Leadership', in: *The Educational Forum*, vol. 68, no. 2, Winter 2004, pp. 108-114.

Sternberg, R.J. (2007), 'A Systems Model of Leadership. WICS', in: *American Psychologist*, vol. 62, no. 1, pp. 34-42.

Stolker, C., *Rethinking the Law School. Education, Research, Outreach and Governance*, Cambridge: Cambridge University Press 2014.

Strawson, G. (2008), 'The impossibility of Ultimate Moral Responsibility', in: Strawson, G., *Real Materialism: and Other Essays*, Oxford: Oxford University Press 2008 (published by Oxford Scholarship Online), pp. 1-19.

Strawson, P.F., *Freedom and Resentment and other essays*, London: Methuen & Co 1974.

Strydom, P. (1999), 'The Challenge of Responsibility for Sociology', in: *Current Sociology*, vol. 47, no. 3, pp. 65-82.

Susskind, R., and Susskind D., *The Future of the Professions. How Technology Will Transform the Work of Human Experts*, Oxford: Oxford University Press 2015.

Susskind, R., *Tomorrow's Lawyers. An Introduction to Your Future*, 2nd edition, Oxford: Oxford University Press 2017.

Sutton-Smith, B. (1997). *The ambiguity of play*. Harvard University Press.

Sutton-Smith B. (2003). Play as a parody of emotional vulnerability. In: D.E. Lytle (Ed.). *Play and educational theory and practice* (pp. 3-18). Westport, Connecticut, Praeger Publishers.

Szadkowski, K. (2017), 'The University of the Common: Beyond the Contradictions of Higher Education Subsumed under Capital', in: Izak et al. (eds.), *The Future of University Education*, London: Palgrave Critical University Studies 2017, pp. 39-62.

Tanis, D.J. (2012). *Exploring play/playfulness and learning in the adult and higher education classroom* (diss. Pennsylvania State University).

Taylor, C.A. (2017), 'Is a posthumanist *Bildung* possible? Reclaiming the promise of *Bildung* for contemporary higher education', in: *Higher Education*, 74, pp. 419-435.

Teixeira, P.N. and Dill, D.D. (2011), 'The Many Faces of Marketization in Higher Education', in: *Public Vices, Private Virtues? Assessing the Effects of Marketization in Higher Education*, Teixeira, P.N. and Dill, D.D, (eds.), Rotterdam: Sense Publishers 2011.

Thayer-Bacon, B.J. (1998), 'Transforming and Redescribing Critical Thinking: Constructive Thinking', in: *Studies in Philosophy and Education*, 17: pp. 123-148.

Thayer-Bacon, B.J., *Transforming Critical Thinking. Thinking Constructively*, New York: Educators College Press 2000.

Thomas, D. and Seely Brown, J. (2011). *A new culture of learning. Cultivating the imagination for a world of constant change*.

Trousdale, R. (2010), 'White Privilege and the Case Dialogue Method', in: *Law Raza*, vol. 1, no. 1, pp. 29-50.

Tomic, W. (1993), 'Behaviorism and cognitivism in education', in: *Psychology*, 30 (3/4), pp. 38-46.

Vargas, M., *Building Better Beings: A Theory of Moral Responsibility*, Oxford: Oxford University Press 2013.

Victor, P.A. (2010), 'Ecological economics and economic growth', in: *Annals of the New York Academy of Sciences, Issue: Ecological Economics Reviews*, 1185, pp. 237-245.

Vincent, N.A. (2015), 'A Compatibilist Theory of Legal Responsibility', in: *Criminal Law and Philosophy*, pp. 477-498.

Vleet, M. van, and Feeney, B.C. (2015), 'Play Behavior and Playfulness in Adulthood', in: *Social and Personality Psychology Compass*, 9/11, pp. 630-643.

Vogel, L. (2001), 'Jewish Philosophies after Heidegger. Levinas and Jonas on Responsibility', in: Davis, W. (ed.), *Taking Responsibility. Comparative Perspectives*, Charlottesville: University Press of Virginia 2001.

Voget-Kleschin, L., Baats, C. and Garcia-Portela, L. (2019), 'Introduction to the Special Issue on Individual Environmental Responsibility', in: *Journal of Agricultural and Environmental Ethics*, no. 32, pp. 493-504.

Vohs, K.D., Redden, J.P. and Rahinel, R. (2012), 'Physical Order Produces Healthy Choices, Generosity, and Conventionality, Whereas Disorder Produces Creativity', in: *Psychological Science*, Vol. 24, No. 9, pp. 1860-1867.

Vries, U.R.M.T. de, (2021), 'Independence of Mind: Moral reasoning and judgment in legal education', in: *European Journal of Legal Education*, June 2021, vol. 2, no. 1, pp. 75-97.

Wahlgren, P. (2005), 'The purpose and usefulness of jurisprudence. Perspectives on jurisprudence: essays in honor of Jes Bjarup', in: *Scandinavian Studies in Law*, 48, pp. 505-516.

Wallace, R.J. (2002), 'Précis of *Responsibility and the Moral Sentiments*', in: *Philosophy and Phenomenological Research*, May 2002, vol. 64, no. 3, pp. 680-681.

Wallas, G., *The Art of Thought*, first published in 1926, Tunbridge Wells, Kent, UK: Solis Press 2014.

Webb, J. (2009), 'Taking Values Seriously: The Democratic Intellect and the Place of Values in the Law School Curriculum' (November 12, 2009), *Warwick School of Law Research Paper*, No. 2009/06. Available at SSRN: http://ssrn.com/abstract=1504582 or http://dx.doi.org/10.2139/ssrn.1504582.

Weber, M. (1904), 'The Protestant Sects and the Spirit of Capitalism', in: Gert, H.H. and Mills, C.W. (eds.), *From Max Weber: Essays in Sociology*, New York: Oxford University Press 1958, pp. 302-322.

Weber, M. (1917), 'Science as a Vocation', in: Gert, H.H. and Mills, C.W. (eds.), *From Max Weber: Essays in Sociology*, New York: Oxford University Press 1958, pp. 129-156.

Weber, M. (1919), 'Politics as a Vocation', in: Gert, H.H., and Mills, C.W. (eds.), *From Max Weber: Essays in Sociology*, New York: Oxford University Press 1958, pp. 77-128.

Weber, M. (originally translated in 1930), *The Protestant Ethic and the Spirit of Capitalism*, London: Routledge 2001.

Weinstein, J. & Morton, L.H. (2003), 'Stuck in a Rut: The Role of Creative Thinking in Problem Solving and Legal Education', in: *Clinical Law Review*, vol 9, pp. 835-877.

Welling, H. (2007), 'Four Mental Operations in Creative Cognition: The Importance of Abstraction', in: *Creativity Research Journal*, vol. 19, nos. 2-3, pp. 163-177.

Wertz jr., W.F. (2005), 'A Reader's Guide to Letters on the Aesthetical', in: *Fifelio*, vol. 14, no. 1-2, Spring-Summer 2005 (Schiller Institute), text available at: https://archive.schillerinstitute.com/fidelio_archive/2005/fidv14n01-02-2005SpSu/fidv14n01-02-2005SpSu_080-a_readers_guide_to_schillers_let.pdf.

White, M.D., *The Decline of the Individual. Reconciling Autonomy with Community*, Cham, Switzerland: Palgrave MacMillan 2017.

Wilson, E.E. (2014), 'Kant's moral Philosophy', in: Garrett, A. (ed.), *The Routledge Companion to Eighteenth Century Philosophy*, London: Routledge 2014.

Witteveen, W. (2005), 'Een brede jurist is een betere jurist', in: Brouwer (ed.), *Wat maakt een goed jurist? Over de academische vorming en het recht*. Den Haag: Boom Juridische Uitgevers 2005, pp. 190-193.

Van der Wolf, M.J.F. (2013), 'Frans Rosier: omgang met grensgevallen begin twintigste eeuw', in: *Gedragskundige rapportage in het strafrecht*, par. 3.3.

Van der Wolf, M.J.F. (2015), 'Oplegging van TBS', in: *Handboek Strafzaken*, par. 53.3.1.

Wolff, E., *Political Responsibility for a Globalised World. After Levinas' Humanism*, Bielefeld: Transcript Verlag 2011.

Wolthuis, A.J. (2007), 'Het spelkarakter van het parlementaire debat', in: *Rechtstheorie en Rechtsfilosofie*, 36(3), 12-33.

Wordsworth, W., *The Collected Poems of William Wordsworth*, With an introduction by Antonia Till, Ware: Wordsworth Editions Limited 1994.

Yeamans, R. (1971), 'Creativity and Legal Education', In: *The Journal of Legal Education*, vol 23/3, pp. 381-398.

Yeats, W.B, *The collected poems of W.B. Yeats*, with an Introduction by Cedric Watts, Ware: Wordsworth Editions Limited 1994.

Young, I.M., *Responsibility for Justice*, Oxford: Oxford University Press 2011.

Zeleza, P. T., *The Transformation of Global Higher Education*, 1945-2015, New York: Springer Nature 2016.

Zepke, N. (2017). *Student engagement in neoliberal times. Theories and practices for learning and teaching in higher education*. Singapore, Springer.

Zheng, R. (2019), 'What Kind of Responsibility Do We Have for Fighting Injustice? A Moral-Theoretic Perspective on the Social Connections Model', in: *Critical Horizons*, 20:2, pp. 109-126.

Zimmerman, M.J., *An Essay on Moral Responsibility*, Totowa, NJ: Rowman & Littlefield Publishers 1988.

Zurita, G., Hasbun, B., Baloian N. and Jerez, O. (2015). A blended learning environment for enhancing meaningful learning using 21st century skills. In: G. Chen, V. Kumar,

Kinshuk, R. Huang and S.C. Kong (Eds.). *Emerging issues in smart learning* (pp. 1-8). New York, Springer.

Zuurmond, A. (2020), 'Critical Thinking, Citizenship, and Vocational Training: Creating a Space for Bildung', in: Montesano Montessori, N. and Lengkeek, G. (Eds.), *Opening up spaces for meaningful engagement in educational praxis*, Utrecht: Eburon 2020, pp. 19-42.

www.ingramcontent.com/pod-product-compliance
Lightning Source LLC
LaVergne TN
LVHW060618300926
849162LV00008B/1648
* 9 7 8 9 0 4 7 3 0 1 8 3 7 *